Literature-Based Instruction: Reshaping the Curriculum

Literature-Based Instruction: Reshaping the Curriculum

Edited by
Taffy E. Raphael and Kathryn H. Au

Credits

Every effort has been made to contact copyright holders for permission to reproduce borrowed material where necessary. We apologize for any oversight and would be happy to rectify them in future printings.

Student samples used with permission.

Figure of Independent Reader Standards, used with permission of Carmel Central School District, Patterson, New York.

Changing Talk About Text: New Roles for Teachers and Students figure, copyright © 1996 by the National Council of Teachers of English. Reprinted with permission.

Figure of Three-Way Conference Guide for Students, Davies, A. Cameron, C., Politano, C., & Gregory, K. (1992). *Together is better: Collaborative assessment, evaluation & reporting.* Winnipeg, Canada: Peguis Publishers Ltd. Used with permission.

Christopher-Gordon Publishers, Inc.
1502 Providence Highway, Suite #12
Norwood, MA 02062
Tel: (800) 934-8322

Printed in the United States of America

10 9 8 7 6 5 4 3 2 1   03 02 01 00 99 98

ISBN: 0-926842-70-6

Contents

●————————●

Seciton II. Curricular Connections

Section III. Assessment within Literature-based Instruction

Essays on The Future of Literature-Based Instruction

Dedication

To Jean B. Raphael and Mun Kyau H. Au

who gave us a love of literature

and continue to share

the wonder of books

with us.

Preface

●————————●

Literacy instruction continues to be one of the most hotly debated topics in education. Progressive forms of instruction, such as literature-based instruction and the process approach to writing, are frequently under attack, as the pendulum swings "back to basics." The critics argue that a return to traditional, skill-and-drill forms of teaching will somehow fix all that is wrong with children's learning to read and write and, by extension, all that is wrong with American education.

We think it vital, in this political climate, to make a strong case for the value of literature-based instruction. The purpose of this book is to make that case. This edited volume provides readers with an overview of the extensive knowledge base supporting literature-based approaches. It should prove worthwhile reading for classroom teachers, resource teachers, curriculum developers, teacher educators, and literacy researchers with applied interests. It is suitable for use in graduate language arts courses.

The use of children's literature in the classroom, not as a fad or a nicety but as the basis for reading instruction, has become a widely accepted practice in the United States. Most teachers use children's literature, in the form of picture storybooks and novels, as well as nonfiction. By the early 1990s, the student anthologies of all the major American basal reading series were composed almost entirely of unadapted works of children's literature. Yet literature-based instruction goes far beyond simply changing the kinds of texts children read. Also required in literature-based instruction are an understanding of children's responses to literature, the value of the experience of reading for reading's sake, the use of literature in the teaching of reading, the content of the literature-based curriculum, and appropriate forms of assessment.

As the authors in this volume demonstrate, literature-based instruction is a well-developed set of approaches to promoting students' appreciation of literature and their proficiency in comprehending and decoding text. Together, these chapters make a unique contribution by giving readers a picture of the "state of the art" as shown through research on literature-based instruction. This broad base of information was not previously available in a single volume. The authors outline the strong theoretical foundation of literature-based instruction, drawing in particular on a sociocultural perspective, and show its grounding in an array of tested classroom strategies.

Most of the chapters in this book began as presentations at three preconvention institutes focused on literature-based instruction, presented at the annual conventions of the International Reading Association in 1994, 1995, and 1996. The ideas in these presentations were revised, reorganized, and sharpened over a four-year period, as the authors interacted with one another and with the editors of this volume. Thus, these chapters do not represent the authors' initial work on these topics, but expert thinking refined over time.

This volume is organized into four sections. The first three sections deal with crucial issues related to literature-based instruction. These issues concern:

- the nature of the literature and of response to literature,
- the nature of the literature-based curriculum, including thematic instruction, curriculum content, teaching strategies, the place of skills, and texts appropriate for use at various grade levels,
- the nature of assessment in literature-based classrooms, including the alignment of instruction and assessment, standards and policy implications, and students' ownership of the assessment process.

The fourth section addresses the future of literature-based instruction and consists of essays by eight highly regarded experts in the field of language arts education.

THE LITERATURE AND RESPONSE TO LITERATURE

The first section, on the nature of the literature and of response to literature, consists of four chapters. The first two provide conceptual lenses with which to view literature. In the opening chapter, Lee Galda suggests that literature can serve as a mirror in which we see the reflection of our own lives, as well as a window through which we can come to understand the lives of others. She distinguishes among the "lived through" experience of reading literature, the "use" of literature as a basis for the language arts curriculum, and the potential "abuse" of literature when it becomes the basis for the reading program. In the next chapter, Violet Harris, writing with author and illustrator Melodye Rosales, addresses the complexities posed by works of literature exploring issues of biracial and multiracial identity. Harris challenges simplistic notions of race and ethnicity in society and as reflected in approaches to multicultural children's literature, and argues for more flexible and sophisticated ways of viewing cultural identity.

The second two chapters focus on reader response and build on the preceding discussion of the literature itself. Lawrence Sipe provides an overview of the many possible theoretical perspectives that can be brought to bear on children's response to literature, including semiotics, psychoanalysis, and poststructuralism. In a close examination of first- and second-grad-ers' responses to literature, he demonstrates the richness and variety of liter-ary understanding that is possible, even for the very young. In the final chapter in this section, Cynthia Brock and James Gavelek propose a theoretical frame-work for reader response based on Vygotsky's sociocultural approach to mind. Using examples from literature-based instruction in a fifth-grade classroom, they show how a sociocultural approach can help teachers foster children's engagement, interpretation, and response, and conclude by outlining five educational purposes served by response.

THE LITERATURE-BASED CURRICULUM

The second section, on the nature of the literature-based curriculum, builds upon the conceptual foundation established in the first section. The first two chapters present frameworks for thinking about the literature-based curricu-lum, in terms of its thematic organization and overall content. Sheila Valencia and Marjorie Lipson outline an approach teachers can follow to organize their teaching around themes, by which they mean challenging concepts and enduring questions, not simply topics. Examples of successful themes are presented, including the literary works highlighted within them. Kathryn Au and Taffy Raphael look at how instruction in literature-based classrooms may be defined from a constructivist perspective, creating multiple roles for the teacher. They outline the five areas of the literature-based curriculum (ownership, comprehension, composition, literary aspects, and language con-ventions) and illustrate the application of this curriculum with examples of instruction from a first- and fifth-grade classroom.

The next two chapters look at intradisciplinary connections among the language arts. Jenny Denyer and Susan Florio-Ruane create an ideal elemen-tary school based on their long history of collaborative work with teachers and students. As they take us on a tour of the school, we visit classrooms and observe teachers, student teachers, and students as they connect their litera-ture study to the teaching and learning of writing. Kathy Highfield describes the influences on her thinking about literature-based instruction as a class-room teacher, and her search for an answer to the question of what children learn through writing about and discussing literature. As she studied her stu-dents' participation in a thematic unit on the Civil War, she found that they showed learning in all five of the curricular areas discussed by Au and Raphael.

The last two chapters in this section deal with selecting literature to meet students' instructional needs at the primary and upper grade levels. Elfrieda Hiebert makes the point that texts for beginning readers must serve as scaf-folds and presents a framework to guide primary teachers in literature-based classrooms, as they make decisions about the texts to be used for instruction.

Arguing that these scaffolds must be temporary, Hiebert discusses characteristics of text, such as the proportion of phonetically regular words, that teachers should consider to promote young children's independence as readers. Laura Pardo, an experienced teacher researcher, addresses the question of how teachers can tell whether a particular work of literature will promote the goals they have for their students. Using examples from her fifth-grade classroom, she discusses three issues: (a) identifying themes around which to organize literature selection and related instruction, (b) finding books with the greatest potential to encourage discussion among her students, and (c) determining the balance between providing students with choice and yet maintaining enough common thematic elements to facilitate discussion across the books chosen.

ASSESSMENT IN LITERATURE-BASED CLASSROOMS

The third section focuses on assessment, one of the most challenging topics facing educators. The first two chapters identify broad issues facing literacy educators, including the goals to be met in innovative assessments, the alignment of assessment and instruction, and the role of state and national standards. Tanja Bisesi, Devon Brenner, Mary McVee, P. David Pearson, and Loukia Sarroub look at efforts to change assessment to better meet the needs of students and teachers in literature-based classrooms. This chapter provides a broad overview of key issues and the progress made in developing new assessments that can meet such criteria as being authentic, equitable for students of diverse backgrounds, and informative to a variety of audiences. Charles Peters and Karen Wixson assert that content (in the form of important ideas) and processes must both be reflected in the language arts curriculum, before the alignment of instruction and assessment can take place. They show how this view of curriculum is reflected in Michigan's English language arts framework and provide examples of a teacher's work with assessment in the context of a thematic unit.

The second two chapters in this section look closely at assessment in literature-based classrooms, tracing the evolution of portfolios and the involvement of students in their own assessment. Susan McMahon describes her collaboration with Jacqueline Wells, a fifth-grade teacher who had begun to use classroom sets of novels and was wrestling with developing appropriate assessments for her students. McMahon discusses how they set goals for student learning, based on the district's goals as well as on Wells' own thinking, and designed instruction and performance-based assessments. Teacher researcher Jo Ann Wong-Kam explains how she helped students in her literature-based classrooms, in both third and fifth grades, learn to evaluate their own progress as readers, instead of relying on the teacher to tell them how they were doing. She explains how she led students to set goals and make plans for achieving their goals, designed instruction to support students in reaching their goals, and had students collect evidence to show what they had learned.

THE FUTURE OF LITERATURE-BASED INSTRUCTION

The essays forming the final section of this volume provide a look at the future of literature-based instruction. Sean Walmsley presents a brief update of his research on the state of literature-based instruction in classrooms and suggests steps to be taken to move this form of instruction forward. Kathy Short sees literature-based instruction as facing the worst of times in the political context, but the best of times in the educational context. Robert Rueda agrees with Short about the dangers in the political context and calls our attention to the needs of students of diverse cultural and linguistic backgrounds and the potential of multicultural literature for addressing these needs. Reflecting on the exclusion of the African American perspective in children's literature of the past, Barbara Diamond explains why multicultural literature is valuable for all children, but cautions that time must be invested in professional development activities that help teachers to use this literature successfully. Barbara Taylor argues that we must preserve what is most vital in literature-based instruction, namely the experiencing and sharing of aesthetic responses to books. Margaret McKeown offers a cognitive perspective, highlighting the importance of discussions of literature for improving students' ability to question the author and make sense of text. Addressing teacher educators, Diane Stephens wonders about teachers who do not use literature-based instruction and argues that professional development activities must be shaped to promote a better match to what teachers (and not just researchers) find significant. Bernice Cullinan concludes that literature will survive, finding hope in several trends (the spread of literature in classrooms, the increase in the number of children's books published each year, the proliferation of bookstores) and honoring literature for its role in preparing a responsible citizenry.

The work of assembling this volume has been a joy from start to finish. We enjoyed the privilege of working with a distinguished group of contributors who showed an extraordinary degree of thoughtfulness and timeliness in preparing their chapters. In addition, we had the pleasure of collaborating with Susanne Canavan of Christopher-Gordon, who moved the book forward in exemplary fashion, while always showing care for its quality.

Can there be literacy without literature? According to this book, the answer is no. Charlotte Huck (1989) notes that, without literature, there might be a minimal, functional kind of literacy. But, she continues, there cannot be the kind of insightful, discerning literacy shown by readers who have had the opportunity to come to know the richness of the human experience, of worlds other than their own, through books. That is the kind of literacy required of citizens in a democracy, who must judge the issues for themselves, and that is the kind of literacy developed by readers, young and old, who have fallen in love with literature.

Taffy Raphael
Kathy Au

REFERENCES

Huck, C. S. (1989). No wider than the heart is wide. In J. Hickman & B. E. Cullinan (Eds.), *Children's literature in the classroom: Weaving Charlotte's web* (pp. 252–262). Norwood, MA: Christopher-Gordon.

Chapter I

Mirrors and Windows:
Reading as Transformation

●————————●

Lee Galda, University of Georgia

Let me tell you a story, one that doesn't begin "once upon a time," but that unfortunately begins anew every day. For 28 years the University of Georgia has sponsored a Children's Book Award Program. I've been teaching at the University for 17 years, and in each of those 17 years I have found myself defending one book or another from an outraged adult who objects to it. This year it's Patricia Polacco's (1994) *Pink and Say,* a moving picture book about one small slice of the Civil War. My son, Adam, a second grader, just loved this book. We read it together and talked about it for days as he sought to understand why bad things happen to good people and what war means to those who do and don't survive. He asked questions about prejudice and justice and courage. Not bad for an 8-year-old! In fact, Adam was so moved by this book that he went to his media specialist and begged her to change his vote for the Book Award from a funny, but lightweight rhyming book to *Pink and Say.* She did. This book that caused my 8-year-old to think about important issues in his life—for prejudice, justice, and courage *are* important issues to 8-year-olds—is under attack by adults who take exception to its content.

Why is this the case? I'll argue that it's because of the potential power that is inherent in reading literature, a power that comes from both book and reader. This power enables readers to transform words-on-a-page into emotional experiences that function as mirrors and windows into our lives and the lives of others. Reader response theory and research, as well as many teacher reports of children reading and responding in their classrooms, attest to the unpredictability, complexity, and power of the act of reading. Indeed, one of the guiding principles of the National Reading Research Center, at both the University of Georgia and the University of Maryland, was *engagement,* a word that describes the kind of reading we would like to see our children doing. The dictionary tells us that the sixth meaning of engagement is to interlock so as to transmit power. Isn't that a wonderful metaphor for what happens when a reader is absorbed in a book?

DESCRIBING ENGAGED READING

What do engaged readers do? Reading is transactional, temporal, social, and cultural. By reading, people turn texts into stories, poems, and meaningful information. By reading, people create meaning for themselves that they can share with others. By reading together, people build communal as well as individual understandings of themselves, others, and the world around them.

As we have studied readers reading literature, we have attempted to answer questions about what goes on in the mind of a reader, about the act of reading and making meaning, and about the social and cultural aspects of reading and responding. We now describe reading as a creative, **transactional** process that involves readers in actively creating meaning under the guidance of the words on the page (Rosenblatt, 1978). The content of any book is not simply the words the author put there but those words as they are infused with meaning by their readers, meaning that reflects the various experience and knowledge that readers bring to their reading.

We have made basic distinctions between aesthetic and efferent reading, or reading for literary and informative purposes (J. Langer, 1996; Rosenblatt, 1978). When reading aesthetically, for literary purposes, a reader is focused on the experience that the text makes possible. This kind of reading is especially appropriate for stories and poems. Aesthetic reading is not to get some information with which to operate in the real world, but to live through an experience. Michael Benton (1983) describes what occurs in the mind of a reader as a journey through the secondary world of story, linking this imaginative secondary world to the imaginative play children engage in long before they learn to read. It is this opportunity for lived-through experience in the secondary world that allows us to learn about ourselves and others when we read.

Reading is a journey because it is **temporal**; the story occurs over time and it is over time that we read. This temporal dimension manifests itself most vividly in a reader's drive to get to the end of the story, in the "narrative lust" that propels many of us when we read a story for the first time. As we are reading aesthetically, Benton argues, we picture characters and events, anticipate actions, think back over what we have read, identify with characters, and make the virtual experience we are shaping part of our lives (1983).

Reading is not only transactional and temporal, it is also **social** and **cultural**. The meaning that readers create as they read, fueled by the reader's own culturally situated experiences, is at once individual and intensely social. The text itself, as language, provides an opportunity for individual meaning making while also promoting shared meaning. Stories are culturally-situated texts, written by authors from particular places and times who hold particular beliefs and have particular ways of looking at the world. Like authors, readers all have unique experiences and feelings. But we all, readers and authors alike, mediate those experiences and feelings through language, and language is a socially constructed system. We share referents within our language, so there is always some amount of shared meaning, while there also may be considerable variation in meaning across readers.

Individuals construct their personal meanings as they read. These meanings are shared with others and become part of a socio-culturally constructed interpretation of a text. We test, alter, and enlarge our constructed meaning as we talk about texts with others, or respond through writing, acting, singing, or drawing. As we share our personal meaning with others, their own responses to the text and to our interpretations become part of our experience and thus of our responses. The meaning we make of a story contains the ideas and images of all those with whom we have talked about the book. Every time we share a book with a class and discuss it, the book becomes a little bigger.

The meaning we create as we read both shapes and is shaped by other texts—those we have read and those we have lived. Robert Scholes (1989) argues that we construct the stories of our lives in much the same fashion as we construct the stories that we read. Our experiences with life and literature mutually inform and influence each other. All that we have experienced, including our experiences gathered through literature, becomes text. New texts in both literature and life are meaningful to us when we link them with our previously constructed texts as well as to our future writings (see Denyer & Florio-Ruane, this volume). Reading thus becomes a constructive, intertextual activity given meaning by its relation to our lives.

READING AS TRANSFORMATION

Just as reading is an act of **transforming** words into meaning, aesthetic reading allows readers the possibility of **transforming themselves** as well. D. W. Harding (1937, 1978) and James Britton (1970) argue that because the kind of experience gained through reading, which Suzanne Langer (1957) calls virtual experience, is not connected to direct action in the real world, readers have an opportunity for contemplation not often available during real-world experiences. Reading aesthetically allows readers to experience, contemplate, and evaluate the attitudes, values, and emotions present in the created story, building not only their own storehouse of experiences but their own value systems as well. This is precisely what Adam was doing with *Pink and Say*.

The luxury of thinking without the necessity of action makes the aesthetic experience one that allows readers to bring texts into their lives in ways that help them define and shape their lives (Britton, 1970). Aesthetic reading makes possible a transformational experience whenever a reader picks up a book. Whether looking at mirrors of ourselves or through windows into the lives of others, our experience during aesthetic reading affords us the opportunity to reconstruct ourselves, to understand living better. This is the transforming power of engagements with story. This is what makes teaching with literature exciting.

What a story is about—ideas that propel the author to write it and that readers generate while reading it—and how it is written make a difference both in the connections that readers make with the story and how they write and talk about it. A story with power can generate powerful, heartfelt responses. A story with power can allow an engagement that lingers over time, as did Adam's engagement with the lives of Pink and Say. A story with power answers the question, Why read? A story with power is dangerous; it can get you into trouble.

This potential for trouble—we call it challenges and censorship—has to do with the transforming power of stories. It is just this potential for transformation, the power that experiences with stories have to change our lives, to make us see, feel, and live a little differently, that makes literature so wonderful and so dangerous. Have you ever wondered why women weren't taught to read but men were? Why slave owners were forbidden to teach their slaves to read? Reading brings power to those who engage in it. That's why we teach with literature, why we all go to great trouble to put powerful books into the hands of our students. That's why we get in trouble, too. Some adults don't want children to be empowered enough to think, to challenge the status quo. Like Jonas in Lois Lowry's *The Giver* (1993), when children are exposed to ideas and experiences beyond those controlled by their communities, they become dangerously individual. They presume to think for themselves.

Challenges and censorship, then, are big issues in literature-based instruction, especially when your goal is to engage children in books in a significant way so that they will want to read, think, and talk about them, so that they will learn from them. Books powerful enough to engage children are the same books that are likely to enrage censors. That is what is happening with *Pink and Say.*

ISSUES IN LITERATURE-BASED INSTRUCTION

But challenges and censorship are not the only issues we face in literature-based instruction. We also must distinguish between the use and misuse of literature in instruction. Hade (1993) describes four reasons that teachers have for using literature in the classroom: teaching reading, developing literary knowledge, developing self-understanding, and developing social responsibility. While these are important—even noble—goals, focusing on these goals often results in our losing sight of the reason for literature, of the potential for powerful engagements that books provide.

Using children's literature to foster reading achievement is now an accepted part of many reading programs. The argument goes like this: Children who read most read best, and engaged readers are likely to become good readers. Therefore, let us give children texts that are likely to engage them and a lot of time to read and they will become better readers. In its best manifestation this might look like Betty Shockley Bisplinghoff's classroom in which children imaginatively engage with narrative by talking, listening, reading, and writing the stories of their lives and those that they find in the many books in their classroom (Galda, Bisplinghoff, & Pellegrini, 1994). As they use language to participate in these stories, they learn to read—and to write, listen, and speak—in narrative forms. In its worst manifestation, literature is seen as a more engaging basal text, and is skilled and drilled exhaustively, with little or no attention to the pleasure and power of the story. When we use books this way, they become the means for learning whatever skill is being studied, and the books themselves get lost in the service of the curriculum. What is even worse, the children who are reading those books are not learning how to become engaged readers. They may be learning how to read, but they are learning in an atmosphere that mitigates against reading for the joy of it, and that shortchanges the individual construction of meaning.

Using trade books as opportunities for decontextualized skills practice works against the very thing that we are trying to promote. Workbook-like exercises and predetermined questions and projects, most of which force readers into reading for information rather than experience, into reading efferently rather than aesthetically, work against our goal of providing children with powerful transformational experiences with literature. This kind of practice forces children to read stories and poems in inappropriate ways that cheat them out of a transforming experience, seriously undermine the pleasure of reading, and enable children to do quite well in school without ever imaginatively engaging with a fictive text. How many children never read the stories that are assigned to them, but rather simply look for the answers to the questions that are assigned simultaneously? Many do, and never have the chance to experience the power of a good book.

The second reason teachers use literature is to develop literary knowledge. This usually has to do with intertextuality, or making connections across life and literature as well as developing understandings about how literature works. We have learned that reading like a treasure hunter digging for the gold called THE MEANING works against reading for pleasure and understanding. This kind of reading often results in dysfluent readers who don't emotionally connect with the texts they read. As an antidote to this, we have sometimes moved to doing very little teaching. We read books, let the kids talk, and then read more books. But when we do only this we are doing our students a great disservice (see Au & Raphael, Chapter 6). Rather than ignore the author's craft in our discussions of books, we need to consider the choices the author has made, and how they have affected our sense making. As Alan Purves (1993) has argued, to ignore this denies the power of the author, something that those of us who work hard to encourage our students to view themselves as authors don't want to do!

We have also come to realize that children can and will connect the stories they read to other texts. When we read we make intertextual connections, linking all that we read with our concept of story, and this helps us learn about literature as verbal art. Often children are neither expected to make these connections nor taught to do so. However, as Highfield describes in Chapter 8, children can make intertextual links across particular literary elements such as characters, events, symbols, and themes; across illustrations; across what they know about the lives of authors and illustrators; and across life experiences. Intertextual links help children see reading as connecting new ideas to previous understandings, help them understand and appreciate the craft of authors, and help them make sense of new literary experiences.

Knowledgeable teachers plan for intertextual links through judicious literature selection (see Pardo, Chapter 10), but even intertextual links can be dangerous. Too often we take the easy way out and link books superficially, such as connecting Phyllis Reynolds Naylor's *Shiloh* (1991) with other dog stories and ignoring the profound moral issues that she presents, or taking a book such as Barbara Williams's *Albert's Toothache* (1974) and putting it in a unit on dental health. Or we may forget that the themes that we create as we read may not be the same themes that our students create (see Au, 1992). *Charlotte's Web* (White, 1952) can be a story about farm life, death and grief, the cycle of life, family, friendship, maturation, or any number of things, depending on who is reading it.

This individual nature of response makes it difficult to know what kinds of intertextual links our students might make. It also makes it difficult to select a book that will provide a powerful reading experience for them. Sometimes we are lucky and we make an inspired choice; other times we select what we think will be a wonderful book to encourage thinking and talking about particular issues and our students refuse us and the book we offer.

If we teach with literature because of the potential for developing self-understanding, then we will want to select books that are potentially powerful experiences for our students, and this is a difficult undertaking (see Pardo, Chapter 10). If we overestimate or underestimate what students are ready to receive, we cheat them. If a book is presented too late, the opportunity for emotional growth and transformation may be lost. And if a book is presented too soon, transformation will not take place. Further, few students will want to return to a book later when it might be meaningful.

Children make sense out of what they are ready to understand. My daughter picked up *The Devil's Arithmetic* (Yolen, 1988) the summer after she finished third grade. Now, she's a strong reader and reads widely and well, but I just didn't think that she was ready for the emotional content in this book even though she could read it with ease. But, since I'm her mother, she didn't listen to me and she read it anyway. And the emotional content *was* too much for her. She simply shut down her thinking, reading to the end to find out what happened but with little evidence of any emotional comprehension. She put the book aside and I feared that she would not read it again when she might be able to really understand what happens in that story. She did take my advice and read Lois Lowry's *Number the Stars* (1989). That book, much less graphic and emotionally wrenching, was just right for her. Fortunately, she likes to reread books and read *The Devil's Arithmetic* again as a fifth grader. She loved it.

This is not to say that we should offer children only emotionally safe books, whatever they may be. If we treat children as if they will be hurt by the strong feelings a story might spark, we cheat them of experiencing the fundamental power of story. So many of us worry about "troubling" children with books, not wanting to disturb them in any way. To not read a book like *Bridge to Terabithia* (Paterson, 1977) to an upper-grade class because it deals with death would cheat students of the potentially rich experience that reading that book has provided many, many children. Of course there are some books that students just don't connect to, no matter how wonderful the book is, and they need to know that it's okay to not like a quite wonderful book that the teacher and perhaps other students do like.

Sometimes students reject a book because of what we do with it in the classroom. Take a book such as *The Great Gilly Hopkins* (Paterson, 1978). If that book is selected because it will teach children not to lie, cheat, or steal, then the lesson will fail! Books aren't meant to teach children how to behave, but rather to allow them to think about how to behave. Katherine Paterson (1982) writes passionately about how horrified she is when she hears from teachers that Gilly is or isn't a suitable "role model" for their students; she says she's not in the business of creating role models or teaching morals but of telling stories. Fiction is about feeling, about meanings and significances, about questions rather than answers. Unlike many authors of the past, most contemporary authors (all the good ones) do not write stories to teach lessons, but rather to transform experience. Certainly fiction deals with values, with morality, but teaching lessons is not what fiction is about. We must be careful not to select books for the purpose of teaching lessons. Powerful books are capable of a much more subtle and effective moral education than that; they are capable of providing mirrors that help us examine our own lives and thus transform them.

Many of us feel a commitment to use literature to enact another kind of transformation: to use books as windows into other lives, to emotionally educate our students about people, cultures, places, and values that reflect the diversity of our country and our world. But of course we can never be sure just what our students will make of a particular book. Cultural differences lead to different voices and different interpretations of life and literature and we all, students and teachers alike, need to learn to hear these different voices (see also, Harris with Rosales, Chapter 2). And while we are learning to listen, we must also remember that if we ask students to understand texts in terms of their own experiences, then we must allow them to do so rather than push them toward understanding texts as we want them to or as we ourselves do.

We all enjoy reading books in which we can see ourselves, and it's easier to see ourselves in a book that is about people who are similar to us. I have listened to children describe how big differences between themselves and their experiences and story characters and events pushed them out of the story. This prevented their empathy, identification, or even anger toward a central character who was simply too different. Sometimes, if differences between life and text experiences are overwhelming, readers read books about other people and places as if they were at a zoo or an aquarium, where they look at but don't live with the characters. And when we're reading books about people whose behaviors, values, and customs are different from our own, we make judgments, which can be negative, about them. This is a problem when one of our goals is to broaden our own and our children's perspectives on life and culture.

At the very least, we all can learn to consider alternative responses and reasons for particular responses, and begin to make distinctions between what we personally like and find comfortable and the value that various books might hold for a variety of readers. In this way we can begin to broaden our perspectives on both literature and life.

At best, reading literature can allow us to understand how alike we all are, even in our differences. Rather than a mirror of ourselves or a window into the lives of others, reading can be like looking through a slowly darkening window. Initially we see through the window into the lives of others, but as we come to know the characters the light slowly dims and their image is replaced by our own (Cullinan & Galda, 1998). Careful selection and sensitive dialogue about our students' reading experiences can help them to experience literature in this way.

We have these four goals, then, of reading proficiency, literary knowledge, self-understanding, and social responsibility. Hade (1993) argues that we, as teachers, tend to hold one as dominant rather than act on all four simultaneously. I would argue that we must act on them simultaneously, and always within the framework of reader response theory (see Brock & Gavelek, Chapter 4). Good teaching with literature seems to me to be an attempt to balance these goals across the days and weeks and months of classroom life, allowing readers the chance to experience the dangerous power that reading can provide, to develop literate voices, to want to read and read more, to spontaneously share and refine their personal responses through self-reflection and social dialogue, and to see the world through the eyes of others.

SELECTING POWERFUL BOOKS

To do this we must be careful about the books we choose. We have so little time to waste that we must choose only the best, because that is what children deserve. Books of value that we connect with can transform us. There are many things to consider when selecting these books of value. Our students' reading ability certainly influences our selection. While partner reading, tape recordings, teacher read-alouds, and extra help for struggling readers allow us to choose books that might challenge some of our students, we must be careful not to challenge them so much that the books defeat the readers. And we must try our best to select books that reflect and stretch the ideas and concepts that are important to our students and that they can understand emotionally. We also need to consider the content of the books we select in terms of community values, selecting wisely so that we might defend ourselves against censorship. How the content relates to our curriculum is also an important consideration when we are using literature in theme-based or integrated instruction.

We must also try to select books that demonstrate how literature reflects the world that we inhabit. Purves (1993) suggests that we use multiculturalism as our selection principle and that, while the individual books that each of us selects may vary, across the years they should represent the best depictions of the many cultural experiences that make up our world (see also Harris with Rosales, Chapter 2).

We will do many things with these books in our classrooms. We will read and understand them individually, certainly, for readers must make sense of what they read before they can consider further the sense they have made. We will also read and explore them as examples of the craft of writing, a craft shared by all good writers regardless of their culture (Purves, 1993).

And we will learn to consider ourselves as culturally-situated readers reading culturally-situated texts. We will do this by reading, writing, talking, and thinking about the ideas, values, beliefs, and questions that are present in the books we read and the responses we create. We will be individuals within a classroom community, working together to understand how artists capture visions of their cultures through the medium of words and how we create our own version of these visions as readers in the company of other readers. By engaging in powerful transactions with books, we will come to know ourselves and others, and to understand and appreciate the power of language and the value of literature in our lives.

CONCLUDING COMMENT

Pink and Say was a transformative experience for my son because it is a powerful book and he is a powerful reader. Those who seek to keep books from others seek to deny them the opportunity to create their own powerful experiences. They're fighting *against* what you are fighting *for*—books that can help shape our lives. The power of literature is perhaps eclipsed only by the power of teachers. What you do with books in your classroom today will make a difference in the lives of your students.

REFERENCES

Au, K. H. (1992). Constructing the theme of a story. *Language Arts, 69* (2), 106–111.

Benton, M. (1983). Secondary worlds. In W. H. Agee & L. Galda (Eds.), *Response to literature: Empirical and theoretical research (Journal of Research and Development in Education), 16* (3), 68–75.

Britton, J. (1970). *Language and learning.* London: Penguin.

Cullinan, B. E., & Galda, L. (1998). *Literature and the child (4th edition).* Ft. Worth, TX: Harcourt Brace.

Galda, L., Bisplinghoff, B. S., & Pellegrini, A. D. (1994). Sharing lives: Reading, writing, talking, and living in a first-grade classroom. *Language Arts, 72,* 334–339.

Hade, D. M. (1993). Books in the classroom: The differences among us. *The Horn Book* (September/October), 642–645.

Harding, D. W. (1937). The role of the onlooker. *Scrutiny, 6,* 247–258.

Harding, D. W. (1978). Psychological processes in the reading of fiction. In M. Meek, A. Warlow, and G. Barton (Eds.), *The cool web: The pattern of children's reading.* New York: Atheneum.

Langer, J. (1996). *Envisioning literature.* New York: Teachers College Press.

Langer, S. K. (1957). *Philosophy in a new key.* Cambridge: Harvard University Press.

Paterson, K. (1982). Reading as a revolutionary activity. *The Advocate, 1* (3), 137–142.

Purves, A. C. (1993). Toward a reevaluation of reader response and school literature. *Language Arts, 70,* 348–361.

Rosenblatt, L. M. (1978). *The reader, the text, the poem.* Carbondale, IL: Southern Illinois University Press.

Scholes, R. E. (1989). *Protocols of reading.* New Haven: Yale University Press.

CHILDREN'S BOOKS CITED

Lowry, L. (1989). *Number the stars.* Boston: Houghton Mifflin.

Lowry, L. (1993). *The Giver.* Boston: Houghton Mifflin.

Naylor, P. R. (1991). *Shiloh.* New York: Atheneum.

Paterson, K. (1977). *Bridge to Terabithia.* New York: Crowell.

Paterson, K. (1978). *The great Gilly Hopkins.* New York: Crowell.

Polacco, P. (1994). *Pink and Say.* New York: Philomel.

White, E. B. (1952). *Charlotte's web.* New York: Harper.

Williams, B. (1974). *Albert's toothache.* New York: Dutton.

Yolen, J. (1988). *The devil's arithmetic.* New York: Viking.

Chapter 2

Biracial and Multiracial Identity: Dilemmas for Children's Literature

●────────●

Violet J. Harris, University of Illinois at Urbana–Champaign
with
Melodye Rosales, Author and Illustrator, Champaign

INTRODUCTION

I teach undergraduate and graduate courses in children's literature. Recently, the daughter of a colleague wanted me to know that I had the best job in our college. She made this comment after perusing the shelves of my offices. Her adoration was cemented when I invited her to borrow books. That's the easy part of what I do, sharing literature with an avid reader. The difficult part is competing with virtual reality pets, Nintendo, and the local mall in order to entice children to the wonderful world of books.

Melodye Rosales is a children's book illustrator and author. She creates art and text that reflect children's need for entertainment and information. Her work appears in textbooks and trade books produced by major and independent publishing companies such as Scholastic, Random House, Pleasant Company, Little, Brown and Company, and Just Us Books, to name a few. One endearing aspect of Melodye's work is her selection of children and adults from our local communities to serve as models for her illustrations. Many of the models have experienced some celebrity as local media interview them or they appear at bookstore signings.

Not surprisingly, we are friends brought together by our mutual love for children's books and our desire to share and create literature that captures the multidimensionality of Black experiences in ways that appeal to children. In order to achieve these goals, we attend conferences such as the National Council of Teachers of English; discuss articles about children's book publishing in journals such as *Publishers Weekly*; critique each other's work; share references; and collaborate on books such as the forthcoming Minnie Series.

Our interest in the topic of this chapter, biracial and multiracial identity, emanates from different sources. Mine evolved out of research with third, fourth, and fifth graders enrolled in an after-school enrichment program. I was intrigued by the insistence of some children that the biracial children self-identify as Black, which they refused to do. My curiosity intensified as more children's books exploring biracial and multiracial identity were published. In contrast to my newly emerging interest, Melodye's concerns grew out of "lived experiences." She is biracial and, to some degree, has grappled with its multiple and sometimes contradictory meanings throughout her life. Our chapter is structured to allow both of our "voices" to emerge. In some ways, Melodye provides the insider's perspective and I assume the stance of an interested observer.

As we traveled throughout the country, we found that others had similar responses to biracial and multiracial identity. We decided to explore the issue as it is constructed today. Our analysis of the contemporary situation draws heavily upon its historic construction. In particular, the historic writings of W. E. B. Du Bois attracted us. Du Bois embodied a multitude of identities and philosophies. He strongly identified as Black but "looked" biracial or multiracial. He wrote insightful and pioneering critiques on race and its use for political subjugation. Du Bois's political beliefs ranged from pacifism to communism to Pan-Africanism. Most importantly for us, he published a children's magazine, *The Brownies' Book* (1920–21), that sought to create new images of Blacks, entertain and inform readers, and imbue children with a sense of social activism and justice. Further, he critiqued his personal experiences and used those to frame national discussions and debates about race, identity, justice, and power. His ideas are relevant today and provide a framework for our ideas. In Du Bois's words:

> Herein lie buried many things which if read with patience may show the strange meaning of being black here in the dawning of the Twentieth Century. This meaning is not without interest to you, Gentle Reader; for the problem of the Twentieth Century is the problem of the color-line (Du Bois, 1903, 1989)

Du Bois wrote these prophetic lines in a collection of essays, *The Souls of Black Folk,* in 1903. Du Bois's piercing intellect crafted ideas about race in a manner that resounds as we enter the 21st century.[1] His essays—such as "Of the Passing of the First-Born" and "The Sorrow Songs"—are passionate and elegant musings about the contradictions of labeling an individual a particular "race" on the basis of physical characteristics and the complex artistic creations that emanate from a group's response to enslavement and oppression. These essays offer pertinent insights for those engaged in analyzing children's literature and critical topics within the discipline such as biracial and multiracial identity and questions about authenticity.

Du Bois's roles as a "public intellectual," political activist, and cultural critic, among many others, required that he produce research, essays, and other documents that would advance the cause of racial justice, political and economic equality, and gain access to power for those who lacked it and were oppressed. Du Bois dedicated his life to these pursuits. He also sought the comforts of a marriage and family. His autobiographies contain numerous references to his family and his love for them is quite evident. Public intellectuals and activists of Du Bois's stature encounter many difficulties trying to reconcile public and private, familial duties; sometimes their spouses and children feel they have been sacrificed to political causes. One recent example that explores the public and familial responsibilities of a public figure is the memoir written by the daughter of a prominent South African political activist (Slovo, 1996).

Du Bois's essay, "Of the Passing of the First Born," captures his mediation of his fatherly love and duties with his intellectual responsibility to analyze his son's life as an example of the manner in which racial stratification affects individuals in myriad ways. Du Bois's son, Burghardt, died before age two. The father's pride and joy are evident in this soulful meditation; yet, the thoughts are tempered by lamentations about the reactions others would display when viewing his son's Nordic and Mediterranean features. Du Bois wrote:

> How beautiful he was, with his olive-tinted flesh and dark gold ringlets, his eyes of mingled blue and brown, his perfect little limbs, and the soft voluptuous roll which the blood of Africa had moulded into his features! I held him in my arms, after we had sped far away to our Southern home,—held him, and glanced at the hot red soil of Georgia and the breathless city of a hundred hills, and felt a vague unrest. Why had not the brown of his eyes crushed out and killed the blue?— for brown were his father's eyes, and his father's father's. And thus in the Land of Color-line I saw, as it fell across my baby, the shadow of the Veil (1903, 1989; p. 170).

Burghardt escaped the awful racial bondage of America of the early 20th century. He did not have to experience the "warring of two souls, the African and the American." Nor would he have to endure questions such as "What are you?", signifying the questioner's need to place him in a discrete racial category. One cannot help wonder which racial category would Burghardt be placed in because of these characteristics: Negro, white, or mulatto? A glance at his parents might cloud the issue further; Du Bois was multiracial (Dutch, French, African) and his wife, Nina, biracial (African and German American).[2]

Similar questions greet many children today. Then, as now, the choices are severely limited, especially for children who have one parent deemed Caucasian, Asian/Pacific Islander, Latino/a, or Native American (and various combinations of these groups) and one parent labeled Black (or African, West Indian, African American, and so forth). Typically, the children of these unions are labeled "Black."[3] Other racial combinations involving the aforementioned groups, with the exception of Black, can choose either category.[4] For example, the child of a Native American and a Caucasian can be identified legally as "White," or Native American along with a specific tribal affiliation. We canvassed four biracial families that featured a European/European American father and a Native American or Asian (the nationalities varied—Thai, Chinese, and Japanese) mother. One parent was questioned from each family; each parent concurred with the statement that two options were available for identifying his children's race on birth certificates and other official documents. Each cautioned, however, that they attempted to provide their children with as much exposure to each racial or ethnic identity as possible.

A recent decision by a federal task force rejected the idea of a "multiracial" category for the U.S. Census for the year 2000 (Associated Press, 1997). The refusal to create another racial category, one which would accommodate biracial or multiracial identity, ensures that the debate will continue as it has for nearly 400 years, especially as interracial marriages increase in number. The task force offered the following as its rationales—"there is no general understanding of what the term means" and the categoric "would, in effect, create another population group and no doubt add to racial tension and further fragmentation of our population" (p. A-6). Racial tension and fragmentation currently co-exist with the reality of biracial or multiracial individuals. Arguing that a multiracial category increases racial tension and fragmentation simply ignores historical truths.

Had the census committee approved a multiracial category, another layer of complexity would have emerged. For example, what fraction of another race should an individual possess before being considered biracial or multiracial? Would 1/64 be sufficient or 1/4?[5] What date would signal an appropriate historical period for labeling an individual biracial or multiracial? According to sociologist F. James Davis, researchers from various disciplines suggest that 75 percent to 90 percent of Blacks have some White heritage and at least 1 percent of Whites have some Black ancestry (Davis, 1991). Are these individuals multiracial? These percentages would shift if Native American heritage were included.

The shadow of the veil, as articulated by Du Bois, permeates children's literature as well. Consider the comments of writer-illustrator Melodye Rosales.

When I was growing up in the 50s and 60s, I didn't have the luxury of choosing the <u>other</u> category, *or,* being thought of as *Biracial.* I was, as many within the Black community, a result of generations of ethnic blending. In my community, I was just "another Negro child."

We who are ethnic blends, naturally accept the "one drop theory" [one drop of "Black" blood makes you Black], often, without questioning its conceptual origin or its historical validity. I, not unlike the many who are the offspring of mixed parentage never met or was acknowledged by my father's <u>white</u> side of the family. My parents met in that unique, cloistered milieu known as "show business." <u>She,</u> a Black chorus girl and <u>He,</u> a White, Jewish record producer. Though my mother and father decided to live separate lives, I never felt the void. Perhaps that was because of our family's strong maternal influence and the natural embrace I felt from the Black community.

Unlike Melodye, other biracial children were confused and felt they did not belong to either racial category. A perusal of *Black, White, Other* (Funderburg, 1994), an oral history, reveals stories similar to Melodye's. Lise Funderburg, the daughter of a White mother and a Black father, sought to determine if biracial children struggled with identity.

My sisters and I, like some biracial people, had home lives relatively uncomplicated by the subject of our race. We were loved by our parents and relatives, never challenged by them on our racial allegiances or entitlements. Outside the family, we have found both black and white people with whom we exchange love and respect, people who may be interested in this odd inheritance, but not threatened or offended by it. Still, many people have felt threatened or offended by our parents' relationship, by our mixed heritage, by the fact that we look white but take pride in being half-black. The camouflage of our skin is disturbing to them, irreconcilable. We are fortunate that the offended have never used violence to express themselves, but their reactions to us have been unsettling and at times, quite painful (Funderburg, 1994, p. 16).

Funderburg interviewed 65 individuals; clearly, these individuals welcomed the chance to share their stories. What becomes apparent as each vignette is read, is that a monolithic biracial or multiracial experience does not exist. The only commonalties are parents of differing races meeting and falling in love and individuals within and outside of the families responding negatively or positively to the interracial unions.

Melodye faces another racial dilemma as she establishes herself as a writer and illustrator. That is, how does she become a candidate for children's book awards that are race-based, for example, the Coretta Scott King Awards (Smith, 1994)? Melodye's problems are two-fold: She does not "look" Black and her married surname suggests an Hispanic heritage. This problem surfaced as we discussed whether her debut work as an author-illustrator, *'Twas the Night B'fore Christmas* (1996) would receive consideration for the CSKA. As a consequence of this discussion, Melodye "outted" herself as a Black person at the 1996 Charlemae Rollins symposium at the NCTE conference. She wanted readers, critics, teachers, and librarians to know that she self-identified as a Black because of the confusion that had previously existed. The experience was somewhat surreal for me as an audience member. Clearly, based on some of the whispered asides that greeted Melodye's comments, several individuals viewed her as a White woman. This experience highlights the uncertainties that some biracial and multiracial individuals face. They must reaffirm their identities, challenge historic assumptions and stereotypes people hold about biracial and multicultural individuals, and maintain some sense of individuality.

Conundrums involving race, and to a lesser extent, ethnicity, have a long-standing history in the study of children's and young adult literature. Typically, research, reviews, and essays focused on racial representation in terms of numbers of books, authors, and illustrators; authenticity; stereotypes; insider/outsider perspectives; authorship by Whites; and the role of literature in celebrating racial differences, ameliorating prejudice, and correcting historical inaccuracies (Brown, 1933; Sinnette, 1965; Muse, 1975; Broderick, 1973; Sims, 1982; Johnson, 1991).

Other writings highlight the benign and less benign ways in which race and ethnicity insert themselves into children's literature. There are at least four. First, they are present in the unmasking of authors who "pass" as a member of another racial or ethnic group other than their own (Gates, 1991). For instance, Forest Carter, the author of *The Education of Little Tree,* was "unmasked" as White, not Native American (Gates, 1991). Second, they matter in arguments supporting the re-publishing of "beloved classics" such as *Epaminondas* (Hendrickson, 1996). Such works were originally banished when other, equally entertaining works were published without stereotypes, instead emphasizing progressive attitudes that rejected pernicious stereotypes as a form of entertainment for children.

Third, race and ethnicity play a role in the manner in which publishers manipulate dust jacket text and photographs. For example, the tribal affiliations of Gayle Ross and Lucy Tapahonso are listed, respectively, in *How Rabbit Tricked Otter* (1996) and *Navajo ABC: A Diné Alphabet Book* (1995). However, the dust jacket information about their tribal affiliation may serve different motivations for author and publisher. Tapahonso, for instance, begins her professional presentations by speaking in Navajo. Her translations of these introductory remarks note that she has indicated her tribal affiliation and her matrilineal and patrilineal descent. In contrast, sometimes publishers, or authors themselves, highlight an author's racial identity in order to forestall questions about the content and whether the content reflects an insider's perspective.

Fourth, racial and ethnic identity are present in the context of the literature itself. Lately, some authors and illustrators create plots that examine the consequences of biracial or multiracial identity or insert visuals depicting biracial or multiracial individuals.[6] Increasingly, biracial and multiracial identities are thematic issues in children's and young adult literature ranging from ground-breaking works such as *Black Is Brown Is Tan* (Adoff, 1973) to more recent works including *More Than Half, Less Than Whole* (Lacapa & Lacapa, 1994), and *The World of Daughter Mcguire* (Wyeth, 1994) and *Ginger Brown: Too Many Houses* (Wyeth, 1996). The scholarly community acknowledges the importance of the topic as well. For example, Rudman (1989) included a section on biracial identity in her volume, *Children's Literature: An Issues Approach.*

In the remaining sections of this chapter, we explore (1) how biracial and multiracial categories are becoming a growing presence in children's literature, especially for those works classified as multicultural; (2) the effects of racial identity; (3) the effects of racial identity on shaping an artist/illustrator's work; (4) concerns about literary issues; and, (5) intended audience.

RACIAL IDENTITY AND MULTICULTURALISM: PROGRESSIVE OR RETROGRESSIVE IDEOLOGY?

Multiculturalism has historical antecedents in the late 1880s and early 1900s (Banks, 1995), though ironically, according to Banks, Eastern, Central, and Southern European immigrants were the groups of concern. Nativist sentiments spread across the country as waves of immigrants seemingly threatened to overwhelm the "White" population with their large families, illiteracy, strange cultural habits, and Catholicism. Assimilation was the preferred method for assuring that these immigrants became Americanized and "White." The intercultural movement emerged in the early 1900s and remained important through the early 1960s. Proponents advanced ideas suggesting that interactions among individuals from various races, ethnicities, and religions could result in meaningful understanding and lessen racial and ethnic discord (Banks, 1995).

The 1960s were a volatile period in which the ethnic studies movement—Black, Native American, and Chicano/a—became a central topic on many college campuses and, later, in elementary and high schools. Unlike the intercultural movement, the ethnic studies movement, along with women's studies, met with vociferous opposition which continues today and affects the efforts of those who advocate multiculturalism. For example, public figures such as Arthur Schlesinger, Jr., Diane Ravitch, Dinesh D'Souza, William Bennett, and George Will excoriate ethnic studies as racial cheerleading, balkanization, fostering national disunity, and intellectually bankrupt.

Multiculturalism is the latest incarnation among efforts to achieve racial reconciliation, justice, power, and equality. Supporters argue that the ideology encourages unity because the cultural contributions of various groups and individuals are recognized and adopted as official knowledge and can result in fundamental reformation of societal institutions (Sleeter & Grant, 1988; Nieto, 1992). Categories such as race, ethnicity, gender, class, language, age, disability, sexual orientation, language, and religion are assessed for their effects on cultural knowledge, institutions, and processes. Multiculturalism is viewed by some as a stop-gap measure that simplifies complex issues about identity, its fluidity, manifestations of power, and the often contradictory relationships that exist within and among groups typically placed under the multicultural umbrella. Anti-racism beliefs and teachings are a more radicalized extension of multiculturalism.

Admittedly, this overview simplifies an ideology and movement with a long and intricate history. For the purposes of this chapter, multiculturalism is conceptualized as an ideology, although not static, that critiques the status of groups who typically have less than full access to cultural institutions, knowledge, power, and capital. Additionally, the groups and individuals have experienced laws and customs that accord them inferior or low status. They also have histories that demonstrate their attempts to assimilate within the dominating culture and the barriers they faced that prohibited full assimilation. This includes creating parallel institutions similar to those that existed within the dominant society. Some of the groups and categories of individuals in our conceptualization include those classified as people of color, women and girls (including those who are usually erased when labeled solely as minority), bilingual or multilingual, elderly, disabled, members of religious minorities, ethnic Whites such as those whose roots are in Appalachia, and gays and lesbians. We expand the categories to include biracial and multiracial individuals, some of whom argue that they have particular concerns. Our focus is not on all of these discrete and intersecting identities; instead we focus on biracial and multiracial individuals, members of an increasingly vocal group.

WHAT'S IN A NAME: MULATTOES, HALF-BREEDS, MESTIZOS, CREOLES, AND BIRACIALS

Today, it is quite fashionable to argue that "race" is a social construct and not a biological reality. Nevertheless, "race" has and remains a legal reality based on historical assumptions about biology. For example, 18th-century census takers counted Negroes as three-fifths of a person; the Naturalization Act of 1790 limited naturalized citizenship to Whites until 1952; the U.S. Supreme Court in *Love* v. *the State of Virginia* overturned the ban on interracial marriages in 1967, especially those involving Blacks and Whites; and the Voting Rights Act of 1964 eradicated, on paper, the disenfranchisement of Blacks. Clearly, those responsible for administering these and other legislative acts did not expect to encounter many difficulties in assigning individuals to various racial categories and limiting their access to Constitutionally guaranteed rights. Race, for them, was a biological fact and reality despite the appearance of biracial and multiracial individuals.[7]

The early history of biracial and multiracial individuals parallels the colonization of the continent by Europeans, the institutionalization of slavery, the subjugation of Native Americans, and the creation of the republic. Any discussion about the historical emergence of a biracial and multiracial population must acknowledge the role of sexual exploitation of women of color, especially women of African descent, literally beginning with initial contact among different racial groups. Sheftall (1990) documents the propaganda created to justify the exploitation of African, and later African American women. Among the beliefs promoted were lies such as the supposed bestial, lascivious nature of the women, the deliberate seduction of White males, the delicate natures of White women that prevented them from fully engaging in sexual intercourse, and the need for White males to find release for their sexual urges. Similar attitudes were advanced about other women of color, including the submissive geisha or the hot-blooded Latina. In most cases, enslaved or oppressed women could not prevent sexual abuse; yet, these erroneous beliefs persisted.

Remarkably, a few children's and young adult books honestly portray these complex "liaisons" as being voluntary or, more typically, forced in the case of enslaved Black women. For instance, Tom Feelings's harrowing depiction of the transatlantic slave trade, *The Middle Passage: Black Cargo, White Ships* (1995), contains illustrations portraying the rape of African women by European and European-American slavers and the subsequent birth of biracial children. *Letters From a Slave Girl* (Lyons, 1992) recounts Harriet

Jacobs's attempts to thwart the sexual advances of her considerably older slave owner. Harriet described how the process began in letters written to her mother:

March, 1828

Dear Mama,

Day has turn to night. The Docter, he been whispering filthy words in my ear. I know what he want, and I am shamed for him and me both. He follow me everywhere. It's got so I look over my shoulder all the time. Today I step out on the piazza for a bit of air. Soon I heared footsteps and a low voice reminding me, You are my property. Lass week I walk over to Providence to lay a bouquet of Snow Drops on your grave. A shadow fall over me when I kneel down. Then I turn and see the Docter, and it scare me so bad I almost run. I wont touch you, he say, but dont forget who you belong to. Then he say, One day you must yeild to me (pp. 33–34).

The Doctor becomes irate when Harriet continues to rebuff him and tells him that she wants to marry a free Black man, "R". This request is denied and Harriet is told that if she *must* have a husband, then it would be a slave. Further, he warns her that he will beat her if she speaks with "R" and that "R" will be shot like a dog (p. 41). Rather than submit to the Doctor, Harriet enters into a liaison with another White male, one who promises to purchase her, as a method for staving off her owner.

The young adult historical series, Brides of Wildcat County, includes the novels *Dangerous: Savannah's Story* (Watson, 1996) and *Tempestuous: Opal's Story* (1996), the tale of a runaway mulatto slave who heads West as a potential bride. Her slave past catches up with her when her owner's daughter, Savannah, is headed West on the same ship in order to escape marriage to a debauched plantation owner. Additional troubles arise when Opal and her sister Ruby reunite and Savannah's brother, Cole Bruneau, comes West, too. Ruby is terrorized by Cole. She reveals to Opal her rape by Cole and their mother's plan to help her daughter escape to freedom so as not to bear slave children for a slave owner. The book is brutally honest in depicting one of the more sordid aspects of slavery, incest. The book's climax occurs when it is revealed that Savannah and Cole are the half-sister and half-brother of Opal and Ruby.

Native Americans also shared some of the same experiences as Blacks. Think about the myths surrounding Pocahontas, Sacajewa, and La Malinche. Each is revered, in part, because she served as a mediator between Indian and European cultures. These women learned European languages, lived among Europeans, and married or engaged in liaisons with Europeans. The offspring of these unions were sometimes derisively referred to as "half-breeds" (Slapin & Seale, 1992). Less negative were labels attached to the children of Indians and Spaniards, for instance, who were called mestizos.

The abolition of slavery did not result in the disappearance of biracial or multiracial individuals. Marriages between Whites and people of color gradually increased but many were not regarded as lawful. Then as now, marriages or liaisons between Whites and Blacks evoke the most umbrage. Less concern is aroused by the marriages or liaisons among Whites and Asian Pacific Islanders, Native Americans, and Latino/as. Indeed, some nationalities (for example, Japanese Americans) tend to marry individuals from other races and nationalities at the same or greater rates as marriages with Japanese Americans. Wong (1993) articulated the confusion and anger of some Asian Americans about the increasing preference of Asian and Asian American women for dating relationships and marriages with Whites. This issue arose in many of the Asian American studies courses Wong taught at the University of California at Berkeley.

Many factors account for the opposition to interracial marriages. Notions of racial superiority and inferiority are certainly a component. The power to control the lives of various groups is another. Racist ideology makes interracial marriages taboo as well as a reason for exacting violence on less powerful groups. As long as humans stratify based on some characteristic, opposition is likely to continue.

Another complicating factor is the inability of biracial or multiracial Black children to assume the legal racial classification as "White." Most of these children are characterized as Black on birth records unless parents intervene or the physical characteristics of the child enable him to "pass" as White. Melodye's experiences as a child in Los Angeles capture the peculiarities of racial identity for Black biracial children.

> Growing up in Los Angeles during my early years, I never thought much about *color*. No one ever seemed to treat me differently. No matter where I went, I just sort of blended in. I guess there was discrimination, but I drank from the same fountain as white children, and they never refused to hold my hand. I never thought that I looked any different from the group I was in at that moment.
>
> It seems it has always been easier for society to assume an identity for me, rather than explain how I came to be who I am, that my my origins are a blending of a variety of cultures and multiple ethnicities. I believe this blending has greatly sensitized my work because my work is a natural reflection of those multiple layers. Layers that are nestled comfortably within the multifaceted Black experience(s).

Melodye does not fit the literary stereotype of the "tragic mulatto." For others, the inability to legally declare oneself biracial or multiracial is a crucial problem. Books such as *The Color of Water* (McBride, 1997) and *Life on the Color Line* (Williams, 1995) painfully chronicle the emotional tug-of-war experienced by some biracial and multiracial individuals. Different reactions greeted golfer Tiger Woods's declaration that he considered himself a "Cablinasian" (*Ebony Magazine,* 1997).[8] Many Blacks celebrated Woods's achievement as an African-American; some castigated him for not declaring himself a Black. Asian Americans claimed him as well (his mother is ½ Thai and ½ Chinese). Woods, however, insisted that he was not privileging one racial identity but acknowledging all the elements that comprised his racial identity. Children's and young adult novels that also depict this struggle for self-identification—for instance *Arilla Sundown* (Hamilton,1976) and *Thief of Hearts* (Yep, 1995)—are equally poignant and revealing.

Despite the on-going national debates about race, some question the need to insert the thorny debate about racial identity into books for children and youth. Imagine reading books and never encountering images that reflect your racial identity or contain information about your heritage. Or, think about the consequences of seeing yourself depicted as a stereotype in print and electronic media. The tragic mulatto is a case in point (Bogle, 1973). The movie *Imitation of Life* is a classic within the cinematic genre. Many biracial and multiracial families confirm that they are not tragic. They simply want literature that includes them. In short, they desire an end to their invisibility.

BIRACIAL/MULTIRACIAL IDENTITY AND THE ARTISTIC OEUVRE

Racial identity, as is true of any physical characteristic, can influence an individual's experiences. These experiences may prove fertile for the artistic imagination. Difference does not necessarily translate into literary or visual excellence. The writer and artist must interpret those experiences in fresh ways. Otherwise, the literature can ease into propaganda or dullness. Melodye shares how she melds personal identity issues with her attempts to tell a good story or create an engaging visual image.

> As an African American, married to an Afro-Cuban, I have painstakingly worked throughout my career to infuse my characters with a true-to-life warmth that, whenever possible, reflects the reality of our experience, achieving our rightful place of dignity and equality in our multicultural society. I have endeavored to do so, even in the harsh context of slavery, without resorting to stereotypical images. An early example was my work on Pleasant Company's first three

Addy books, in which I used my oldest daughter as the model for the main character, an escaped slave who overcomes a series of challenges, making a new life in the North. Most recently, I reached back to my great grandmother, Ellen Weathersby, a slave near Prentiss, Mississippi, as the model for the Godmother character in *Irene Jennie and The Christmas Masquerade: The Johnkankus* (Small, 1995). I was fortunate to have met the late Reverend Earl Kennedy, a former pastor of St. Luke Christian Methodist Episcopal Church, who served as my model for St. Nicholas in *'Twas The Night B'fore Christmas* (Rosales, 1996), before his unfortunate death this year. Real people. Real lives. The reality of the Black experience, even if fancifully told. It is this devotion to promoting positive images in even the most disturbing, but no less enlightening circumstances, that has guided my career as a children's book illustrator for the past 10 of the 17 years I have worked as a commercial artist. Thanks to the Johnson Publishing family and *EBONY JR!* in particular, I was able to begin a career as a children's book illustrator at a time when no other publisher was willing to take a chance on me.

Melodye articulates a dilemma faced by many writers and illustrators of color. For some, their racial or ethnic identity is a crucial part of their artistic creations (Greenfield, 1974; Clifton, 1981; Feelings, 1985). Their commentaries elucidate a personal aesthetic that emphasizes the multiple functions the art and literature serve. Among these are the personal expression of ideas and imagination, provision of literary and artistic role models, correction of historical distortion, models of social action, and entertainment. Other illustrators and authors, such as Allen Say, view their racial or ethnic identities as important but not necessarily central (Rochman, 1993). Say approaches the matter in a wry manner: "I know that I'm categorized as an ethnic, as a multicultural artist, but that's not really where I'm coming from. All I'm trying to do is art. I consider myself a uniquely American artist and author" (p. 351). On the question of where does he fit, Say commented: "On the one hand, I feel I can live anywhere, and on the other hand, I know I will always be rootless. My home is in my work" (p. 351).

A few, among them Virginia Hamilton (Rochman,1992), Laurence Yep (1993), and Walter Dean Myers (Sutton, 1994), critique the fluidity of racial and ethnic identity by assessing how it shapes being an American, male or female, resident of a particular geographic locale, holder of a specific worldview, family history, and participant in ongoing social and historical processes. Poet Janet Wong illustrates how bi-ethnic identity shapes an individual's experiences in *A Suitcase of Seaweed* (1996). One of the last poems in the volume describes a person who is Chinese, Korean, Alsatian, and German. Add sexual identity to the volatile mixture of characteristics that shape identities and you have the contradictory, parallel, and intersecting attributes that inform writers such as Jacqueline Woodson (1995).

DIDACTICISM OR INFOTAINMENT?

Are racial or ethnic identity themes sufficient to garner readers? For some, it is enough. Many readers actively seek the literature because they crave affirmation of their identity, wish to bolster self-esteem, or simply want access to works about themselves. However, simply creating a book to foster a particular perspective is not sufficient. The authors and illustrators need to be held to standards of excellence. Flat, stereotyped, or cardboard characters suggest a lack of talent, especially for a topic rife with possibilities. Themes should move beyond tragic mulattoes or racial misfits. The cultural milieu should accurately reflect the mores, customs, and worldviews of a historical period, not some romanticized past. Additionally, the language should possess a vibrancy reflective of the language styles found among disparate communities and racial enclaves. Granted, there are some shared language and cultural patterns, because we are Americans. Differences exist as well. Melodye addresses the artistic considerations.

> My passion is doing period work. Imitating and reconstructing words and images that were a part of our past, our history which often include stereotypes and pieces of history that we, as a society, would like to forget. One of my immediate goals is to make contemporary society understand that it is important not to judge historical incidents, prejudices, and racist attitudes by modern standards.
>
> As a creative person, a person who recreates realities, it is not for me to make judgments about why an individual, group, or society inflicted offensive acts on another cultural group or individual. Though our contemporary sensibilities may judge particular words, languages, phrases, or images as offensive, done in bad taste or with reckless disregard for today's political correctness, certainly one would agree we cannot bury our past as if it were nonexistent. We must be reminded that the attitudes, values, and morals of certain periods in time shaped the knowledge that was taught, the language that was spoken, and the visuals that were shown. I support wholeheartedly the concerns of educators and parents who hesitate to explore books that may introduce children to controversial subject matter or stories that highlight a particularly horrendous period in our society or history. But, it is my responsibility to recreate these images and scenarios that will include enough realistic information on the subject matter to be a valuable resource for our children. It is the responsibility of the consumer to explore with young readers the

subject's historical significance and the issues of the time. Together, we can help children become better informed. Informed children will then begin to read books about the multicultural experience, whether it is historical or contemporary, through educated eyes. Often I sign my books simply: Remember. Our history is our future. Reminding my readers that we cannot rewrite our history, but through it, we can all learn about ourselves. Perhaps, one day, *with the increasing number of major publishers beginning to broaden their sensitivities,* the idea of *cultural* correctness will overshadow the current trend, toward *political* and *commercial* correctness. Until then, I will relentlessly pursue and execute stories I feel not only can make a difference and that need to be told, stories that bring us all one step closer together.

Not all writers and artists would agree with Melodye's decision not to make judgments about the historical past. In some ways, this view has pervaded children's literature, especially when applied to historical accounts about people of color. Others have made judgments and those decisions resulted in selective explanations of historic events. For example, slavery was portrayed as beneficial to Blacks in books such as *Amos Fortune, Free Man* (Yates, 1950). Historic fiction written by Laurence Yep—for example, *Dragon's Gate* (1995)—contradicted the myth that the Chinese were not an integral factor in the laying of the transcontinental railroads. These views have been corrected in numerous books by those who have decided to make some judgments about the past. Again, the contradictions are many.

Melodye and other writers and illustrators mediate a fine line between didacticism and imaginative, thought-provoking, and entertaining literary fare. The instrumental and, occasionally, didactic purpose of literature is evident in several picture and photo-essay books about biracial and multiracial identity. *Less Than Half, More Than Whole* (Lacapa & Lacapa, 1994), *The Two Mrs. Gibsons* (Igus, 1996), and *Jalapeno Bagels* (Wing, 1996) explore biracial identity. The characters in these books are part of loving, gentle families. Their parents talk about biracial identity as problematic only for those within the society who object to interracial marriages or harbor prejudicial feelings. Because these are picture books intended for a younger age group, complex issues are presented in a less complicated fashion.

Two examples of books that depict unusual biracial families in engaging and insightful ways are Faith Ringgold's *Bonjour, Lonnie* (1996) and Angela Johnson's *The Aunt in Our House* (1996). Ringgold's fictionalized history takes the reader on a veritable journey through African American history, covering topics such as WWI, WWII, and the Jewish Holocaust, and French fascination with African American culture, notably jazz and entertainers such as Josephine Baker and Bricktop. Interspersed is the tale of Lonnie's African

American father and European, Jewish mother and his subsequent escape from Europe and adoption into an African American family. Whew! The inclusiveness of information makes the book suitable for older readers unfamiliar with pivotal historic moments.

In contrast, Johnson takes an unusual tack in *The Aunt in Our House*. The biracial family features a White father and a Black mother. Their two children are varying shades of brown. This biracial family is presented in a matter-of-fact fashion. Race is not mentioned in the text; only the visuals convey biracial identity.[9] The emphasis of the story is the father's sister, the aunt in the title. She is somewhat mysterious. Something has happened in her life, necessitating the move to her brother's home. There is the suggestion of mental illness but no concrete clues are offered. Instead, the reader focuses on the possible causes for the move and the comfort and support the aunt receives from her relatives.

Novels and short story collections enable authors to explore biracial and multiracial identity in a more complex fashion. *Thief of Hearts* (Yep, 1995) presents the main character, Stacy, with an intriguing mix of physical features including blondish hair and green eyes in a "Chinese face." Neither her Chinese nor European heritage is central to her identity. She is a "typical" California pre-teen interested more in clothing and friends. Racial identity is thrust upon her when a Chinese girl, Hong Ch'un, enrolls in her school and is assigned to her class. Immediately, Stacy's peers and friends assume that they should have some kinship because of their Chinese ancestry. Stacy rejects this notion. Yet, a nascent interest in her Chinese heritage is awakened and she seeks knowledge from her grandmother. Grandmother Tai-Paw takes her to Chinatown to help locate Hong Ch'un and share some memories of her life, and that of Stacy's mother, Casey.

One of the more poignant ways in which the desire for a biracial or multiracial identity manifests itself is evident in the yearning for "Caucasian" physical features, especially blonde, straight hair and blue or green eyes. This theme appears more as transracial adoptions increase in frequency. *If It Hadn't Been for Yoon Jun* (Lee, 1993) and the short story collection *American Eyes* (Carlson, 1994) vividly depict the oppressive nature of beauty standards. Alice Larsen, the protagonist in *If It Hadn't Been for Yoon Jun*, was adopted as an infant in Korea. Her adoptive parents are White and live in Minnesota. Alice does not think of herself as Korean or Asian. In her mind's eye, she desires blonde hair and blue eyes. Once again, the enrollment of another Korean forces her to come to terms with her racial identity along with being called a "gook" at a school function. One short story, "Blonde," in *American Eyes* chronicles an Asian American girl's wish for blonde hair similar to a Barbie doll. Her parents do their best to fulfill her wish by purchasing a blonde wig. The "Mongolian" face with a blonde wig causes unrestrained laughter from the narrator's parents.

Intragroup color differences figure in several novels written by African Americans, such as *Let the Circle Be Unbroken* (Taylor, 1981). The Logans' biracial cousin serves as a catalyst for potential racial violence when White males desire the cousin and mistake her for a White woman. They are angry when they discover that she is "passing." The hierarchical ranking that privileges light skin and straight hair is evident in *The Shimmershine Queens* (Yarbrough, 1989). *The Shimmershine Queens* demonstrates the negative consequences of internalizing racist stereotypes.

Girls are the ones overwhelmingly concerned with their physical features. Perhaps this stems from the greater value society places on female beauty and desirability as a component of value. This is rather disheartening given that the idealized features, for example those associated with media-hyped supermodel Claudia Schiffer, are often impossible for some biracial and multiracial individuals as well as those who are racially unmixed.

Although writers and artists create for varying reasons, they share one fact in common. They seek an audience for their creations. Placing a creative work in the public sphere almost insures critical scrutiny, particularly for unique or controversial topics. Books portraying biracial or multiracial characters or exploring themes related to identity usually garner critical reviews. One can expect the critical scrutiny to continue as biracial and multiracial individuals seek recognition, acknowledgement, and power.

The critical response to the works varies. A perusal of major review journals—for instance, *Booklist, The Bulletin, Horn Book Magazine,* and *School Library Journal*—suggests that reviewers are willing to praise or pan a book when warranted. The very nature of the topic, perhaps, demands serious treatment. Frequently, didacticism overwhelms plot, especially in the picture books. Other times, the layering of issues along with the question of biracial or multiracial identity seems too much. A nearly grave seriousness seems to pervade a few. Humor is mainly absent, with occasional exceptions, such as the short story, "Blonde." Gaiety, ironic humor, or satire in one or more works might serve to encourage less monolithic themes.

None of this matters if the authors are unable to attract readers. If the writers create engaging and well-written works, then the books may garner a broad-based readership. Other forces, however, may help create the perspective that the books are intended for a limited, specialized, niche readership. These forces, which include marketing strategies, book reviews, library selection practices, author or illustrator name recognition, book's content, and format, will determine whether the books remain in publication. The taboo nature of the topic may seal its fate for a special audience. As Meloyde explains, writers and illustrators strenuously object to this belief.

A QUESTION OF AUDIENCE

When I asked Melodye, "for whom do you intend your work?," she responded:

Everyone. I feel this way, perhaps because of my eclectic cultural and ethnic make-up. I believe it is important for children to be exposed to diverse images of classic characters, *both fictional and non-fiction,* throughout their formative years. For example, my *Santy* character in *'Twas The Night B'fore Christmas,* was *my* first attempt at altering both the images and text of a beloved classic folk hero. I tweaked it just enough to accommodate a broader audience without diluting the richness and cadence of this timeless tale.

After moving to Chicago during the mid-60's, I remember begging my mother to take me to see the *real* Santa Claus. He was the White one I read about in storybooks, the one with rosy red cheeks. It was bitter cold. My Mom didn't own a car so that meant catching the elevated train and a city bus. You see, the white Santa sat way up high, on a golden throne in Marshall Field's, a downtown department store. His red velvet suit draped his round, jolly form in grandeur. Field's Santa was what I had come to know and believe in, as Christmas. In contrast, the Black Santa, who made his wish station at our neighborhood Wieboldts department store seemed unauthentic because he was absent from my storybooks. I can still see his gray scratchy beard peeking out from underneath the silly white one he wore on top. He sat amidst the last-minute Christmas frenzy and among the rows of discount tables. This Santa didn't sound like the majestic, soft spoken White one I saw the year before in Marshall Field's. In fact, his HO! HO! HO! sounded like the Hallelujah-Amens I heard on Sunday mornings in my grandfather's Baptist church. I remember thinking, "I can go hear my preacher any Sunday, but Santa only comes once a year."

Because of the dominant images in books that I was exposed to as a child, I had no other basis on which to make a judgment. These books developed the idea that a real Santa Claus *had* to be white. *'Twas The Night B'fore Christmas* was my way of allowing children from my neighborhood to dream their own dreams, to let them know that their dreams had just as much magic and excitement as any that were told to them before.

But my version of *'Twas The Night B'fore Christmas* was not meant just for African American readers. It was designed to welcome all children to reflect on Santa Claus as the spirit of giving, to be reminded of his magic, that it can be found by anyone, anywhere, and at anytime.

> In creating stories and images that are rooted in African American culture, whether it is the retelling of fairy tales, recreating mythical characters, reintroducing historical backdrops, or just reminding us that we are all part of everyday events, I want children to begin understanding their similarities. We are far more alike than we are different.
>
> Through my books I want children to learn that although we all come from unique and diverse backgrounds, whether it is because of culture, ethnicity, religion, or ordinary family values, we need to begin to find that common thread which hold our fragile world together. It is up to our children to begin to understand our similarities in order to bridge our differences. I am by no means advocating a monocultural society or existence. Rather, through my books, and other books like mine, we can let children know it is all right to cross those bridges and play on the other side, that there are no evil trolls lurking down below. Perhaps through these books, our adventurous youth will see that, though we may be different, we all have *common needs*—the need for love, friendship, and understanding—all key components in making a sturdy, lasting bridge.

Melodye is quite hopeful that books can serve as catalysts for major societal changes. Yes, human beings share many things in common. However, differential, hierarchical status in various cultural institutions ensures significant differences in experiences. Historically, these differences have been harnessed to prevent equal access to Constitutionally guaranteed rights. Literature should not bear the burden of insuring that readers learn to treat each other in a civil or humane fashion. Quite simply, the task is too overwhelming. Literature can encourage empathy and expand a reader's knowledge while providing a satisfying aesthetic experience. One example of a book that achieves these goals is Roll of Thunder, Hear My Cry (Taylor, 1976). It is regarded by many as an excellent example of historical fiction and a riveting recreation of a quintessential African American experience. And it garners readers year after year. A similarly successful book exploring biracial or multiracial identity has yet to emerge. However, the small body of works beginning to appear may contain a potential classic.

CONCLUDING COMMENTS

Race remains one of the most important and volatile issues of the century. Children's literature is necessarily affected by race because it is shaped by dynamic societal forces. Each human problem eventually finds its way, whether welcomed or not, into a children's book. The literature can withstand the onslaught of what has been labeled extra-literary concerns. A protective, hothouse environment is not required. Clearly, biracial and multiracial identity will become increasingly prominent as more individuals appropriate this identity and argue for literature reflecting the racial heritages and cultural and historical experiences of the groups. Racial categories in children's literature, if they were ever tidy, will become messier and more problematic.

The vast majority of the 20 or so books discussed in the chapter focus on the Black biracial or multiracial child. Perhaps biracial Asian, Latino/a, and Native Americans find this a less salient issue because individuals within those groups have the option of identifying as White. However, some Asian American (Maria Lee and Laurence Yep) and Native American (Michael Dorris) authors capture some of the realities of biracial identity, as the issue becomes more salient in their communities, in ways understandable for children and adolescents. Some common thematic issues have emerged such as finding a place for oneself when one's identity stems from two different racial groups and the search for cultural connections with one's heritage.

Many of the problems and perils associated with multiculturalism affect this body of literature. Biracial and multiracial identity are typically not a part of the race categories found in conceptions or definitions of multi–culturalism. Proponents of the ideology will have to argue for or against its designation as a subcategory. Another potential "biracial identity" issue reflects the growth in trans-racial adoptions. Several books, for example, *Allison* (Say, 1997), make explicit the emotional turmoil of possessing physical features diametrically opposite to those of one's adoptive parents. Authors will have to tread carefully in order to avoid having their works labeled as too exotic or remote for a general audience. Marketing campaigns, undoubtedly, will focus on the biracial and multiracial components of the books; however, in order to transcend possible pigeon-holing, those campaigns must all emphasis characters, style, plots, and creative language as well. *Authenticity* and insider/outsider perspectives are two of the thornier aspects of multicultural literature. Imagine the possible debates that will arise out of works about or created by biracial and multiracial individuals. Authors, poets, and illustrators such as Melodye Rosales, Janet Wong, and Floyd Cooper, with their melange of cultural *and* racial identities, illustrate how complex and potentially absurd the issue can become. However intellectually intriguing biracial and multiracial identity are as themes, one central task remains—securing a place in school curricula, libraries, and scholarly journals for the literature. Success can result in the institutionalization of the literature; failure means its relegation to bargain-book tables and out-of-print lists.

ENDNOTES

1. Attempting to define or describe a particular racial category is difficult if not foolhardy. So much about the ways in which race has been traditionally defined is under debate. Nevertheless, terms such as Colored, Negro, Black, Afro-American, and African American are used to identify persons of African descent. Asian American/Pacific Islander refers to individuals from the more than 14 Asian countries and Pacific Islands as well as descendents of individuals from those countries. Latino/a identifies individuals from the Caribbean, Central and South America. Native Americans are individuals who are descendents of members of one of the more than 300 officially recognized nations.

2. Significant physical variation exists among Blacks. Many volumes have been written that attempt to explain the differences and characterize individuals on the basis of hair texture and skin color, for example. One of the more intriguing volumes is Day, C. B. (1932; 1970), *A study of some Negro-white families in the United States*, Westport, CT: Negro Universities Press. Day's sociological study is a profile of several "Negro" families and includes mind-boggling data such as proportions of Negro, White, and Indian ancestry, numerous samples of hair textures, measurements for lip and nose size, as well as commentary about the history and progress of each family member. A biography, Leslie, K. (1995), *Woman of color, daughter of privilege,* Athens, GA: University of Georgia Press, illustrates the social, political, and legal difficulties encountered by one "woman of color"—a slave—who could have passed for White.

3. Relying on physical characteristics to determine racial identity is problematic. The contradictions that emerge are discussed in volumes such as Davis, F. J. (1991), *Who is Black?* College Station, PA: The Pennsylvania State University Press and Williams, P. (1995), *Life on the color line,* New York: Dutton.

4. Asian American Coalition. (1996), *Children of Asia America,* Chicago: Polychrome Publishing Co. is a photo-essay volume that includes some discussion of biracial identity.

5. Day, op. cit.

6. Several years ago, illustrator Trina Schart Hyman, in a presentation at the Ohio State University Children's Literature Conference, discussed her new understanding of the criticisms she received for some of her illustrations. A

few were criticized as perpetuating stereotypes. Hyman attributed her insight to the birth of a biracial grandson, one who would could possibly feel the sting of stereotypes about Blacks. Vera Williams' *More, More, More, Said the Baby* (1990), New York: Greenwillow, includes an illustration of what looks to be a White grandmother and a Black child. The illustration has been a source of interesting discussions in children's literature classes taught by Harris. Similarly, artist David Diaz deliberately created ambiguous physical features for the characters in Eve Bunting's *Smoky Nights* (1995), New York: Harcourt Brace.

7. Several individuals discuss identity in such a manner that the paradoxes and absurdities are revealed. Of course, W. E. B. Du Bois made the study of race and, by extension, identity a central part of his work. For example, his autobiography (1968) *Dusk of Dawn,* New York: Schocken Books is subtitled, *An essay toward an autobiography of a race concept by W. E. B. Du Bois*, and the essay "Miscegenation" in the Aptheker volume, position race in relation to ideas about power, oppression, and the institutionalization of racism. Albert Murray (1970), *The omni-Americans: Black experience and American culture,* New York: Da Capo Press, characterized the "Negro as half Anglo-Saxon." He is sometimes quoted as saying that American culture is half Negro. Cornel West (1993), *Prophetic reflections: Notes on race and power in America,* Monroe, ME: Common Courage Press, posits three dimensions for identity: self-conception, political aspect, and the moral component. bell hooks (1992), *Black looks: Race and representation,* Boston: South End Press and (1995), *Killing rage, ending racism,* New York: Henry Holt dissects the ways in which race identity is politicized, demonized, and appropriated.

8. The July 1997 issue of *Ebony* magazine contains a cover photograph of Tiger Woods and his father, Earl Woods. The accompanying article, for which Tiger Woods declined to be interviewed, contains a series of commentaries from prominent Blacks such as Jesse Jackson, Congresswoman Maxine Waters, Kwesi Mfume, director of the NAACP, and actress Salli Richardson, herself biracial. Needless to say, their opinions vary.

9. Williams, V. and Bunting, E., op cit.

REFERENCES

Aptheker, H. (Ed.). (1985). *Against racism. Unpublished essays, papers, addresses, 1887–1961, W. E. B. Du Bois.* Amherst, MA: The University of Massachusetts Press.
Asian American Coalition. (1996). *Children of Asia America.* Chicago: Polychrome Publishing Co.

Banks, J. (Ed.). (1995). Multicultural education: Historical development, dimensions, and practice. In J. Banks (Ed.), *Handbook on research on multicultural education.* New York: Macmillan.

Banks, J. (1997, July). Black America and Tiger's dilemma. *Ebony, LII,* 28–34.

Bogle, D. (1973). *Toms, coons, mulattoes, and mammies.* New York: Viking.

Broderick, D. (1973). *The image of the Black in children's literature.* New York: R. R. Bowker.

Brown, S. (1933). Negro character as seen by white authors. *Journal of Negro Education, 2,* 179–203.

Clifton, L. (1981). Writing for Black children. *The Advocate, 1,* 32–37.

Davis, F. J. (1991). *Who is Black?* College Station, PA: The Pennsylvania State University Press.

Day, C. B. (1932; 1970). *A study of some Negro-white families in the United States.* Westport, CT: Negro Universities Press.

Du Bois, W. E. B. (1903; 1989). *Souls of Black folk.* New York: Penguin Books.

Du Bois, W. E. B. (1968). *Dusk of dawn.* New York: Schocken Books.

Feelings, T. (1985). Illustrations is my form, the Black experience my story and content. *The Advocate, 4,* 73–82.

Funderburg, L. (1994). *Black, White, Other.* New York: Morrow.

Gates, H. L. (1991, November 24). 'Authenticity,' or the lesson of Little Tree. *New York Times Book Review, 1,* 26–30.

Greenfield, E. (1975). Something to shout about. *The Horn Book Magazine, 51,* 624–626.

Hendrickson, L. (1996). Whatever happened to *Epaminondas? Children's Literature Review, 22,* 1–5.

hooks, b. (1992). *Black looks: Race and representation.* Boston: South End Press.

hooks, b. (1995). *Killing rage, ending racism.* New York: Henry Holt.

Johnson, D. (1991). *Telling tales: The power and pedagogy of African American literature for youth.* Westport, CT: Greenwood Press.

Leslie, K. (1995). *Woman of color, daughter of privilege.* Athens, GA: University of Georgia Press.

McBride, J. (1997). *The color of water.* New York: Riverbend Books.

Murray, A. (1970). *The omni-Americans: Black experience and American culture.* New York: Da Capo Press.

Muse, D. (1975). Black children's literature: Rebirth of a neglected genre. *Black Scholar, 7,* 11–15.

Nieto, S. (1992). *Affirming diversity.* New York: Longman Publishing Group.

Rochman, H. (1992, February 1). The *Booklist* interview: Virginia Hamilton. *Booklist, 88,* 1020–1021.

Rochman, H. (1993, October 1). The *Booklist* interview: Allen Say. *Booklist, 89,* 350–351.

Rudman, M. (1984). *Children's literature: An issues approach.* New York: Longman.

Sheftall, B. (1990). *Daughters of sorrow: Attitudes toward Black women, 1880–1920.* New York: Carlson Publishers.

Sims, R. (1982). *Shadow and substance.* Urbana, IL: National Council of Teachers of English.

Sinnette, E. (1965). *The Brownies' Book:* A pioneer publication for children. *Freedomways, 5,* 133–142.

Slapin, B., & Seale, D. (Eds.). (1992). *Through Indian eyes: The native experience in books for children.* Philadelphia: New Society Publishers.

Sleeter, C., & Grant, C. (1988). *Making choices for multicultural education.* Columbus, OH: Merrill Publishing Co.

Slovo, G. (1996). *Every secret thing: My family my country.* Waltham, MA: Little, Brown & Co.

Smith, H. (1994). *The Coretta Scott King Award Books: From vision to reality.* Chicago: American Library Association.

Sutton, R. (1994, June). Interview with Walter Dean Myers. *School Library Journal, 40,* 24–28.

West, C. (1993). *Prophetic reflections: Notes on race and power in America.* Monroe, ME: Common Courage Press.

Williams, P. (1995). *Life on the color line.* New York: Dutton.

Wong, S. (1993, November). Beyond Bruce Lee. *Essence, 23,* 64.

Woodson, J. (1995, November/December). A sign of having been here. *Horn Book Magazine, 71,* 711–715.

Yep, L. (1993). *American dragons.* New York: HarperCollins.

CHILDREN'S BOOKS CITED

Adoff, A. (1973). *Black is brown is tan.* New York: Harper & Row.

Bryant, S. (1907; 1938). *Epaminondas.* Boston: Houghton Mifflin.

Carlson, L. (Ed.). (1994). *American eyes.* New York: Fawcett Juniper.

Carter, F. (1976). *The education of Little Tree.* Albuquerque, NM: University of New Mexico Press.

Feelings, T. (1995). *The Middle Passage: Black cargo, white ships.* New York: Dial Books.

Hamilton, V. (1976). *Arilla sundown.* New York: Greenwillow.

Hamilton, V. (1993). *Plain city.* New York: Blue Sky Press.

Igus, T. (1996). *The two Mrs. Gibsons.* San Francisco: Children's Book Press.

Johnson, A. (1996). *The aunt in our house.* New York: Orchard.

Lacapa, K., & Lacapa, M. (1994). *Less than half, more than whole.* Flagstaff, AZ: Northland Publishing.

Lee, M. (1993). *If it hadn't been for Yoon Jun.* New York: Houghton Mifflin.

Lyons, M. (1992). *Letters from a slave girl.* New York: Aladdin.

Ringgold, F. (1996). *Bonjour, Lonnie.* New York: Hyperion.

Rosales, M. (1996). *'Twas the night b'fore Christmas.* New York: Scholastic.

Ross, G. (1995). *How rabbit tricked otter.* New York: HarperCollins.

Say, A. (1997). *Allison.* New York: Houghton Mifflin.

Small, I. (1995). *Irene Jennie and the Christmas masquerade: The Johnkankus.* Boston: Little, Brown & Co.

Tapahonso, L. (1995). *Navajo ABC: A Dine' alphabet book.* New York: Simon & Schuster.

Taylor, M. (1976). *Roll of thunder, hear my cry.* New York: Dial Books.

Taylor, M. (1981). *Let the circle be unbroken.* New York: Dial Books.

Watson, J. (1995). *Dangerous: Savannah's story.* New York: Aladdin Paperbacks.

Watson, J. (1996). *Tempestuous: Opal's story.* New York: Aladdin Paperbacks.

Wing, N. (1996). *Jalapeno bagels.* New York: Atheneum.

Wong, J. (1996). *A suitcase of seaweed.* New York: Margaret McElderry Books.

Wyeth, S. D. (1994). *The world of daughter Maguire.* New York: Delacorte Press.

Wyeth, S. D. (1996). *Ginger Brown: Too many houses.* New York: Random House.

Yarbrough, C. (1989). *The shimmershine queens.* New York: G. Putnam's Sons.

Yates, E. (1950). *Amos Fortune, free man.* New York: Dutton.

Yep, L. (1995). *Thief of hearts.* New York: HarperCollins.

Yep, L. (1995). *Dragon's gate.* New York: HarperCollins.

Chapter 3

First- and Second-Grade Literary Critics: Understanding Children's Rich Responses to Literature

●————————●

Lawrence R. Sipe, University of Pennsylvania

When you think of a literary critic, you may picture an English professor, complete with tweed coat and elbow patches and pipe, lecturing on Shakespeare or Melville or Proust. When I think of a literary critic, my image is of a tow-headed first-grader named Brad. Here is a vignette (from a recent classroom study of mine) that shows this wonderful child critic in action:

> *It's three months into the school year, and the teacher is reading James Marshall's (1989) version of* The Three Little Pigs *to her class of first- and second-graders. She shows them the cover, with its illustration of the three pigs bowing on the stage of a theater, with drawn curtains on either side. Then she opens the book and shows the plain, brick-red endpages, which are the same color as the curtains on the front cover.*

> Brad: Well, it's like a curtain, like on the front cover, the curtain's open, the curtain's red, and, um, then the endpages, they're red, too, and it's like, like the curtain's closed, and you're gettin' ready for the play to start.

And, indeed, the play will begin—with the first page of the book—and when it ends, the "curtains" (in the form of the back endpages) will close again. It's interesting to speculate on what Brad must know in order to make such an astonishing literary interpretive comment. Brad takes nothing for granted in the picturebook—not even those plain-colored endpages. Like Gerald Genette (1980) and other French critics, he knows that the *peritext*—all the parts of the book other than the printed text—carry meaning, too. He uses his knowledge of what a theater looks like before a play begins, and links this to the two visual experiences of the front cover and the endpages.

He connects the teacher's reading of the picturebook with the performance of a play. He expects that everything in the picturebook will have meaning: in semiotic terminology, that all will function as *sign,* and that the signs will interrelate to each other and inform each other. For Brad, all the world's a sign, raw material waiting for his own construction of meaning.

Brad's statement was all the more marvelous to me because, less than a year before, in a doctoral seminar on picturebooks, I had heard a guest speaker, the professional illustrator Will Hillenbrand, use *exactly the same metaphor* of endpages as the stage curtains for a book. And here was a first-grader *inventing* it.

Although we may marvel at the idea that children can be literary critics, this notion has been used for over twenty years, beginning with the publication of Glenna Davis Sloan's *The Child as Critic* in 1975; and, as children's literature has assumed more and more prominence in many primary and elementary classrooms, the issue of literary understanding by young children has also become increasingly important. The art historian and aesthetic theorist Ernst Gombrich (1960) wrote, "To marvel is the beginning of knowledge, and when we cease to marvel, we may be in danger of ceasing to know" (p. 8). So, too, our wonder—at the sensitivity and perception of young children as they respond to literature—may be the beginning of our understanding of them as literary critics.

As the vignette indicates, my view of literary understanding is that it is a lot more complex than the traditional, somewhat sterile concepts of plot, setting, characters, and theme. During the rest of this chapter, I first highlight some of the many theoretical possibilities for conceptualizing literary understanding, then sketch the research that has been part of the professional conversation about this topic. Third, I'll share some data from my own research on young children's literary understanding and reflect on some of the implications it may have for educators concerned with children and their literature. Fourth, I'll step back from my research and suggest some connections between literature and literacy: why should we want children to become critics, anyway?

THEORETICAL PERSPECTIVES ON LITERARY UNDERSTANDING

What are some possible theoretical frameworks we could use to view literary understanding, particularly the literary understanding of a picturebook (like *The Three Little Pigs*), which is the most common form in which young children experience literature? In constructing a view of literary understanding, I have cast my net as widely and eclectically as possible, drawing from the many contemporary theories of literary criticism and other disciplines. My intention here is merely to toss several conceptual balls into the air to give an indication of the diverse possibilities.

Formalism and Structuralism: A Search for Patterns

From the perspective of the literary critical schools of formalism (Brooks, 1947) and structuralism (Scholes, 1974), we might look at literary understanding as a search for patterns. For example, many stories for children have the pattern of things happening in groups of three. Jack climbs up the beanstalk three times; in some versions of the *Cinderella* story, the main character makes three trips to the ball; Goldilocks tries out three things in the three bears' house: porridge, chairs, beds. Somehow, threes are very satisfying. When children know that things often happen in threes, they can anticipate, predict, and follow the structure of a story. But there are hosts of other patterns, too. There's the common "home-away-home" pattern in which the main character begins at home, in familiar surroundings; has some sort of adventure; and returns home again. Stories as different as *Peter Rabbit* (Potter, 1902) and *Where the Wild Things Are* (Sendak, 1963) share this pattern. And in practically every story, the end circles around to the beginning, somehow, even though the circling may not be the "home-away-home" form. In *Smoky Night* (Bunting, 1994), a story about the Los Angeles riots, the first page of the story shows a picture of a boy holding his cat. At the end of the story, after the boy's family is forced to evacuate their house, the boy is reunited with his pet, which had been lost. So the end circles around to the beginning.

Sometimes, this circling job is done by the illustrations. In Peter Spier's (1977) *Noah's Ark,* the opening illustration shows Noah working in his vineyard on the right-hand page, while the destructive qualities of humanity (in the form of a conquering army leaving a city in flames) are depicted on the left-hand page. In the background are the cedars of Lebanon, the symbols of peace, righteousness, and endurance. The last illustration in the book again depicts Noah, this time on the left-hand page. He is planting a vineyard in the soggy soil. Instead of the red and orange flames of the burning city, we see the red and orange of a rainbow, with the cedars of Lebanon flourishing under it. The images of death have been replaced by images of life and hope, and Noah is engaged in the same occupation as before. This circling round to the beginning brings the story to a satisfying closure, and is one of the principal ways the book achieves resolution and completion.

Yet another type of pattern we might explore is the ways in which binary opposites (like good and evil or light and darkness) function in a text. Many traditional stories are virtually built around binary opposites. Think of the binaries in *Cinderella*: love and hate; beauty and ugliness; hard work and laziness; poverty and riches; royalty and commoners; innocence and deception; magic and reality.

Semiotics: Interpreting Sign Systems

Taking a semiotic perspective on picturebooks seems natural and appropriate, given that semiotics assumes that language (written and spoken) is, as Deborah Wells Rowe (1994) puts it, "only one subset of the many forms of communication used by humans to construct meaning about their world" (p. 2). In picturebooks, the sequence of illustrations carries just as much meaning as the words of the story. In semiotic terms, the illustrations constitute a visual "sign system," and these signs can be interpreted and integrated with the verbal sign system of the words. Also, a semiotic perspective provides a foundation for viewing children's literary understanding as the beginning of the same process of sign interpretation used by adults.

William Moebius (1986) has analyzed commonly occurring codes (clusters of conventional signs) in picturebooks. For example, Moebius refers to the code of "position" in illustrations, noting that how far up a character appears on the page "may be an indication of an ecstatic condition or dream-vision or power," whereas low placement on the page may suggest a character's "low spirits" or "unfavorable social status" (p. 139). Semiotics provides a theoretical basis for understanding how we might move from one sign system to another, using the sign system of the illustrations to interpret the sign system of the verbal text of the picturebook, and vice versa. Charles Suhor (1984) calls this ability to translate information from one sign system to another "transmediation." Perry Nodelman's *Words About Pictures* (1988), which is probably the fullest treatment so far of picturebook theory, takes a semiotic perspective.

Psychoanalytic and Subjective Criticism: A Mirror for Readers

From psychoanalytic (Holland, 1975) and subjective (Bleich, 1978; Steig, 1989) theories of literary criticism, we could take the idea of reading one's own identity theme or basic personality into a piece of literature: literature as a protean mirror of each reader. Research I've done (Sipe, 1994) with children's responses to Maurice Sendak's (1993) recent picturebook, *We Are All in the Dumps with Jack and Guy,* has suggested that children may read their own identity themes into literature. I read the book to two children, both little boys. Brian was the son of professional parents and lived in a loving and secure home. Alan lived in poverty with his ailing grandmother, and only rarely saw his mother, who was addicted to drugs. In Sendak's story, there is a little boy who is looking for a family and a home. Does it surprise you that Brian found elements of humor in the story, while Alan heard every word with intense seriousness? And does it surprise you that Alan was the one who, at several points in the story, asked me, "But where's his mom? I wanna know where his mom is!" This is just one example of how different readers may tend to read themselves into a story. At least part of literary understanding involves this tendency.

Reader Response Theories

From the range of critical approaches under the umbrella term "reader re-sponse" criticism (Beach, 1993), we could take the crucial understanding that meaning does not reside in the text, but in the reader, in the reader's own personal interaction or (to use Louise Rosenblatt's term) *transaction* with the text. On this view, there is no one definite literary interpretation that takes precedence over another. Readers are different, and bring different experiences to a text, so interpretations will naturally differ. This idea is similar to the basic assumption of schema theory (see Sipe, 1995b, for a comprehensive review), that what we take away from reading depends heavily on what we bring to it in prior knowledge.

Rosenblatt (1978) argues that a reader's "stance" determines what sort of experience the reader will have, and she distinguishes between efferent and aesthetic stances. If we read *Moby Dick* to find something out about whaling, we are, in Rosenblatt's terminology, engaging in efferent reading— reading for the information we can take away. If we read *Moby Dick* as a "lived through experience," allowing its power to affect us emotionally, we are engaging in aesthetic reading (see Galda, Chapter 1). Rosenblatt claims that many teachers of literature encourage or even force their students to adopt an efferent stance. Teachers who use children's literature solely for the information it will provide for the children, who ask endless "comprehension" questions, or who try to analyze texts to death, are forcing the children into an efferent stance.

From other forms of reader response criticism, we might also consider Wolfgang Iser's (1978) and Roman Ingarden's (1973) notion of indeterminacies or gaps in text. Iser argues that literary understanding involves the filling in (by the reader) of the conceptual and affective gaps in the text, by generating inferences. Readers assure that their ongoing gap-filling is consistent with the information they have encountered previously in the text, and may revise their inferences as they come upon new information. In picturebooks, text and illustrations help to fill in each other's gaps. Iser also writes of the reader's "wandering viewpoint," as the reader interprets events and situations from the viewpoints of various characters, and "revisits" previous events in the narrative from the perspective of subsequent events.

The Social Contexts of Response

From the work of the literary critic Stanley Fish (1980), and from socio-psycholinguistics and speech-act theory, we can reflect on the deep embeddedness of language in social contexts, including talk about literature. Fish believes that the norms for literary interpretation and what counts as literary response are formed by each social group. He calls this an "interpretive community," because the community sets the standards for what literary understanding means. We might consider the classroom as a particular kind of interpretive community, asking what norms are set for reading literature and response to it, and how these norms are negotiated among the teacher and the students.

Visual Aesthetic Theory

The literary experience of young children is mainly with *picturebooks,* where illustration is as important as the text. Thus, we should consider aesthetic theory: theories of form, shape, line, color, balance, and so on, and the emotional effect of these design choices on the viewer. Barbara Kiefer (1983, 1995) has researched children's developing understanding of these visual aesthetic elements of picturebooks. We also could investigate the potential of various art media, such as watercolor, tempera paint, and collage, which are used in picturebook illustrations. My own collaborative research with a second-grade teacher and her class (Sipe, 1995a) suggests some ways in which the *process* of working with various art media contributes powerfully to children's understanding and interpretation of picturebooks. Other researchers (Madura, 1996) have examined how young children engage in discourse patterns that parallel the steps of art criticism described by Eisner (1994): description, interpretation, evaluation, and thematic issues.

Other Critical Approaches

From critical, cultural, feminist, or Marxist theories, we might consider how a reader's response is conditioned by class, race, gender, or culture and is therefore always partial and positioned by the reader and by others. Bronwyn Davies's (1989, 1993) work with preschoolers suggests how children's responses to stories can be differentiated along gender lines. We also may try to understand a text's underlying, implicit ideological assumptions, and how it may reinscribe (or even *resist*) prevailing cultural assumptions and norms. In *Language and Ideology and Children's Fiction,* John Stephens (1992) shows how many forms of children's literature, including picturebooks, socialize children into the prevailing ideologies of mainstream culture. This is one of the theoretical underpinnings of the view that *multicultural* literature for children is important for its ability to trouble and challenge the hegemonic ideologies with the perspectives of what Virginia Hamilton (1989) has called "parallel cultures" (see also Harris & Rosales, Chapter 2).

Finally, lest we get too heavy-handed, some poststructuralist and deconstructive literary theories give us the engaging idea of the literary text as a playground or a carnival (Bakhtin, 1981), where readers can make whatever meaning they want, becoming lost in the sheer pleasure of enjoying the text (Barthes, 1976) in their own idiosyncratic ways. Those of us who deal with young children know all too well that what they perceive or appreciate in a text may not be what we want them to see. When children talk about stories without the supervision of an adult (and sometimes even with supervision), the discussion resembles a rollercoaster of ideas rather than any kind of carefully constructed sequence of linked meanings. And there is an undeniable zaniness—a laugh-till-you-pee-in-your-pants quality—to young children's free literary responses that subverts our good intentions. We want them to learn a lesson; they gleefully subvert us and set their own agendas.

The bottom line is this: The richer, the more *textured* our view of literary understanding, the more we will see when we consider how children respond to literature. Every one of these approaches and perspectives can be a heuristic lens for understanding young children's responses.

SOME RESEARCH PERTAINING TO LITERARY UNDERSTANDING

I've identified three clusters of research that take various perspectives on literary understanding: story grammar research, research on reader stance, and research on literature discussion groups.

Schema Theory and Story Grammar

Schema theory (Anderson & Pearson, 1984), used in various ways by researchers with backgrounds in reading, psychology, and/or linguistics, has been used to produce a large number of models of the structure of stories, variously called "story grammars," "story maps," or "story schemas" (reviewed in Meyer & Rice, 1984; and Graesser, Golding, & Long, 1991). One of the newest of these models is Golden and Rumelhart's (1993) model of story comprehension and recall, which posits that the reader's main job is to inferentially "fill in the gaps" in the narrative trajectory; this is quite similar to the notion of reading as filling in gaps propounded by Iser.

These grammars, maps, and models attempt to describe how narrative structures are represented in the mind; thus they are sometimes called theories of *narrative representation*. Researchers have found that, as complicated as all these models are, even young children display a working under-standing of story structure which is, if anything, more complex than reflected in the models (Mandler & Johnson, 1977; Stein & Glenn, 1979). More recent research has found that explicit instruction in story-map-ping—making a visual representation of the events in the story—has a positive effect on the understanding of narrative (Fitzgerald & Spiegel, 1983; Spiegel & Fitzgerald, 1986; Dimino, Gersten, Carnine, & Blake, 1990), and on children's writing abilities (Fitzgerald & Teasley, 1986; Gambrell & Chasen, 1991). Working with first-graders, Baumann and Bergeron (1993) were the first to study story-mapping with children who were younger than grade three, and concluded that explicit instruc-tion in story-mapping is effective in helping first-graders to understand "central narrative elements" such as characters, plot, setting, problem, and resolution.

There seem, however, to be some difficulties in applying all of this theory and research to picturebooks: (1) the models are often based on very simple, written-for-the-occasion stories that don't reflect the length or the complexity of real books for children; (2) no attention is paid to the meaning-bearing qualities of illustration; and (3) the understanding of "narrative elements" seems to be limited to the traditional elements of plot, characters, setting, and so on.

Stance Research

So far, I've been discussing research having mainly to do with character-istics of text; I now turn to work that focuses mainly on the readers. The research that clusters around reader stance makes direct use of the work of Louise Rosenblatt (Cox & Many, 1992; Wiseman, Many, & Altieri, 1992; Zarillo & Cox, 1992) and, to a lesser extent, James Britton (Galda, 1982, 1990). Judith Langer (1990) is notable for deriving a new theoreti-cal approach to stance—a model of "envisionment"—from her data. Stance research demonstrates that teachers frequently constrain the responses of their students toward the efferent end of the continuum. However, children's responses do range from the efferent to the aesthetic, and, with the teacher's guidance, go far beyond superficial plot summaries or "like and dislike" lists to focus on substantive issues of life. There is evidence that literature can be a life-informing and life-transforming experience (McGinley & Kamberelis, 1996). Some of this research is problematic, in that it tends to dichotomize the efferent and aesthetic stances, rather than viewing them as a continuum. Moreover, it does not tell us a great deal about the teacher's positive role as scaffolder, extender, and refiner of children's responses.

Literature Discussion

There is a growing body of research on classroom literature discussion in small groups, also called "literature circles," "booktalks," "bookclubs," or "grand conversations" (Daniels, 1994; Hill, Johnson, & Noe, 1995; Short & Pierce, 1990; McMahon & Raphael, 1997; Roser & Martinez, 1995). This work is fairly recent, and may be said to begin with the research of Eeds and Wells (1989), who conducted discussions about literature with fifth- and sixth-graders. They argue that much of classroom literature takes the form of "gentle inquisitions," where the teacher probes for understanding of what is read in an efferent manner. What they propose is a form of discussion that they call "grand conversations," which focuses on child-centered talk and personal response that reflects aesthetic reading. One of their important findings was that "the elements of literature can be expected to emerge naturally as children and teacher talk about the book together" (p. 23). Eeds and Wells also highlight the importance of the teacher taking advantage of "teachable moments" in the conversation to point out literary elements.

The success of the "grand conversations" approach with upper-elementary and secondary students has led researchers to investigate the use of the approach with younger children. Lea McGee (1992; 1995; McGee, Courtney, & Lomax, 1994) is one of the few researchers who has studied the grand conversations of emergent readers and writers (in first grade), and has analyzed the role of the teacher and the interpretive questions she may ask, as well as the types of literary responses these young children make.

I haven't referred to the voluminous research on storybooks read aloud to children. Although *learning to read* and *learning to read literature* cannot be easily separated (Sawyer, 1987), research on storybook reading has rarely focused on literary understanding. A notable exception is Marilyn Cochran-Smith's (1984) study of storybook read-alouds to preschoolers, which takes a more inclusive view of the reading process. She examined how the teachers mediated the experience of the story for the children, and found that the children frequently made connections between the story and their own lives, in the form of "life-to-text" connections (where children used some experience in their own lives to understand the story) and "text-to-life" connections (in which children used their knowledge of a story to understand something in their own lives).

FIRST- AND SECOND-GRADE CRITICS IN ACTION

My own research has been with first- and second-grade children as they listen to picture storybooks read aloud and offer their comments, questions, and responses. This "tale from the field" (Van Maanen, 1988), is based on data gathered over a period of seven months in a first- and second-grade classroom in an elementary school with a twenty-year history of using children's literature in creative ways. The school's population was middle class and lower-middle class—mostly blue collar; as a group, these were not children of privilege. The 27 children belonged to diverse racial and cultural groups, including European-American, African-American, Native American, and a number of children with Appalachian backgrounds. The teacher, Ms. Tracey Bigler-McCarthy, had never used a basal to teach reading, relying instead on trade books. Although response to literature permeated this classroom—in creative play, drama, art, writing, and many other ways (Hickman, 1981), I limited myself to the teacher's and children's *talk* before, during, and after storybook read-alouds. I looked at this talk in three contexts: in Tracey's read-aloud sessions with the entire class; in read-alouds that I did with two small groups of five children each; and in one-to-one storybook read-alouds that I did with each of the ten children in the two small groups. My researcher stance, therefore, ranged on the continuum from "participant-observation" (Spradley, 1980) to "observant participant" (Erickson, 1992). Averaging three classroom visits per week, I collected observational field notes and audiotapes for a total of 83 read-alouds. I transcripted the read-aloud tapes myself, and chose 45 complete transcripts for in-depth conceptual analysis.

The research focused on what constituted literary understanding for the children, and how the teacher scaffolded this developing understanding. The data I discuss below is intended to convey a rich description of what "literary competence" (Culler, 1975) meant for this interpretive classroom community. Although a great number of books were used in the study, focus will be on children's discussions of four books: Paul Galdone's (1978) traditional version of *Cinderella*; a gender-reversed spoof of Cinderella called *Prince Cinders*, by Babette Cole (1987); Christopher Coady's (1991) version of *Red Riding Hood*; and Jon Scieszka's (1992) book of deconstructed fairy tales, *The Stinky Cheese Man*.

You'll note from Table 3.1 that these were substantial discussions—around 40 minutes in length—with many conversational turns. There is data from two discussions of *Prince Cinders* (by the two small groups of five children each) and, because *The Stinky Cheese Man* is so long, the discussion was done in two successive days. In the representations of the children's conversation, overlapping speech (two speakers talking at once) is indicated by single (/) and double (//) slashes. The teacher's talk is indicated by a "T," and children I couldn't positively identify are indicated by a "?".

Cinderella: Analysis and Interpretation of Textual Gaps

In the reading of the Galdone version of *Cinderella*, the teacher had just reached the point in the story where Cinderella tries on the glass slipper that

Table 3.1

Picturebook	Length of Discussion in Minutes	Number of Conversational Turns
Cinderella (Galdone)	46	230
Prince Cinders (Cole)	40 (group 1) 38 (group 2)	156 132
Red Riding Hood (Coady)	42	205
The Stinky Cheese Man (Scieszka)	38 (day 1) 26 (day 2)	150 95

she lost at the ball. This is the point at which Mickey asks an intriguing question:

Mickey: Why doesn't the slipper disappear?

Teacher: Why doesn't it disappear? I haven't figured that out yet, Mickey, either. Maybe,

[H1]   Cal: Maybe it's when, it turns into a very small size.

[H2]   ?: 'Cause it's glass.

Teacher: That's why it doesn't disappear? Because I've always wondered; the rest of her clothing disappears. Why not her slippers?

[H3] Gordon: Because, um, the fairy godmother gave it to her to keep.

Teacher: Do you think that was in the plan, then, when the fairy godmother designed /her outfit?

[H4] Gordon: Maybe not.// Maybe it just didn't disappear; maybe, maybe it didn't have to be on her. Maybe she'd have to take it off or something for it to disappear.

[H5]   ?: Maybe she'd have to have both of them.

Teacher: For them to disappear? And because she doesn't have the one, the magic doesn't work all the way? Terry.

[H6]   Terry: I think I know why they didn't disappear. Because she didn't make 'em, she probably bought 'em. They probably got 'em from the stepsisters.

	Teacher:	You think they were the stepsisters' shoes, originally?
	Kevin:	No, because they were old, dirty shoes to begin with.
	Teacher:	Kevin?

[H7]   Kevin: They were probably old dirty shoes and the fairy god-mother touched 'em and turned 'em into glass slippers.

Teacher: So why, when the clock struck midnight, did the shoes not turn back into raggedy shoes like her, /the rags she was wearing?

[H8]   Kevin: I know why.// Because um, um, she probably ran out of power. Her wand ran out of power.

Teacher: So the magic stopped on the shoes.

Kevin: Yeah.

[H9]   Trudy: I know why it didn't disappear, because she had one and it was in her pocket, and she forgot it was in her pocket, and so the fairy must've knew about it 'cause she wanted her to marry the prince.

Teacher: Do you think it could have been in the fairy godmother's plan all along to get these two together, and so she made that happen with the shoe, do you think she could have planned all that out, and knew that Cinderella was going to indeed marry the prince, someday? And so she planned it.

[H10]   Cal: Maybe she planned that she would lose it.

Teacher: Yes, so maybe it wasn't an accident, after all.

Terry: Maybe she knew it fell off, but she didn't want to go back and get it, because it, she didn't want to get caught by the prince.

Cal: She didn't want to get caught by the prince in her old clothes.

Why doesn't the slipper disappear at midnight, along with the rest of Cinderella's magic clothing? This represents what Iser would call a gap in the text; the text does not tell us. And the illustrations don't help to fill in this gap, either. After the teacher validates Mickey's question, some of the other children generate a series of hypotheses (which are marked with an H). Cal (H1) thinks it has to do with the *size* of the slipper; a child I couldn't identify (H2) suggests that the material—glass—has something to do with it. Gordon (at H3 and H4) introduces the idea of the fairy godmother's *intentions*, and another child (H5) suggests that maybe the slippers have to be together to disappear. At H6, Terry suggests that maybe the glass slippers weren't the fairy godmother's doing at all; maybe Cinderella got them from the stepsisters. Kevin disputes this, *because the text says* that they were Cinderella's old, dirty shoes to begin with.

Kevin then generates two more hypotheses (H7 and H8); the second one might be called the "Energizer Bunny" hypothesis: maybe the wand ran out of power. Trudy's hypothesis at H9 moves the discussion back to Gordon's previous idea of the *godmother's intentions*: maybe the godmother *planned it all along*. The teacher supports this and expands on it. At H10, Cal suggests that the godmother *planned* that Cinderella would lose the slipper, and after Terry shifts the discussion again to *Cinderella's* intentions—that she didn't want to get caught by the prince—Cal backs this up by suggesting that she didn't want to get caught in her old clothes. The discussion actually went on for a few more minutes, moving from Cinderella's embarrassment at the prince seeing her in her old clothes to the idea that the prince must have been a pretty superficial guy if he only liked her for her clothing!

I've included this long vignette for several reasons. First, it demonstrates the typical, extended discussion that is encouraged by the teacher *during* the reading of the book. Second, it shows the way the teacher honors a child-generated question, and the way the teacher then manages, contributes, scaffolds, extends, and refines the children's thoughts. Third, it shows the social construction of meaning in which this interpretive community is engaged; the children are scaffolding and building upon each others' interpretations. Fourth, this is all text-based talk, rather than reader-based talk: the children aren't relating this to their own lives, *but they are actively engaged*. Some of the research on stance and reader response seems (at points) to imply that the only worthwhile discussions are ones in which the children relate the story to their own lives. This vignette shows how intrigued children can be by textual, interpretive, gap-filling questions, if those questions are generated by *them* in a supportive environment, and in the context of the story. Within the frame of the story, the children were analyzing and interpreting the actions and motivations of story characters.

Prince Cinders: Personal and Intertextual Connections

Now I'll move to segments of the discussions about Babette Cole's *Prince Cinders*, a gender-reversed spoof of the classic *Cinderella* story. In this book, Prince Cinders is small, scruffy, and skinny. He has three big, hairy brothers who are always teasing him, and make him do all the work, while they go to the Palace Disco with their girlfriends. The following moment occurred during the discussion of the first page. What I read and said is indicated by the L's; and the bold type-face is the text of the book.

> L: **Prince Cinders was not much of a prince. He was small, spotty, scruffy /and skinny.**
>
> ??: [laughter]]//
>
> Gordon: I told ya he was skinny!
>
> **[1]** Sally: Not even my cousin Brandi's that skinny. My cousin Brandi's not even that skinny, and she's skinnier than a stick.
>
> L: So he's even skinnier /than your cousin Brandi?
>
> Charles: My sister's skinnier.// My sister's skinnier than a tooth-pick. Or a needle.
>
> L: He had three big hairy brothers who were always teasing him about his looks.
>
> **[2]** Charles: Ha, ha, you ugly, you skinny, you funky [chanting, like a rap song]
>
> ??: [laughter]

At number 1, we notice that Sally makes a life-to-text connection, by comparing Prince Cinders to her own cousin Brandi; Charles tries to top this by an unflattering comparison to *his* sister. They are personalizing the text by interpreting it in terms of their own life experience. In the whole data set, one out of every ten conversational turns by the children contained a personalizing connection.

After I read about the three big, hairy brothers, Charles (at number 2) assumes the voice of those brothers:

> "Ha, ha, you ugly, you skinny, you funky!"

He takes on the role of those characters, and this is a type of gap-filling, as well, because the text doesn't tell us what the brothers said to tease; and Charles leaps into that breach. The Russian literary critic Bakhtin (1981) would say that Charles is reveling in the *polyphony* or *heteroglossia*—the multiple voices—of this text; and adding his own distinctive voice. I found that Charles frequently gave a voice to characters in a story; in fact, this type of response was so consistent with him that I began to trace (and found) other "signature" responses of individual children. This is significant, because it suggests that individual literary response styles may develop early.

In the next vignette, I continued reading:

> L: **They spent all their time going to the Palace Disco with princess girlfriends. They made poor Prince Cinders stay behind and clean up after them.**

Charles: Oh, this is just like Cinderella. They called Cinderella "cinders." So that should be,

Sally: Her real name was Ella.

L: Um, her real name was Ella in the David Delamare version, wasn't it?

Charles: They call him Cinders:

Sally: Ella.

L: So you think there's a connection, Charles?

[1] Charles: They call him Cinders, and they called Cinderella Cinder. And see, this is just like Cinderella, 'cause he do all the work, but he's a boy. He has to scrub and to the /stuff.

Gordon: There's// something way /different.

Charles: I'm not// done. I'm not even done!

L: Wait a second.

Gordon: He's even skinnier than Cinderella.

[2] Charles: He's like Cinderella, 'cause he do all the work and stuff, and they go out and hassle 'im and go somewhere, they probably goin' to the ball.

Here, only two pages into the book, Charles makes an intertextual connection to the traditional *Cinderella* story. Sally supports this, and I amplify Sally's comment, remembering that, in David Delamare's (1993) version, Cinderella's real name is Ella, but that she's given the name *Cinder*-ella by her mocking stepsisters. In two subsequent comments, marked 1 and 2, Charles justifies his intertextual connection. Here he demonstrates that he has something akin to a *schema* for Cinderella.

The plot of *Prince Cinders* thickens when he meets a fairy who says that she'll make him big and hairy like his brothers, so that he can go to the Royal disco, too. But she's a rather inept fairy, and he's changed by mistake into a big, hairy gorilla. He goes to the disco, but he can't fit through the door, and he decides to wait at the bus stop for a ride home. Here he meets Princess Lovelypenny, who is frightened by the big, hairy monkey; but, no sooner does she see him than the clock strikes midnight, and Prince Cinders changes back into himself. He's very shy, though, and runs away, losing his trousers in the rush.

L: **Luckily, midnight struck and Prince Cinders changed back into himself.**

Charles: Lookit, his pants fell off!

   ??: [laughter]

   L: The princess thought he had saved her by frightening away the big hairy monkey. "Wait!" she shouted, but Prince Cinders was too shy. He even lost his trousers /in the rush!

[1] Charles: I know what!// They gonna say, whoever fit the pants, they be the prince!

  Julie: Yeah!

   L: Why do you think that?

[2] Charles: 'Cause, he just, 'cause his pants fell off, like the slipper fell off, and he see the princess.

   L: Oh, so you're making a /connection to

[3] Charles: And in the other one// a girl, in that one, her slipper fell off, and there was a *man* who say, "Wait, come back."

   L: Ah, so this is kind of like Cinderella but not really.

  Julie: Yeah, but it's a boy.

   L: OK, so what do you think will happen now?

[4] Charles: She gonna find, gonna go up to the houses, where who, whoever could fit in it.

At this point, at number 1, Charles uses his "Cinderella schema" to make a prediction: whoever fits the pants will be the husband of the princess. In numbers 2 and 3, he engages in what I call "intertextual analysis"—he is analyzing the connections between this gender-reversed spoof and the traditional version of Cinderella. In number 3, he is actually able to make an explicit analysis of the role reversal: in what he calls "the other one," the traditional version, a *female* loses a *slipper*, and it's a *male* who calls to her to come back, whereas in this version, it's a *male* who loses *trousers*, and a *female* who calls him to come back. In number 4, he amplifies on his previous prediction about how the princess will find the owner of the trousers.

The making of intertextual connections was a common occurrence in my data; in fact, in the whole data set, one out of every ten conversational turns by the children contained an intertextual connection. This was evidence of their rich exposure to many books. I suggest that these connections are crucial to the children's developing literary understanding. Hearing multiple versions of the same tale lets children make these connections easily; this allows them, as cognitive flexibility theory (Spiro, Coulson, Feltovich, & Anderson, 1994) suggests, to build up knowledge gradually across cases, in the ill-structured domain of story knowledge, and to use that knowledge to make predictions. It also allows children to raise the discussion to a higher level of sophistication, as the next vignette shows:

> L: **The princess was none other than the rich and beautiful Princess Lovelypenny. She put out a proclamation to find the owner of the trousers.**
>
> Krissy: Yep. She's gonna kiss him.
>
> L: **The Princess Lovelypenny decrees that she will marry whoever fits the trousers lost by the prince who saved her from being eaten by the Big Hairy Monkey:**
>
> Krissy: Oh, it's like, um, Mr. Sipe, what is it?
>
> Jake: *Cinderella*?
>
> Krissy: No.
>
> Jake: *Smartypants*?
>
> Krissy: No, it's *Ugh. Ugh.* It reminds me of *Ugh.* Whoever, whoever rides this bike, bicycle, they get to be king.
>
> Brad: /It's just like *Cinderella*, too
>
> Trudy: It's like *Princess Smartypants//* and *Cinderella*, too.
>
> L: Why is it like *Cinderella*?
>
> Trudy: Because she, uh, had the slipper, and had to try it on, and:
>
> Krissy: And he had to put on the pants.
>
> Brad: Let's hope she does not kiss his pants! Kiss his butt!

In this vignette, Krissy, Jake, Brad, and Trudy intertextually connect *Prince Cinders* with three other texts: a traditional version of *Cinderella*; *Ugh*, a Cinderella variant by Arthur Yorinks (1990), in which the role of the slipper is played by a newly invented bicycle; and *Princess Smartypants*, another book by Babette Cole (1986), in which the princess is successful in *not* marrying a prince, by kissing him and turning him into a frog. This four-way comparison leads to Brad's comment: "Let's hope she does not kiss his pants!" I think this is a sophisticated moment. Notice the language here: "Let's hope!" Here Brad uses the group's intertextual connections to position himself so that he can, as it were, *speak above* all the character's heads, to even speak above the *narrator's* head: to survey them all from a superior position—a position of irony and humor. This ability to take on various characters' viewpoints, to even place oneself on an entirely different plane from the characters and the narrator, is not uncommon in my data, and represents an instantiation of what Iser (1978) calls the "wandering viewpoint" of the reader. Incidentally, the bathroom humor in Brad's last remark shouldn't surprise anyone who knows first- and second-grade children. There's practically no research on the subversive and transgressive nature of children's responses to literature.

Little Red Riding Hood:
The Power of Illustration and Teachable Moments

I now turn to two vignettes from a discussion of a much more serious book: Christopher Coady's *Red Riding Hood*. Coady follows Charles Perrault's version of the Red Riding Hood story, which ends abruptly and shockingly with the death of Red Riding Hood; in this version, no woodsman comes to save either the little girl or her grandmother. Coady's illustrations are correspondingly dark and foreboding. What follows is part of the discussion about the front cover.

	Krissy:	I like the pictures.
	T:	Krissy, you like the pictures?
[1]	Krissy:	Yeah, it looks like watercolors.
	Alice:	No, it isn't.
	T:	Alice, you say no it isn't. What do you think it is?
[2]	Alice:	It could be tissue paper.
	T:	It's not as light as tissue paper or watercolor, is it? I think it's more like a paint called acryllics or oils. And that:
[3]	Krissy:	And that makes it scratchboard. [making several short, jerky motions with her hand]
	?:	It's got like scratches all over.
	?:	Scratchboard!
	T:	Oh, it does have a texture like scratchboard.
	Krissy:	You scratch it, like that book by Jerry Pinkney.
	T:	[nodding] That's scratchboard. Scratchboard is different-looking than this. This is oils or acryllic, and when you paint with oils or acryllic, it's a real thick paint, even thicker:
[4]	?:	I still think it's scratchboard.
	T:	Well, no, that's just the brushstrokes. But it's even thicker than the tempera paint we paint with.

During the discussion about the cover, Krissy says, "I like the pictures," and, at number 1, suggests that the illustration was done in watercolor. At 2, Alice disagrees, thinking it might be tissue paper. When the teacher explains that it was probably done with acryllics or oils, Krissy suggests (at number 3) scratchboard, and several children agree. Krissy reinforces her point by comparing the texture to the scratchboard technique used by another artist (she had actually confused Brian Pinkney with his father Jerry Pinkney, whose work she also knew). My purpose in sharing this vignette is to show another strong theme in my data: serious and informed discussion about illustrations. The children are very sensitive to illustrational style, and frequently speculate on which art media were used in an illustration. They are confident enough of their knowledge to disagree with the teacher, as in number 4.

Identifying and understanding the media used in illustrations is certainly part of the literary understanding of picturebooks. But the children and the teacher are also concerned about the *semiotic significance* of illustration, as the next vignette will show.

The title page of *Red Riding Hood* contains a rather sinister oval illustration of a bare tree and a full moon. In the colored illustration, the image is rendered more disturbing by the use of red in the tree branches and the lower border. The following is part of the discussion about this illustration:

[1]   Sean: At first, there's some red strokes over the moon.

        T: Some red strokes over the moon.

        Sean: And down here, too [pointing to the curved lower border of the vignette]

[2]   Nicole: Because it's Red Riding Hood.

[3]   Mickey: Because when, um, the hunter cuts him open, there's blood in the story.

[4]   T: Do you think that might be something we call foreshadowing, to let you know? Foreshadowing is what allows you to predict what might happen. Because when the illustrator and the author give you little clues to foreshadow what will happen next, and to let you know what will happen next. Julie?

[5]   Julie: It's October because the leaves aren't on the tree.

        T: And look at that moon: a full moon.

[6]   Charles: It's a warning of blood from the wolf that's goin' to eat the grandma.

At 1, Sean notices the red strokes (notice his use of the word "strokes") over the moon and along the border. At 2, Nicole suggests that the color is appropriate for Red Riding Hood. At 3, Mickey connects the red to the blood in the story. At 4, we see the teacher taking advantage of the children's observations to make a point about foreshadowing: this is a "teachable moment," as Eeds and Wells (1989) suggest. At 5, Julie remarks that it must be the fall of the year, and the teacher adds a reference to the moon. Then, at 6, Charles sums it all up: "It's a warning of blood from the wolf that's goin' to eat the grandma."

The code of color (to use William Moebius' terminology) is important in picturebooks. Red can mean excitement and joy; but it can also be a sign (in the semiotic sense) for danger, or warning, or blood. The children are learning how to "read" these visual metaphors and symbols: this *visual text*. They're also learning that the opening illustration can set the stage for the book, giving us an idea of the tone of what follows.

The Stinky Cheese Man:
Deconstruction and Performative Response

My data suggest that certain genres with certain textual features tend to evoke particular types of response. Jon Scieszka's *The Stinky Cheese Man* (1992) is witty, tongue-in-cheek, and plays with language and the conventions of the picturebook, telling such bizarre stories as "Little Red Running Shorts" and "The Princess and the Bowling Ball." Even the endflap is intriguing, exhorting us to buy the book.

ONLY
$16.99!
USA
56 action-
packed pages.
75% more than
those old 32-page
"Brand-X" books.

10
COMPLETE
STORIES!

25
LAVISH

NEW!
IMPROVED!
FUNNY!
GOOD!
BUY!
NOW!

PAINTINGS!

Just after I read the endflap, the following discussion occurred:

> L: ... **New! Improved! Funny! Good! Buy! Now!**

[1]   Terry: Why?

[2]   Julie: It got a medal, too!

[3] Gordon: "Why," just say "why," just say "why," Mr. Sipe, just say it.

> L: What? OK, "Why?"

[4] Gordon: How come? Because! Where? When? Who? [dissolves into giggles]

> L: [laughing, playing along] OK. **New! Improved! Funny! Good! Buy! Now!**

[5]   Terry: I don't wanna go "bye" now! I don't wanna go bye-bye now!

> Gordon: Me neither!

> ??: Bye-bye!

[6]   Terry: I don't want to go to the bathroom, and the stinky cheese man!

> ??: [uproarious laughter]

[7]   Sally: [laughing] Enough of this goofiness!

At 1, Terry interrogates the text: why should we buy the book, just because the text says so? Julie tries to keep us on track with her comment at 2, but the other children are having none of it. At 3 and 4, Gordon sets up an imitative display of the language in the book: "How come? Because. Where? When? Who?", which I feed into by rereading part of the text. At 5 and 6, Terry makes moves that the deconstructive critic Geoffrey Hartman would be proud of, punning and using the text as a springboard for his own transgressive text-to-life connection. At 7, Sally brings us back to earth. So you can see that the sheer wackiness of the book influences the children's responses: To use the French critic Roland Barthes's (1976) term, this is a text of bliss—"jouissance"—for the children; they become happily lost in it, and, like little deconstructionists, they treat the text as their playground. In this vignette, we can also see that, as Barthes says, the text of their lives interweaves with the text of the book. They assume the carnivalesque (Bakhtin, 1981) tone and spirit of this crazy book, and we haven't even gotten to the endpages yet!

The children's zany responses here are an example of what I call "performative response." They are using the text as a platform for the expression of their own creativity. In a sense, they are subverting the text, manipulating it for their own playful purposes. In some classrooms, these types of responses might not even be considered a response at all. This "goofiness" (as Sally put it) might be considered simply "off task" behavior. On the other hand, it's also possible to understand these responses as a very sophisticated form of response, where the book becomes a catalyst for the children's own expressive aesthetic impulse.

CONCLUSIONS AND IMPLICATIONS

In this presentation of data, I've shown the children as literary critics who demonstrate a range of response: from "mastering" the text (as in the long discussion of why Cinderella's slipper didn't disappear at midnight) to *transcending* the text in this last vignette. I've also indicated what I think is new and important. To summarize:

1. This research shows the importance of letting young children talk during storybook reading by the teacher.

Since the children's responses are so often *of* the moment and *in* the moment, to hold the response until the end of the reading would be in many cases to lose it. In Hoffman, Roser, and Battle's recent study (1993) of storybook reading practices, the category of discussion *during* reading doesn't even occur—only discussion before and after, as a indication of how little it may happen in classrooms. And researchers have rarely studied talk during storybook reading. Virtually all the research on literature discussion, for example, deals with discussion that takes place after a book has been read.

By allowing children to talk during read-alouds, teachers can assist children in their making of meaning as that meaning is in the process of being constructed. They can also observe how the children assist each other in making meaning. If children invariably understand read-alouds as a time to sit quietly and listen to the story, discussion afterward may be less rich. Whole categories of response (for example, performative response) may simply disappear. In the study, two-thirds of the discussion took place during the read-alouds, while just one-third occurred afterward. One of the reasons the teachers in this study didn't have to "prime the pump" with questions was that the children understood the storybook read-aloud situation to be a collaborative effort at interpretation and understanding. When our discussions ranged too far afield, and the sense of the story was in danger of being lost, it was the children themselves who said, "Can we get on with the story now?"

2. The data suggest that discussion about illustration and illustrational style results in a great deal of meaning-making by the children, which can be analyzed semiotically.

In other words, we can closely look at the ways in which the children interpret the illustrations in terms of the text, and the text in terms of the illustrations. Close examination of illustration is a potentially rich source of understanding; but teachers need to appreciate this richness themselves before they can help children to access it. Fortunately, there are very teacher-friendly resources for those who want to learn more about how illustrations work in picturebooks. Kiefer (1995), Stewig (1995), Bang (1991), and Doonan (1993) have all produced interesting and jargon-free books.

  3. The making of intertextual connections acts as a crucial conceptual pivot, allowing the children to respond by analysis, to take on the role of characters, and to position themselves above the dynamics of the narrative.

To alter the metaphor a little: intertextual connections may be one of the major joints in the scaffold that assists children in constructing literary understanding. Realizing the critical importance of intertextual connections, teachers can model by pointing out connections to other books themselves, and can praise and probe the connections the children make. One of the simplest ways of ensuring that the children can easily make intertextual connections is to read multiple variants of a single tale. The *Cinderella* tale, for example, exists in many forms and across many cultures. There are African (Steptoe, 1987), Chinese (Louie, 1982), Native American (Martin, 1992; San Souci, 1994), and Russian (Winthrop, 1991) versions, in addition to the many western European and English forms (Brown, 1971; Huck, 1989; Jacobs, 1989; Delamare, 1993). Hearing many versions like this, children will naturally begin to relate them to each other in an increasingly rich and complex web of meaning.

  4. At least some children may have a cluster of typical responses that constitute their "signature."

Aside from Galda's work (1982) with three fifth-graders, there is virtually no empirical evidence for this with children of primary and elementary age. With exposure to many books, children may, indeed, develop individual styles of response quite early. Teachers can watch for and encourage individual children's development of particular interests, knowing that a diversity of response styles can only enrich the social construction of literary meaning in the classroom. In the classroom I studied, Kenny viewed stories as an opportunity to tell his own (frequently very funny) stories; Krissy and Gordon were our experts on illustrational media and style; Jim drew together the threads of the discussion by making wonderful thematic generalizations; and Sally contributed her strong sense of social justice and fairness.

  5. Different texts—varying by genre and openness to differing interpretations—may evoke quite different responses.

The Stinky Cheese Man seemed to evoke many "performative" responses, for example. It may be most powerful for children's developing literary understanding if they are exposed to many varieties of literary genres, styles, and forms. In this way, a wide range of responses may be elicited.

6. We should be wary of postulating any type of developmental scale or sequence in the matter of literary understanding.

This research suggests, rather, that young children's literary understanding is heavily dependent on the role of the teacher, or expert others, as well as the social construction of meaning by the group (Berk & Winsler, 1995). It also seems clear that children do not develop literary understanding simply by being "exposed" to the reading of books. In the study, the teacher acted as manager, clarifier/prober, fellow wonderer/speculator, and extender/refiner. She took advantage of "teachable moments" to extend or refine a child's response. Terms she used, like *foreground*, *background*, and (in the data I've presented) *foreshadowing* were picked up by the children and used in subsequent discussions. She was an active participant in the discussion, though she rarely asked a direct question. When she did ask a question, it was one that she really wondered about, and for which she didn't already have a firm answer. She did not play that game teachers often play, called "What's on My Mind?" Although the children actively scaffolded each others' understanding, the teacher's interventions seem crucial as well. She didn't just watch the flowers unfold. The key to the teacher's role seemed to be her ability to perceive the rich potential inherent in the children's responses, and to capitalize on it.

7. The insights and perspectives provided by literary criticism of many different types—not just so-called "reader-response" criticism—give us new ways of understanding young children's responses during storybook read-alouds, and thus new ways of viewing literary understanding.

For example, the whole concept of "performative response," which uses a text as a launching pad for the reader's (or listener's) own flight of aesthetic creativity, was something I didn't understand as a type of response *at all* until I conceptualized it in terms of the "carnivalesque" (Bakhtin, 1981) and as a type of intense pleasure (Barthes, 1976).

THE LITERATURE-LITERACY CONNECTION

I've tried to show in what sense and to what degree young children can be critics. There seems no doubt that children can develop rather sophisticated literary understanding. But why would we want to encourage this in classrooms? What good is it in learning how to read and write? And what good is it for "doing life" (Erickson, 1993)?

According to Margaret Meek (1988), "To learn to read a book, as distinct from simply recognizing the words on the page, a young reader has to become both the teller (picking up the author's view and voice) and the told (the recipient of the story, the interpreter)" (p. 10). Thus, children learn that there would be no story without them. For example, only the reader can make sense of the interaction of text and illustration. Further, literature provides beginning readers with crucial lessons in narrative that teach "how texts work" even as they motivate children to read to the end.

Children with developed literary understanding are children who *write* with a strong sense of structure and rhetorical purpose: children who write like readers and read like writers (Smith, 1984). The literature-writing connection is very powerful.

Children with developed literary understanding are children who are alive to the force and value of multiple interpretations of what they read, and who know how to engage in a critical exchange of views with their peers.

They are children who read thoughtfully and inferentially, and who can interrogate or resist a text, not accepting it at face value, probing its underlying ideological assumptions.

They are children who know how to pleasurably surrender to the power of the text (Scholes, 1985), while also using their developing literary understanding to *heighten* their pleasure.

They are children who have the transmediational skill—the ability to move between several sign systems—which is very important for such new textual entities as hypertext.

Finally, there is the importance of narrative as a way—perhaps a primary way—of structuring reality itself. According to many cognitive psychologists and anthropologists (Bruner, 1980, 1986, 1990; Geertz, 1973; Wolf & Heath, 1992), the experience of literature may be one of the most powerful ways of imposing order and meaning on the world. We know that experience shapes language (and literature); but language (and literature) can also shape experience, by engaging what Robert Coles (1989) calls the "moral imagination." Various writers in the human sciences and the humanities (Hardy, 1978; Polkinghorne, 1988; White, 1980) have argued that narrative is a crucial factor in the formation of identity and the constitution of what Jung called the Self, to the extent that the human mind may be seen as a mechanism for turning the "raw data" of day-to-day experience—the "booming, buzzing confusion" of life—into narratives, thereby rendering reality understandable and meaningful (Ricoeur, 1980). According to some psychoanalysts (Spence, 1982), one of the main ways we understand an event or a situation is by turning it into a story. To understand stories and how they work is thus to possess a cognitive tool that not only allows children to become comprehensively literate, but also to achieve their full human potential.

REFERENCES

Anderson, R. C., & Pearson, P. D. (1984). A schema-theoretic view of basic processes in reading comprehension. In D. Pearson (Ed.), *Handbook of reading research*, Vol. 1 (pp. 255–291). New York: Longman.

Bakhtin, M. (1981). *The dialogic imagination* (C. Emerson & M. Holquist, trans.). Austin: University of Texas Press.

Bang, M. (1991). *Picture this: Perception and composition.* Boston: Little, Brown.

Barthes, R. (1976). *The pleasure of the text* (R. Miller, trans.). New York: Hill & Wang.

Baumann, F. J., & Bergeron, B. S. (1993). Story map instruction using children's literature: Effects on first-graders' comprehension of central narrative elements. *Journal of Reading Behavior, 25*(4), 407–437.

Beach, R. (1993). *A teacher's introduction to reader response theories.* Urbana, IL: National Council of Teachers of English.

Berk, L. E., & Winsler, A. (1995). *Scaffolding children's learning: Vygotsky and early childhood education.* Washington, D.C.: National Association for the Education of Young Children.

Bleich, D. (1978). *Subjective criticism.* Baltimore: Johns Hopkins University Press.

Brooks, C. (1947/1968). *The well-wrought urn: Studies in the structure of poetry.* London: Methuen.

Bruner, J. (1980). The narrative construction of reality. *Critical Inquiry, 7*(1), 1–21.

Bruner, J. (1986). *Actual minds, possible worlds.* Cambridge: Harvard University Press.

Bruner, J. (1990). *Acts of meaning.* Cambridge: Harvard University Press.

Cochran-Smith, M. (1984). *The making of a reader.* Norwood, NJ: Ablex.

Coles, R. (1989). *The call of stories: Teaching and the moral imagination.* Boston: Houghton Mifflin.

Cox, C. (1994, April). *Young children's response to literature: A longitudinal study, K–3.* Paper presented at the annual meeting of the American Educational Research Association, New Orleans.

Cox, C., & Many, J. (1992). Beyond choosing: Emergent categories of efferent and aesthetic stance. In J. Many & C. Cox (Eds.), *Reader stance and literary understanding* (pp. 103–126). Norwood, NJ: Ablex.

Culler, J. (1975). *Structuralist poetics: Structuralism, linguistics, and the study of literature.* London: Routledge.

Daniels, H. (1994). *Literature circles: Voice and choice in the student-centered classroom.* York, ME: Stenhouse.

Davies, B. (1989). *Frogs and snails and feminist tales: Preschool children and gender.* Boston: Allen & Unwin.

Davies, B. (1993). *Shards of glass: Children reading and writing beyond gendered identities.* Cresskill, NJ: Hampton Press.

Dimino, J., Gersten, R., Carnine, D., & Blake, G. (1990). Story grammar: An approach for promoting at-risk secondary students' comprehension of literature. *Elementary School Journal, 91,* 19–32.

Doonan, J. (1993). *Looking at pictures in picture books.* Stroud, Eng.: The Thimble Press.

Eeds, M., & Wells, D. (1989). Grand conversations: An exploration of meaning construction in literature study groups. *Research in the Teaching of English, 23*(1), 4–29.

Eisner, E. (1994). *The educational imagination: On the design and evaluation of school programs* (3rd ed.). New York: Macmillan College Publishing Company.

Erickson, F. (1992, April). *Post-everything: The word of the moment and how we got here.* Paper presented at the annual meeting of the American Educational Research Association, San Francisco.

Erickson, F. (1993). Foreword to M. Cochran-Smith & S. L. Lytle, *Inside/Outside: Teacher research and knowledge.* New York: Teachers College Press.

Fish, S. (1980). *Is there a text in this class? The authority of interpretive communities.* Cambridge: Harvard University Press.

Fitzgerald, J., & Spiegel, D. L. (1983). Enhancing children's reading comprehension through instruction in narrative structure. *Journal of Reading Behavior, 15,* 1–17.

Fitzgerald, J., & Teasley, A. B. (1986). Effects of instruction in narrative structure on children's writing. *Journal of Educational Psychology, 78,* 424–433.

Galda, L. (1982). Assuming the spectator stance: An examination of the responses of three young readers. *Research in the Teaching of English, 16*(1), 1–20.

Galda, L. (1990). A longitudinal study of the spectator stance as a function of age and genre. *Research in the Teaching of English, 24*(3), 261–278.

Gambrell, L. B., & Chasen, S. P. (1991). Explicit story structure instruction and the narrative writing of four- and fifth-grade below-average readers. *Reading Research and Instruction, 31,* 54–62.

Geertz, C. (1973). *The interpretation of cultures.* New York: Basic Books.

Genette, G. (1980). *Narrative discourse* (trans. J. Lewin). Ithaca: Cornell University Press.

Golden, R., & Rumelhart, D. (1993). A parallel distributed processing model of story comprehension and recall. *Discourse Processes, 16*(3), 203–237.

Gombrich, E. (1960). *Art and illusion.* Princeton, NJ: Princeton University Press.

Graesser, A., Golding, J. M., & Long, D. L. (1991). Narrative representation and comprehension. In R. Barr, M. Kamil, P. Mosenthal, & P. D. Pearson (Eds.), *Handbook of reading research,* Vol. II (pp. 171–205). New York: Longman.

Hamilton, V. (1989). "Anthony Burns." Acceptance Speech for Boston Globe/ Horn Book Award. *The Horn Book, 129,* (March/April), 183–185.

Hardy, B. (1978). Narrative as a primary act of mind. In M. Meek, A. Warlow, & G. Barton (Eds.), *The cool web: The pattern of children's reading* (pp. 12–23). New York: Atheneum.

Hickman, J. (1981). A new perspective on response to literature: Research in an elementary school setting. *Research in the Teaching of English, 15,* 343–354.

Hill, B. C., Johnson, N. J., & Noe, K. L. S. (1995). *Literature Circles and response.* Norwood, MA: Christopher-Gordon.

Hoffman, J. V., Roser, N. L., & Battle, J. (1993). Reading aloud in classrooms: From the model to a "model." *The Reading Teacher, 46*(6), 496–503.

Holland, N. (1975). *5 readers reading.* New Haven: Yale University Press.

Ingarden, R. (1973). *The cognition of the literary work of art* (trans. R. A. Crowly & K. R. Olson). Evanston: Northwestern University Press.

Iser, W. (1978). *The act of reading: A theory of aesthetic response.* Baltimore: Johns Hopkins University Press.

Kiefer, B. (1983). The responses of children in a combination first/second grade classroom to picture books in a variety of artistic styles. *Journal of Research and Development in Education, 16*(3), 14–20.

Kiefer, B. (1995). *The potential of picturebooks: From visual literacy to aesthetic understanding.* Englewood Cliff, NJ: Prentice Hall.

Langer, J. (1990). The process of understanding: Reading for literary and informative purposes. *Research in the Teaching of English, 24*(3), 229–260.

Madura, S. (1996, December). *"Her life was aglow; she was so loved": Transitional readers' and writers' responses to literature through discussion, writing, and art.* Paper presented at the National Reading Conference, Charleston, SC.

Mandler, J. M., & Johnson, N. S. (1977). Remembrance of things parsed: Story structure and recall. *Cognitive Psychology, 9,* 111–151.

McGee, L. (1992). An exploration of meaning construction in first graders' grand conversations. In D. Leu & C. Kinzer (Eds.), *Literacy research, theory and practice: Views from many perspectives* (pp. 177–186). Chicago, IL: National Reading Conference.

McGee, L. (1995). Talking about books with young children. In N. L. Roser & M. G. Martinez (Eds.), *Book talk and beyond: Children and teachers respond to literature* (pp. 105–115). Newark, DE: International Reading Association.

McGee, L., Courtney, L., & Lomax, R. (1994). Supporting first graders' responses to literature: An analysis of teachers' roles in grand conversations. In C. K. Kinzer & D. J. Leu (Eds.), *Multidimensional aspects of literacy research, theory, and practice* (pp. 517–526). Chicago, IL: National Reading Conference.

McGinley, W., & Kamberelis, G. (1996). Maniac Magee and Ragtime Tumpie: Children negotiating self and world through reading and writing. *Research in the Teaching of English, 30,* 75–113.

McMahon, S. I., & Raphael, T. E., with Goatley, V. J., & Pardo, L. S. (1997). *The Book Club Connection: Literacy learning and classroom talk.* New York: Teachers College Press.

Meek, M. (1988). *How texts teach what readers learn.* South Woodchester, Stroud, Eng.: The Thimble Press.

Meyer, B. J., & Rice, G. E. (1984). The structure of text. In P. D. Pearson (Ed.), *Handbook of reading research* (pp. 319–351). New York: Longman.

Moebius, W. (1986). Introduction to picturebook codes. *Word and Image, 2*(2), 141–158.

Nodelman, P. (1988). *Words about pictures: The narrative art of children's picture books.* Athens: University of Georgia Press.

Polkinghorne, D. (1988). *Narrative knowing and the human sciences.* Albany: SUNY Press.

Ricoeur, P. (1980). Narrative time. *Critical Inquiry, 7*(1), 169–190.

Rosenblatt, L. (1978). *The reader, the text, the poem: The transactional theory of the literary work.* Carbondale, IL: Southern Illinois Press.

Roser, N. L., & Martinez, M. G. (Eds.). (1995). *Book talk and beyond: Children and teachers respond to literature.* Newark, DE: International Reading Association.

Rowe, D. W. (1994). *Preschoolers as authors: Literacy learning in the social world of the classroom.* Cresskill, NJ: Hampton Press.

Sawyer, W. (1987). Literature and literacy: A review of research. *Language Arts, 64*(1), 33–39.

Scholes, R. (1974). *Textual power.* New Haven: Yale University Press.

Short, K., & Pierce, K. (Eds.). (1990). *Talking about books: Creating literate communities.* Portsmouth, NH: Heinemann Educational Books.

Sipe, L. R. (1993). Using transformations of traditional stories: Making the reading-writing connection. *The Reading Teacher, 47*(1), 18–26.

Sipe, L. R. (1994). Alan and Brian respond to *We Are All in the Dumps with Jack and Guy. Ohio Journal of the English Language Arts, 35*(2), 5–11.

Sipe, L. R. (1995a). Connecting visual and verbal literacy: Second graders learn about art techniques in picture books. *Teacher Research: The Journal of Classroom Inquiry, 2*(2), 61–73.

Sipe, L. R. (1995b). The roots and branches of schema theory: A historical overview. *Educational Reports No. 25.* Columbus, OH: The Martha L. King Language and Literacy Center, The Ohio State University.

Sloan, G. D. (1975). *The child as critic.* New York: Teachers College Press. [1st ed.].

Smith, F. (1984). Reading like a writer. In J. M. Jensen (Ed.), *Composing and comprehending* (pp. 47–68). Urbana, IL: ERIC clearinghouse in Reading and Communication Skills and National Conference on Research in English.

Spence, D. (1982). *Narrative truth and historical truth: Meaning and interpretation in psychoanalysis.* New York: W. W. Norton.

Spiegel, D. L., & Fitzgerald, J. (1986). Improving reading comprehension through instruction about story parts. *The Reading Teacher, 39,* 676–682.

Spiro, R. J., Coulson, R., Feltovich, P., & Anderson, D. (1994). Cognitive flexibility theory: Advanced knowledge acquisition in ill-structured domains. In R. Ruddell, M. R. Ruddell, & H. Singer (Eds.), *Theoretical models and processes of reading* (4th ed.). Newark, DE: International Reading Association.

Steig, M. (1989). *Stories of reading: Subjectivity and literary understanding.* Baltimore: Johns Hopkins University Press.

Stein, N. L., & Glenn, C. G. (1979). An analysis of story comprehension in elementary school children. In R. O. Freedle (Ed.), *New directions in discourse processing* (pp. 53–120). Norwood, NJ: Ablex.

Stephens, J. (1992). *Language and ideology in children's fiction.* London: Longman.

Stewig, J. W. (1995). *Looking at picture books.* Fort Atkinson, WI: Highsmith.

Suhor, C. (1984). Towards a semiotics-based curriculum. *Journal of Curriculum Studies, 16,* 247–257.

Van Maanen, J. (1988). *Tales of the field: On writing ethnography.* Chicago: University of Chicago Press.

White, H. (1980). The value of narrativity in the representation of reality. *Critical Inquiry, 7*(1), 5–27.

Wiseman, D. L., Many, J. E., & Altieri, J. (1992). Enabling complex aesthetic responses: An examination of three literary discussion approaches. In C. K. Kinzer & D. J. Leu (Eds.), *Literacy research, theory and practice: Views from many perspectives* (pp. 283–289). Chicago, IL: National Reading Conference.

Wolf, S., & Heath, S. B. (1992). *The braid of literature: Children's worlds of reading.* Cambridge: Harvard University Press.

Zarillo, J., & Cox, C. (1992). Efferent and aesthetic teaching. In J. Many & C. Cox (Eds.), *Reading stance and literary understanding: Exploring the theories, research, and practice* (pp. 235–249). Norwood, NJ: Ablex.

CHILDREN'S BOOKS CITED

Brown, M. (1971). *Cinderella or The little glass slipper.* New York: Charles Scribner's Sons.

Bunting, E. (1994). *Smoky night.* San Diego: Harcourt Brace.

Coady, C. (1991). *Red Riding Hood.* New York: Dutton Children's Books.

Cole, B. (1986). *Princess Smartypants.* New York: G.P. Putman's Sons.

Cole, B. (1987). *Prince Cinders.* New York: G.P. Putnam's Sons.

Delamare, D. (1993). *Cinderella.* New York: Simon & Schuster.

Galdone, P. (1978). *Cinderella.* New York: McGraw-Hill.

Huck, C. (1989). *Princess Furball.* New York: Greenwillow.

Jacobs, J. (1989) *Tattercoats.* New York: G. P. Putnam's Sons.

Louie, A. L. (1982). *Yeh-Shen: A Cinderella story from China.* New York: Philomel.

Marshall, J. (1989). *The three little pigs.* New York: Dial.

Martin, R. (1992). *The rough-face girl.* New York: Scholastic.

Potter, B. (1902/1987). *The tale of Peter Rabbit.* London: Warne.

San Souci, R. (1994). *Sootface.* New York: Bantam Doubleday Dell.

Scieszka, J. (1992). *The stinky cheese man and other fairly stupid tales.* New York: Viking.

Sendak, M. (1963). *Where the wild things are.* New York: Harper & Row.

Sendak, M. (1993). *We are all in the dumps with Jack and Guy: Two nursery rhymes with pictures.* New York: HarperCollins.

Spier, P. (1977). *Noah's Ark.* New York: Dell.

Steptoe, J. (1987). *Mufaro's beautiful daughters: An African tale.* New York: Lothrop, Lee, & Shepard.

Winthrop, E. (1991). *Vasilissa the beautiful: A Russian folktale.* New York: HarperCollins.

Yorinks, A. (1990). *Ugh.* New York: Farrar, Straus and Giroux.

Chapter 4

Fostering Children's Engagement with Texts: A Sociocultural Perspective

Cynthia H. Brock, Texas Woman's University
and
James R. Gavelek, Oakland University

Mrs. Weber is a fifth-grade teacher in an urban school district in the Midwest. Like many teachers, she has moved from exclusively using a basal reading program to including authentic literature (i.e., trade books) in her literacy instruction. Like many teachers, she is concerned about using literature in meaningful ways with her children. In particular, she wants to foster her students' abilities to effectively engage with texts, through both their personal response and their ability to make sense of or interpret what they've read. As teacher educators and literacy researchers, we believe that children's responses to texts are crucial aspects of literature-based instruction. Further, we believe that a sociocultural theoretical perspective sheds light on how teachers can facilitate readers' interpretations of texts and support their development of response.

In this chapter, we examine children's text response and interpretation as played out during literacy instruction in Mrs. Weber's classroom. We begin by describing Mrs. Weber's use of literature and her beliefs about the relationship between readers, texts, and authors. Beliefs about this relationship merit consideration because our underlying beliefs and assumptions about the relationship between readers, texts, and authors influence the ways we use literature with our children (Beach, 1993). Next, using scenarios from Mrs. Weber's classroom, we illustrate how a sociocultural conception of textual engagement provides a rich framework for fostering and extending students' interpretation of and responses to texts. However, such instruction is not without its challenges. Therefore, we draw on several examples within Mrs. Weber's classroom to detail not only the opportunities for fostering *engagement, interpretation,* and *response,* but also the sources of "missed opportunities" that may reduce students' potential for such engagement.

MRS. WEBER: AN INTRODUCTION

Mrs. Weber wants her children to actively engage with texts, constructing powerful interpretations of and responses to them. To help her children develop these competencies, Mrs. Weber studies the texts themselves and their authors. Additionally, she strives to get to know her children well. She attempts to assess their literacy learning strengths and needs, and know her children and their families as unique individuals. Mrs. Weber draws on her knowledge of different texts and authors, as well as her knowledge of her children as learners, to develop a framework for literacy instruction that involves actively engaging her children as thinkers and decision-makers during literacy lessons.

Mrs. Weber's use of literature in her classroom draws on, though is not limited to, a reader response approach described by literary theorists such as Rosenblatt (1938, 1978) and Beach (1993). Historically, major movements in literary theory have privileged either the role of the author (e.g., romanticism) or the role of the text (e.g., new criticism) with respect to where meaning lies when interpreting texts (see Eagleton, 1983). However, contemporary educational approaches to reading, and literary theory in general, have increasingly recognized the role of the reader in constructing meaning while reading (e.g., Anderson & Pearson, 1984; Beach, 1993). Advocates of reader response theory argue that meaning does not reside exclusively "in" the text, nor "in" the author's intentions; rather, as Galda suggests in Chapter 1, meaning emerges from readers' transactions with texts (Beach, 1993; Rosenblatt, 1938, 1978; Tompkins, 1980).

Mrs. Weber works to create opportunities for such transactions to occur, using her knowledge of texts, authors, and her students. Her goal is to design meaningful literacy lessons where her students engage effectively with texts. Teachers such as Mrs. Weber can be helped to achieve their goals when guided by theories that can inform their instructional planning. As Gee (1990) has argued, the instructional decisions we make are based on our theories about how teaching and learning occur best. Our tacit theories about teaching and learning must be made explicit, questioned, and informed by others' theories so that we may design and continually improve quality instructional programs for our children.

Careful attention to a sociocultural theoretical perspective toward textual response and engagement can help us, as educators, address questions such as: How do children learn to engage effectively with and respond to texts, and what role can I play in facilitating that development? What can I do to help students develop a repertoire of responses to texts? What social settings in the classroom would help children learn to respond effectively to texts? What cultural and experiential knowledge shapes children's abilities to learn to engage with and respond to texts? In the following section, we lay out our definition of response, offer an overview of different approaches to reader response theory, and explain why a sociocultural perspective toward response merits consideration by educators.

READER RESPONSE: A DEFINITION AND OVERVIEW OF MULTIPLE PERSPECTIVES

As Sipe describes in Chapter 3, response is defined and studied from many different prespectives. Drawing on Rosenblatt (1989), we present a definition of response that we find useful for our work. Response relates to the kind of stance—either efferent or aesthetic—that a reader assumes when reading a text. Readers never exclusively assume one stance or the other when reading; however, in general, when assuming an efferent stance while reading, readers are primarily concerned with "what is to be carried away or retained *after* the reading event" (p. 159, emphasis in original). An aesthetic stance, on the other hand, refers to the emotions, tensions, ideas, scenes, and so forth, that are being "lived through" during the reading experience (p. 159). "Response" refers to the evocation that occurs as a result of engaging with text either efferently or aesthetically.

Typically, readers who assume a predominately efferent stance while reading are concerned with the public aspect of meaning-making. For example, readers concerned with the main idea of a text or passage assume an efferent stance while reading. Generally, when educators speak about comprehension, they refer to an efferent stance toward text. Readers assuming a predominately aesthetic stance toward text, conversely, tend to be concerned with the individual aspect of meaning-making. For example, readers who assume an aesthetic stance might focus on the emotions evoked while engaging in the act of reading.

We suggested earlier that reader response is typically conceptualized from the perspective of literary criticism. Literary critics are primarily concerned with relationships between readers, texts, and the reading process (Scholes, 1985). However, reader response is also conceptualized from different psychological perspectives. Those studying reader response from a psychological perspective are concerned not only with relationships between reader and text. They are also concerned with learning and development that occurs as a result of readers engaging with texts. An important question emerges: Why should teachers consider response from a psychological perspective, and what does such a perspective "buy for us" as educators?

As educators, we believe that we must be interested in a comprehensive psychology of response—one that considers the importance of understanding human learning and development—because we must be concerned with facilitating our children's literacy learning. This is especially important since teachers are increasingly using literature in their classrooms and focusing on children's response to literature (see, for example, Roser & Martinez, 1995; McMahon & Raphael with Goatley & Pardo, 1997). We, as a profession, must think carefully about how we can use literature to effectively foster student literacy learning.

While we believe that it is worthwhile to consider response from a psychological perspective, in our view, not all psychological perspectives are equal. Most psychological perspectives imply that the process of constructing meaning from text is an individual one. However, like Bloome (1986) and Gee (1990), we believe readers are situated in complex social networks. Thus, a major problem with individualistic conceptions of reader response is that they do not take into account the social, cultural, and historical dimensions of mind and its development. A sociocultural approach to reader response, however, includes these important dimensions of meaning-making. From a sociocultural perspective there exists an unavoidable tension between the social and the individual in a person's response to a text.

Teachers using a literature-based approach to literacy instruction would benefit from considering a sociocultural conception of textual response and engagement that integrates social, cultural, and historical dimensions of mind and meaning-making. These dimensions, when considered collectively, have important consequences for teaching reading and understanding and facilitating student literacy learning. A sociocultural approach can (1) shed light on how to facilitate rich transactions between readers and texts, (2) provide a developmental explanation for how children learn to engage with and respond effectively to texts, and (3) shed light on the role of culture in teaching children to engage with and respond to texts. In the following section, we lay out a sociocultural conception of reader response. We conclude the chapter by identifying five key educational purposes of response that can be derived from a sociocultural perspective toward response.

A SOCIOCULTURAL PERSPECTIVE ON READER RESPONSE

The influence of Vygotsky's sociocultural theory in education has grown steadily over the past two decades, even though Vygotsky, a Russian developmental psychologist, died over sixty years ago. More than any other theory of human development, Vygotsky's theory implicates the role of language in relating instruction to cognitive and affective development (Vygotsky, 1978, 1986). There are three interrelated lines of thought in a Vygotskian sociocultural theoretical perspective that we draw on to frame our conception of the development of readers' textual response and engagement (Wertsch, 1985). First, to understand any phenomenon (e.g., reader response), we must understand both its origin and the processes by which it is acquired. This is known as a genetic or developmental analysis (Vygotsky, 1978). Second, mind is social in nature; that is, mind develops through our interactions with others. Third, human action is mediated by signs and tools—primarily psychological tools such as language (Wertsch, 1985).

Developmental Analyses

A developmental analysis addresses the origins and development of psychological processes, such as those associated with response to, engagement with, and interpretation of literature. Vygotsky proposed four interdependent temporal dimensions for studying development (Wertsch, 1985):

1. the development of our species,
2. our cultural and historical development,
3. the development of the individual, and
4. the short-term development of psychological processes over relatively brief periods of time, such as within a lesson.

Dimension One: The Development of the Human Species. The first and widest-angle lens refers to the development of humans as a species and the characteristics that distinguish humans from other species. Bruner (1972) writes of the "evolution of educability." Unlike any other species, we have evolved many ways to educate our young in the history of our species, so that each generation builds on the accomplishments of previous eras. Because we engage in deliberate teaching and learning, *experience*—not genetic transmission—is the major medium of change. Moreover, as both Bruner (1972) and Vygotsky (1978) suggest, humans are unique in their ability to make meaning through language. Therefore, unlike other species, humans are uniquely predisposed to create, respond to, and interpret written texts.

Dimension Two: Cultural History. Cultural history, the second developmental dimension, is especially important for teachers to consider because students' textual responses and interpretations depend upon their cultural and historical frame of reference. For example, with respect to response, the generally accepted notion that the reader plays an active role in meaning-making is relatively new despite the existence of seminal work such as Rosenblatt's 1938 book (Beach, 1993; Tompkins, 1992). Nonetheless, from a sociocultural perspective, we must first understand readers' "locations" both culturally and historically in order to understand the ways in which they respond to and interpret texts.

Realizing that students' cultural and historical backgrounds shape both their engagement with and interpretations of texts helps teachers make sense of the different responses and interpretations students offer (see also Harris with Rosales, Chapter 2). Such knowledge can influence how teachers assist children in interpretation and response. Students' diverse responses and interpretations can become positive learning opportunities when they have occasions to share and explain their unique backgrounds, experiences, and interpretations with others. However, if teachers fail to realize the different frames of reference from which diverse children interpret texts and activities that invite response to text, then children from diverse backgrounds can be placed at a disadvantage in the classroom. We draw on a vignette from Mrs. Weber's classroom to illustrate these points.

Mrs. Weber's Classroom: *The Maniac Magee* Hand Scene[1]

During the spring semester, Mrs. Weber and her children read the text Maniac Magee—*engaging in whole-group lessons and small-group activities as they read. This vignette focuses on one episode during a whole-group lesson when the class was approximately half-way through the book. During whole-group lessons, the class (approximately 21 students) typically sat in a semi-circle around Mrs. Weber and discussed the text as they read it aloud together. On this particular day, the children had already read that Maniac, the main character in the story, was unofficially "adopted" by the Beale family in Two Mills, Pennsylvania. A characteristic of Two Mills was that all of the Black families lived on the east end of the city and all of the White families lived on the west end of the city. Since Maniac (a Caucasian boy) lived with the Beales (an African-American family) on the East End, he looked different from others in the community. Maniac was perceptive and noticed those around him and the ways they described themselves. Mrs. Weber read the excerpt below about Maniac's perceptions:*

"Maniac loved the colors of the East End, the people colors. For the life of him, he couldn't figure why these East Enders called themselves black. He kept looking and looking, and the colors he found were gingersnap and light fudge and dark fudge and acorn and butter rum and cinnamon and burnt orange. But never licorice, which, to him, was real black" (Spinelli, 1990, p. 51).

Mrs. Weber paused shortly after reading the above segment and said, "I want to stop there for a minute and I want to go back to the colors. That was a significant passage in that the author wants you to know that Maniac didn't see the ultimate of contrasts—black and white. He couldn't figure out why Blacks called themselves black. He looked at skin tones and he said, 'I see cinnamon.' What do you think about when you think about cinnamon?"

The class discussed Spinelli's use of descriptive words for colors and how some of those words (e.g., cinnamon, acorn, etc.) made them feel. Then the teacher said, "I want you to put your hands out right here." She told the children that she wanted to look at all the different shades of their hands. The children and the teacher moved off of their chairs into the center of the circle and began to hold out their hands. Because the class was ethnically diverse with African-American, Hispanic, Caucasian and Asian children, there was a stunning array of different colored hands in the center of the circle. One child, Bill, said, "Oh cool, it goes from light to dark." After several students noted that no one was all black, Tran and Sally responded that no one was all white either. Then the class discussed the colors of their own hands. They talked about butterscotch, cinnamon, flan, etc. Mrs. Weber mentioned the beauty of variations and closed this discussion episode by suggesting, "I have the feeling that the author wants you to know that Maniac spends time looking at the person rather than at the skin tone."

Mrs. Weber uses the Hand Scene Episode to promote a number of aspects of response: connecting students' lives to the text, problematizing themes that are present in the literature they read, and considering how the author uses his craft to invite particular responses by readers. By asking students to look closely at the colors of their own skin—reflected in their hand colors—Mrs. Weber helps them to connect their own diversity to that of the children in the novel. Bill's comment about how "cool" it is that their skin tones go from light to dark reflects his personal response to this connection. She also invites them to critique the story characters' position about race—specifically their polarization of black and white. By having students look closely at both the author's choice of words to describe color and their own skin variations, she helps them raise questions about issues of "black and white." Moreover, part of personal response involves being able to appreciate the author's craft. By highlighting the passage about East Enders and West Enders and specific words within the passage such as cinnamon and nutmeg, Mrs. Weber raises students' awareness of important social issues as well as the author's use of language to sensitize readers to these social issues. Thus, this short activity provides students with opportunities to think about challenges that face citizens living among diverse peoples, raises questions about the underlying causes of prejudice, and highlights the author's crafting of the text. Students' comments—such as those made by Bill, Tran, and Sally—illustrate that many students responded personally to this activity associated with the text.

However, such opportunities may not be uniformly effective in supporting all students' response to the text. In fact, for one student in Mrs. Weber's class, Deng,[2] the activity did little to engage him with the literature or support his personal response. Interpreting Mrs. Weber's request to look at their hands as a literal command, he thought that Mrs. Weber simply wanted to know the colors of the students' hands.

Examining Deng's interpretation of the Hand Scene from a cultural perspective provides insights into why this activity was not as meaningful for Deng as it was for many of his classmates. First, Deng was from Laos and had only been in the United States a short time. During an interview (conducted in his native language of Hmong with an interpreter fluent in both Hmong and English), he revealed that he was not familiar with the American "school story" of racism between African-Americans and Caucasians. Second, interviews with Deng also revealed that schooling in Asia for him involved rote memorization and literal recall. Schooling, from his cultural perspective, was not about relating personally to texts, making inferential judgments, or offering warranted assertions for his unique interpretations of and responses to texts and school-like events.

Understanding individual students' cultural backgrounds is an important aspect of supporting their personal engagement with and response to literature. If Mrs. Weber had known that Deng was not clear about racial tensions in America—especially between African-Americans and Caucasians—she might have elaborated on this issue in the class discussion and spent more time making explicit connections between her children, the text, and racial issues in America. We return to our discussion of this episode later in the chapter and discuss other possible ways that Mrs. Weber might have supported Deng's learning.

Dimensions Three and Four: Long-Term and Short-Term Individual Development. Within the third dimension, Vygotsky emphasizes the uniqueness of each person's life trajectory or biography—the developmental differences between individuals across time. While the second dimension—cultural history—frames or channels experiences, it does not determine them. Individuals with common cultural and historical backgrounds still have unique life experiences that impact their individual development and their readings of texts. Thus, even individuals within common cultures and time frames may respond to and interpret texts very differently.

The fourth developmental dimension relates closely to the third, but reflects a more microscopic lens for viewing development—it refers to the individual episodes that constitute the development of psychological processes within the individual. The unique life trajectories of individuals (the focus of the third developmental dimension) are made up of countless individual episodes (the focus of the fourth developmental dimension), and they are organized through cultural experiences (the focus of the second dimension).

However, human development cannot be reduced to a chronological suc-
cession of the individual episodes that make up the unique life trajectory of
the individual. Not all of the countless individual episodes across individuals' lives affect an individual's overall development in the same ways. For
example, a particular event in a story may leave a lasting impact on an individual, and yet other complete books may recede from memory. We draw on
the following excerpt from a discussion about *Maniac Magee* in Mrs. Weber's
classroom to illustrate key aspects of both dimensions three and four.

On the final day of the unit pertaining to *Maniac Magee,* in their small
peer-group discussion, Chris, Tran, and Deng reflected on the way the story
ended. At the end of the story, Maniac was homeless and living in a buffalo
pen in the local zoo. Maniac's friend Amanda told him in no uncertain terms
(by both yelling at and kicking him) that he should leave the zoo and move
back in with her family, where he had once lived. After Amanda's tirade,
Maniac acquiesced. Tran said that if he had been Maniac, he would not have
responded as Maniac did to Amanda, even though Amanda was inviting
Maniac to come back to live with her family.

> Tran: But, what I don't understand, Maniac, I would not go back, be-
> cause see Amanda, if I was Maniac and Amanda was trying to hit
> me, and kick me, no way. I was like, come back in a couple weeks
> when you're calmed down.
>
> Chris: It's like, you know,
>
> Tran: I know, she had to kick Maniac and everything, I was like, come
> back when you're in a better attitude.

Chris responds differently to the situation, thinking that anything would be
preferable to living at the zoo. In contrast to Tran's assuming Maniac's position, Chris seems to have taken Amanda's point of view.

> Chris: It's like . . . like Maniac was living in a deer pen, and wouldn't you
> rather be pulled up by your ear and brought home?
>
> Tran: No, Amanda could've just asked politely.
>
> Chris: But, in that situation, you don't want to ask politely, you want to
> be persistent and get him home.

A key point with respect to the third dimension is that even though individuals may have common cultural and historical backgrounds, their unique
life experiences can impact their different responses to texts. For example,
although Tran[3] and Chris were both fifth-grade boys raised in American
middle-class homes, they respond differently to the story event described
above. Tran argues that he would not have left with Amanda if she had ordered him the way she ordered Maniac. Chris, on the other hand, felt that

Amanda had a right to be pushy because the stakes were so high for Maniac. The discussion continued with Tran emphasizing his empathy for Maniac, and drawing on earlier interactions between the characters to explain his position. Further, he enlists Deng's support, and together they appear to convince Chris that, at the very least, Maniac had good reason to refuse to go home with Amanda. Chris and Tran's responses are typical of what Laura Pardo (1997) has described as being "in the character's shoes," metaphorically donning a character's shoes to judge events and consequences from his or her perspective.

When given the guidance to learn to express personal responses to texts and when given opportunities do so, children will respond differently to the same texts owing to their individual differences and backgrounds. Teachers must also realize that they can and should play a central role in facilitating their children's literacy learning by understanding their responses and perspectives and helping children to understand the responses and perspectives of others. For example, both Tran and Chris had reasonable responses to the text events, influenced by their own experiences and the character through whose eyes they had viewed the event. They shared the same historical point in time. They had different ethnic backgrounds, but shared a great deal: gender, academic competence, as well as linguistic, economic, and cultural backgrounds. Their differing responses—both valid—could be supported by evidence from the text, from experiences as friends and family members, and from connecting to other texts they had read. Thus, when teaching children to respond to and engage with text, teachers should (1) encourage diverse responses, (2) encourage children to offer warranted assertions for their interpretations of texts, and (3) encourage children to strive to understand the perspectives of others.

In terms of the fourth temporal dimension—the individual episode or event—teachers would be concerned, for example, with the moment-to-moment unfolding of how a child or group of children respond to text. A focus on the individual episodes that shape children's psychological development underscores the importance of being attuned to "the teachable moment." Teachers should capitalize on opportunities to help students engage in powerful learning experiences that could significantly influence their engagement with and response to text and their engagement with others around text.

By providing children with the opportunity to talk together in small groups, suggesting important topics for the students to discuss (i.e., parts of the story that made a significant impact on them), and modeling personal response to and engagement with the text, Mrs. Weber set the stage for her children to engage in meaningful personal discussions about the text. However, while setting the stage is important, a useful extension occurs when students are brought together as a whole class at the end of their small-group discussions.

In the large-group setting, students can share and discuss the issues that they found to be particularly relevant in their small-group discussions. Further, Mrs. Weber can highlight aspects of the small-group discussions that are important for the whole group to consider. Both types of discussions provide powerful "teachable moments" for extending children's learning about response and engagement with text after small-group discussions. (See McMahon & Raphael with Goatley & Pardo, 1997, for additional ways to teach children to respond effectively to texts in large-group and small-group discussions.)

THE SOCIAL ORIGINS OF MIND

Whereas the developmental line underscores the multiple and interacting sources of the *origin* of response, the second major line in Vygotsky's thinking—the importance he attributed to social interaction—addresses the *process* by which response emerges within the individual (Wertsch, 1985). Vygotsky (1978) suggests that higher psychological processes, such as those involved in reading and writing, are acquired initially through our interactions with others and gradually over time take place within the individual.

Harré (1984) proposes what he terms the Vygotsky Space as a schematic model to portray the ways that higher psychological processes, such as engaging with and responding to texts, are individually acquired (see Gavelek & Raphael, 1996, for a more complete description of the Vygotsky Space). The Vygotsky Space is formed by the overlaying of two independent dimensions, one public ←→ private, and the other social ←→ individual (see Figure 4.1). Together these dimensions describe a space consisting of four quadrants: (1) public-social; (2) private-social; (3) private-individual; and (4) public-individual. At any given time, an individual's cognitive functioning may be located in one of these four quadrants. Harré proposes that individuals move cyclically through these quadrants in the course of their development. Harré further identifies four processes that characterize these successive developmental transitions between quadrants.

The process of *appropriation* refers to the movement of thinking from the public to the private domain (i.e., Q_I to Q_{II}). *Transformation* (i.e., Q_{II} to Q_{III}) refers to the process by which individuals personalize and make these earlier social ways of thinking and feeling their own. *Publication* (i.e., Q_{III} to Q_{IV}) refers to the process by which the individuals' now transformed and individualized ways of thinking are once again made public for others to respond to. And, *conventionalization* (Q_{IV} to Q_I) describes the process by which individuals' public manifestations of thinking and feeling may be incorporated as part of the conventions of the language communities within which they participate.

Figure 4.1   The Vygotsky Space (Gavelek & Raphael, 1996; adapted from Harré, 1984).

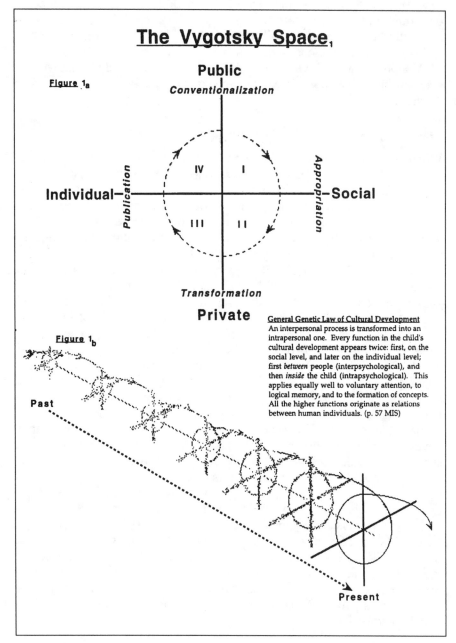

The Vygotsky Space₁

Figure 1ₐ

Public

Conventionalization

Individual — **Social**

Appropriation

Publication

IV   I

III   II

Transformation

Private

Figure 1_b

Past

Present

General Genetic Law of Cultural Development
An interpersonal process is transformed into an intrapersonal one. Every function in the child's cultural development appears twice: first, on the social level, and later on the individual level; first *between* people (interpsychological), and then *inside* the child (intrapsychological). This applies equally well to voluntary attention, to logical memory, and to the formation of concepts. All the higher functions originate as relations between human individuals. (p. 57 MIS)

The Vygotsky Space is a rich heuristic for conceptualizing how individuals appropriate and transform that which they experience in the public/social realm. The model highlights the public and social roles of discourse; it is in public and social domains that meanings are "out in the open" so they may be appropriated and transformed within individuals, subsequently becoming the subject of discussion between individuals.

For Vygotsky, "mind" emerges from, but is not reducible to, these social interactions. In terms of reader response, the ability to offer up response is born through interactions with others—both text-based interactions and interactions with others around text. Response is not reducible to these interactions; it neither lacks individual creativity, nor reflects uniformity of thought. Bakhurst (1982) eloquently illustrates this point:

> . . . the 'social interaction' of child with his elders is not simply the origin of particular beliefs, desires, hopes, intentions, etc., but the source of the child's very capacity to believe, to desire, to hope, to intend. 'Socialization', the all-pervading influence of the community upon the child, is not conceived as that which in principle limits individuality, but as that which makes possible the child's emergence as a self-determining subject (p. 117).

Thus, due primarily to different social, cultural, and life experiences, individuals appropriate and transform that which they experience in social encounters in their own unique ways.

The Vygotsky Space serves as a valuable tool for highlighting the process by which students learn to engage with and respond to texts. We draw on Deng's involvement in the Hand Scene Episode to illustrate how a teacher could use knowledge of the Vygotsky Space framework to explore Deng's understanding of the lesson and enhance Deng's opportunities to meaningfully engage with and respond to *Maniac Magee*.

Mrs. Weber invited her students to engage personally with the text by asking them to participate in the Hand Scene Episode as she drew attention to Spinelli's descriptive discussion of skin color and related the activity to broader societal issues about racism. These social events occurred "in the open" in quadrant I of the Vygotsky Space (i.e., the public/social space). Deng participated in the activity as did his peers; however, his level of understanding was minimal. He appropriated the idea that Mrs. Weber wanted to note the differences in children's skin color, and, in doing so, was left with little to transform that might be meaningful to his response to the literary selection. Further, there was little opportunity for Deng to make his thinking *public,* nor was there opportunity for *conventionalization* of his thoughts or ideas. This reflects a missed opportunity for both Deng and his peers.

For Deng, opportunity to share his thinking publicly might have elicited the instructional support he needed to make sense of the Hand Scene Episode and provided the necessary background for a richer response to and engagement with the text. For example, one key piece of knowledge Deng needed was cultural knowledge about relationships between African-Americans and Caucasians in American society. That is, Deng needed "the public referents of the verbal signs" for "African-Americans" and "Caucasians" in the Hand Scene Episode (Rosenblatt, 1989, p. 159). These "public referents" were common cultural knowledge for Deng's mainstream peers. Moreover, Rosenblatt suggests that knowledge of "common public referents" influences whether readers adopt either an efferent or aesthetic stance toward text. And, as we have already suggested, the stances readers adopt while reading influence their response to texts. Consequently, the more readers know about common cultural "public references to verbal signs" the richer their opportunities for engagement with and response to text. For Deng's peers, this was a missed opportunity to recogize racial discord between African-Americans and Caucasians in the United States as a cultural phenomenon.

A question worth exploring is: What might have made involvement in the Hand Scene Activity a more meaningful experience for Deng, as well as for his peers? We draw on the Vygotsky Space as a tool to explore one alternative scenario. Say, for example, that the episode played out exactly as it was described in the vignette, except that Mrs. Weber provided for a follow-up activity after the episode. The events that occurred in quadrants I, II, and III of the Vygotsky Space (i.e., the manner in which Deng initially experienced, *appropriated,* and *transformed* the experience) would have remained the same; however, if Deng had had the opportunity to make his thinking (in this case, his lack of understanding about the full significance of the episode) public, Mrs. Weber would have been alerted to Deng's interpretation of the activity and his need for more support and guidance. By doing so, the question of the social construction of racist attitudes might have emerged in the students' discussions, pushing their thinking and enhancing their personal and critical response to *Maniac McGee.*

The opportunity for *publication* plays an important role in student learning. When students make their thinking public through venues such as writing, talking, role playing, and so forth, they have an opportunity to influence—and be influenced by—others. *Conventionalization* can occur when individuals' thoughts and/or ideas are made public and there is community uptake on those ideas. In Deng's case, if Mrs. Weber and Deng's peers had realized his need for instructional assistance with respect to the Hand Scene Episode, they may have inferred that he also needed instructional assistance in other cases, and a community norm could be established whereby community members check one another's understanding during lessons and encourage one another to make confusions public so that everyone could work together to promote learning. Moreover, his views of racism may have led to important ways of thinking about sources of discrimination and a greater appreciation for Maniac's beliefs and values as students continued reading and discussing the story.

MEDIATION WITH SIGNS AND SYMBOLS

The nature of language-in-use and the various analytical ways of looking at language-in-use become important when teaching children to respond effectively to texts. The third major line of thought in Vygotsky's sociocultural theory refers to the importance attributed to mediation with signs and symbols (e.g., the guidance and support teachers provide to students through language). While there are many different sign systems, language is a central sign system in literacy education, and the one on which Vygotsky primarily focused (1978). Vygotsky asserted that mind emerges in interactions with others, however, it is not simply social interactions, but language-based social interactions that shape mind (Vygotsky, 1978). Thus, this third line of thought builds upon the second by focusing on the central role of language in social interactions to promote learning, in general, and response and engagement with texts, in particular.

A meaningful distinction made by Vygotsky that relates to language use in social interactions and the notion of response is his distinction between meaning and sense (Vygotsky, 1986). Meaning is the collective—the agreed upon dictionary definition—or, in the case of literary texts, it is the canonical interpretation. Meaning refers to agreed-upon underlying conceptions of words and ideas that people in particular cultures and time frames hold in common. Sense, on the other hand, includes the "meaning" that individuals construct from their unique transactions with texts. As such, sense incorporates the autobiographical dimension of an individual's understanding of texts. Thus, for Vygotsky, meaning is collective—and relative to the second developmental dimension, it relates to cultural and historical "norms." In contrast, sense incorporates an individual's unique "meanings" and relates more to the third and fourth developmental dimensions. Meaning is based on the shared understandings of texts and sense includes an individual's particular knowledge of texts.

Vygotsky's sense/meaning distinction also relates closely to Rosenblatt's distinction between efferent and aesthetic stances toward texts (see also Galda, Chapter 1). Readers who adopt a primarily efferent stance toward text are interested in the ideas they can "take away" from their reading of the text. This notion aligns with Vygotsky's notion of meaning—the typical or canonical interpretations of texts. In contrast, readers who adopt an aesthetic stance toward text are primarily concerned with their "lived through" experience while reading the text. This relates to Vygotsky's conception of sense—the unique and autobiographical meanings that readers construct while reading.

We return to the Hand Scene Episode introduced earlier to serve as a backdrop for discussing meaning/sense and efferent/aesthetic distinctions and their relevance to teachers interested in children's textual response and engagement. Cindy interviewed Deng—with the help of Vue (a Hmong/English interpreter)—after Deng's involvement in the lesson containing the Hand Scene Episode. While Deng made it clear that he understood the visual distinctions between African-Americans and Caucasians, he apparently understood little else from the activity. When asked why Mrs. Weber had the children engage in the Hand Scene Episode, the following discussion ensued:

Deng: Because the teacher want to know the Black and the White people their hands, what color are their hands.

Cindy: Are there any other reasons?

Deng: Because the teacher want to know what color the kids in the classroom are?

Thus, Deng understood the dictionary definition of African-American and Caucasian. He recognized the visual (i.e., skin color) differences between African-Americans and Caucasians—he understood the "meaning" of Black and White. However, his "sense" of the differences between African-Americans and Caucasians in American culture was very different from that of many of his mainstream American classmates and Vue, the high school Hmong interpreter who had been in this country for eight years and was interpreting for Deng and Cindy.

After the short interchange above, Deng and Vue began speaking in Hmong, and a few minutes later Deng added that Mrs. Weber asked the children in the classroom to participate in the Hand Scene Episode because she wanted the Black people and the White people to be friends and not fight. When asked if Deng thought of that idea by himself or if Vue helped him think of it, Vue responded, "Actually, I just gave him some ideas. He knows that too, but I just gave him some ideas" (Transcript, 2/6/1996). Because Vue had been in America much longer than Deng, his "sense" of the cultural differences between Blacks and Whites in America was much different from Deng's. Vue understood that racial discord between African-Americans and Caucasians existed both historically and in contemporary American society.

As the example with Deng and Vue above illustrates, children bring unique and individual experiences to their engagement with texts and, consequently, they may transact with and respond to texts very differently. Two people can know the same dictionary meaning for words, but have very different senses of words owing to their unique life experiences. The sense/meaning distinction has important ramifications for teachers—both in terms of knowing what "sense" children make of texts and in knowing how to guide them to transact with and respond to texts in a variety of different ways.

It is also important for teachers to be aware of the different stances readers might assume toward texts. Moreover, through particular types of language-based social interactions, teachers can promote different stances toward texts—which, in turn, can promote particular types of textual response and engagement. While texts can lend themselves to particular types of readings (e.g., undoubtedly, many readers adopt a primarily efferent stance when reading an encyclopedia), teachers play a central role in guiding readers to adopt different stances toward texts. For example, if a teacher asks her students to answer a series of literal and inferential questions at the end of each chapter of a trade book, she is prompting her children to assume an efferent stance toward literature. If children are primarily prompted to respond to texts from an efferent stance, it is less likely that they will experience texts from an aesthetic stance.

At the beginning of this chapter, we suggested that teachers' instructional decisions are influenced by their underlying beliefs about learning and how literature should be used to facilitate student literacy learning. Thus far, we have presented a sociocultural framework for teaching children to engage with, respond to, and interpret texts. We suggest that this framework can serve as a useful tool for informing teachers' understanding about textual response and engagement and their instructional decision making. We draw on this sociocultural framework as a basis for examining five educational purposes for teaching children to respond and engage with texts.

TEXTUAL RESPONSE AND ENGAGEMENT: EDUCATIONAL PURPOSES

The educational purposes of textual response and engagement that we present in this section are derived from, and further extend, the sociocultural conception of response we have articulated. We divide this section of the chapter into two general categories: (1) how literature used within a response and engagement framework facilitates children's understanding of the human condition (see also Galda, Chapter 1), and (2) how literature used within a reader response framework facilitates children's understanding of both literature and literacy processes (i.e., reading and writing).[4] In actuality, these purposes and the respective categories into which we have grouped them are intertwined with and interdependent upon one another; however, we separate them here to highlight important issues that we believe merit teachers' consideration.

Facilitating Children's Understanding of the Human Condition

In this section, we suggest that by teaching perspective-taking, facilitating civil discourse, and facilitating social, cultural, and historical awareness, teachers help children respond to and engage with texts in more complex and meaningful ways while simultaneously developing deeper understandings of the human condition.

Teaching Perspective-Taking. Teachers can use literature and a response framework to help children understand perspective-taking, or what it might feel like to "walk in another's shoes." For example, some of Mrs. Weber's reasons for using *Maniac Magee* with her children included helping them understand the plight of homeless people and those who are the targets of racism or prejudice. Further, she wanted her children to see how dialogue and understanding helped characters overcome racism and prejudice. One example of how Mrs. Weber taught perspective-taking was modeling questions that the children might ask themselves and one another during the course of reading and discussing the text—questions such as: "How do you think Mars Bar (an African-American character in the story) felt when he was treated unfairly at Russell and Piper's (two Caucasian characters in the story) house?"

Modeling such questions points to teaching a particular type of perspective-taking: teaching the language of emotions. Teachers can use literature discussions as venues for teaching students the normative nature of emotions—the range of emotions people ought to experience in particular situations and contexts. Empathy, and the perspective that it presupposes, do not come naturally to children but are learned in the myriad of encounters that they have with others. These interactions include both face-to-face ones as well as ones that occur through their transactions with texts. While we would argue that there are many different responses that may be warranted by particular situations or events, there are some that conventional wisdom suggests are appropriate. For example, in response to learning about victims of prejudice, one might feel surprise, anger, sadness, confusion, desire to take action, and so forth. In contrast, feelings of joy, humor, or happiness would be considered inappropriate. In the above example, Mrs. Weber helped her children understand that people should feel empathy for others when they are the victims of prejudice. Further, people ought to take positive action when such occasions arise.

When teaching perspective-taking, teachers must realize the potential for multiple perspectives presented within a text, and multiple ways of interpreting those perspectives. Also, children's social, cultural, and language backgrounds will inform the perspectives they assume and the interpretations they render. Children must be guided to construct persuasive arguments for their interpretative responses to texts. Moreover, they must be taught to understand that others may not necessarily accept their interpretations as valid, but all parties in a conversation are best served when conversants strive to flesh out others' meanings and interpretations. Thus, teaching perspective-taking involves helping children strive to understand different perspectives of story characters as well as the perspectives of others with whom they are discussing the story. We further develop the latter point below.

Facilitating Civil Discourse. The second dimension intertwines with the first, but relates primarily to the immediate context of children responding to texts and discussing their responses. It is important for teachers to foster the notion of civility when sharing perspectives and ideas during literature discussions. Understanding that children's different social and cultural backgrounds and individual life trajectories shape both the manner in which they interpret text and interact with one another around text can alert teachers to the necessity of teaching children appropriate and useful patterns of interacting. For example, teachers can model how to (a) be respectful when taking turns, (b) show a genuine interest and concern for peers' ideas, and (c) revoice others' ideas (O'Connor & Michaels, 1996). In short, teachers must teach their children that they have the right to render and present their own unique interpretations of texts, but when discussing their responses to and interpretations of texts, children must be aware that others also have that right. Coupled with the right to be heard is the responsibility to listen to others.

Facilitating Social, Cultural, and Historical Awareness. Teachers can use literature and response as a venue to help children understand that authors write in particular cultural, historical, and political contexts that shape the nature of the texts they create. And, while response deals with the images, emotions, and ideas evoked from a reader's engagement with text, the nature of the text itself plays an important role in the transaction between reader and text (Rosenblatt, 1989). Moreover, readers are situated in particular cultural, historical, and political contexts that influence the manner in which they respond to and interpret texts. Thus, not only can different readers within the same context respond differently to texts, but readers from different cultures and from different time periods can respond to and construct different meanings of texts. So, texts themselves can vary culturally and historically, as can the nature of the readers reading and responding to them.

It is important for teachers to be aware of the cultural, historical, and political complexities of readers and texts. Such an awareness can influence teachers' text choices and teaching practices. For example, one theme of the text *Maniac Magee* is the importance of racial harmony. Reading and discussing the story heightened Deng's awareness that there was, and still is, racial discord between some African-Americans and Caucasians in America. On the other hand, through interactions and discussions, Deng's classmates (which included Asian-Americans, Caucasians, Hispanic-Americans, and African-Americans) were able to see African-American/Caucasian racial tensions in America through the eyes of someone from a different culture. That is, because Deng was not aware that there were racial conflicts between Blacks and Whites in America, his peers had an important opportunity to learn the cultural bases of racial conflicts and tensions. Heightened awareness of issues with appropriate teacher guidance could propel students to begin tackling social injustices within their own schools and neighborhoods.

Promoting Children's Understanding of Literacy and Literature

Children's personal response to texts can be used as a vehicle for teaching them about literacy and literature as a subject matter that can, in turn, facilitate richer response to and engagement with texts. Children can learn about the various literary structures and practices that contribute to the processes of meaning-making (e.g., making intertextual connections and understanding authors' uses of different textual features and devices) when their teachers encourage and teach them to personally respond to and engage with texts.

Facilitating Intertextual Connections. Scholes (1989) asserts that an important characteristic of reading is the process of making connections between our lives, the author's words, and other texts—that is, making intertextual connections. Scholars (e.g., Hartman, 1990; Scholes, 1989) propose that we define "texts" broadly to include linguistic signs, art, music, drama, gestures, and so forth. Hartman argues that readers make meaning while reading as they "transpose texts into other texts, absorb one text into another, and build a mosaic of intersecting texts" (1990, p. 50). Thus, reading is, in part, the process of bringing life to the author's words by the rich textual connections readers make with the words on the page. The teacher can play a central role in using children's responses to texts to facilitate such intertextual connections.

Consider our earlier discussion of the social origins of mind. We suggested that the classroom teacher plays an important role in guiding her children's thinking by making her own thinking and responses to texts public—as illustrated by the public/social space in quadrant I of the Vygotsky Space—and providing opportunities for children to make their thinking and responses to texts public—as illustrated by individual/social space in quadrant IV of the Vygotsky Space. Through the iterative process of teachers and children engaging in public dialogue about their experiences with texts, teachers can guide children to construct meanings as they read by helping them learn to engage in activities such as (a) discerning relationships and comparing ideas within and between text,[5] (b) comparing ideas within and across texts, and (c) contrasting one text with another.

For example, engaging in dialogue involves reading, speaking, listening, and writing. Through writing and speaking, in particular, students have opportunities to demonstrate how they have responded to texts and made intertextual connections. Prior to reading *Maniac Magee,* Mrs. Weber's class reviewed what they had learned about Dr. Martin Luther King during Black History Month. Additionally, the class read, discussed, and listened to an audiotaped version of Dr. King's "I Have a Dream" speech. Mrs. Weber felt that these experiences would provide valuable background knowledge as her students read about and discussed issues of prejudice and racism between African-Americans and Caucasians in *Maniac Magee.* After the students read, listened to, and discussed Dr. King's famous speech, she asked them to write about their reaction to his speech in their journals. The following is an excerpt of Tran's written response:

> My feelings about this speech is, what he said was great. He put things and compared them with others. It affected me because It made me want to help prejidice people to think like Dr. Martin Luther King.[6]

This excerpt of Tran's writing illustrates his response to Dr. King's speech and the personal connections he made between his life and the ideas presented by Dr. King, including how he wants to help others learn to treat people with respect as Dr. King proposed. Mrs. Weber could extend this writing activity by using her knowledge of Tran's response to Dr. King's speech in the broader classroom community to discuss specific ways that the children could promote racial harmony and respect for others in their own personal lives.

Teaching Children about "Literariness" and Literacy. The literacy teacher has two important goals: (1) facilitating children's growing knowledge about literature and how literature works, and (2) facilitating children's literacy learning. First, teachers need to teach children how authors use different textual features and devices (e.g., figures of speech, genres, unique and creative word choices, etc.) to heighten readers' reactions and responses to text and to shape readers' interpretations in particular ways. Recall that in the Hand Scene Episode, Mrs. Weber highlighted Spinelli's use of descriptive words (e.g., dark fudge, butter rum) to describe African-Americans' skin tones. She encouraged students' personal response by noting and discussing the different shades of their own hands. She then drew her children's attention to the way Spinelli used these descriptive words about skin tone to help readers understand that people's personalities vary as widely as their skin tones.

Second, teachers help their children to become better readers and writers. Mrs. Weber recognized the need to focus on the social dimensions of the text *Maniac Magee*, as well as the literary aspects of the work and her children's literacy learning. Throughout the overall unit, she focused on (a) social issues such as racism, prejudice, and homelessness, (b) literary issues such as the genre of the tall tale and Spinelli's use of figures of speech in the text, and (c) further developing her children's comprehension abilities of predicting, summarizing, and drawing on prior knowledge to respond to and interpret text.

CONCLUDING COMMENTS

We value literature as the basis for literacy instruction. We value response as a means of heightening students' awareness of how texts work, of making connections between texts and their own lives, and of promoting students' interest in engaging with a wide range of texts. Further, we urge educators who opt to use literature within their literacy programs to continually examine, nurture, and revise their own theories about literacy learning and teaching—especially as they relate to student response to and engagement with text. In our estimation, the framework we have presented here provides a crucial starting point. As teachers, teacher educators, and literacy researchers apply the framework in their own work, the framework can be continually modified and elaborated. These modifications and elaborations will stem from their own reading and responding to texts—including the texts of their own lives, their students' lives, and the written texts about literacy teaching and learning that they read and create.

ENDNOTES

1. From C. Brock (1997). "Exploring a Second Language Student's Literacy Learning Opportunities: A Collaborative Case Study Analysis." Unpublished doctoral dissertation, Michigan State University, East Lansing, MI. pp. 128–130.

2. Deng and his family had immigrated to the United States from Laos via Thailand when he was in the third grade. Thus, at the time of the Hand Scene Episode, Deng had been attending school in America for about two years.

3. Tran was a Korean-American child adopted shortly after his birth and raised by middle-class Caucasian parents.

4. The distinction we present here aligns with a distinction Rosenblatt has made. For example, in her seminal work, *Exploration of Literature* (1938), she highlights the reader's response to and engagement with text. In her text, *The Reader, the Text, and the Poem* (1978), she highlights the role that literature and response can play in facilitating children's understanding of literature.

5. We use the term "texts" broadly to include written texts and the texts of readers' lives.

6. The text is typed exactly as it was written in Tran's journal.

REFERENCES

Anderson, R. C., & Pearson, P. D. (1984). A schematic theoretic view of basic processes in reading comprehension. In P. D. Pearson (Ed.), *Handbook of reading research* (pp. 255–292). New York: Longman.

Bakhurst, D. J. (1982). Action, epistemology and The Riddle of the Self. *Studies in Soviet Thought, 24,* 185–209.

Beach, R. (1993). *A teacher's introduction to reader-response theories.* Urbana, IL: NCTE.

Bloome, D. (1986). Building literacy and the classroom community. *Theory into Practice, 25*(2), 71–76.

Bruner, J. S. (1972). The nature and uses of immaturity. *American Psychologist, 27*(8), 1–22.

Eagleton, T. (1983). *Literary theory.* Minneapolis: University of Minnesota Press.

Gavelek, J., & Raphael, T. (1996). Changing talk about text: New roles for teachers and students. *Language Arts, 73,* 182–192.

Gee, J. P. (1990). *Social linguistics and literacies: Ideology in discourses.* London: Falmer Press.

Harré, R. (1984). *Personal being: A theory for individual psychology.* Cambridge, MA: Harvard University Press.

Hartman, D. K. (1990, December). *Readers composing inner texts: The intertextual links of able high school students reading five passages.* Paper presented at the meeting of the National Reading Conference, Palm Springs, CA.

McMahon, S. I., and Raphael, T. E. with Goatley, V. J., & Pardo, L. S. (1997). *The Book Club connection: Literacy learning and classroom talk.* New York: Teachers College Press.

O'Connor, M., & Michaels, S. (1996). Shifting participant frameworks: Orchestrating thinking practices in group discussion. In D. Hicks (Ed.), *Discourse, learning, and schooling* (pp. 63–103). Cambridge: Cambridge University Press.

Pardo, L. S. (1997). Reflective teaching for continuing development of Book Club. In S. I. McMahon and T. E. Raphael, with V. J. Goatley and L. S. Pardo. (1997). *The Book Club connection: Literacy learning and classroom talk* (pp. 227–247). New York: Teachers College Press.

Rosenblatt, L. M. (1938). *Literature as exploration.* New York: Appleton-Century.

Rosenblatt, L. M. (1978). *The reader, the text, the poem: The transactional theory of the literary work.* Carbondale, IL: Southern Illinois Press.

Rosenblatt, L. M. (1989). Writing and reading: The transactional theory. In J. M. Mason (Ed.), *Reading and writing connections* (pp. 153–176). Boston: Allyn and Bacon.

Roser, N. L., & Martinez, M. G. (1995). *Book talk and beyond: Children and teachers respond to literature.* Newark, DE: International Reading Association.

Scholes, R. (1989). *Protocols of reading.* New Haven: Yale University Press.

Tompkins, J. P. (1992). The reader in history: The changing shape of literary response. In J. P. Tompkins (Ed.), *Reader-response criticism* (pp. 201–232). Baltimore: The Johns Hopkins University Press.

Vygotsky, L. S. (1978). *Mind in society.* Cambridge, MA: Harvard University Press.

Vygotsky, L. S. (1986). *Thought and language* (A. Kozulin, Trans.). Cambridge, MA: MIT Press.

Wertsch, J. V. (1985). *Vygotsky and the social formation of mind.* Cambridge, MA: Harvard University Press.

CHILDREN'S BOOKS CITED

Spinelli, J. (1990). *Maniac Magee.* New York: Harper.

Chapter 5

Thematic Instruction: A Quest for Challenging Ideas and Meaningful Learning

●————————●

Sheila W. Valencia, University of Washington
and
Marjorie Y. Lipson, University of Vermont

Literature-based instruction lays the perfect foundation for teaching thematically. It is difficult, if not impossible, to imagine thematic instruction without the range of trade books, textbooks, reference materials, periodicals, documents, and media found in literature-based classrooms. But, more than that, the ideas and concepts of good literature provide students access to substantive content from which they can build new ideas, concepts, and understandings about subject matter, the world, and themselves (Pappas, Kiefer, & Levstik, 1995; Morrow, Pressley, Smith, & Smith, 1997; Walmsley, 1994). High-quality literature is compelling; it presents endless possibilities for interpretation, critical thinking, and problem solving. As Stevens (1993) notes, "Worthwhile literature, whether nonfiction, fiction or poetry, is about life itself. It is embedded with universal themes that are common to the human condition . . . [themes] transcend subject areas by providing natural frameworks for unifying the curriculum. They can become windows of learning whereby students perceive connections among themselves, their education, and their world" (p. 3). So, on one hand, thematic instruction would lose much of its power and appeal without linkages to good literature. On the other hand, linking good literature together through themes increases the likelihood that students will extend their engagement with the literature itself, encouraging them to delve into meaning-making, knowledge building, and understanding of multiple perspectives (Hoffman, Roser, & Farest, 1988; Morrow, O'Connor, & Smith, 1990).

Together, good literature and thematic instruction can open the world of knowledge and exploration to students. However, knowing THAT the world is open is little comfort to teachers who are trying to determine HOW to open the world through thematic instruction. Although thematic instruction is widely endorsed and, it appears, widely practiced, there is little consensus about the definition of thematic instruction and little guidance to help teachers make good decisions when planning and implementing thematic instruction in their classrooms (Lipson, Valencia, Wixson, & Peters, 1993).

In this chapter, we suggest a framework for creating effective thematic instruction—a way to bring challenging ideas and meaningful learning into the classroom. We begin with a brief overview of the advantages and cautions associated with thematic instruction. Then we suggest a strategy for planning powerful thematic units that, we believe, facilitates the advantages and minimizes the cautions. Our framework requires attention to three essential building blocks for thematic instruction:

1. focus—criteria for good themes and theme selection;
2. coherence—designing unifying themes and helping students make connections;
3. instruction—providing students with instruction in subject-matter and language arts.

Throughout our discussion, we offer examples of thematic instruction designed to promote meaningful learning.

BACKGROUND

Thematic instruction has its origins in both literature-based instruction and integrated curriculum (Tchudi, 1994). Whether it includes intradisciplinary integration within the language arts of reading, writing, listening, speaking, and viewing, or interdisciplinary integration between two or more disciplines such as social studies, science, and language arts, thematic teaching is viewed as a means of teaching more powerful content, higher-level thinking, and meaningful application of skills. The goal is to help students become knowledgeable, capable, and thoughtful; to use that knowledge and skill effectively for personal and public purposes, now and in the future. To achieve this goal, students must be able to read and write a variety of types of texts, and they must acquire and use both subject-matter knowledge and language arts abilities. They must be able to carry their knowledge and skill flexibly into new learning situations and into their lives (Bruner, 1960; Spiro, Vispoel, Schmitz, Samarapungavin, & Boerger, 1987). As a result, thematic instruction must attend to both language arts and subject matter (see Peters & Wixson, Chapter 12, for a more in-depth discussion of the importance of subject matter). These are ambitious goals but ones that are clearly at the heart of all educational enterprises.

Advantages of Thematic Instruction

Advantages of thematic teaching are extolled in the professional literature and, apparently, they have been embraced by many practicing teachers. In fact, a survey of teachers from all 50 states revealed that 95 percent of them devote a portion of their instructional time to teaching in thematic units (Valencia, Lipson, Wixson, & Peters, 1994). They report four main reasons for organizing their instruction around themes: (1) in-depth learning for students, (2) better connections across subjects and within the language arts, (3) increased student interest and motivation, and (4) better use of time. All four reasons parallel the advantages cited in the professional literature.

In-depth learning. The most compelling advantage of thematic teaching is the potential for more meaningful and in-depth student learning that is fostered as students study powerful ideas and concepts. By focusing student learning on conceptual knowledge, flexible, higher-level thinking is privileged (Ackerman, 1989; Alleman & Brophy, 1993; Case, 1991; Spiro et al., 1987). Students use complex psychological tools such as analyzing and synthesizing information, asking questions, identifying and solving problems, weighing and gathering various perspectives, using multiple sources, taking a critical stance, and transferring knowledge and skills to new situations. They gain insights about complex phenomenon; they inquire and construct knowledge rather than simply gather it (Case, 1991; Short & Burke, 1996). The hope is that through thematic instruction, students will learn to think in a new way about more complex issues and to transfer those abilities to other contexts.

Connections. Thematic instruction fosters three types of connections for students. First, it helps students see and experience the connections among all the language arts—reading, writing, listening, and speaking (Walmsley, 1994). Because thematic instruction brings the language arts together around authentic purposes rather than separating them into distinct lessons, new skills and strategies are learned together and they are learned to serve a real purpose (i.e., gather information, research a question, solve a problem). A second type of connection promoted through thematic teaching is the connection across subject areas (e.g., language arts, social studies, science, math). Students see how subject-matter knowledge and language arts strategies are used together to grapple with important ideas and questions (Willis, 1992; Pearson, 1994). A third type of connection helps students see broader connections to the world and to other learning. As they learn to use knowledge and skills flexibly, students are able to connect and extend what they have learned to new situations (Hughes, 1991; Lipson et al., 1993).

Motivation. Because themes are organized around relevant, whole chunks of learning, they are thought to be more engaging, more "fascinating," for students (Lipson et al., 1993; Pappas, Kiefer, & Levstik, 1990; Perkins, 1989). In addition, students may have more choice and a wider range of options during thematic instruction, engaging them in learning that is personally interesting to them. A growing body of research indicates that students learn more and persist longer when reading and studying information that is interesting to them (Hidi, 1990). Anderson and his colleagues (1987) identified several factors that contribute to students' interest in text, two of which are especially noteworthy given the nature of good thematic instruction: identification with characters and presence of a universal or real-life theme.

Time. Advocates argue that thematic instruction may be more efficient than traditional forms of instruction because it folds together aspects of the curriculum that are typically treated separately (Willis, 1992). By combining portions of the curriculum, both the amount and quality of the time should be enhanced. Teachers are particularly hopeful about the potential for increased time, especially as they struggle to meet growing curricular requirements and a wider range of student abilities.

Although the advantages are compelling, they are not easy to realize. Thematic instruction requires thoughtfully developed and carefully implemented themes; not just any theme will do.

Cautions about Thematic Instruction

Along with the endorsements and the popularity of thematic teaching are cautions about its potential to go awry. The cautions are both conceptual and logistical.

Means not an end. Many educators and researchers caution that thematic teaching is a means to the advantages outlined above, not an end in itself (Alleman & Brophy, 1993; Case, 1991; Parker & Jarolimek, 1997); that thematic instruction is not the panacea for all curriculum or instruction. It has the *potential* to guide students toward important and meaningful learning but this depends on the worthiness of the goals and the quality of the learning experiences and instruction. Thematic instruction that is focused on unimportant or superficial themes should not be the objective. Thematic instruction must focus student attention on worthwhile and powerful ideas. Our time is better spent teaching worthwhile curriculum that is not organized thematically than teaching unimportant curriculum that is "thematically" linked.

Thematic teaching sometimes leads to the creation of "themes of convenience" (Lipson et al., 1993) that superficially join together activities simply to demonstrate a connection. Routman (1994) refers to this as correlation rather than integration, and Jacobs (1989) refers to it as the "potpourri" problem. Although some of the activities associated with themes may be fun and engaging for students, they may not necessarily advance powerful ideas or connect meaningfully with other activities. For example, we have seen topics such as kites, birds, clouds, and the moon joined together in a primary grade theme simply because they are all in the sky. Similarly, we have found "themes" on bears used in such a way that students learned about how bears hibernate, read *Goldilocks and the Three Bears,* and counted gummy bears in groups of ten. The problem, in these cases, is not merely the arbitrary selection of content or the superficial links and limited opportunities to build deep, flexible thinking across activities but, as we point out above, the lack of a powerful unifying idea. In addition, time and energy are diverted away from teaching genuinely important content and skills. Theme activities must be worthwhile because they fill curricular purposes, not just because they are interesting to children or cut across subject-matter lines (Alleman & Brophy, 1993; Parker & Jarolimek, 1997).

Limited learning in content areas and literature. Thematic instruction is designed around central ideas, often related to science and social studies. But not all subject-matter experts believe this is a good thing. Alleman & Brophy (1993) caution that sometimes thematic instruction leads to curricular "invasion" rather than integration! By this they mean that important content is lost at the expense of superficial content that appears to be related to the theme. For example, students may read *Johnny Tremain* (Forbes, 1942) and *My Brother Sam Is Dead* (Collier & Collier, 1974) as part of a theme on the complexities of war. Although reading both books may help students build background and make the revolutionary period more alive to them (Alvermann, 1994), it doesn't replace students' need to know, for example, about the competing interests that led to the Revolutionary War. Historical fiction does not replace historical facts or important historical concepts, it enriches them. A teacher who views reading these excellent books as a way to cover social studies content about the Revolutionary War would be doing an injustice to the disciplinary knowledge required of social studies. From Alleman and Brophy's perspective, social studies would have been invaded!

A related concern has been raised about literary understanding. Just as subject-matter experts fear that their content will be marginalized, some in the field of literacy fear that literature will be marginalized in thematic instruction. Pearson (1994) is concerned that the essence of literature, aesthetic and efferent responses to literature, and literary understanding may be lost if texts are selected only on the basis of how well they serve a particular subject-matter. He fears there may be an overreliance on non-fiction and a narrowing of the range of texts and purposes for which students read. Similarly, Alvermann (1994) and Pearson (1994) caution that if literature is overused for teaching language arts skills and strategies in context and for integrating the language arts in intradisciplinary themes, reader response and literary experience may be ignored and the literature may become "contaminated." Loss of disciplinary integrity can happen in language arts as well as in subject areas.

Quantity and quality of instruction.   Another caution is related to the amount and quality of instruction provided to students during thematic teaching. Although well-planned projects and activities can provide important learning experiences for students, explicit teaching is often necessary to help students develop new skills, strategies, and subject-matter knowledge. This is of particular concern in the area of language arts.

In our survey, approximately 70 percent of the K–6 teachers spent more than three-fourths of their language arts instructional time teaching through themes or integrated curriculum (Valencia, Lipson, Wixson, & Peters, 1994). This suggests that many teachers believe they are accomplishing most of their language arts instructional goals during thematic teaching. However, simply encouraging or even requiring students to use existing reading and writing abilities during theme projects or activities may not help them acquire new skills and strategies, or further develop existing ones. Ackerman (1989) cautions us about hoping that learning will simply "rub off." Carefully planned lessons, modeling, and practice may be required. Unfortunately, our survey also indicates that many teachers do not list language arts goals when asked about their theme goals. Instead, they suggest that through themes, students are meaningfully *using* and *integrating* their language arts skills as they work on theme projects. We suspect that, many times, students are receiving instructions about how to carry out specific theme activities but are receiving relatively little explicit instruction related to the reading and writing skills and strategies they are expected to use. If students are not provided with needed instruction, especially at the early stages of literacy development, we fear that students who bring "rich" literacy abilities to thematic instruction will continue to get "richer" and those who bring "poor" literacy abilities will simply get "poorer" (Stanovich, 1986).

Time.   Although advocates suggest that teaching thematically can save time, teachers are frequently cautioned that developing meaningful thematic units takes a substantial amount of time, knowledge, and experience (Wiggins in Willis, 1992). Routman (1994) reports that it has taken many teachers 3 to 5 years to feel comfortable with thematic instruction. It is challenging to understand all the facets of strong thematic instruction, time consuming to develop the units and find the resources, and difficult to orchestrate its implementation in the classroom. On the other hand, even if teachers do take the time to develop and implement thematic instruction, Lipson and colleagues (1993) caution that it won't save time if it is simply added to the curriculum already in place.

Given the ambitious goals, potential advantages, serious cautions, and lack of direction in the professional literature, it is no surprise that many existing themes fall short of expectations. If thematic instruction is to realize its full potential, teachers need strategies for planning or adapting worthwhile themes. We believe that with strategic attention to three building blocks—focus, coherence, and instruction—teachers can develop worthwhile themes that enhance student learning.

BUILDING BLOCKS FOR THEMATIC INSTRUCTION

Figure 5.1 provides a conceptual display of how focus, coherence, and instruction can guide the development of strong thematic instruction. In general, we begin with a thematic focus, a big idea or enduring question, and then identify two or more relevant examples or cases for study. Several coherent, related activities grow out of each case, and the instruction is planned around specific activities related to each case. Students are guided to make important connections across the various activities and across the various cases to help them think about the big idea or the enduring question. We describe each of the building blocks in detail in the next section.

Focus

Criteria for good themes. The most important aspect of planning is selecting a good theme. To be sure, there are different points of view about what makes a good theme and each point of view has implications for what students learn. Our criteria are intended to help students achieve the advantages associated with thematic instruction we describe above. Broadly stated, a theme is a central idea (Haggitt, 1975). More specially, we believe good themes meet three criteria. First, they are organized around significant and worthwhile ideas—important curricular goals rather than trivial ones (Case, 1991; Parker & Jarolimek, 1997). Second, they represent rich, complex ideas that require deep understanding and flexible use of knowledge. Third, themes have relevance and importance beyond the immediate situation so that what students are learning and how they are learning to think can be useful in other parts of their lives.

To meet all three criteria, we suggest thinking about themes as "big ideas" or "enduring questions" that have relevance for the people of a diverse society in many aspects of their lives, both in and out of school.

Figure 5.1

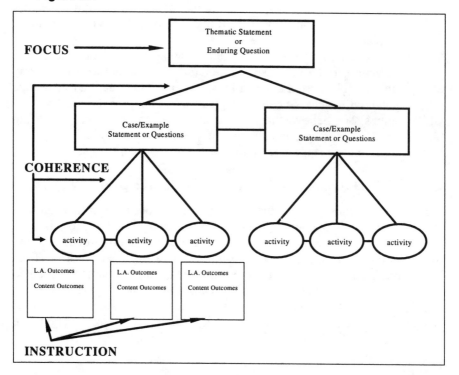

First, we turn to "big ideas." "Big ideas" are powerful concepts or generalizations written in the form of a statement rather than specific topics, particular texts, limited concepts, or genres. Surely, students can study a topic
(e.g., chocolate, World War I, Valentine's Day, Martin Luther King), a single
text or author (e.g., *Ira Sleeps Over* [Weber, 1972], *The Giver* [Lowry, 1993],
Patchwork Quilt [Flournoy, 1985], Ezra Jack Keats, Lois Lowry), a limited
concept (e.g., kites, bears, plants, endangered species, friendship), or a literary genre (e.g., historical fiction, poetry, personal narrative). In fact, there
may be times when we would want to concentrate students' efforts on one of
these ideas. However, they don't constitute themes—they will not help students achieve the goals associated with good thematic instruction. They simply don't go far enough. By our criteria, these topics, single texts, limited
concepts, and genres don't exemplify educationally significant goals; don't
require deep, higher-level thinking; and will not have far-reaching application to other aspects of students' lives and students' thinking. As we will
demonstrate below, they could be *part* of a thematic unit or a stepping stone
in the planning, but, by themselves, they don't constitute big ideas.

We suggest thinking beyond topics, texts, and single concepts to thematic statements. Thematic statements express a relationship between two or more worthwhile curricular concepts. They are engaging statements that drive student thinking deeply and broadly, beyond the immediate examples they study, to other contexts. For example,

- Living in a diverse society requires respect, cooperation, and negotiation;
- Culture and life experience influence how people respond to challenges they face;
- Humans' interactions with the environment have intended and unintended consequences.

Each of the thematic statements above presents a relationship between two or more worthwhile concepts (i.e., diversity, society, and respect, cooperation and negotiation; culture, life experience and challenge); the relationship is powerful, complex, and far-reaching. However, not all statements or generalizations are good themes. Consider the following statements, which parallel those above:

- Friends must learn to get along;
- People took different sides during the Civil Rights movement;
- Recycling is good for our planet.

Although these statements contain multiple concepts, they lack power and complexity. In contrast to the first set of thematic statements, the second set of statements represents ideas that are more narrowly defined, less transferable to other situations, less likely to engage students in higher-level thinking and learning and, in some cases, they are less educationally significant.

Thematic statements are clearly different from individual topics, texts, or genres; however, they are also different from limited concepts. For example, studying the limited concept of endangered species or the broader concept of interdependence might lend itself to more important, engaging, and deeper learning than simply studying the topic of the Great White Whale. And, you can imagine that learning the distinguishing characteristics of endangered species, how various species adapt or fail to thrive in different environments, and why we should be concerned about endangered species or humans' role in preserving endangered species would cause students to think more deeply about important ideas than simply learning about one or two examples of endangered species. However, in our opinion, even concepts such as endangered species or broader concepts such as interdependence need more direction and more breadth to become meaningful, workable themes. We suggest that teachers need to ask themselves, "What do I want my students to learn about endangered species or interdependence? How can this theme become a worthwhile and significant curricular goal that requires deep, rigorous thinking? How can this theme help students build knowledge and skills that will transfer to other parts of their lives? How can these theme experiences help students develop ways of thinking—their 'habits of mind' (Meier, 1996)?" These questions can lead teachers to form statements that will add focus and clarity to their themes.

We focus next on "enduring questions" that also can embody the criteria for a good theme. Thematic questions, like statements, must center around significant educational goals, engage students in rigorous learning and higher-order thinking, and have endurance or long-lasting application to students' lives. Unlike theme statements, theme questions ask students to use the information and skills they will develop in the thematic unit to take a position on an issue, suggest a solution to a problem, or answer a critical question. For example,

- Should nations interfere in the civil affairs of other nations?
- How do different communities adjust to, adapt to, or resist the diversity of their members?
- What is the human responsibility for caring for one another?

Strong theme questions push students to learn and think about worthwhile, complex ideas as well as the relation between ideas. In contrast, weak questions such as

- What would you have done if you had been drafted during the Vietnam war?
- How are people the same and how are they different?
- How does our city take care of homeless people?

are too specific, too simple, or too factually oriented to be considered enduring, thematic questions. As we explore below, these questions could be part of a theme study but do not, by themselves, fit the criteria of a good theme.

Some teachers combine the use of big ideas and enduring questions when they plan a theme. For example, consider the following thematic statement and the accompanying thematic questions adapted from Smith and Casteel (1996) for use with fourth-grade students:

Thematic Statement: People have a responsibility to consider the rights of others when making community changes.

Theme Questions: What determines whether a community change is positive or negative?
Does the environment exist to be used by humans?
Can special interests be reconciled for the common good?

Both intradisciplinary and interdisciplinary themes can be organized around big ideas or enduring questions. For example, intradisciplinary literary themes often focus on understanding humanity (ourselves and others) by exploring our various experiences, values, and cultural practices. The content here is literary understanding and the materials are drawn only from literature, rather than from primary documents, reference materials, and textbooks. Themes of this type might focus on a big idea such as "Personal change often involves interpersonal and intrapersonal conflict" or a question such as "How can humans reconcile personal integrity and group norms?" On the other hand, there are themes that could be more interdisciplinary in nature, such as "What is the role and responsibility of people in positions of power?" or "How do cultural beliefs and survival needs influence humans' relation with their environment?" that pull in curricular goals from social studies and science. Interestingly, it is not obvious simply from the big idea statements or questions which particular themes might have an interdisciplinary focus and which might have an intradisciplinary focus. The differences become apparent at the next two levels of our framework, coherence and instruction, where specific learning outcomes are identified.

Regardless of whether themes are interdisciplinary or intradisciplinary, and regardless of whether they are designed around big idea statements, enduring questions, or a combination, the focus should be on helping students explore and grapple in-depth with the relationships between worthwhile concepts. Unfortunately, most professional material (Lipson et al., 1993) and most teachers (Valencia, Lipson, Wixson, & Peters, 1994) do not conceptualize themes in this way. In our survey, fewer than 1 percent of 375 themes that teachers reported they had used could be classified as big ideas or enduring questions, while 91 percent could be classified as topics (e.g., chocolate, Egypt, potatoes, Christmas). The discrepancy between the criteria for a good theme and these classroom findings indicate that teachers may need some help in selecting powerful themes.

Selecting Themes. As we have worked with teachers developing thematic units, we have observed two different approaches to selecting themes: (a) bottom-up and (b) top-down. In a bottom-up approach, teachers begin with required texts or topics and work with those resources to build an expanded and coherent set of activities focused on a big idea or enduring question. For example, a first-grade teacher wanted to teach about classroom rules. Because this is a worthwhile, common curricular goal for first graders, the teacher had little trouble thinking of important concepts and generalizations she could use to create a worthwhile theme. She asked herself, "What are the concepts and big ideas that students should learn related to classroom rules?" She knew she wanted to focus on community and codes of conduct or fair play.

She asked, "How can I create a theme that requires deep, rigorous thinking about these ideas? How can this theme help students build knowledge and skills that will transfer to other parts of their lives? How do I want my students to use this theme to develop new ways of thinking?" She came up with one overarching thematic question and several related questions:

Theme Question: How do different members of a diverse community take care of themselves and others?

Sub-questions: What is a community?
What are different kinds of communities?
What are the responsibilities of community members?
How are different communities governed?
How do different communities solve their problems?
How do different communities deal with new members or people different from themselves?

Through this theme, the teacher was able to engage students in a more thoughtful and far-reaching study of classroom rules—why we need them; what makes rules fair; how class members can develop, implement, and monitor their effectiveness. She also was able to include animal communities as one of the units in her theme, which allowed her to cover a portion of the science curriculum—how different adult animals take care of their young. Including the animal unit did not marginalize the science content; in fact, it strengthened it because students were encouraged to look at different kinds of communities and the factors (norms, instinctual behavior, environment, beliefs, etc.) that influence group and individual behaviors.

Another teacher planned to cover the fourth-grade curriculum on plants. Although she had always done a "theme" on plants, she wanted to transform the work into a more powerful theme. She recognized that "plants" didn't have a big idea; that she might be limiting the content, thinking, and skills her children could learn. The teacher's first step was to think beyond the topic of plants to important concepts she wanted her students to learn about plants that might also have application to other parts of their lives. She decided to focus on how plants grow and change and the factors that influence their growth and change. The concept of "Change" could apply to plants and also apply to other important learnings for her fourth graders (how we are growing and changing; changes in our state, community, families, etc.). Her thinking had expanded from a topic to a broad concept—"Change." Now she had to provide specificity and direction to "Change" by creating a thematic statement and/or enduring questions. She asked herself, "What are the big ideas or questions in the curriculum that students should explore about change?" She asked, "How can I create a theme that requires deep, rigorous thinking about these ideas? How can this theme help students build knowledge and skills that will transfer to other parts of their lives? How do I want my students to use this theme to develop new ways of thinking?" She came up with several ideas: "What causes things to change or grow?" "Change in one part of a system often affects the other parts of the system." "How do living things adapt to change?"

As this teacher thought about another "theme" she had always done, "Washington State," she realized that instead of approaching the topic through a series of student research reports on the resources, geography, and people of the state, she could also include this unit as part of her theme. Specifically, she could have students explore the question, "How do geography, natural resources, and culture influence how regions develop and how they change over time?" By rethinking this unit on Washington State, the teacher was able to include portions of the required curriculum (history and geography of the state) in a deeper, more thoughtful way. Students were guided to consider how the people and resources in the state had changed over time and how and why different regions within the state had developed in different ways. In addition, she was able to capitalize on students' local interests regarding salmon fishing and logging debates and to consider these dilemmas in terms of the geography, natural resources, culture, and economic needs. She also was able to integrate a portion of the science curriculum that focused on renewable and nonrenewable resources by exploring resources in Washington and its neighboring states.

Both the community example and plant/Washington State examples demonstrate how teachers can use a bottom-up approach to theme selection, rethinking existing curriculum so that it becomes more powerful, in-depth, and far-reaching for students. At the same time, teachers can capitalize on students' interests by expanding the examples and cases students study as they explore the big idea of the theme.

In a top-down approach to theme development, teachers begin with a big idea, enduring question, or a universal concept they develop on their own or adapt from other sources. Then they work appropriate parts of their curriculum into the themes. Sometimes the top-down approach begins with a grade level or school-wide focus on a universal concept, such as interdependence, change, systems, or democracy. As we suggest above, teachers need to add specificity and generalizability to these concepts by asking what they want their students to learn about that particular concept and related concepts. For example, a team of middle school teachers wanted to work on the concept of democracy. They developed several big ideas and questions, any one of which could focus their planning. For example,

How can we deepen our understanding of democracy such that diversity is not marginalized?

Can the people rule themselves or are strong authorities needed?

For democracy to thrive in heterogeneous societies, cultural diversity (race, class, ethnicity, gender) must coexist with the common good.[1]

Democracy is the worse form of government imaginable except for all the alternatives.[2]

Their final decision about whether to focus on one statement or question, or to incorporate several depends on several factors: resources, time, students' knowledge and abilities, and the specific elements of the curriculum they want to cover in the theme.

Teachers don't need to start from scratch in developing big ideas and enduring questions. Several resources related to national standards, benchmarks, state standards or literary themes can be helpful (see Table 5.1). Although most of these resources don't define themes in precisely the same way as we've described, they do offer very useful information on what students should know and be able to do in various disciplines. With this information as background, theme statements and enduring questions are more easily developed.

The critical issue with both the bottom-up and top-down approaches to theme selection is to be sure that students will spend their time engaged with worthwhile, rigorous learning that can be applied in other contexts. As we have demonstrated, there are alternative paths to this end. Some teachers find it easiest to begin with a topic, then think about a broader concept, and then move to thematic statements or questions. Others begin with a powerful concept and then move to thematic statements or questions. And still others prefer to begin with thematic statements or questions. Whatever path you take, the objective is to ask, "What is important for my students to learn? What enduring questions are important for them to explore?" The process of identifying a good theme is difficult. However, working through thematic statements and questions will make the next steps, planning a coherent set of experiences and instructional opportunities (see below), flow more smoothly.

Coherence

We use the term coherence to address two aspects of thematic instruction: (1) content selection within the theme (what cases and activities students will study), and (2) helping students make connections across cases and activities. The point of both aspects of coherence is to help students use the subject-matter knowledge and language arts strategies they acquire during the theme study to develop the cognitive flexibility they will need to build the big idea or join the enduring question. Careful content selection assures that activities are not disjointed or only tangentially related to the big idea—

Table 5.1

Sources for Thematic Ideas

California History-Social Science Framework, California State Board of Education.

Curriculum Standards for Social Studies, National Council for the Social Studies.

Geography for Life: National Geography Standards 1994, National Geographic Society.

Lehr, S. (1988). The child's developing sense of theme as a response to literature. *Reading Research Quarterly, 23*(3), pp. 337–357.

Lukens, R. (1995). *A critical handbook of children's literature.* New York: HarperCollins.

Michigan Framework for English Language Arts, Michigan Department of Education.

Michigan Framework for Social Studies, Michigan Department of Education.

National Issues Forums, National Issues Institute.

National Standards for Civics and Government, Center for Civic Education.

National Standards for History, grades K–4; available from National Center for History in the Schools.

National Standards for the English/Language Arts, International Reading Association.

National Standards for United States History, grades 5–12, National Center for History in the Schools.

National Standards for World History, National Center for History in the Schools.

Science for All Americans, Benchmarks for Science Literacy (nicknamed, "Benchmarks" and "Project 2061").

---

that meaningful connections are possible. Even so, students will not necessarily draw meaningful connections across activities simply because the *teacher* understands that important connections exist. Coherence among the cases and the activities must be carefully planned and explicitly explored with the students. The lines connecting each component of our theme (see Figure 5.1) indicate all the ways coherence is needed in a thematic teaching.

Content selection. Decisions about which specific cases or projects to include in a theme are critical to their effectiveness. Students should have experiences with more than a single instance, or case, of the concepts and relationships included in the theme. They must explore ideas from various perspectives or investigate several contexts in which ideas take different form. For example, let's return to a common thematic statement:

> Humans' interactions with their environment produce both intended and unintended consequences.

As the teacher plans, he must decide on the specific cases, or examples, he will use to help students develop an understanding of this theme. The possibilities are rich. Students might explore logger and environmental debates, factors that influence the determination of an endangered species and the resulting actions taken by our government, local decisions regarding urban sprawl and open space, or other cases of the theme. Additional cases can be drawn from students' interests or grow out of the theme as it develops. The teacher would carefully select two, three, or more cases, so students are able to use knowledge and skills across cases. Cases should not be selected simply because they share a topic or author, or because students will enjoy them, but, rather, because they advance thinking about the theme. In the same way, multiple activities are selected because, as a group, they help students develop the same flexible understanding and perspective gained by studying multiple cases.

This process of selecting cases and activities is quite different than many of the suggestions found in the literature. One of the most common recommendations made to teachers for developing themes is to use a spider web or a wheel for planning. At the center of the web is the "theme," and around the web are activities, often organized by subject area. For example, a space exploration "theme" may have web spokes leading to social studies (history of space travel), art (solar system mobile), science (experiments on weightlessness), math (calculate your weight on different planets), and language arts (write about your experiences as an astronaut). Although "space exploration" doesn't fit our definition of a big idea, the example is typical of how theme activities are frequently developed. When theme activities are developed this way the connections often are superficial and only topically related. Furthermore, there is rarely any substantive coherence among the various activities. In our opinion, it is unrealistic for all, or most, subject areas to fit substantively in all themes. It is important, nonetheless, to think about how meaningful cases can be drawn from various subject areas, but always with an eye toward the big idea and conceptual, rather than superficial, coherence.

We present three examples of coherent cases and activities. As Figure 5.1 indicates, we begin by thinking about the big idea and the cases students will explore to build the big idea. Several activities grow out of each case.

For example, a first grade teacher wanted to teach a theme on humans' impact on the environment and, rather than select individual activities such as reports on endangered species, a visit to a recycling plant, and planting a garden, she organized her theme into meaningful, in-depth cases of human interaction with different aspects of the environment (see Figure 5.2). Each case offers another perspective on human interaction with the environment to help students understand various facets of the big idea. The focus questions included with each case help the teacher and the students stay focused and they assure that the case remains connected to the larger theme. As the teacher worked with students to think *across* these cases, they learned to think critically and analytically as they formulated generalizations and responses to the theme question.

Another teacher began with the concept of friendship, a favorite "theme" for her third grade intradisciplinary theme. She thought about the worthwhile big ideas undergirding friendship that were important for her students to explore. Then she developed a thematic question and two cases, each of which was developed around literature-based activities (see Figure 5.3). Notice that one of her cases addressed the interpersonal nature of change by focusing on friendships while the other explored the internal conflicts people experience as they make decisions and changes in their lives. The cases present two, sometimes conflicting, perspectives in children's lives. Alternatively, the teacher could have decided to explore the concept of interconnectedness, and generated different thematic statements to focus the theme. The sample of possible activities demonstrates how a well-thought-out set of activities can help students explore important concepts within each of the cases, and, as a result, help them build knowledge about the big idea.

Figure 5.2

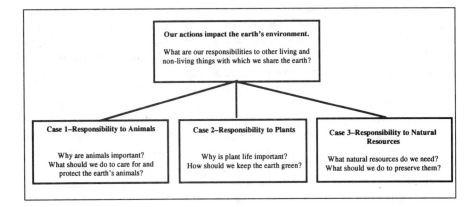

Our actions impact the earth's environment.

What are our responsibilities to other living and non-living things with which we share the earth?

Case 1–Responsibility to Animals

Why are animals important? What should we do to care for and protect the earth's animals?

Case 2–Responsibility to Plants

Why is plant life important? How should we keep the earth green?

Case 3–Responsibility to Natural Resources

What natural resources do we need? What should we do to preserve them?

Figure 5.3

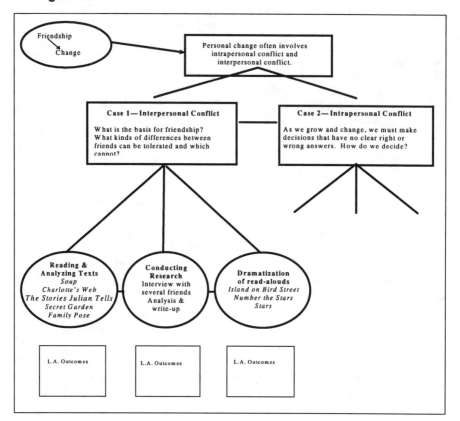

In this language arts intradisciplinary theme there are three activities: (1) a literary exploration of how different characters deal with conflict between friends who may be quite different from themselves; (2) a process writing activity in which students interview two friends to explore their similarities and differences, analyzing differences that are valued; and (3) a second, more complex, literary exploration of characters who are faced with moral dilemmas concerning friends. The first activity includes five books about friends who are different from each other—four realistic fiction and one fantastic narrative; however, nonfiction books such as *Brian's Song* (Blinn, 1972) or other biographies could have been included as well. These five books were selected to provide a range of reading difficulty and to offer different perspectives on friendships. The second activity provides a meaningful context for students to learn and apply the writing process and interviewing strategies as they explore the focus question on friendships and the larger theme question on personal change. With an eye on these questions, the writing activity takes on a new purpose (information gathering to explore an important question) and students are encouraged to think in new ways. The literature in the third activity is very difficult—likely too difficult for most of these third-grade students—yet the teacher selected it because she wanted to use historical fiction to introduce the students to the genre of historical fiction and life-and-death sorts of dilemmas that sometimes occur within friendships. She chose to use these texts as read-alouds. The focus on genre in this activity works well because the literature was selected to support the theme statement and the particular case.

The final example is an intermediate grade interdisciplinary theme on the tensions between self-rule and authority (see Figure 5.4). The cases span several perspectives—an historical perspective (the Revolutionary War, which is required curriculum), local perspective (the classroom), and community perspective (police)—although, as we note, many other cases are possible. The focus questions within each case keep it connected to the theme. By exploring the theme question through all these lenses, students need to consider a wide range of factors and contexts; they come to understand the complexity of the questions and to thoughtfully consider a range of responses. The activities under Case 1 exemplify how a set of activities can provide important information and perspectives. Two of the activities require students to use textbooks and reference material to learn historical information; one focuses their attention on the pros and cons of the American Revolution, the other on interpreting different rationales for war offered by people on the same side—Henry, Paine, Jefferson. A third activity combines the study of historical fiction with personal perspectives and experiences of young people involved on both sides. The fourth activity also highlights genres study, this time biographies of people who argued different sides of the question. The combination of literary-oriented and social studies-oriented activities demonstrates how both can contribute to in-depth student learning when they are selected to serve a powerful theme.

Helping students make connections. Developing a powerful big idea and selecting a coherent set of cases and activities creates the potential for students to make meaningful connections. However, we have found that teachers need to plan opportunities, and often guide students, to make these connections both across cases and across the activities within a case. For example, although the cases developed for the human/environment theme (see Figure 5.2) form a coherent set of experiences, students may not automatically see the connections among them or their connection to the theme. Several approaches are possible. For instance, after studying each case, the teacher could have students make a list of ways people can protect animals, plants, and natural resources. They could then do a chart of similarities and

Figure 5.4

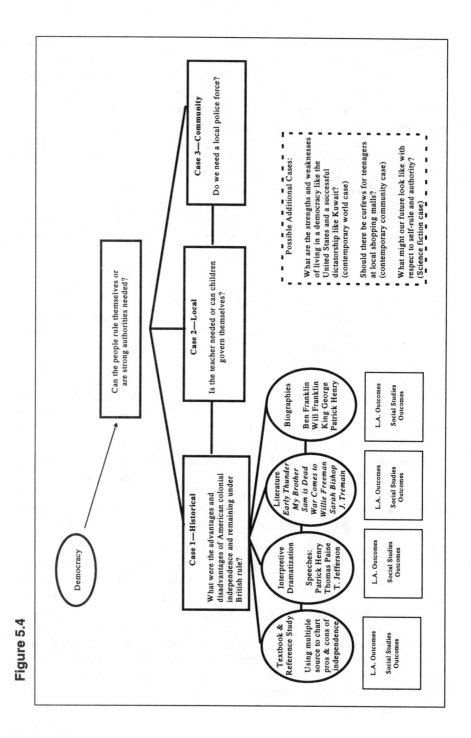

differences, comparing how certain actions would help to preserve more than one element. They might also discuss a specific example in which actions to preserve one (for example, animals) might threaten another (plants). Then they could use their knowledge and skills to formulate positions on this controversial issue. Alternatively, students could do theme projects in which they take personal action regarding their responsibilities to the earth's environment. Using the information gathered during the theme study, they could provide a statement of the problem, a personal plan of action (including evidence-based rationale), and then a long-range plan for assessing their effectiveness. They could then implement their plans, discuss the experiences, and revisit the theme question. These types of culminating theme projects are discussed in more detail by Peters & Wixson in Chapter 12 as a meaningful way to assess student performance.

Students also need guidance in making connections among activities within a case. The activities in Figure 5.4 might seem to be only superficially related to the students, but again, teachers can help them understand the deeper connections. After completing two or more activities, students could, for example, use a data retrieval chart (see Parker & Jarolimek, 1997), to keep track of the advantages and disadvantages of independence, charting evidence separately for the British, the Loyalists, and the Patriots. This would help them understand different perspectives and how the same information can be used to support different points of view. Students might also be encouraged to compare pros and cons from the perspective of an individual and the perspective of what might be good for the entire country. In addition, they could distinguish reasons presented in different sources—historical fiction, primary documents, textbooks, reference materials, and biographies to see if different reasons are emphasized, thus also studying the attributes of various genres. Making connections across these activities helps students develop a deep understanding of the Revolutionary War period and issues of self-rule and authority during that time in history. Then, those specific understandings need to be connected to the broader theme question. And, as students explore other cases in-depth (self-rule and authority in the classroom, the local police force, etc.) more connections are fostered and they are helped to build an understanding of the big idea across different contexts.

Making meaningful connections among activities, among cases, and between cases and the big idea is essential in thematic teaching. Sometimes, this may simply require focused discussion in which students are using information and insights from several experiences or sources. Other times, it will require more deliberate and structured activities such as those we've described. Whatever the approach, thinking across instances is a primary objective of thematic teaching, and one that is critical to deepening students' understanding.

Instruction

Instruction is the last of our essential building blocks for thematic teaching. It appears last in our model because instruction is easier to think about in terms of specific learning activities than in terms of big ideas or cases. If thematic teaching is taking the place of language arts instruction or social studies instruction, for example, then students must do more than use and practice their existing abilities. They must also be guided to acquire new abilities.

The lesson plan boxes in Figure 5.4 depict the importance of attending to language arts instructional outcomes and subject-matter outcomes within each activity. This means that teachers should think about what students will learn from participating in each activity and how they will receive the instruction and guidance they need. For example, the first activity listed under the American Revolution case in the self-rule/authority theme might include the following learning outcomes:

Language Arts Outcomes:

- Understand main ideas and important supporting details when reading textbooks and other sources (e.g., encyclopedia, CD ROM, nonfiction trade books)
- Synthesize information from two or more sources
- Summarize information from multiple sources
- Identify similarities and differences, and points of view among various perspectives

Social Studies Outcomes:

- Understand the events that led up to the American Revolution and why the war was fought
- Identify and compare the different positions of the Loyalists, British, and Patriots
- Analyze the results of the war in terms of the different initial positions

These language arts and social studies outcomes demonstrate that important skills, strategies, and subject-matter knowledge can be addressed through a well-structured activity. In addition, by identifying outcomes, teachers can be sure to provide instruction when needed. In the example above, students might need a lesson on how to synthesize information from more than one source, including teacher modeling and practice, or they might need several lessons and support to understand different points of view. Furthermore, teachers can address the various reading levels of their students by varying the texts students are reading or providing appropriate background knowledge and support for the reading. Our point is that teachers can provide the same level of instruction during theme activities as during separate language arts or social studies instruction. They can model, guide, and scaffold; work with large groups, small groups, and individuals. And students can work directly with a teacher, collaboratively with peers, or independently.

The same process of identifying outcomes can be applied to all activities, those with an intradisciplinary focus as well as those with an interdisciplinary focus. Consider the following learner outcomes for the interview research project in the intradisciplinary theme on personal change (see Figure 5.3):

Language Arts Outcomes:

- Learn about and conduct interviews (developing questions, being a good interviewer, taking notes, writing a report from notes)
- Use the writing process to plan, draft, revise, edit, and share interview reports
- Understand use of quotations to communicate people's exact words
- Analyze interview information to determine similarities between self and friends
- Evaluate those differences that can be sustained and those that threaten a friendship
- Examine diversity issues and their impact on important similarities and differences among people

Notice that with this intradisciplinary theme, there are two different types of language arts outcomes. The first three outcomes address language arts strategies and skills similar to the language arts outcomes in the interdisciplinary activity on the American Revolution. The second three address outcomes related to the content of the literature that is tied to the case and the theme statement. Because this theme is not interdisciplinary, the content focus is not related to social studies or science; it is related to literary understanding.

Directing attention to instruction accomplishes several purposes: (1) important curricular goals are addressed, (2) students are provided with language arts and subject-matter instruction as needed, (3) activities are planned to accommodate different student needs, and (4) students are more likely to enjoy and succeed at the activities, and therefore more likely to benefit from the theme. Many teachers with whom we have worked appreciate this focus on instruction. As one remarked, "Planning this theme has made me realize how difficult it is to teach deliberately." Another teacher put it this way: "I found that I was always asking, 'What do I want the students to learn from this theme and from this activity? How can I help them learn these things?' " Such a focus on instruction will undoubtedly enhance student learning.

CONCLUDING COMMENTS

We have described a process for planning effective thematic instruction, one that we believe will lead to challenging ideas and meaningful learning. The framework we propose and the examples we provide are intended to be descriptive rather than prescriptive; there are other ways to realize the benefits and to attend to the cautions of thematic instruction. We believe that with a clear understanding of thematic focus, coherence, and instruction, teachers will be able to design powerful themes. We close with three recommendations for implementation.

First, themes, as we have described them, are rich enough to explore over months, years, or even lifetimes, but any theme that goes too long, no matter how interesting, is likely to lose its appeal. We are not advocating year-long themes or even ones that take months. While possible, they are not advocated or required by this model. Nor are we suggesting that all teaching must be thematically linked. We are suggesting that regardless of length, themes must represent powerful ideas and questions that engage students in important, in-depth learning.

Second, you must consider the words, or language, you will use to present big ideas and enduring questions to your students. The statements and questions we have developed for the themes and cases in this chapter are not written in student language. Although we have attended to the developmental appropriateness of the ideas and outcomes, we have not considered how to phrase or present the big ideas and questions to students. We have directed this chapter to you, the teacher. Themes that are too abstract, complex, or removed from students' lives are unlikely to engage them. Themes that are too specific or simple are likely to drift into topics. You will need a balance of complexity to foster flexible thinking and simplicity to engage students. We offer three alternative solutions to presenting thematic ideas to students. One is to develop thematic statements and questions for your own planning and then revise them to present to students in language they can understand. Another approach is simply to create a label or phrase for a theme that will have meaning for your students (e.g., Living in our world; Growing and changing; Self-rule and authority). However, as the teacher, you will still need to attend to specificity in focus, coherence, and instruction in your planning. A third approach is to let the big idea grow out of a set of coherent cases and activities rather than to introduce it to students at the beginning of the theme. This gives the children time to acquire knowledge and experiences that will lead them, under your guidance, to form the big idea. Remember, though, if students are going to address an enduring question, they will need to know that question at the beginning of the theme.

Finally, we recommend that you use every opportunity to capitalize on students' interests when designing and carrying out your theme. Although we have presented examples in which both curriculum and instruction are teacher generated, this need not always be the case. There is room for student choice and individual projects within themes. Our objective is not to force students into a lock-step theme or to ignore their individual interests. However, teachers should guide content selection so that students are working toward developing big ideas rather than working on projects that are tangential or unrelated to the theme. In this respect, we agree with Dewey (1906, 1938), who advised teachers to capitalize on students' experiences and interests but within a curriculum designed largely by the teacher. He reminded us that the teacher needs to select and organize the subject-matter for children to study, not merely draw it from them. There is a difference, he argued, between utilizing students' experiences and interests in the development of a continuing line of study, which he advocates, and "trusting them to provide the chief material of learning," which he does not (p. 79). It would be difficult, if not impossible, to develop a powerful theme, to plan for transfer and flexible use of knowledge or to insure attention to instructional outcomes without careful teacher planning; at the same time, it is important to link the theme to students' interests and experiences.

Thematic teaching can be an engaging and powerful tool for student learning, and it can be an engaging and powerful tool for teaching. Yet, many popular themes and recommendations for thematic instruction are unlikely to put this powerful tool to work. Themes must be carefully planned to help students think deeply and carefully about important ideas; cases and activities must be selected to help students make meaningful connections and apply their knowledge flexibly; and instruction must be provided to help students learn and effectively use language arts abilities and subject-matter knowledge. By attending to these three building blocks—focus, coherence, and instruction—we believe that effective thematic teaching is possible. This is challenging work, to be sure, but work that will reap rewards for both teachers and students.

ACKNOWLEDGMENT

We gratefully acknowledge generous collaboration and feedback from Walter Parker, Karen Wixson, and Charles Peters.

ENDNOTES

1. See Parker, Walter C. (1996). Advanced ideas about democracy: Toward a pluralist conception of citizen education. *Record, 98*(1), 104–125.

2. Adapted from Sir Winston Churchill, Speech, Hansard, November 11, 1947.

REFERENCES

Ackerman, D. B. (1989). Intellectual and practical criteria for successful curriculum integration. In H. H. Jacobs (Ed.), *Interdisciplinary curriculum: Design and implementation.* Alexandria, VA: Association for Supervision and Curriculum Development.

Alleman, J., & Brophy, J. (1993). Is curriculum integration a boon or a threat to Social Studies? *Social Education, 57,* 287–291.

Alvermann, D. (1994). Trade books versus textbooks: Connections across content areas. In L. M. Morrow, J. K. Smith, & L. C. Wilkinson (Eds.), *Integrated Language Arts: Controversy to consensus* (pp. 51–70). Needham Heights, MA: Allyn and Bacon.

Anderson, R. C., Shirey, L. L., Wilson, P. T., & Fielding, L. (1987). Interestingness of children's reading material. In R. E. Snow & M. L. Farr (Eds.), *Aptitude, learning, and instruction; Vol. III. Cognitive and affective process analyses* (pp. 287–299). Hillsdale, NJ: Erlbaum.

Bruner, J. (1960). *The process of education.* Cambridge, MA: Harvard University Press.

Case, R. (1991). *The anatomy of curricular integration* (Tri-University Integration Project 5). Simon Fraser University, Burnaby, British Columbia.

Dewey, J. (1906). *The child and the curriculum.* Chicago: University of Chicago Press.

Dewey, J. (1938). *Experience and education.* New York: Collier Books.

Haggitt, E. M. (1975). *Projects in the elementary school.* London: Longman.

Hidi, S. (1990). Interest and its contribution as a mental resource for learning. *Review of Educational Research, 60*(4), 549–572.

Hoffman, J. V., Roser, N. L., & Farest, C. (1988). Literature sharing strategies in classrooms serving students from economically disadvantaged and language different home environments. In J. E. Readence & S. Baldwin (Eds.), *Dialogues in literacy research. 37th yearbook of the National Reading Conference* (pp. 331–338). Chicago: National Reading Conference.

Hughs, M. (1991). *Curriculum integration in the primary grades: A framework for excellence.* Alexandria, VA: Association of Supervision and Curriculum Development.

Jacobs, H. H. (1989). The interdisciplinary model: A step-by-step approach for development of integrated units of study. In H. H. Jacobs (Ed.), *Interdisciplinary curriculum: Design and implementation* (pp. 53–66). Alexandria, VA: Association for Supervision and Curriculum Development.

Lipson, M. Y., Valencia, S. W., Wixson, K. K., & Peters, C. W. (1993). Integration and thematic teaching: Integration to improve teaching and learning. *Language Arts, 70,* 252–262.

Meier, D. (1996). *The power of their ideas: Lessons for America from a small school in Harlem.* Boston: Beacon Press.

Morrow, L. M., Pressley, M., Smith, J. K., & Smith, M. (1997). The effect of a literature-based program integrated into literacy and science instruction with children from diverse backgrounds. *Reading Research Quarterly, 32*(1), 54–77.

Morrow, L. M., O'Connor, E., & Smith, J. (1990). Effects of story reading program on the literacy development of at risk kindergarten children. *Journal of Reading Behavior, 22,* 255–275.

Pappas, C. C., Kiefer, B. Z., & Levstik, L. S. (1995). *An integrated language perspective in the elementary school.* New York: Longman.

Parker, W. C., & Jarolimek, J. (1997). *Social studies in elementary education* (10th ed.). Upper Saddle River, NJ: Prentice-Hall.

Pearson, P. D. (1994). Integrated Language Arts: Sources of controversy and seeds of consensus. In L. M. Morrow, J. K. Smith, & L. C. Wilkinson (Eds.), *Integrated Language Arts: Controversy to consensus* (pp. 11–31). Needham Heights, MA: Allyn and Bacon.

Perkins, D. N. (1989). Selecting fertile themes for integrating learning. In H. H. Jacobs (Ed.), *Interdisciplinary curriculum: Design and implementation* (pp. 67–76). Alexandria, VA: Association for Supervision and Curriculum Development.

Routman, R. (1994). *Invitations: Changing as teachers and learners K–12.* Portsmouth, NH: Heinemann.

Short, K. G., & Burke, C. (1996). Examining our beliefs and practices through inquiry. *Language Arts, 73*(2), 97–104.

Smith, E., & Casteel, J. (1996). English language arts vignette. In *Michigan curriculum framework* (Section IV: Teaching and learning, pp. 11–19). Lansing: Michigan Department of Education.

Spiro, R. J., Vispoel, W., Schmitz, J., Samarapungavin, A., & Boerger, A. (1987). Knowledge acquisition for application: Cognitive acquisition for application: Cognitive flexibility and transfer in complex content domains. In B. Britton & S. Glynn (Eds.), *Executive control processes in reading* (pp. 177–199). Hillsdale, NJ: Erlbaum.

Stanovich, K. E. (1986). Matthew effects in reading: Some consequences of individual differences in the acquisition of literacy. *Reading Research Quarterly, 21,* 360–407.

Stevens, A. D. (1993). *Learning for life through universal themes.* Portland: Northwest Regional Educational Laboratory.

Tchudi, S. (1994). *Integrating language arts in the elementary school.* Belmont, CA: Wadsworth.

Valencia, S. W., Lipson, M. Y., Wixson, K. K., & Peters, C. W. (1994). *A national survey of practices in thematic language arts instruction*. In S. Florio-Ruane (Chair), Thematic/Integrated language arts instruction: From theory to practice. Symposium conducted at the meeting of the American Educational Research Association, New Orleans, LA.

Walmsley, S. A. (1994). *Children exploring their world: Theme teaching in elementary school*. Portsmouth, NH: Heinemann.

Walmsley, S. A., & Walp, T. P. (1990). Integrating literature and composing into the language arts curriculum: Philosophy and practice. *The Elementary School Journal, 90*(3), 251–274.

Willis, S. (November, 1992). Interdisciplinary learning: Movement to link the disciplines gains momentum. *Curriculum Update,* 1–8.

CHILDREN'S BOOKS CITED

Blinn, W. (1972). *Brian's song*. New York: Bantam Books.

Burnett, F. H. (1989). *The secret garden*. New York: Viking.

Cameron, A. (1981). *The stories Julian tells*. New York: Knopf.

Collier, J. L., and Collier, C. (1974). *My brother Sam is dead*. New York: Four Winds.

Collier, J. L., and Collier, C. (1983). *War comes to Willy Freeman*. New York: Delacorte.

Flournoy, V. (1985). *The patchwork quilt*. New York: Dial.

Forbes, E. (1943). *Johnny Tremain*. Boston: Houghton Mifflin.

Fritz, J. (1975). *Where was Patrick Henry on the 29th of May?* New York: Coward.

Fritz, J. (1967). *Early thunder*. New York: Coward-McCann.

Fritz, J. (1982). *Can't you make them behave, King George?* New York: Coward.

Hughes, D. (1989). *Family pose*. New York: Atheneum.

Lowry, L. (1989). *Number the stars*. Boston: Houghton Mifflin.

Lowry, L. (1993). *The Giver.* Boston: Houghton Mifflin.

Meltzer, M. (1988). *Benjamin Franklin: The new American*. New York: Watts.

O'Dell, S. (1989). *Sarah Bishop*. Boston: Houghton Mifflin.

Orlev, U. (1984). *Island on Bird Street*. Boston: Houghton Mifflin.

Peck, R. N. (1974). *Soup*. New York: Knopf.

Weber, B. (1972). *Ira sleeps over.* Boston: Houghton Mifflin.

White, E. B. (1952). *Charlotte's web*. New York: Harper & Row.

Chapter 6

Curriculum and Teaching in
Literature-Based Programs

●————————●

Kathryn H. Au, University of Hawaii
and
Taffy E. Raphael, Oakland University

Times change. We continually learn more. But, as citizens in an increasingly complex society, we face ever-changing and ever-increasing demands, ones that require higher levels of skills than ever before. This is as true for reading education as it is for medicine, space exploration, or building construction. These higher demands and increased complexities underscore the importance of updating our practices in literacy instruction. We want to ensure that our richly diverse students acquire the necessary literacy skills and dispositions to read and to think critically about the texts that they read and write.

In this volume, contributors (e.g., Galda, Chapter 1; Harris with Rosales, Chapter 2; Denyer & Florio-Ruane, Chapter 7) argue persuasively for the importance of literature as the basis for such instruction. In Chapter 4, Brock and Gavelek underscore the importance of social interactions of all kinds, from formal instruction to informal discussion, for enhancing children's response to literature. Still others (e.g., Sipe, Chapter 3) have presented new information on the kinds of knowledge bases readers draw upon, beyond the traditional areas of decoding and comprehension. These chapters strongly suggest the importance of re-examining what we mean by *instruction* in literature-based instruction.

In this chapter, we argue that conventional definitions of instruction and curriculum in the field of reading must be expanded dramatically if we are adequately to prepare students to read, understand, and interpret text. First, we discuss changing visions of instruction and related changes in forms of instruction. We suggest that in preparing students effectively, teachers will engage in different types of instruction, from explicitly instructing to simply participating in conversation with students. Second, we focus on changing visions of the curriculum, or the content, of literacy instruction. Third, we describe first- and fifth-grade literature-based classrooms that reflect these changing views of literacy instruction. In the concluding section, we consider the implications of this view of instruction and the curriculum for teachers moving toward literature-based instruction.

NEW VIEWS OF INSTRUCTION

In new views of instruction, which grow from constructivist (Spivey, 1997) or sociocultural perspectives (Brock & Gavelek, Chapter 4), the student is not seen as an empty vessel that the teacher must fill with knowledge. Rather, teachers in literature-based classrooms recognize that students come to school with rich backgrounds of experience, interests, and motivations that can and should be tapped in the reading and interpretation of literature. The purpose of instruction in these classrooms is to engage students in active meaning-making with literature, to give them the ability both to learn from and to enjoy literature throughout their lives.

We define instruction as *the process of getting students interested and involved in an activity, then providing necessary support to complete the activity successfully.* This definition of instruction begins with students' engagement in an activity they find interesting. In the literature-based classroom, students will be engaged in reading a picture storybook or novel, either of their own choice or chosen by the teacher. Once students are engaged, perhaps because they are intrigued by the characters or interested in knowing what happens next, they are in a position to hear and make sense of the support their teacher provides to be successful in reading the text. Teacher support varies according to students' needs. For example, first graders may require help with decoding new words, while fourth graders may be confused because part of the plot is presented in a flashback. The skills and strategies of word identification and comprehension are taught when students can see their usefulness in the reading of the literature.

The value of literature to students' reading development is reinforced by this new view of instruction. When we say that reading instruction is literature-based, we mean that teaching centers on reading good books. It is hard to capture students' interest with contrived texts, composed using restricted vocabulary and choppy sentences. Literature provides the meaningful, motivating context that enables teachers to further students' learning to read and their reading enjoyment. The starting point for reading instruction in literature-based classrooms is students' engagement with good books. Once students are captured by the magic of books, teachers have the opportunity to provide them with instruction in any skills and strategies that may be needed.

Forms of Instruction

In literature-based classrooms, the teacher engages in at least five different forms of instruction, as shown in Figure 6.1. The first form of instruction is explicit teaching in which the teacher transmits knowledge to students. In conventional views of literacy instruction, this form of instruction tends to be emphasized over all others. While explicit teaching certainly has a place in the literature-based classroom, its role is more limited. On one hand, explicit teaching has the advantage of allowing the teacher to impart information to students in an efficient manner. On the other hand, listening to a lecture has the disadvantage of tending to promote a passive attitude toward learning and does not encourage students actively to construct their own understandings. In the literature-based classroom, teachers use explicit teaching when they present students with mini-lessons. Mini-lessons are brief lessons, usually no longer than 10 minutes. During a mini-lesson (for example, on the topic of symbolism), teachers acquaint students with the knowledge, strategies, and skills mature readers use to interpret novels.

Figure 6.1

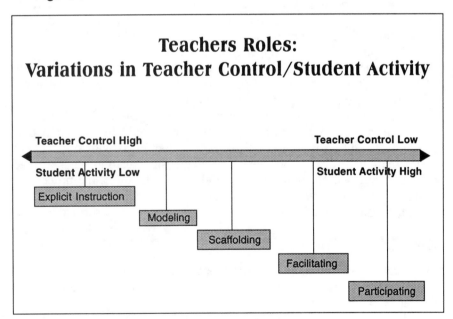

Teachers Roles:
Variations in Teacher Control/Student Activity

Teacher Control High

Teacher Control Low

Student Activity Low

Student Activity High

Explicit Instruction

Modeling

Scaffolding

Facilitating

Participating

Modeling is the second form of instruction seen in literature-based classrooms and involves teacher demonstrations of literate behavior. For example, teachers share their own written responses to literature, so students can see how a mature reader responds to a novel. Teachers demonstrate their enjoyment of and involvement with books when they read aloud to the class. They share their own tastes and preferences as readers, for professional and recreational purposes, so that students know that reading goes beyond the walls of the classroom.

The third form of instruction is scaffolding, in which teachers provide temporary and adjustable support as students engage in literate behavior. For example, during literature discussions, teachers may ask questions to lead students toward considering possible themes in the novel. Teacher questions promote students' engagement in deeper levels of discussion than they are capable of achieving on their own and prepare students to conduct literature discussions independent of the teacher. Or, if a child struggles with an unknown word, the teacher may ask the child to think of a word that begins with the same letter or that follows the same spelling pattern.

The fourth form of instruction, facilitating, has to do with encouraging and assisting students as they engage in literate behavior. Facilitating differs from scaffolding in that students are at the point where they do not require much help from the teacher. The teacher is smoothing the way but does not need to engage in lengthy interactions with the students. For example, if students are participating in a literature discussion, the teacher may ask the group to think about connections between the novel and their own lives. Or if a child is attempting to read a challenging text, the teacher may have the child engage in partner reading with a peer who is a capable reader. Finally, teachers may facilitate whole-class or large-group discussions simply by orchestrating turn-taking among a large number of participants.

The fifth form of instruction is participating, in which the teacher engages in the same activities as the students. For example, teachers may participate in literature discussions, sharing their own ideas with students but not dominating the discussion. During sustained silent reading, teachers read books of their own choosing, just as students do. In short, the process of teaching in literature-based classrooms is complex, because teachers are required to engage in the five different forms of instruction described here.

CONTENT OF THE LITERATURE-BASED CURRICULUM

In this section, we outline the content of the literature-based curriculum in a manner that we believe reflects all that our field has learned in the past 50 years of research (see also, Peters & Wixson, Chapter 12). We then present examples of first-grade and fifth-grade classrooms in which a comprehensive literature-based curriculum is brought to life.

In literature-based classrooms, we see that the nature of the curriculum and ideas about what counts as a skill or strategy have changed. If our goal is to help students understand and enjoy literature and to use literacy in everyday life, we must take a much broader perspective on skills and strategies than we have in the past. Typical reading scope and sequence charts have tended to emphasis word identification skills (such as initial consonant sounds or base words) and comprehension skills (such as prediction or cause and effect). While these skills have a place in the literature-based curriculum, we now recognize that students must acquire a far larger range of skills, strategies, and concepts if they are to understand and appreciate literature. For example, students in literature-based classrooms should be able to write in response to literature. They should be able to use the context of the sentence, passage, and text as a whole to infer the meanings of new vocabulary. They should be familiar with the characteristics of different genres of literature. They should be able to think critically about what they are reading, for example, noticing the particular slant an author gives to events.

Unfortunately, in recent times, we have seen skills and strategies (e.g., phonics first) pitted against response and interpretation (e.g., meaning first)— as if one can substitute for the other. In the popular press (e.g., Levine, 1994) and in professional journals such as the *American Educator* (Summer, 1995) published by the American Federation of Teachers, instruction is cast as a great debate between phonics and meaning. Creating such false dichotomies leads to simplistic approaches to reading instruction. Our position is that it makes as little sense to ignore instruction in decoding skills as it does to base an entire reading program on teaching decoding.

As implied above, the literature-based curriculum is broad and comprehensive. As shown in Figure 6.2, the curriculum encompasses the following areas: (a) ownership, (b) comprehension, (c) composition, (d) literary aspects, and (e) language conventions. Of course, these areas are not discrete. They overlap and are closely and complexly related to one another. The arrows indicate that development in any one of these areas contributes to development in all of the others.

Ownership

We define ownership as students' valuing of literacy (Au, 1997). Students with ownership have positive attitudes toward literacy and the habit of using literacy in their daily lives, in the home and community as well as in school. In the literature-based classroom, students who have ownership of literacy:

- Enjoy reading
- Have confidence and pride in their reading
- Share their reading with others

Figure 6.2

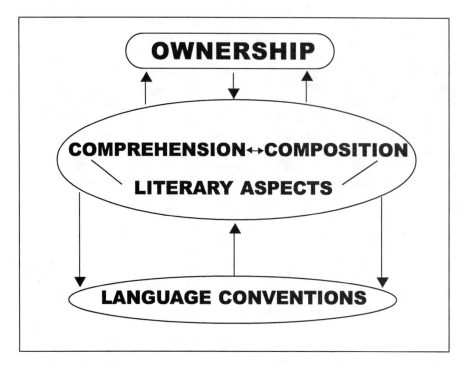

- Choose to read for their own purposes, both in and out of school
- Make personal connections to literature
- Set goals and evaluate their own progress as readers

Students display positive attitudes both by willingly engaging in reading themselves and by taking an interest in others' reading by, for example, recommending a book to a friend. Students engage in literacy at home as well as at school—for example, by reading books of their own choosing, writing in journals, or corresponding with relatives and friends. While some activities, such as journal writing, may have been introduced by teachers, students continue these activities even when they are not assigned as homework.

Considerable research supports the importance of ownership of literacy, motivation to read, and active engagement in literacy. Guthrie and Wigfield (1997) cite four supporting areas of research. First, studies of cognitive strategy development for reading demonstrate that strategy use is a deliberate, demanding activity, requiring a great deal of conscious effort. Strategy use does not occur easily or automatically, but requires an act of will on the part of the individual. These studies raise the question of the individual's motivation for applying taught strategies. Second, studies of students' reading activities show a strong relationship between amount—or volume—of reading and reading achievement (e.g., Anderson, Wilson, & Fielding, 1988), and book reading seems particularly beneficial (Fielding, Wilson, & Anderson, 1986). The relationship between wide, independent reading and achievement appears to be maintained regardless of factors such as students' grade level, reading ability, gender, or socioeconomic status.

Third, research by motivation theorists (e.g., Wigfield & Eccles, 1992) shows how motivational and cognitive processes combine to promote achievement. However, these researchers have not yet looked specifically at motivation for reading. Fourth, sociolinguistic research (e.g., Bloome & Green, 1992) conducted from a social constructivist perspective shows how interaction with others in the social context of the classroom can foster growth in reading, especially in the ability to participate in literate activity. Guthrie and Wigfield note that "[t]he acquisition of motivational goals through social mediation promises to be a fruitful area for inquiry" (p. 5).

In addition to the lines of inquiry noted by Guthrie and Wigfield, support for the place of ownership in the literature-based curriculum comes from accounts of the process approach to writing and from whole language (Dudley-Marling & Searle, 1995). A commitment to ownership is seen when students are allowed to decide upon their own topics during the writers' workshop, the form of their written responses during the readers' workshop, or the questions to be addressed during science inquiry.

Comprehension

In literature-based curricula, comprehension is fundamental to students engaging in response, critical analysis, and connecting the text to their own lives. Comprehension involves

- using background knowledge to make sense of and interpret text characters and events
- using text-processing strategies (e.g., sequencing, summarizing) to construct the story-line and its key events, and
- monitoring the sense-making process, clarifying potential confusions.

These three aspects of comprehension are supported by a range of research (see Dole, Duffy, Roehler, & Pearson, 1991; Pearson & Fielding, 1991; Pressley, Johnson, Symons, McGoldrick, & Kurita, 1989; Tierney, Readance, & Dishner, 1990). Students across ages and literacy competencies benefit from being taught about comprehension and comprehension monitoring strategies (e.g., Beck, McKeown, Sandora, Kucan, & Worthy, 1996; Ogle, 1986; Raphael & Wonnacutt, 1985).

Comprehension instruction and strategy use closely intertwine with response to literature. Langer's (1995) description of the process of literary understanding supports such connections. She suggests that readers create an envisionment, or text-world. For example, readers of *Walk Two Moons* (Creech, 1994) enter the world of Salamanca Tree Hiddle, her friends and family, a word of intrigue and mysterious parallels between Sal and her friend Phoebe. The process of understanding this world involves four stances: (a) stepping into the world, (b) moving through the world as the story unfolds, (c) stepping back from the world as readers think about the ways the story impacts them personally, and (d) stepping out of the world to examine it more closely, critique the text, and make connections to other texts. Adopting each stance requires readers' use of comprehension strategies as they engage with the literature.

Drawing on Background Knowledge. Readers draw on background knowledge, and teachers help them acquire relevant knowledge, at different points in their journey through their newly encountered text-world. As readers begin the story, they step into a new world, looking at the covers of the book, reading the title, looking at chapter titles, and reading about the author to activate background knowledge. As the text unfolds and readers move through the text-world, they continue to rely on background knowledge. A chapter title like "Pandora's Box" suggests that background knowledge about myths may be useful. Students may have such knowledge or, if not, teachers may provide instruction so students can appreciate subtleties that they may otherwise miss as they read the book. Frameworks such as K-W-L (Ogle, 1986) and Experience-Text-Relationship (Au, 1979; Au, Carroll, & Scheu, 1997) emphasize ways teachers highlight readers' background knowledge as they enter a text-world and begin to explore new concepts.

Readers draw on background knowledge as they step back from the world, making connections to their own lives, as one young reader illustrated after reading about a tense moment between Sal and Phoebe:

> I can relate to Sal about Peeby because some of my friends I just want to strangle. And they are all ways bothering me and bugging me Augh! They just say my room is messy, my bed is lumpy and I did not vacuum and a hole lot of other stuff! And all the time they just mess my room up and I don t like it. [Sheila, 11/27/96, age 11]
> (from Raphael, Pardo, Highfield, & McMahon, 1997, p. 203).

Sheila's entry indicates comprehension of Sal's emotions, the text event that created tension between the two characters, and the temporary nature of the friends' struggle. Learning to draw upon and to share background knowledge is a pervasive aspect of comprehension that teachers must highlight as part of the instructional curriculum. Other aspects support the use of background knowledge as readers process the text they encounter.

Processing Text.   Moving through the text-world involves time-honored comprehension strategies for remembering characters and events, determining the meaning of new words or words used in unfamiliar ways, and constructing a story interpretation. Dole et al. (1991) believe that strategies are used to determine important information, summarize information, and draw inferences. Conventional comprehension strategies such as sequencing continue to be important to understanding literature. For example, students reading *Tuck Everlasting* (Babbitt, 1975) can sequence story events to help trace the main character's changing emotions. Teaching summarizing, identifying important information, and asking and responding to a range of questions is as crucial within a literature-based curriculum as it would be in any instructional program.

Monitoring Comprehension.   In a literature-based curriculum that encourages students' independence in reading and talking about books, it is particularly important to foster monitoring strategies. A long line of research in reciprocal teaching (Palincsar & Brown, 1984, 1989) underscores the value of students' learning to identify confusing aspects of the text and ask clarifying questions of the peers and their teacher. Current research in Questioning the Author (Beck et al., 1996) suggests that students benefit from learning about ways in which texts may fail to make sense, and how to distinguish between a difficulty caused by the way the text is written from one that may stem from within themselves. Similarly, learning to differentiate sources of information for seeking clarification has proved beneficial (Raphael & Wonnacutt, 1985).

In short, the strong research base underlying comprehension instruction supports helping students develop a wide repertoire of strategies to apply across a wide range of books and for a variety of reading purposes. Comprehension instruction is grounded in engaging with meaningful texts and connects to both composition and response to literature.

Composition

Composition in the literature-based classroom refers to writing in all its varied forms and functions (see also Denyer & Florio-Ruane, Chapter 7). Forms of writing include personal narratives, fiction, poetry, research reports, essays, letters, journal entries, and lists. These may serve the functions of reflecting upon one's life, expressing feelings, synthesizing information from multiple sources, maintaining or developing relationships with others, convincing, and aiding memory. Composition involves short-term reflective writing, characteristic of response logs and free-writes, as well as the sustained writing required to create essays or reports.

Teachers in literature-based classrooms address both the forms and functions of writing that are important in the real world (such as letter writing), as well as those with particular relevance for school (such as research reports).

Composition in the literature-based curriculum includes the writing process, or students' ability to plan, draft, revise, edit, and publish their work (Graves, 1983). Writing conventions, such as spelling, punctuation, and grammar, are taught in connection with the editing phase of writing.

In a review of research on writing, Dyson and Freeman (1991) emphasize studies in three major areas. First, they discuss research highlighting the importance of social context (including historical, economic, and religious factors) to the way that people use writing (e.g., Heath, 1983). They note that "written language is always 'embedded'—it always figures into particular kinds of communicative events" (pp. 755–756). The approaches that teachers use to structure their interactions with students (for example, in writing conferences), or to structure students' interactions with one another (for example, in peer conferences) may have a powerful effect on students' development as writers (Graves, 1983). Second, Dyson and Freeman address research on the composing process. These studies portray composition as a complex process involving the orchestration of many different skills (e.g., Hayes & Flower, 1980). Certainly, the complexity of this process points to the need to provide students with considerable instruction in composition, as well as with many opportunities to write.

Third, Dyson and Freeman review research on the development of writing (e.g., Dyson, 1989). Some of these studies focus on the broad developmental phases that may be discerned in students' writing (e.g., Clay, 1975). However, other studies demonstrate that, within these broad phases, students follow their own individual paths as composers (e.g., Graves, 1983). At any given moment, students' performance may be influenced by the demands of the social context and their own preferences and motivations, as well as by the complex nature of the writing process. Dyson and Freeman imply that effective instruction requires close observation on the part of the teacher. Instruction requires identifying the writing skills already under students' control and leading them to build upon these skills. For example, if students understand that sentences may be rearranged, they may be led to the understanding that paragraphs may be also be rearranged.

A form of composition central to the literature-based classroom is written response to literature. In many classrooms, students compose these responses in preparation for meeting with a literature discussion group or book club. When the group meets, students share their responses as a way of getting the discussion started. Written responses to literature serve at least two functions, personal and social. First, they allow students to express and record their feelings, thoughts, and questions about the literature. Second, when written responses are shared, they serve the function of promoting interaction around the literature.

Teachers assist students by providing instruction on the many and varied forms that written responses may take. For example, the writing component of Book Club (an approach to literature-based instruction) helps students see that their ideas about novels can be recorded, added to, and revised over time (Raphael & Boyd, 1997). At the beginning of the year, the teacher introduces students to a range of possible approaches for writing reading log entries in response to the novels they are reading. These approaches include character map (how the character looked, likes and dislikes about the character), special story part (including reasons why this section of the text stood out), me and the book (personal connections to the text), and book/chapter critique (things the author did well or might have done better). As students gain experience in writing reading log entries, they combine these approaches in their own ways. They learn to synthesize ideas across the novel as a whole, instead of responding in a chapter-by-chapter manner, and make intertextual connections (such as noting similar themes across two novels). When students write about literature and discuss literature with classmates, they develop an increasingly sophisticated understanding. By reviewing students' written responses, teachers know what students are understanding and what points in a novel, or comprehension skills and strategies, may require further attention.

Literary Aspects

To use—not abuse—the literature in a literature-based reading program, teachers have a responsibility to teach about the literary side of the literature. Literary aspects include literature's content, its elements, and readers' response to literature.

The Content of Literature. As Lee Galda suggested in Chapter 1, and Peters and Wixson discuss in Chapter 12, literature's content is to raise consciousness about what it means to be human and to provide windows into distant people, places, times, and events. Through literature, we tesseract through time to the planet Camazotz as we read L'Engle's (1962) *A Wrinkle in Time*. We immerse ourselves in the pre-Civil Rights era of the rural South as we read Taylor's *Roll of Thunder, Hear My Cry* (1991) and *Mississippi Bridge* (1990). In focusing on literature's content within literature-based instruction, we develop themes that help us understand humanity as well as build our students' literacy competencies.

Literary Elements. Literature works through authors' successful manipulations of its elements: theme, point of view, plot, characters, and setting. Instruction highlighting literary elements can help increase students' story understanding, their appreciation, and their ability to use literature as models for their own writing. Lukens (1990) describes theme in terms of a story's significant truth that serves to comment on society, human nature, or the human condition. The author's purpose is revealed in the story theme (Huck, Hepler, & Hickman, 1987). In her research, Lehr (1991) notes that readers' understanding of themes grow out of their life experiences with stories, which they then, in turn, apply to a particular story at a given time. Thus, part of literature-based instruction should focus on uncovering the range of themes stories offer.

Point of view is defined as "the eyes and mind of the character from whose vantage point we are reading the story and seeing events unfold" (Raphael & Hiebert, 1996, p. 148). A part of the instructional focus, then, is to introduce young readers to the existence of different points of view, and to help them develop an appreciation for what a particular point of view buys the author.

Plot has been studied extensively by comprehension researchers interested in helping students understand the narrative structure common to the stories they read (e.g., Fitzgerald, 1992; Graesser, Golding, & Long, 1991). This research highlights typical story structure as including an initiating event, internal response, action, consequence, and reaction. Such studies have led to many instructional strategies that teach students to map out the story structure and use this knowledge to make sense of the sequence of events, the characters' motivations, and the consequences of characters' actions (e.g., Baumann & Bergeron, 1993; Beck & McKeown, 1981; Idol & Croll 1987). From a literary tradition, however, plot is assumed to be somewhat more complex, involving various forms of conflict (e.g., character's internal conflict, character against the social order, character against a natural phenomenon), various patterns of action (e.g., explanation, constant suspense, foreshadowing), and various plot types (e.g., progressive plots that build to a climax and denouement, episodic plots linked by a theme). We shortchange our students if we treat plot simply as a sequence of actions.

Two literary elements—setting and character—provide young readers early entré into exploring the art of literature. Unlike the more complex elements of plot and theme, very young children can identify, and identify with, story characters and place. Of course, not all characters and settings are equally well-developed. Some stories are character-driven, others action-driven, others driven by a sense of place.

Learning about literature's content and elements provides a much needed basis for engaging in literary response. Through the study of literature's content and elements, students develop the concepts and the vocabulary to experience and share their personal response, as well as to engage in a range of literary critique (see Sipe, Chapter 3; Brock & Gavelek, Chapter 4).

Response to Literature. The study of literature, within a literature-based curriculum, would not be complete without attention to reader response. Instructing students in a range of responses intersects with instruction in writing (e.g., reflecting on text read or on discussions that relate to shared readings), as well as teaching students conventions for interacting around texts (e.g., in student-led discussion groups, literature circles). This is because the primary means for students to go public with their personal responses are through writing and through conversations among peers. We can identify three categories of literary response: personal, creative, and critical. However, in practice, these often are combined. Teaching students about ways of instantiating each type of literary response is important, as is teaching the metaknowledge that allows readers to combine these different ways of responding as they read and engage with texts.

Personal response to literature includes readers' impressionistic response to the text, their first reactions and the reasons underlying their reactions. These often take the form of readers' initial reactions to the story, or how they relate to specific story events. Sheila's response to a *Walk Two Moons,* writing that she could relate to Sal's feelings because "some of my friends I just want to strangle," is one such example. Personal response is grounded in the aesthetic reaction to literature that others (e.g., Rosenblatt, 1978; Sipe, Chapter 3; Taylor, in Section IV) have described.

Creative response to literature captures readers' play with the texts they are reading. Such responses involve asking questions of the text, such as, What if a particular event had occurred differently? For example, after reading the final chapter of *Tuck Everlasting,* students in Laura Pardo's fifth-grade classroom responded with wondering what if Winnie had sipped the water, instead of pouring it over the frog? Students may also engage in creative response as they develop dramatizations of favorite stories or story parts.

Critical response to literature represents readers' analysis of the effectiveness of a text. Did it work for them as readers? What models did it provide for them as writers themselves? What purpose did it seem to serve? Did it change the way they were thinking? Critical response involves stepping out of the text-world, making the text an object of study. This can occur as students read a text or when they have completed it. Critical response is illustrated by the following example by Steve, a student in Kathy Highfield's fifth-grade classroom, as he read *Last Summer with Maizon* (Woodson, 1990) early in the school year. He criticized the author for including a poem by the main character of the story:

> . . . A thing that made me think is why Margaret wrote that poem. Especially the beginning "My pen doesn't write anymore". That is one weird beginning. I mean, who in the world would write some-

thing like that beginning? If I wrote that, I would (think) I was crazy or something. But to put it this way, it's just down right, absouloutely (sic), positively, crazy weird. "Phew." Know what? I bet the Author did this to confuse us. (Steve, 9/13/96, from Raphael et al., 1997, p. 74)

Language Conventions

The curriculum in a literature-based classroom is certainly expanded, in comparison to the curriculum in a traditional classroom, when areas such as ownership and literary aspects are added. Teachers might wonder, then, about the place of skills and strategies, such as phonics, spelling, and grammar. These skills and strategies are encompassed in language conventions. The area of language conventions is a broad one, involving the various kinds of knowledge students need to read and write effectively and to participate in literacy activities. These include word identification, text conventions, and conventions for interaction. In terms of word identification, students must understand concepts about print, decoding, and spelling. In terms of text conventions, students need a working knowledge of grammar, punctuation, and other mechanics. In the literature-based classroom, the texts students are reading and writing provide the basis for instruction in word identification and text conventions. In terms of conventions for interaction, students should know how to engage appropriately in different literacy contexts, such as literature discussion circles or writing conferences.

Word Identification. Particularly in the primary grades, teachers will spend considerable time teaching students word identification or decoding. Instruction in decoding is supported by numerous studies pointing to the importance of fluency in word identification to the development of effective reading (Stanovich, 1984). Proficiency in word identification is the key characteristic distinguishing good readers from poor readers. If students find it difficult to identify words, all of their attention must be devoted to this task, and they plod through the text in a labored manner, word by word. Little or no attention is then available for comprehension.

While there is little debate about the need to include word identification in the curriculum, the question of how best to teach decoding is perennially debated. In literature-based classrooms, instruction in word identification grows from the texts children are reading. A picture book such as *My Best Shoes* (Burton, 1994), which describes the types of shoes children wear each day of the week, provides the teacher with an opportunity to give a lesson on consonant digraphs (such as /sh/), because the word shoes has become salient. Literature offers the context by which skills such as consonant digraphs can be made meaningful to children. The teacher helps children realize that knowing these skills will enable them to read books on their own.

Picture books with rhyming words give teachers the opportunity to teach students decoding by analogy. Research indicates that proficient readers decode unfamiliar words by comparing them to words they already know (Stanovich, 1984). Teachers help children use this same strategy when they come to new words (Gaskins, Gaskins, & Gaskins, 1991). For example, in the story, *My Best Shoes,* children come across the word "snap." First, the teacher asks them to think of a word that begins like this new word. The children come up with snack, which appears in their daily schedule. Then the teacher asks them to think of a word that has the same spelling pattern and rhymes with the new word. The children think of "cap," a word they know from having read *Caps for Sale* (Slobodkina, 1947). By using this process of comparison and contrast, they can identify the word as snap.

Text Conventions. Similarly, literature offers opportunities to teach about text conventions such as grammar, and these lessons can help students appreciate the author's craft. *My Best Shoes,* for example, lends itself to a lesson on adjectives or "describing words." Teachers can ask children to choose the pair of shoes they liked best and to find all the words and phrases the author used to tell them just how those shoes looked. Students can be invited to write descriptions of their own favorite pairs of shoes, using language patterns similar to those in *My Best Shoes.*

In short, the reading of literature can lead logically into instruction in word identification and text conventions. During such lessons, teachers ask students to take a close, analytical view of the text. This process of analysis is intended to help students understand what Mason, Herman, and Au (1991) call the systematicity of the English language: how letters are patterned to form words, as well as how authors use words to create particular effects.

Interaction Conventions. Another important area under the broad category of language conventions is students' knowledge of the interactional skills necessary for participating appropriately in literacy events. The Book Club approach, for example, centers on student conversations about literature (Raphael & McMahon, 1994). In general, students have not had previous experience discussing literature without the teacher's guidance, and they can benefit from instruction that improves the quality of their conversations. The teachers in the fourth- and fifth-grade classrooms described by Raphael and McMahon used a number of strategies to make students aware of the interactional skills they needed to use. Students liked listening to audiotapes of their book clubs, so teachers sometimes played short sections of the tapes and had students evaluate the conversation. At other times, students reviewed transcripts of book clubs to identify strengths and areas for improvement. Students also used book club transcripts for role playing to illustrate problems (e.g., one person ordering others around) or exemplary behaviors (e.g., someone inviting others into the conversation). As they guided students through these activities, teachers started by emphasizing positive points (e.g., several students had contributed good ideas), before they worked on suggestions for improvement (e.g., involving everyone in the group). As this overview suggests, the social context for literacy learning enters into all areas of the literature-based curriculum, from ownership to language conventions.

A FIRST-GRADE CLASSROOM

The majority of the 22 children in Jean Araki's first-grade classroom in a rural school in Hawaii are of Native Hawaiian ancestry. Almost all the children are from low-income families, and they speak Hawaii Creole English (a nonmainstream variety of English) as their first language. On this day in March, as on other days, the readers' workshop in Mrs. Araki's room begins with a child leading the class in the reading aloud of several favorite poems. The leader uses a magic wand, pointing to each word on the chart or in the big book, and all the children join in. Mrs. Araki believes the rereading of favorite poetry helps the children to begin the day with pride in their reading ability. This activity builds a sense of community and ownership of literacy, and it promotes fluency in word identification and a knowledge of language conventions. Because the children were familiar with this activity, Mrs. Araki relies on facilitating and participating as the forms of instruction.

After the poems have been read, Mrs. Araki calls the "yellow" group to meet with her at Center 1, the semi-circular table she uses for small-group lessons. The children are divided into four small groups for reading instruction, and they follow a schedule with four different activities: a lesson with the teacher, a follow-up writing assignment, independent reading, and learning centers.

The children in the yellow group have just finished reading *The Little Red Hen* (Galdone, 1973). Mrs. Araki calls their attention to the pocket chart. On large file cards, she has drawn pictures of items in the story, including a sack of flour, a loaf of bread, and a sickle. She has the children identify the items and tell her how they should be arranged in the pocket chart, to mirror the sequence of events in the story. The children point out, for example, that the sickle should come before the sack of flour. They explain that the sickle had to be used to cut the wheat, before the wheat could be taken to the mill and ground into flour. Mrs. Araki uses this opportunity to build the children's vocabulary and to develop their understanding of the sequence of events, both important aspects of comprehension. The forms of instruction Mrs. Araki uses are explicit teaching, modeling, and scaffolding.

Mrs. Araki passes out copies of the book, and she asks the children to do some choral reading. She reminds the children to be sure to track the print, and she encourages them to point to the words with their fingers, if that will help. At one point, the text describes how the Little Red Hen asks who will help her take the wheat to the mill. The children read the word mill as miller. Mrs. Araki stops the group and asks the children to look carefully at the word. "Is that word mill or miller?" she asks. One of the children says it must be mill, because it ends with l. Mrs. Araki writes the two words, mill and miller, on the chalkboard, so the children can see the difference. This part of the lesson allows Mrs. Araki to observe the children's progress in word identification and to focus their attention on the details of print or language conventions. The forms of instruction she uses are scaffolding and facilitating.

To prepare the children for their written follow-up assignment, Mrs. Araki poses the question, "What is the Little Red Hen's problem?" In many previous lessons, Mrs. Araki has discussed the idea of a problem with the children, using examples from stories as well as real life. Today, she asks the children to give their answers in a complete sentence. She wants the children to rehearse orally the sentences they will later write down. Keoni says, "Her problem is she doesn't want to share." Kanani has a different opinion. "The pig, the dog, and the cat don't want to help the Little Red Hen." Mrs. Araki repeats both answers and praises the children for sharing their ideas. She tells the children what they should do when they leave Center 1. First, they will reread the story with a partner. Then they will write their ideas about the problem in complete sentences. Mrs. Araki passes out sheets of paper headed by the question, "What is the Little Red Hen's problem?" The discussion and writing about the problem in the story contribute to the children's comprehension and knowledge of story elements or literary aspects. The assignment involves them in composition and language conventions (complete sentences). In setting up the reading and writing assignments, Mrs. Araki uses facilitating.

The children leave Center 1 to reread the book with partners. One pair settles on the carpet at the front of the classroom, while others read together at their seats. This activity builds fluency and reinforces word identification skills. When the children are finished, they go to their desks to write. Although they converse and check on one another's work, they take pride in composing their own responses. Keoni reads his response to another child: "She did not share. She did not like to share." Kanani sits quietly composing her response, which shows her use of invented spelling:

> Dy dd not hlp the hn. So she hk dt bi hr slf. She bkd bi hr slf. She at it bi hr slf. (They did not help the hen. So she had to do it by herself. She baked by herself. She ate it by herself.)

These first graders use what they know about letter sounds to record their ideas on paper. Later, when they publish their writing about the story in a group booklet, Mrs. Araki will work with them on conventional spelling. In these story-related activities, Mrs. Araki has created opportunities for the children to work on comprehension, literary aspects, composition, and language conventions. The pride the children take in composing their own original responses reveals their ownership of literacy.

When the children have finished their written responses, they choose books to read with a partner. Books are all around the classroom. Several shelves are filled with boxes of books, one for each of the children's favorite authors: Frank Asch, Norman Bridwell, Eric Carle, and others. Books the children have written themselves are placed in a bin near the author's chair at the front of the classroom. On a rack are easy predictable books the children have read many times before. Big books and picture story books, such as *Peanut Butter and Jelly* (Wescott, 1987), are also displayed. Mrs. Araki has marked many books with colored dots, to indicate how difficult the book is likely to be. She has asked the children in the yellow group to look for books with blue dots, because she feels they will able to handle the text in these books. Mrs. Araki wants to make sure her students interact with text and don't just "read" the pictures. When the children have finished their books, they record the date, title, and their partner's name in their reading logs. This further opportunity to read lets the children apply their knowledge of comprehension, literary aspects, and language conventions. Because they can choose the books they read, their ownership of literacy is reinforced. The children in the yellow group now go to one of the learning centers set up in the room: the listening center, library center, poem and song center, writing center, math manipulatives center.

As the readers' workshop draws to a close, Mrs. Araki calls the children together on the carpet, and they discuss what went well and what could be improved tomorrow. Mrs. Araki praises children who have done good thinking or helped others. Then she reads the children a story, modeling reading. Today, because several reading groups have been discussing the importance of cooperation, she reads *Swimmy* (Lionni, 1963). Several children clap their hands happily, because they are already familiar with the story. During the discussion, Mrs. Araki encourages the children to make connections between *Swimmy* and the stories they have been reading, facilitating this process of meaning-making. Before school ends for the day, each child selects one or two books to read at home. Mrs. Araki makes sure that one of these is a book the child can read independently. Often, children take home the book they are reading at Center 1. Reading and writing are challenges for most of the first-graders in Mrs. Araki's class, but the varied forms of instruction she provides address all aspects of the curriculum and extend the children's engagement in literacy beyond the classroom to the home.

A FIFTH-GRADE CLASSROOM

It is the spring semester, and Mrs. Pardo and her fifth-grade students are in the second phase of a two-phase unit. During Phase 1, they studied the events surrounding the American Civil War, framed in terms of the theme of human rights. In the second phase, they are reading historical fiction set during this era. The fifth-graders reflect the diversity of mid-Michigan: African American, Latino, Asian American, and Caucasian students, many of whose parents work in nearby automobile-related factories or in rural areas just north of the school. The language arts program features Book Club and the writers' workshop as its two primary contexts. Book Club (see McMahon & Raphael, with Goatley & Pardo, 1997; Raphael & McMahon, 1994) centers around the small, student-led discussion groups for which the program was named, supported by whole-class community share (the site for large-group discussion and instruction), reading, and writing activities. The sustained writing that is part of the writers' workshop often reflects the themes that have emerged through the students' readings. Similarly, books read during Drop Everything and Read (the sustained silent reading program) often reflect the themes, authors, and genres students have studied within Book Club.

On this day in early May, as students filter into the room to start the day, they pull out their dialogue journals and begin to write. On the board is the question, "What is your worst habit? How have you tried to get rid of it? What else can you try?" followed by "or you may free-write on a topic of your choice." While Mrs. Pardo completes typical morning work (e.g., lunch count, attendance), students write. Three volunteers each go, in turn, to the Author's Chair to share one of their entries for that month. Mrs. Pardo believes it important for each student to share something from their journal at least once a month, as a way of helping her students know each other and to build a sense of community. Journal writing develops ownership as well as composing ability. Mrs. Pardo often brings in short pieces of her own reflective writing to model both writing and sharing.

After about 20 minutes, Mrs. Pardo signals the beginning of Book Club. Four students take out their own copies of Hunt's (1964) *Across Five Aprils,* the book that Mrs. Pardo begins to read aloud to the students; the four follow along by choice as the rest of the class listens. Mrs. Pardo describes three reasons for the read-aloud for this unit. First, this book is a shared novel for the class, particularly important since each book club group is reading a different novel. Second, it is an exciting and moving story related to the unit's theme, but one most of her students would find too frustrating to read themselves. Third, the density of reference to events of the Civil War provides natural points to reprise the knowledge base they had begun to generate through the first phase of the unit, as they did whole-group, small-group, and individual projects about the Civil War (see Raphael & Hiebert, 1996, for a more detailed description of the unit).

Mrs. Pardo reads for 10 minutes, pausing occasionally to think aloud. As she reads a section from the book where the main character has sent a letter to his family, she comes to the word, "ironclads," and pauses. She muses, half to the class and half to herself, "What's that? It's something we've come across before." Several students chime in to remind Mrs. Pardo of a student report on this topic and of what they had learned. A little later, Mrs. Pardo is reading a segment where soldiers are marching in the heat and drop their bedrolls. She says aloud, "Mmm, they haven't thought ahead." Ali adds, "Like the grasshopper and the ant." Mrs. Pardo smiles encouragingly; she has emphasized intertextual connections throughout the year. The read-aloud provides important opportunities for Mrs. Pardo to model strategies for comprehension and interpretation (e.g., figuring out words, making connections to other texts).

Mrs. Pardo segues from the read-aloud to the opening community share, which usually involves instruction related to ownership, comprehension, composition, literary aspects, and/or language conventions. Today, the focus is on language conventions, specifically the questions that support a good book discussion. This lesson is an extension of several earlier lessons on questioning: (a) questioning the author to sort out confusions (see also, Beck, McKeown, Hamilton, & Kucan, 1997), (b) questioning oneself to promote reflections about the story, and (c) questions to write in reading logs to remember issues as well as points of confusion.

Mrs. Pardo maintains a journal of reflections and observations of students' progress. While reading her entries about students' recent book clubs, she had noticed a disturbing pattern. She felt that students had fallen into using what she felt were formulaic questions: How did this story make you feel? Do you like this story? While such generic questions may be useful at times, she felt that students needed to be challenged to ask each other more meaningful questions in their groups—ones that were specific to the texts they had read that day and ones they were sincerely interested in exploring.

During the course of the 10-minute mini-lesson, Mrs. Pardo explicitly teaches about: (a) the difference between meaningful questions and ones that were used simply to pass the time or use up one's turn for speaking, (b) questions designed to promote discussion rather than ones that elicited single-word responses, and (c) questions that might be helpful when a Book Club is experiencing a breakdown. She then moves to scaffolding, presenting several questions related to the read-aloud book, *Across Five Aprils,* and asking students to critique the question's ability to generate discussion and the question's specificity to that section of the book. Finally, she models generic questions that might be used to jump-start a conversation if everyone seems stuck about where to begin, listing these questions on the overhead as she speaks. She suggests that as students read their section for that day's Book Club discussions, they think about questions that they genuinely would like to discuss, and record them in their reading logs so they can be remembered.

Because each group is reading a different book, Mrs. Pardo suggests that the students get together with their group prior to silent reading and make sure they are reading or rereading the section they had agreed to discuss that day. By scaffolding their initial interactions, she is able to emphasize one of her goals for the unit—to promote students' planning and monitoring their progress. Desks tops are raised as students take out their books and reading logs, then regroup into the Book Clubs at various places in the room—a round table, a rug area, sections of the room where desks have been put together. One group moves to the hallway outside the classroom. Mrs. Pardo facilitates this process, guiding movement around the room as the Book Clubs get to work.

Students in each Book Club group are allowed to select how they will read for the next 15 minutes. Many read silently, but some students pair up for buddy reading, some read in small groups of three, and two students read with Mrs. Pardo. As in most classrooms, these students reflect a range of reading levels, from two to three years below to a year or two above grade level expectations. To support all students' participation, Mrs. Pardo uses several strategies. Some students have a copy of the book that they leave at home to read ahead with a parent, sibling, or guardian. Some students read ahead with the resource room teacher. Some listen to the book on tape as they read along. Some read as much as they can during the Book Club allotted time, then finish that day's section during Drop Everything and Read.

As they finish reading or rereading that day's section of their book, the students turn to their logs and record their responses. Although the focus at this time is reading, composition plays an important part in capturing thoughts about the books. Not surprisingly, many students responses include questions they want to raise during Book Club and closing community share discussions. However, since Mrs. Pardo encourages multiple responses each day, a scanning of students' log entries reveals character analyses, personal response, connections from the book to their own lives, and so forth. After allowing approximately 10 minutes for writing, Mrs. Pardo announces quietly that they may begin their Book Club discussions.

The room buzzes with a steady hum as children begin to talk. Mrs. Pardo monitors the different groups, although there is little need at this point in the year for her to facilitate the discussions. In the group reading *Turn Homeward Hannalee* (Beatty, 1984), Charles shares a picture from his log entry about a key event in the story. This leads to a debate about whether one of the main characters should have revealed that he had been masquerading as a girl. Noting that this character was taken away from his sister, students engage in a spirited discussion. Some argue that he should have kept his identity hidden and stayed with his sister, while others suggest that it didn't matter. One boy states emphatically that, like the character in the story, he wouldn't want to pretend he was a girl. This conversation ebbs and flows, but eventually moves to a discussion of the hypocrisy of the Northerners—buying the Confederate children and former workers while denouncing slavery. Another debate emerges about whether the war was fought over slavery or over the North's rights to dictate terms to the South. To engage in this discussion, students must apply comprehension strategies and knowledge of literary aspects, in addition to background knowledge about the historical era. The sophistication of the discussion shows the benefits of much of the instruction that Mrs. Pardo has provided throughout the unit, on point of view, human rights, states' rights, and character development.

Because groups of students are reading different books, community share discussions are devoted to highlighting three different types of information. First, there are thematic connections among the books (e.g., family support in difficult times, human rights issues that override differences between races, North and South, captors and prisoners, soldiers and deserters). Second, there are links from the historical fiction to what they are learning about the Civil War era (e.g., states' rights, importance of key historical figures, battles and their significance). Third, by asking each group to reiterate briefly what is happening in their stories, Mrs. Pardo is able to provide authentic reasons to practice summarization and to highlight literary elements such as character, setting, plot, and point of view. However, the specific agenda of the closing community share is determined largely by what has occurred within the students' Book Club discussions.

Today, Mrs. Pardo begins by asking each group to share what happened in their story. This surfaces a confusion in one group about who is now telling the story, generating an impromptu discussion about point of view and the purpose it serves in moving a story forward. During this community share, Mrs. Pardo often facilitates students' discussions, occasionally scaffolds learning through questioning, and sometimes simply participates as a member of the group. As the community share draws to a close, Mrs. Pardo reminds students that they may continue reading their novels later in the day, during Drop Everything and Read time.

These two classroom examples show how experienced teachers address all aspects of the literature-based curriculum on a daily basis. Instruction to promote ownership, comprehension, composition, literary aspects, and language conventions are not compartmentalized but all occur around the reading of picture books and novels. In both classrooms, teachers do not hesitate to transmit knowledge to students, but whole-class lessons are brief and to the point. Rather than spending most of their time listening to the teacher, students are actively involved in reading literature, writing responses to literature, and discussing literature. Teachers support students in these activities by flexibly shifting back and forth among the various forms of instruction: explicit teaching, scaffolding, modeling, facilitating, and participating.

CONCLUDING COMMENTS

We have argued in this chapter for an updated and expanded view of instruction and curriculum in literature-based classrooms. We began by presenting a new definition of instruction, consistent with a constructivist or sociocultural perspective, emphasizing students' engagement in motivating literary activities. Once students are engaged, teachers follow up with instruction to ensure students' success in completing these activities. Instruction is not viewed as a straightforward process of transmission but is seen to involve dynamic interactions among teachers and students. Teachers employ different forms of instruction in order to meet students' needs. For example, if students are quite proficient in an activity, such as composing written responses to literature, teachers may facilitate their writing. If students have little proficiency, as when they first begin to participate in literature discussions, teachers may model and scaffold.

The nature of the curriculum in literature-based classrooms must also be rethought. When literature is the basis for instruction, reading is no longer seen as a mechanistic process, and affective as well as cognitive goals for student learning are required. Ownership becomes part of the curriculum, along with comprehension, composition, and language conventions. When students read picture books and novels, they have the chance to grapple with rich content rather than skimming over the shallow words of contrived texts written only to teach reading. To appreciate, comprehend, and interpret this rich content, students must learn literary aspects such as character development and theme and must recognize the features of different genres of literature.

To be effective, teachers in successful literature-based classrooms obviously must do much more than switch materials, from contrived texts to authentic literature. What we really mean by literature-based instruction is deep changes in thinking, to a constructivist or sociocultural perspective. We mean deep changes in instruction, beginning with student engagement and the moving toward the flexible application of at least five different forms of teaching. We mean deep changes in the content of the curriculum, to include ownership and literary aspects, along with comprehension, composition, and language conventions. What we really mean by literature-based instruction is giving students the power to make books their own, and this outcome makes all the time and effort required by these changes worthwhile.

REFERENCES

American Educator, 1995, 19(2), 3–25.

Anderson, R. C., Wilson, P. T., & Fielding, L. G. (1988). Growth in reading and how children spend their time outside of school. *Reading Research Quarterly, 23*(3), 285–303.

Au, K. H. (1979). Using the experience-text-relationship method with minority children. *The Reading Teacher, 32*(7), 677–679.

Au, K. H. (1997). Ownership, literacy achievement, and students of diverse cultural backgrounds. In J. T. Guthrie & A. Wigfield (Eds.), *Reading engagement: Motivating readers through integrated instruction* (pp. 168–182). Newark, DE: International Reading Association.

Au, K. H., Carroll, J. H., & Scheu, J. A. (1997). *Balanced literacy instruction: A teacher's resource book.* Norwood, MA: Christopher-Gordon Publishers.

Baumann, J. F., & Bergeron, B. S. (1993). Story map instruction using children's literature: Effects on first graders' comprehension of central narrative elements. *Journal of Reading Behavior: A Journal of Literacy, 25*(4), 407–437.

Beck, I. L., McKeown, M. G., Sandora, C., Kucan, L., & Worthy, J. (1996). Questioning the Author: A yearlong classroom implementation to engage students with text. *Elementary School Journal, 96*(4), 385–414.

Beck, I. L., McKeown, M. G., Hamilton, R. L., & Kucan, L. (1997). *Questioning the Author: An approach for enhancing student engagement with text.* Newark, DE: International Reading Association.

Bloome, D., & Green, J. L. (1992). Educational contexts of literacy. *Annual Review of Applied Linguistics, 12,* 49–70.

Clay, M. (1975). *What did I write?* Auckland: Heinemann.

Dole, J. A., Duffy, G. G., Roehler, L. R., & Pearson, P. D. (1991). Moving from the old to the new: Research on reading comprehension instruction. *Review of Educational Research, 61*(2), 239–264.

Dudley-Marling, C. (1995). Complicating ownership. In C. Dudley-Marling & D. Searle (Eds.), *Who owns learning: Questions of autonomy, choice, and control* (pp. 1–15). Portsmouth, NH: Heinemann.

Dyson, A. H., & Freeman, S. W. (1991). Writing. In J. Flood, J. M. Jensen, D. Lapp, & J. R. Squire (Eds.), *Handbook of research on teaching the English language arts* (pp. 754–774). New York: Macmillan.

Dyson, A. H. (1989). *Multiple worlds of child writers: Friends learning to write.* New York: Teachers College Press.

Fielding, L. G., Wilson, P. T., & Anderson, R. C. (1986). A new focus on free reading: The role of trade books in reading instruction. In T. E. Raphael (Ed.), *Contexts of school-based literacy* (pp. 149–162). New York: Random House.

Fitzgerald, J. (1992). Reading and writing stories. In J. W. Irwin & M. A. Doyle (Eds.), *Reading/writing connections: Learning from research* (pp. 81–93). Newark, DE: International Reading Association.

Gaskins, R. W., Gaskins, J. C., & Gaskins, I. W. (1991). A decoding program for poor readers—and the rest of the class, too! *Language Arts, 68,* 213–225.

Graesser, A., Golding, J. M., & Long, D. L. (1991). Narrative representation and comprehension. In R. Barr, M. L. Kamil, P. B. Mosenthal, & P. D. Pearson (Eds.), *Handbook of reading research* (Volume 2) (pp. 171–205). New York: Longman.

Graves, D. (1983). *Writing: Teachers and children at work.* Exeter, NH: Heinemann Educational Books.

Guthrie, J. T., & Wigfield, A. (1997). Reading engagement: A rationale for theory and teaching. In J. T. Guthrie & A. Wigfield (Eds.), *Reading engagement: Motivating readers through integrated instruction* (pp. 1–12). Newark, DE: International Reading Association.

Hayes, J. R., & Flower, L. S. (1980). Identifying the organization of writing processes. In L. W. Gregg & E. R. Steinberg (Eds.), *Cognitive processes in writing* (pp. 3–30). Hillsdale, NJ: Erlbaum.

Heath, S. B. (1983). *Ways with words: Language, life, and work in communities and classrooms.* Cambridge, Eng.: Cambridge University Press.

Huck, C. S., Hepler, S., & Hickman, J. (1987). *Children's literature in the elementary school.* New York: Holt, Rinehart, & Winston.

Idol, L., & Croll, V. J. (1987). Story-mapping training as a means of improving reading comprehension. *Learning Disability Quarterly, 10*(3), 214–230.

Langer, J. A. (1995). *Envisioning literature: Literary understanding and literature instruction.* New York: Teachers College Press.

Lehr, S. S. (1991). *The child's developing sense of theme: Response to literature.* New York: Teachers College Press.

Levine, A. (1994). The great debate revisited. *The Atlantic Monthly, 274*(6), 38–44.

Lukens, R. J. (1990). *A critical handbook of children's literature.* Glenview, IL: Scott, Foresman.

Mason, J. M., Herman, P. A., & Au, K. H. (1991). Children's developing knowledge of words. In J. Flood, J. M. Jensen, D. Lapp, & J. R. Squire (Eds.), *Handbook of research on teaching the English language arts* (pp. 721–731). New York: Macmillan.

McMahon, S. I., & Raphael, T. E., with Goatley, V. J. & Pardo, L. S. (1997). *The Book Club connection: Literacy learning and classroom talk.* New York: Teachers College Press.

Ogle, D. M. (1986). K-W-L: A teaching model that develops active reading of expository text. *The Reading Teacher, 39*(6), 564–570.

Palincsar, A. S., & Brown, A. L. (1984). Reciprocal teaching of comprehension-fostering and comprehension-monitoring activities. *Cognition and Instruction, 1*(2), 117–175.

Palincsar, A. S., & Brown, A. L. (1989). Classroom dialogues to promote self-regulated comprehension. In J. Brophy (Ed.), *Advances in research on teaching* (pp. 35–72). Greenwich, CT: JAI Press.

Pearson, P. D., & Fielding, L. (1991). Comprehension instruction. In R. Barr, M. L. Kamil, P. Mosenthal, & P. D. Pearson (Eds.), *Handbook of reading research* (pp. 819–860). New York: Longman.

Pressley, M., Johnson, C. J., Symons, S., McGoldrick, J. A., & Kurita, J. A. (1989). Strategies that improve children's memory and comprehension of text. *The Elementary School Journal, 89,* 301–342.

Raphael, T. E., & Boyd, F. B. (1997). When readers write: The Book Club writing component. In S. I. McMahon & T. E. Raphael (Eds.), *The Book Club connection: Literacy learning and classroom talk.* (pp. 69–88). New York: Teachers College Press.

Raphael, T. E., & Hiebert, E. H. (1996). *Creating an integrated approach to literacy instruction.* Ft. Worth, TX: Harcourt Brace Publishers.

Raphael, T. E., & McMahon, S. I. (1994). "Book Club": An alternative framework for reading instruction. *The Reading Teacher, 48*(2), 102–116.

Raphael, T. E., Pardo, L. S., Highfield, K., & McMahon, S. I. (1997). *Book Club: A literature-based curriculum.* Littleton, MA: Small Planet Communications.

Raphael, T. E., & Wonnacott, C. A. (1985). Heightening 4th grade students' sensitivity to sources of information for answering comprehension questions. *Reading Research Quarterly, 20,* 282–296.

Rosenblatt, L. M. (1978). *The reader, the text, the poem: The transactional theory of the literary work.* Carbondale, IL: Southern Illinois University Press.

Spivey, N. N. (1997). *The constructivist metaphor: Reading, writing and the making of meaning.* New York: Academic Press.

Stanovich, K. E. (1984). The interactive-compensatory model of reading: A confluence of developmental, experimental, and educational psychology. *Remedial and Special Education, 5,* 11–19.

Tierney, R. J., Readence, J. E., & Dishner, E. K. (1990). *Reading strategies and practices: A compendium* (3rd ed.). Boston: Allyn and Bacon.

Wigfield, A., & Eccles, J. S. (1992). The development of achievement task values: A theoretical analysis. *Developmental Review, 12,* 265–310.

CHILDREN'S BOOKS CITED

Babbitt, N. (1975). *Tuck everlasting.* New York: Farrer, Straus, & Giroux.

Beatty, P. (1984). *Turn homeward, Hannalee.* New York: Troll.

Burton, M. R. (1994). *My best shoes.*Ill. by J. E. Ransone. New York: Tambourine Books.

Creech, S. (1994). *Walk two moons.* New York: Harper Trophy.

Galdone, P. (1973). *The little red hen.* New York: Seabury.

Hunt, I. (1964). *Across five Aprils.* New York: Berkley Books.

L'Engle, M. (1962). *A wrinkle in time.* New York: Bantam Double Dell Books for Young Readers.

Lionni, L. (1963). *Swimmy.* New York: Random House.

Slobodkina, E. (1947). *Caps for sale.* New York: HarperCollins.

Taylor, M. (1990). *Mississippi bridge.* New York: Bantam Skylark.

Taylor, M. (1991). *Roll of thunder, hear my cry.* New York: Puffin Books.

Wescott, N. B. (1987). *Peanut butter and jelly.* New York: Dutton.

Woodson, J. (1990). *Last summer with Maizon.* New York: Dell Publishing.

Chapter 7

Contributions of Literature Study to the Teaching and Learning of Writing

●————————●

Jenny Denyer, Michigan State University
and
Susan Florio-Ruane, Michigan State University

INTRODUCTION

Learning to write involves learning both the conventions of our language and the composition strategies supporting drafting and revision (Calkins, 1994, 1991; Graves, 1994, 1983; Murray, 1979; Atwell, 1987). Perhaps less evident is the importance of literature study for writing development. Mastering the forms and function of written discourse involves learning appropriate uses of written language to perform a range of meaningful social and cultural functions, as well as forming grammatical sentences. Sociolinguist Dell Hymes dubbed this learning the acquisition of "communicative competence" (Hymes, 1974). As teacher educators who also study the language of teaching and learning in classrooms (see, for example, Denyer & Florio-Ruane, 1995; Florio-Ruane, 1990), in our chapter we emphasize ways to help students learn and practice a rich range of written forms and functions. We argue that studying literature as part of a writing curriculum can help youngsters discover how writing works as a tool for communication within our society.

LITERATURE IN THE WRITING CURRICULUM

In many classrooms youngsters experience limited and uneven instruction in composing and comprehending texts for a range of functions. Rather, contemporary writing instruction tends to be guided by procedure or process. While this attention to process has the advantage of not truncating students' writing into drill and practice of isolated skills, it can default into "mere" process if teachers do not address matters of curriculum and instruction (Calkins, 1994; Florio-Ruane & Lensmire, 1989; Peters & Wixson, Chapter 12). Our curriculum for writing education needs to introduce learners explicitly to a range of the forms and functions for writing for two reasons. First, communicative competence in writing is more than the sum of its constituent skills, and second, the skills and sub-processes of writing differ depending on text structure and function (see Applebee, 1986). In this chapter, we look primarily at curricular issues, focusing on the potential role of reading and literature discussion for helping students learn this dimension of communicative competence in writing. We illustrate why and how teachers might enhance students' experience and skill in writing by engaging them in the study of written texts authored by others in a wide variety of forms, for a wide variety of functions or purposes, and in order to communicate with diverse audiences.

Literature is potentially a powerful means by which to expand the experiences of student writers. As many authors in this volume describe, literature offers readers access to a variety of experiences fundamental to learning how—and why—we write. Yet, when literature is taught as part of language arts or reading, it is often taught in a way that is unassociated with children's own writing. On those occasions when literature is connected to children's writing, the predominant and limited metaphor for that connection is the "springboard." This metaphor speaks primarily to literature's power to motivate writing, but we would argue that literature is more than a springboard. Literature is, in our view, not only a source of motivation for student writing, but also a dynamic medium offering models of written text as well as experiences of how that text "means" for writing.

In this chapter, we have created an imaginary school within which we visit four classrooms. However, far from being crafted from our imagination or some idealized sense of what we would like to see in writing instruction, these classrooms are composites of the many and varied examples of classroom instruction we have witnessed as teacher educators and researchers working in collaboration with preservice and inservice teachers for over 15 years. Through our teaching and research relationships, we have been able to serve as participant observers across many and varied classrooms. As we tour our imaginary school, we provide snapshots of teachers and students working together in classrooms that reflect various writing practices that exist in very real classrooms across grade levels, schools, and districts. Before we begin our tour of classroom writing instruction, we offer a map of the territory, describing the conceptual foundations of the teaching you will see along the way.

LITERATURE AND WRITING IN CLASSROOMS

In his work on writing development, Britton created a typology of functions for which people in our society write. His typology provides insight into both text structure and the context in which a text is crafted and shared.

Thus, he highlights the idea that to learn to write one needs experience with context as well as text—with social activities and relationships within which a writer expresses herself in written language (Britton, 1982).

While his is surely not the only way to slice the pie, the function categories he identifies give us a helpful way to think about literature's role in the writing curriculum for youngsters. This is the case because he challenges us to think about *what* to read, *how* to read it, and *what to notice* about literature as we study it. In this light, literature is not a transparent medium to which readers respond, but the artifact of a process and a relationship wherein text is crafted by a writer in a social context in order to communicate with others.

Using Britton's typology, we can identify three functions for writing. Writers sometimes write to conduct transactions with others—the "business" of everyday life in the world which is undertaken by written texts. Alternately, writers craft texts with aesthetic purposes and in which language is used figuratively to convey values and feeling states. Finally, writing can serve chiefly a vocative function wherein a writer writes to articulate (and perhaps to sort out) life experiences (Temple, Nathan, Burris, & Temple, 1988).

When we read and discuss literature inside the classroom, we can similarly look at the how and why of writing from the perspectives of author, reader, and context. Paralleling writers' functions are categories of response. For example, Raphael, Pardo, Highfield, and McMahon (1997) refer to "creative," "personal," and "critical" response to literature which must be taught and learned (for examples, see Raphael et al., pp. 6 and 27). How does this text "work" to express meaning? How does its reader make sense of it? What are the sociolinguistics resources brought to bear by each person in this transaction? How does a person's time, place, social identity, and background knowledge figure in this mix? In what sense does the text exceed or fail fully to realize an author's intentions? How is writing (and reading) in some sense "larger" than mere message transfer? (see, for example, Scholes, 1989).

These may seem lofty questions not easily linked to the elementary classroom or its instructional imperative to help students learn to wield the tools of written language. But our examples aim to show that, in fact, this lofty work is part and parcel of classroom literacy events. Further, we illustrate that what makes these activities educational is the teacher's attention to pedagogy—including how the learning environment is organized and provisioned, how instructional support is provided, and how youngsters are guided to read, discuss, and make written text.

Looking within the four sample classrooms in our imaginary school, one can see elements of various dimensions of written literacy: personal response to literature, reading like a writer, critical response to the author's craft, intertextual investigation, and writing as a cultural tool. The teachers in this school work hard with their students to teach them how they, as writers, can learn their craft from literature. They have created contexts in which students are engaged in real reading and writing for real purposes—purposes that range from learning and writing about their histories and the histories of their classmates, to creating a piece of fiction, to learning about the lives of the published authors they read, to becoming real authors themselves, from drawing pictures and telling the story of those pictures to writing to organize their thoughts and communicate important information to others.

In this school, the study of literature is not supplemental to, nor is it apart from, the study of writing; it is central to learning to write. The teachers in this school believe and teach their students that writing is a social and intellectual tool that can be used in a variety of social contexts, for a range of purposes, in a number of forms, and to give expression to various aspects of the human experience. Writing is an integral part of reading instruction— and literature is an integral part of writing instruction. We now visit four of the classrooms.

MR. GRAY'S FIFTH-GRADE CLASSROOM: FOCUS ON PERSONAL RESPONSE

Mr. Gray uses a particular framework for his literature-based instruction, Book Club (McMahon & Raphael, with Goatley & Pardo, 1997), which is comprised of four inter-relating contexts: reading, writing, literary circles or student-led book clubs, and whole-class discussion or community share. As we enter this fifth-grade classroom, we can see that all the students are engaged in silent reading and individual writing. Mr. Gray believes that his students need opportunities to write in response to literature. Here, where writing is focused on understanding and creating literature, he sees an opportunity to engage students in an exploration of literature's purpose and function, writers' craft, the literary elements, and the readers' experiences with text.

In the far corner of the room, we see one of the students look up from his book, stare out the window for a moment, pick up a pen, and begin to write in his notebook. For his Book Club log entry on this day, Michael has zeroed in on looking at the writer's craft and how it affects his experience of reading this text. We can see in his writing that he is not only working to make sense of how the words that Paula Fox has chosen to use in her text impact him as a reader, but he is also making intertextual links, specifically to Lois Lowry's (1989) *Number the Stars,* around how authors use language to create images in text and involve the reader in the characters' experiences. Michael has been reading Fox's (1991) *Monkey Island* and writing in his response log in preparation for tomorrow's student-led literature discussion, a regular part of his classroom's daily routine. While the students in this classroom have many options to choose from when responding to literature, today Michael has chosen to combine two kinds of responses, and is writing about "wonderful words" and "the writer's craft" (see McMahon & Raphael, with Goatley & Pardo, 1997, for further descriptions of literature response within Book Club). As Michael writes, he opens his book a few times, rereads parts of it, and then returns to this writing:[1]

> It seems funny to say that the author's words here are wonderful, because they sure don't make me feel wonderful. They make me feel sad. I feel like I'm walking down that street with Clay, hearing the car alarm go off, seeing the lights of the movie theater go off, and feeling cold when he woke up on the stairs of that building. I'm almost scared when Clay sees the park with all the people sleeping in cardboard boxes and on the benches, and then a little relieved that maybe he can sleep there too and be okay, and then scared again when those two guys, Buddy and the old man, start talking about him.
>
> It's kind of hard to explain about these being wonderful words because it's almost hard to read this book because it seems so real. I guess that's what I'm trying to say. Paula Fox is a good writer because she makes me feel like I'm walking down the street with Clay— because I feel like I can hear the car alarm shriek, and feel the cold air in the park. That's what makes them good words to use in a story. It's like when we read *Number The Stars* last year with Mrs. Wilkerson and we were talking about how Lois Lowry made us feel like we were standing next to Annemarie in her house when the Nazi soldiers came to see why so many people were in her house. And we could almost feel the slap when one of the soldiers hit Annemarie's mother. That writing didn't make me *feel* wonderful but it did make me feel like I was there. I guess that's what a good writer does. That's what the author's craft is.

Michael puts his pen down, and with a frown on his face, picks up his book and begins to read again.

Michael and his classmates often use the literature that they read as a springboard for their writing. As they write in response to what they read, these students have opportunities to consider their own experiences as readers and how the authors that they read use powerful language to craft images for readers—images that pull the reader into the text, into the experiences of the character. Today Michael will read on, and perhaps write a bit more in the few remaining minutes before he joins his classmates and Mr. Gray to talk about the book and what he has written about it.

Mr. Gray and his students have spent many of their community share discussions talking about how to pay attention to the writer's craft. He and his students actually get in and "muck around" with text—literature written by authors outside the classroom walls as well as the students' own original text as they play with questions such as

- Why do people create literature, how do writers use language to craft literary text?
- How do readers make sense of or experience literature?
- What is the nature of the transaction that happens among the author, the reader and the written work?

MRS. WILKERSON'S FOURTH-GRADE CLASSROOM: READING LIKE A WRITER

As we enter Mrs. Wilkerson's fourth-grade classroom, we see a small group of students hunched closely together around a table strewn with several of Chris Van Allsburg's picture books: *The Garden of Abdul Gasazi* (1979), *The Wreck of the Zephyr* (1983), *The Stranger* (1986), and *The Wretched Stone* (1991). Along with the picture books are several pages of the children's originally-authored text. The text has been written in pencil and in multiple students' handwriting. Clearly work-in-progress, it contains arrows and scribbles along with the words. The children are engaged in an intense discussion, pointing alternately to a set of pages in one of the picture books and to the pencil scribbled pages of text that are lying at the center of the table—and they have learned to have this kind of discussion because it is one very important part of what Mrs. Wilkerson teaches her students to do.

Like Lucy Calkins (1986), Mrs. Wilkerson wants her students to learn to "see the author behind the writing." As we listen in on this small group of students working with the set of Van Allsburg's book, we will see them doing just that. The children are interrogating these texts in order to understand how this author uses foreshadowing to create suspense in his books. They move among the texts, looking for examples in one book, then another, then another. They move back and forth between text and illustrations in one book to see how the author creates a synergy between the two. And they wonder aloud how they as writers can try out this same technique in their own story. As they interrogate the text, they are, in effect, interrogating the author, trying to get inside his written text to understand it, and to learn from it. Let's listen in:

Erik: Our story isn't very exciting.

Maria: What do you mean?

Erik: Well, when somebody reads this, I want them to be really scared, even nervous about what's going to happen next. Like when you read *Jumanji*. Every time a new animal appears, I keep wondering what's going to happen next. Will more animals appear? What will they do to the house, or even to the kids?

Yen: Maybe we could try to do some, oh, what we were talking about the other day with Mrs. Wilkerson? You know when the author gives you a hint about something that's going to happen but really doesn't come right out and say it.

Maria: Oh, yeah . . . foreshadowing.

As we listen to what these students are saying, we can see that they know quite a bit about what it means to be an author. They know that authors must consider their audience as they write: they worry that people will not find their story exciting. They have learned that there are certain literary techniques that authors use in their writing: they remember that they have learned about foreshadowing in an earlier lesson with Mrs. Wilkerson. They know that they can look to other authors for models of good writing: they look to see how Van Allsburg creates suspense in his books. Let's go back to their conversation as Maria continues to draw the group's attention to foreshadowing:

Maria: Van Allsburg uses some of that foreshadowing. See, here on this page. This is where I first get the idea that something not so good might happen to Peter and Judy. Listen [reads aloud from one of the books] "Look," said Peter, pointing to a note taped to the bottom of the box. In a childlike handwriting were the words "Free game, fun for some but not for all. P.S. Read instructions carefully."

Erik: And then on the next page, the last part of the instructions that say the game won't be over till someone reaches the golden city, they're printed all in capital letters. Why would the author do that except to hint that *something* weird is going to happen?

Maria: And it does, on the next page when the lion appears on top of the piano.

Dylan: Oh. I get what you mean. It's like at the end of the book when there's that picture of the two kids leaving the park with the game under their arms. He doesn't come right out and say the same thing's going to happen all over again.

Yen: No, but he hints at it in words on the page next to the picture . . . in this one part . . . [begins to read aloud from the book]

"Such a hard puzzle," she said to the children. "Daniel and Walter are always starting puzzles and never finishing them." Daniel and Walter were Mrs. Budwing's sons. "They never read instructions either. Oh well," said Mrs. Budwing, turning to rejoin the guests, "I guess they'll learn."

Both children answered, "I hope so," but they weren't looking at Mrs. Budwing. They were looking out the window. Two boys were running through the park. They were Walter and Danny Budwing, and Danny had a long thin box under his arm.

Dylan: And then the story ends. It's like he's foreshadowing another book.

Erik: Yeah. He does that same thing in the *The Wretched Stone* when you get the feeling that something weird is going to happen to the crew when they start staring at the stone—and then it does when they all start turning into monkeys. That's a really weird book.

Maria: Okay, but what are we going to do with our story. Should we try to do some of this foreshadowing?

Yen: How would we do it?

Dylan: Good question.

Here we see the children involved in interrogating this text. In this interrogation, we actually see the students move back and forth between talk *about* the text and *diving into* the text as they reread it to see what they can learn from this model. They have been able to see that Van Allsburg creates suspense not only by using foreshadowing in the words he writes but also in the illustrations he draws. We even see the children making intertextual links between the text they are currently reading and the books in this text set (Calkins, 1991) they have been looking at. As they engage in this interrogation, these students are able to get inside the written language of the text—to explore the linguistic building blocks of a literary text, to compare and contrast these building blocks across texts and genres, and in light of authors' purposes.

Why are they doing this? Why are they so intent on this interrogation? They are doing this because they, too, are authors. They are creating their own picture book and, in so doing, find themselves faced with authors' question, like, "How do we create suspense so that our readers are on the edge of their seats?" This question is a real question for this group of writers, and it takes them to Van Allsburg's books to consult with a fellow author as they read, reread, wonder, notice and appreciate this text. These children are reading like writers. They are using one author's books as a set of models from which they can learn how to write.

Yen: Wait!! I've got an idea!! Maybe here, when the three kids are about to enter the haunted house, we could draw a picture with someone looking out of the upstairs window.

Erik: Yeah!! That's a great idea! And in the words we can say something like, "As Jake started to walk up the stairs to the old mansion, he felt like someone was watching him." That way when somebody reads the words, they can start to wonder what's going to happen . . .

Yen: Yeah—and then when they look at the picture, they can see this mysterious person—or whatever it is, peeking out of the window!

Dylan: Cool!

The children laugh, and turn to the papers in front of them. One of the children starts to draw the picture, sketching the old house with the curtain being drawn back from the window on the top floor. The other two work on the wording of the text for this same page.

Mrs. Wilkerson has been standing near the group listening in to their conversation—and feeling pretty excited. She has really worked hard with her students to get them to the point where they can have this kind of conversation. She believes that literature provides students with models of good writing, and she works hard to engage them in conversations about those models to help them develop their own skills as writers. She spends a lot of time helping her students learn to read like a writer (Tierney & Pearson, 1983; Smith, 1990), an experience that she believes is a potentially powerful one for her students. Early in the year, as she reads aloud to her students, she often engages them in discussion about the text that helps them to see the author behind it. They talk about the words the author uses to create images for readers. She teaches them about different literary techniques—like foreshadowing—that authors can employ. They talk about why authors write books and how they consider the audiences for their writing. And throughout all of these discussions, she helps the students to see that as authors themselves, they will need to think about these same issues—and even learn some new writing techniques as they think about their writing and their audiences. Mrs. Wilkerson and her colleague down the hall, Miss Davis, have been working together to help their students read like readers. Let's see what's happening in that classroom.

MISS DAVIS'S FOURTH-GRADE CLASSROOM: DISCOVERING THE AUTHOR'S CRAFT

In this classroom there is a quiet hum of many groups working around the room. Off to the right side, we see Miss Davis sitting with one of the small groups gathered on the rug usually used for classroom meetings. She is reading aloud the prologue from Natalie Babbitt's (1975, p. 3) novel, *Tuck Everlasting,* as the students follow along in their own books:

The first week of August hangs at the very top of summer the top of the live-long year, like the highest seat of a ferris wheel when it pauses in its turning. The weeks that come before are only a climb from balmy spring, and those that follow a drop to the chill of autumn, but the first week of August is motionless, and hot. It is curiously silent, too, with blank white dawns and glaring noons, and sunsets smeared with too much color. Often at night there is lightning, but it quivers all alone. There is no thunder, no relieving rain. These are strange breathless days, the dog days, when people are led to do things they are sure to be sorry for after.

As she finishes reading, Miss Davis initiates a book discussion with her students by asking, "So, what do you think of that opening paragraph?"

Marcia: It makes me hot. When she says that August is "motionless and hot" and the days are "breathless," it makes me feel all sweaty like when I've been out riding my bike really fast and my face gets red, and I have to run into the house and get something cold to drink cause I'm sooo thirsty.

Steven: I wish it was summer.

Dominque: Sometimes my sister and I watch the lightning from our bedroom window and we think it's going to rain but it never does. My grandma always says she wants the rain because it will make it cooler, but the rain doesn't come—and my sister and I are happy.

Jill: I felt like I was stuck in a ferris wheel at the very top. My mom always gets mad at me when I lean over and look at the ground, but it's so cool to look down on everybody. People look like ants—and it's not so noisy at the top like when the author said, "curiously silent." And when we go to Cedar Point it's always hot and the sun's shining.

Miss D.: Sitting here listening to all of you makes me think that Natalie Babbitt has done a pretty good job of setting the mood for her story. You all have described ways in which the words she uses have triggered pictures in your minds about what it's like in the summer—from actually riding a ferris wheel, to being really hot and sweaty in August, to watching the lightning that comes with no rain. She made me think about summer, too, actually the whole year when she writes about how the first week of August hangs at the top of summer like the highest seat of the ferris wheel. (Miss Davis turns toward the board behind her and draws a ferris wheel, putting August at the top and writing "spring" around the cars on the left and "autumn" around the cars on the right.) Babbitt is using the metaphor of a ferris wheel to describe how she sees August as the, what does she say? Here it is: "the top of the live-long year."

Emily: That kind of makes August the best time of the year.

Miss D.: What makes you say that, Emily?

Emily: Well, it's at the top, like being on top of the hill or being on top of the world. It's just a cool place to be.

Miss D.: So you think Babbitt is using the metaphor of the ferris wheel to describe the first week of August as the best part of the year. That makes sense.

Here we can see Miss Davis and her students wonder together about how words affect readers, how words help readers create images, and how authors choose words and craft text to evoke those images. They talk about the literal images that Babbitt's words evoke—that of being on a ferris wheel in the middle of summer at the local fair. And they talk about the possibilities that the metaphorical ferris wheel might suggest—that of the cycle of a year with August being the very best part. Teacher and students are looking together at the ways in which this author uses her words to create these images— but their talk does not stop there. Miss Davis wants to nudge her student writers along:

Miss D.: I've been noticing that several of you have been using metaphors in your writing, too. Jose described the main character in his football story as a streak of lightning as he ran down the field with the football. Lisa wrote that her bedroom looked like a disaster area the day after a tornado.

Steven: I said my brother was a pig when he eats pizza.

Miss D.: That certainly is descriptive! We have examples from several authors who have used metaphors to create vivid pictures in our minds. You might try using a metaphor in your current writing, and you could consult with Jose or Lisa about how they came up with their metaphors, or you could reread how Natalie Babbitt uses this metaphor.

Anthony: But Ms. Davis, I don't get what the author means when she says, "people do things they'll be sorry for later." Is something bad going to happen?

Miss D.: Good question, Anthony. What do you think?

Anthony: I'm not sure. I think that's a hint that something's going to go wrong, but I don't know what it will be.

Jose: Maybe something good is going to happen since she thinks the first week in August is the best time of the year.

Miss D.:   You know what I think? I think Natalie Babbitt has done it again. I think she picked those words on purpose so that readers like us would wonder what she meant. That sentence is kind of mysterious: "These are strange and breathless days, the dog days, when people are led to do things they are sure to be sorry for after." I'm certainly curious. Good authors do that. They write their stories so that we want to keep reading. Sometimes they put in mysterious sentences like this one to pique our curiosity.

Jose: So, can we keep reading?

Miss D.:   Sure.

Miss Davis uses this opportunity to link this use of metaphor in the writing of Natalie Babbitt to the children's own writing, identifying examples of the writings of the members in the group—Jose's football character who ran like a streak of lightning and Lisa's bedroom that looked like a tornado disaster area. She encourages her students to try out some metaphors in their writing—and to consult with authors like Natalie Babbitt, Jose, and Lisa.

These kinds of conversations in which teachers elicit students' responses to text, explore with students the images created in the texts, and help students notice how authors use language to craft these images and their text are conversations in which teachers are helping students learn to read like writers. These are the kinds of conversations that the students in Mr. Gray's and Mrs. Wilkerson's classroom have had throughout the year. These are the kinds of conversations that have prepared the last group of students we visited who were writing their own picture book to be able to have those conversations without the teacher present—and they are the kinds of conversations that prepare students to have these conversations with themselves as Michael, the first student we visited, was able to do as he wrote in his reading log. These children are learning not only to appreciate literature as pieces of text, but they are also learning to appreciate literature as models of good writing—models upon which they can draw as they write themselves.

It seems important to note here, that not only do students need opportunities to learn how to look at books as models of writing, to have opportunities to get in and muck around with texts to see what's there. Teachers also need to spend some time noting, and—as one of our colleagues, Eliot Singer suggests (personal communication, 1995)—"fondling its details."[2] This carefully paying attention to text, looking for patterns in language, noting unusual (and usual) ways that authors draw readers into texts, develop characters, structure plots, create settings—all of this paying attention to a text helps a teacher think about all that a text offers her and her students. Singer suggests that teachers actually develop what he calls a "crib sheet" in which they note these details and patterns for themselves. He cautions against using the crib sheet to march students through attention to these same ideas in a lockstep fashion. Instead, it becomes an important resource upon which teachers like Miss Davis can draw as she prepares to talk about a book with her students—or as she helps them think about themselves as writers.

MRS. MATHEWS'S THIRD-GRADE CLASSROOM: WRITING TO EXPLORE CULTURE

As we walk in the door, we almost collide with a group of three students who are hurrying to the large bulletin board by the drinking fountain to post a notice that announces the performance of their original play the following day. The announcement, complete with painstakingly printed letters in big bold colors, invites all their classmates to join them for a performance:

COME ONE

COME ALL

TO SEE OUR NEW PLAY

LEO'S DANGEROUS ESCAPE FROM THE ZOO

BE ON THE CARPET AT EXACTLY 2:15 TOMORROW

YOU WON'T WANT TO MISS OUR PLAY

IT'S GRRRRRRRRRRREAT!!!!!!!!

This group hurries back to their table and makes last-minute lists of needed props, and costumes—and puts the finishing touches on the written invitation for the principal before they take it down to her office. Sasha's job is to check the spelling, and Terrence will check to make sure they have capital letters and periods in the right places.

Mrs. Mathews creates opportunities for her third-grade students to learn and practice writing to organize their thinking and communicate with others. In the beginning of the year, she and her students talked a lot about how writing is one of the tools people use within cultures and societies to communicate messages to one another. Together they wrote a weekly classroom newsletter to their parents to tell them all about the different things they were learning, the variety of activities they were engaged in, and to notify parents of important upcoming events. As teacher and students collaborated on these newsletters, Mrs. Mathews used this opportunity to teach the children about one of the many forms that writing can take and the functions these forms can serve. It served as an opportunity to help her students understand the importance of and to practice the conventions of language use that help us to communicate clearly—the conventions of spelling, grammar, and usage. With this experience beginning early in the year, Mrs. Mathews was able to create other "occasions for writing" (Florio & Clark, 1981, 1982) that are functional within the classroom, school, and larger community. These occasions included inviting fifth graders to visit the new gerbils that are part of the classroom science exploration center, and writing to thank the local grocery store owner for donating gerbil food. As Sasha, Randall, and Terrence make last-minute arrangements for their performance, they are using what they have learned about writing as a tool for communication for a real purpose.

Students in this classroom are also engaged in using writing as a tool for learning about themselves and developing their own cultural understandings. As we've been standing at the board, another student places her announcement—this one detailing the names of four guest speakers and the dates of their classroom visits. The last part of the announcement reminds students to have their questions ready to ask the guests. The class has been studying immigration in the early 1900s. Mrs. Mathews has been reading *Journey To America* (Levitin, 1970), and autobiographies of immigrants to the United States. These books have prompted them to want to interview people in their community who were born in other countries.

The students have identified four guest speakers from the extended families of the students in their class. One is a grandfather from Egypt; another is a grandmother from Ireland. Another's parents come from Mexico. The last guest is the great-great-grandson of slaves who came from West Africa. After listening to these guests tell their stories, the class will have a chance to ask them questions. Then students will write the history of their own families, doing their research by interviewing adult relatives and looking at "artifacts" treasured in their family, such as photographs and books and other mementos.

Here we see another example of how Mrs. Mathews works to create opportunities for her students to use writing as a tool for learning and communicating with others. Just as the young playwrights and actors are using writing both to communicate to others about their upcoming performance—peers and the principal, this second notice announces another such opportunity. As the students prepare for the visits of their guest speakers, they are organizing their thoughts by writing their questions. Then, once they have heard from their guests, they will create a set of interview questions that they will use to talk with their own family members to learn more about their own histories. And the writing won't stop there.

As students craft accounts of their histories, they will use writing to extend what they already know about themselves and their families as they organize and write about the new information they have learned. And finally, as they share these accounts with their classmates, writing becomes a tool for communicating with others about one's cultural understanding and identity. These texts that the students will create and share with their peers reflect the cultural contexts that have helped to shape these children, and these texts have helped these students express and transform their sense of themselves in the world.

LEARNING TO TEACH IS HARD: A LOOK INSIDE MS. STONE'S CLASSROOM

On our way out of the building, there's one more classroom we will stop by. It's a second-grade classroom where Ms. Stone, a student teacher, is in the midst of student teaching—working hard to learn how to help her students see the connections between the texts that they read and their own writing. Ms. Stone has been learning in her teacher preparation classes that it is important to have students work together in small groups to get in and muck around with text, so on this day she has divided her students into several small groups. We can see the children scattered around the room looking at and talking about books at their tables, and we can see Ms. Stone walking around the room making sure that students are getting started on their mucking around. For a couple of groups she has needed to focus their conversation, reminding them that they are supposed to be talking about their books, not the soccer game at recess.

One group of children has just picked up a set of books from the shelf and is taking them to a round table by the window where they can look at the books. Their stack includes *The Pain and the Great One* (Blume, 1974), *The True Story of the 3 Little Pigs* (Scieszka, 1989), *Alexander and the Terrible, Horrible, No Good, Very Bad Day* (Viorst, 1972), and *Two Bad Ants* (Van Allsburg, 1988). Ms. Stone had noticed that some of her students were beginning to include different points of view in some of their writing, so she wanted to provide some models for them to consult so that they could see how other authors worked with point of view in their texts. Ms. Stone has put this text set (Calkins, 1991) together because all the authors have written their books from very distinct points of view: from the point of view of an older sister and a bratty younger brother, from the point of view of the much maligned wolf, from the point of view of a little boy for whom nothing goes right, and from the point of view, literally, of two adventurous ants who go about exploring—even though they've been warned not to. Ms. Stone is particularly interested in hearing what this group has to say about these books—and she is hoping to hear the students make the connection to their own writing. As she sits at a nearby desk and begins to listen, it seems that the children are already familiar with some of these books:

Shawn: This is one of my favorite books! I like the two different parts of the book. First you get to hear from the older sister about what a pain her little brother is. And she's right. My little brother's a pain, too. Then it switches and the little brother tells about how he gets tired of hearing about his sister—the great one.

Allan: I like Alexander better because he sounds just like my little brother. He just keeps talking and talking and whining. Look how long this sentence is: [reading aloud] "On the way downstairs the elevator door closed on my foot and while we were waiting for my mom to get the car Anthony made me fall where it was muddy and then when I started crying because of the mud Nick said I was a crybaby and while I was punching Nick for saying crybaby my mom came back with the car and scolded me for being muddy and fighting." Whew! That's even hard to read because there's no period. There's not even a comma so you can take a breath. How come the author gets to write like that? I'd be in big trouble with Mrs. Stone if I wrote a sentence like that.

Kerry: I like *The True Story of the 3 Little Pigs*!!!! It is sooooooo gross. Have you seen these pictures? Look at this one with the sandwich. There's a rat tail and bunny ears and a nose and some paws.

Serina: That is so gross!!

Kerry: Yeah—but I feel sorry for the wolf. Like he says, "It's not my fault wolves eat cute little animals like bunnies and sheep and pigs. That's just the way we are. If cheeseburgers were cute, folks would probably think you were big and bad too." I never really thought about it from his side, but maybe he was—

Alex: The other day I saw this dead raccoon on the side of the road—it was really gross. There was blood everywhere and its guts were spread out all over the road.

Kerry: Cool! My older brother almost ran into a deer on his way home the other night. He was telling me how it ran into the road in front of his car and he almost didn't see it and—there was this other car that was right alongside him and he didn't have any place to go except into the ditch and . . .

   As Ms. Stone listened as this group was getting started, she was pleased to hear them noticing everything she had hoped. They were commenting on Judith Viorst's telling of the same story from two different points of view— and about how realistic that made the story seem. Shawn and Alex were even making connections between the texts and their own lives—talking about how two of the books made them think about their own brothers. This was great!

She was even more excited when she heard Kerry talk about how he felt sorry for the wolf and how he hadn't ever thought about the story "from his side." Things were going really well. Any moment now she expected them to start making connections to their writing. She could just imagine that Kerry would tell his group about the story he's writing about the bank robbery. He would tell them that instead of just writing it from the point of view of the bank teller, he was also going to include the robber's point of view—maybe even write it so you could see that the robber was really scared instead of fearless and mean, as the teller thought. Ms. Stone could almost hear these ideas coming out of Kerry's mouth while she was busy making notes to include in the paper she had to write about engaging students in talking about literature and thinking about their own writing.

And then it happened. Her friends had told stories about it happening to them. It never seemed to happen to her collaborating teacher or the other teachers in the building whom she had observed. She had always hoped it wouldn't happen to her, but here it was! Her students weren't making the connections she wanted them to make. Kerry wasn't spinning out ideas for how to incorporate a different point of view in his bank robbery story. Her students were talking about dead animals along the side of the road!! What now? She had to think quickly and she knew she had to step into the conversation, but how would she bring it around to what she thought the students should be talking about?

Ms. Stone began to think carefully about what she had heard. The students had a good sense of how to identify point of view in a story, yet they hadn't used that term. She wanted them not only to learn it, but also to think about using this technique as writers. The students were making connections between the texts and their own experiences and that was important. The trick would be for her somehow to make a bridge from the connections they were making to the connections she wanted them to make. Hmmm . . . point of view and stories about dead animals. Well, it was a stretch, but she thought she might give it a try before the conversation got so far away from the books that she would never be able to bring it back. So she jumped in:

Ms. S.: So, what did I hear about a deer on the side of the road?

Kerry: I was just telling them about my brother almost running into a deer . . .

Alex: And I was telling 'em about a dead raccoon I saw on the side of the road.

Ms. S.: Interesting. I'm curious about how the deer and the raccoon came up in your conversation about these books.

Alex: I don't know.

Kerry: Well, I guess, umm, we were talking about the gross pictures in this book.

Ms. S.:   Oh, I see. Yeah. These pictures are a lot different from what you'd expect. Why do you suppose the illustrator put those in?

Serina: To be gross!

Alex: No, if he really wanted to be gross he would of put a dead bunny all . . .

Ms. S.:   Well, I think he put them there for another reason. Maybe he wanted us to think about this story from the wolf's point of view. What do you think?

Students: Mmmhmmm.

Ms. S.:   You know, I heard Kerry say that he felt sorry for the wolf. Why did you feel sorry for the wolf?

Kerry: I don't know. I just did.

Ms. S.:   Okay, well let's think about the story for a minute. Where's one place that you felt sorry for him? Serina? Alex? Kerry? What do you think?

Serina: Well, I guess I kinda felt sorry for him 'cause he had a cold.

Ms. S.:   Okay.

Alex: Ms. Stone, it's time for recess.

Ms. S.:   Already? Okay, let's talk about this tomorrow.

Well, Ms. Stone didn't quite get to where she had hoped. In fact, as she talked with her collaborating teacher later that day, she talked about how hard it is to get students engaged in the kinds of conversations she wants them to have about books. She wants her students to have opportunities to give their personal responses to literature—to make connections to their own experiences. She wants them to learn to read like writers, to make intertextual links, to critically examine an author's craft, and to come to see writing as a cultural tool. And she wants them to learn to do all of this because she believes it will make them better writers. At the end of the day, as Ms. Stone sits down to plan for tomorrow's lessons, she begins by writing, "This teaching is really hard!!!"

HELPING TEACHERS CONNECT TALK ABOUT TEXT AND WRITING

As teacher educators working with preservice and experienced teachers, we agree with Ms. Stone that teaching in the ways she and the other teachers in her building are teaching is hard—and we believe that this kind of teaching is an important way to support the development of children as writers and readers. We recognize that many teachers have had little opportunity to interact with text and think about writing in the ways that they are being asked to teach children, so we work hard to engage our preservice and experienced teachers in the kinds of experiences with literature that we hope they will engage their own students in.

Burbules (1993), an educational philosopher, argues that while teachers are encouraged to teach by means of democratic, discourse pedagogies, rarely do they have opportunities to learn this way, and more rare still is the opportunity to examine their own experiences as learners in these conversations. It seems sensible then, that if we want teachers to engage students in educative conversations about books and about their original writing, we as teacher educators must find ways to engage teachers in the same kinds of conversations around their teaching. We need to help teachers develop an image of what these kinds of conversations look, sound, and feel like, to explore their potential and complexity. We need to help them experience the joy, pleasure, frustration, and hard work of coming together with others to make sense of text—whether that text is *The True Story of the 3 Little Pigs,* Kerry's original text about the bank robbery, or the text of Ms. Stone's teaching.

One of the ways we help teachers develop these images of the possible is in our work with preservice and experienced teachers. We and our students are often seen pouring over and mucking around with sets of picture books, or chapter books for children, or autobiographies for adults. Together, we notice details we may not have seen before, we laugh at interesting twists in a plot, or puzzle over odd but intriguing word choices. We revel together about how authors such as Maya Angelou and Jill Kerr Conway so skillfully chose to reveal their characters bit by bit through dialogue, and we wonder about their poignant experiences (Florio-Ruane, Raphael, Glazier, McVee, & Wallace, in press; Florio-Ruane & De Tar, 1995).

We also have recently been exploring the use of videotape in our work with teachers learning to talk with children about text—teachers just like Ms. Stone. In particular, Jenny and the teachers with whom she works have been examining videotaped teaching episodes of just the kind of messy situation in which Ms. Stone finds herself above (see Denyer, 1997; Denyer & Pfeiffer, 1996). These messy situations are what Schon would call "indeterminate zones of practice" (1987)—those situations in which there is no one clear-cut way of proceeding but rather multiple avenues for a teacher to pursue. These are situations in which the teacher and students must work together to "muck around" in the text, play with ideas, try out alternative ways of interpreting or composing the text, and, in Ms. Stone's case, work hard to find ways to help students connect the texts they are reading with the texts they are writing. These situations are particularly tricky because it is not readily apparent to the teacher which of the avenues will prove fruitful for discussion and educative for students (Denyer, 1993).

Videotapes of these "messy situations" stop the action of the text discussions, essentially freezing the action to be revisited at a later time. Then, as teachers and teacher educators take up this opportunity to revisit the talk, they engage in a careful examination of the situation and in a deliberation and consideration of possible alternative actions. This collaborative analysis of the videotape creates a kind of "conversational workspace" (Denyer, 1997; Denyer & Pfeiffer, 1996) for teachers and teacher educators to have their own educative conversations as they engage in a close examination of teaching talk and action as a stimulus for thought, reflection, and new action. This collaborative analysis has the potential to support the efforts of teachers like Ms. Stone as they explore ways to engage their students in educative talk about text as a way to support their students' growth and development as writers.

In Ms. Stone's words, "Teaching like this is hard." It requires teachers to learn new ways of talking with children about text for new purposes. By creating conversational workspaces for Ms. Stone to examine the text of her teaching with us, her teacher educators, and with her colleagues, we are creating opportunities for all of us to explore the status quo of teacher-student discourse, and consider alternative ways of organizing talk in classrooms (Denyer, 1994, 1997; Florio-Ruane, 1989; Michaels & O'Connor 1990). Little (1993) and Lord (1994) call for teachers to talk openly and critically about their teaching practices as a means for creating meaningful changes in classrooms. This collaborative analysis of videotaped book discussions provides just such an opportunity for this kind of talk.

CONCLUDING COMMENT

As we get ready to leave our school, we can see Ms. Stone still sitting at her desk working on tomorrow's plans—and thinking hard about how she will shape her conversation with Kerry, Serina, and Alex. As we look over her shoulder, we can see her playing with several ways of approaching the conversation as she writes in her notebook. She's even considering videotaping tomorrow's discussion so that she can revisit it with one of her instructors and her collaborating teacher.

How will Ms. Stone get the conversation started tomorrow? Where will the discussion take these students and their teacher? How will Ms. Stone help them make the connection between the writing in *The True Story of the 3 Little Pigs,* and their own writing? As much as we would like to, we haven't time to stay and hear what happens next, but lots of possibilities are dancing around in our heads—and yours, we hope. What would you do if these were your students? Some food for thought as we make our way out of the build-ing and back to our own classrooms . . . wherever they may be.

ENDNOTES

1. All students' examples and all conversations have been created or recon-structed based on our observations, fieldnotes, and conversations with teach-ers and their students.

2. Singer borrows this phrase from Nabokov.

REFERENCES

Applebee, A. L. (1986). Problems in process approaches: Toward a reconceptualization of process instruction. In A. K. Petrosky & D. Bartholomae (Eds.), *The teaching of writing: 85th yearbook of the National Society for the Study of Education* (pp. 95–113). Chicago: University of Chicago Press.

Atwell, N. (1987). *In the middle.* Portsmouth, NH: Boyton/Cook.

Britton, J. (1982). Spectator role and the beginnings of writing. In M. Nystrand (Ed.), *What writers know: The language, process, and structure of written discourse.* New York: Academic Press.

Burbules, N. (1993). *Dialogue in teaching: Theory and practice.* New York: Teachers College Press.

Calkins, L. (1986). *The art of teaching writing.* Portsmouth, NH: Heinemann.

Calkins, L. (1994). *The art of teaching writing,* 2nd ed. Portsmouth, NH: Heinemann.

Calkins, L. (1991). *Living between the lines.* Portsmouth, NH: Heinemann.

Denyer, J. (1997). *What happens when the conversation falls apart?: The potential for collaborative analysis of talk about text.* Paper presented at the annual meeting of the American Educational Research Association, Chicago.

Denyer, J. (1994). *Questioning, listening, telling, and showing: A teacher candidate balances the demands of an educative conversation about text in a writing conference.* Paper presented at the annual meeting of the American Educational Research Association, New Orleans, Louisiana.

Denyer, J. (1993). *Teaching by talking, teaching by listening: The conversational complexity of learning to engage children in educative conversations about text in the writing conference.* Doctoral dissertation, Michigan State University. (University Microfilms No. 26675).

Denyer, J., & Florio-Ruane, S. (1995). Mixed messages and missed opportunities: Moments of transformation in writing conferences and teacher education. *Teaching and Teacher Education 11*(6), 539–551.

Denyer, J., & Pfeiffer, L. (1996). *Mining images in learning to teach: The role of videotape and conversation in teachers' identity development.* Innovative symposium presented at the Ethnography in Education Research Forum, University of Pennsylvania, Philadelphia.

Florio, S., & Clark, C. (1982). The functions of writing in an elementary school classroom. *Research in the Teaching of English, 16*(2), 115–130.

Florio, S., & Clark, C. (1981, October). *Pen pals: Describing an occasion for writing in the classroom.* Paper presented at the Midwest Regional Conference on Qualitative Research in Education, Kent State University, Kent, Ohio.

Florio-Ruane, S. (1990). Instructional conversations in learning to write and learning to teach. In B. Jones & L. Idol (Eds.), *Educational values and cognitive instruction: Implications for reform* (Vol. 1, pp. 365–386). New York: Erlbaum.

Florio-Ruane, S. (1989). Social organization of schools and classrooms. In M. Reynolds (Ed.), *Knowledge base for beginning teachers: A handbook* (pp. 163–177). Oxford: Pergamon Press.

Florio-Ruane, S., &. De Tar, J. (February, 1995). Conflict and consensus in teacher candidates' discussion of ethnic autobiography. *English Education, 27*(1), 11–39.

Florio-Ruane, S., & Lensmire, T. (1989). The role of instruction in learning to write. In J. Brophy (Ed.), *Advances in research on teaching.* Greenwich, CT: JAI Press.

Florio-Ruane, S., Raphael, T. E., Glazer, J., McVee, M., & Wallace, S. (in press). *Article in NRC Yearbook, 1997.*

Graves, D. (1994). A fresh look at writing. Portsmouth, NH: Heinemann.

Graves, D. (1983). *Writing: Teachers and children at work.* Portsmouth, NH: Heinemann.

Hymes, D. (1974). *Foundations in sociolinguistics: An ethnographic approach.* Philadelphia: The University of Pennsylvania Press.

Little, J. W. (1993). Teachers' professional development in a climate of education reform. *Educational Evaluation and Policy Analysis, 15*(2), 129–151.

Lord, B. (1994). In N. Cobb (Ed.), *The future of education: Perspectives on national standards in America.* New York: College Entrance Examination Board.

McMahon, S. I., Raphael, T. E., with Goatley, V. J., & Pardo, L. S. (1997). *The book club connection: Literacy learning and classroom talk.* New York: Teachers College Press.

Michaels, S., & O'Connor, M. C. (1990). *Literacy as reasoning in multiple discourses: Implications for policy and educational reform.* Paper presented for the Council of Chief State School Officers 1990 Summer Institute: Restructuring Learning.

Murray, D. (1979). The listening eye: Reflections on the writing conference. *College English 41,* 13–18.

Raphael, T. E., Pardo, L. S., Highfield, K., & McMahon, S. I. (1997). *Book club: A literature-based curriculum.* Littleton, MA: Small Planet Communications, Inc.

Scholes, Robert (1989). *Protocols of reading.* New Haven: Yale University Press.

Schon, D. (1987). *Educating the reflective practitioner.* San Francisco: Jossey-Bass.

Smith, F. (1990). *To think.* New York: Teachers College Press.

Temple, C., Nathan, R., Burris, N., & Temple, F. (1988). *The beginnings of writing.* Boston: Allyn and Bacon.

Tierney, R. J., & Pearson, P. D. (1983). Toward a composing model of reading. *Language Arts, 60*(5), 568–589.

CHILDREN'S BOOKS CITED

Babbitt, N. (1975). *Tuck everlasting.* New York: Farrar, Straus & Giroux.

Blume, J. (1974). *The pain and the great one.* New York: Dell Publishing.

Fox, P. (1991). *Monkey Island.* New York: Orchard Books.

Levitin, S. (1970). *Journey to America.* New York: Aladdin Books.

Lowry, L. (1996). *Number the stars.* New York: Dell Publishing.

Scieszka, J. (1989). *The true story of the 3 little pigs.* New York: Viking Penguin.

Van Allsburg, C. (1981). *Jumanji.* Boston: Houghton Mifflin.

Van Allsburg, C. (1979). *The garden of Abdul Gasazi.* New York: Houghton Mifflin.

Van Allsburg, C. (1986). *The stranger.* New York: Houghton Mifflin.

Van Allsburg, C. (1988). *Two bad ants.* New York: Houghton Mifflin.

Van Allsburg, C. (1983). *The wreck of the Zephyr.* New York: Houghton Mifflin.

Van Allsburg, C. (1991). *The wretched stone.* New York: Houghton Mifflin.

Viorst, J. (1972). *Alexander and the terrible, horrible, no good, very bad day.* New York: Atheneum.

Chapter 8

Evidence of Literacy Learning in a Literature-Based Reading Program

•————————•

Kathy Highfield, Holly Elementary School

In 1991, after my first year of teaching upper elementary school, I decided to return to Michigan State University to pursue a Master's degree in literacy instruction. During my studies, I learned about a literature-based reading program called Book Club (see Raphael & McMahon, 1994; McMahon & Raphael with Goatley & Pardo, 1997). The Book Club program is centered around small, student-led discussions about texts (i.e., chapter books, short stories, nonfiction). It was developed to promote the integration of the English language arts and to create opportunities for students to engage in and take ownership for meaningful discussions of text. Supported by my participation in a teacher research group (Goatley, Highfield, Bentley, Pardo, Folkert, Scherer, Raphael, & Grattan, 1995), I extended the Book Club program to integrate literacy with social studies (see Highfield & Folkert, 1997).

Within a typical day of Book Club in my classroom—like most Book Club classrooms—my students begin by reading their Book Club book, and then responding to literature through written entries in their response logs. Students then discuss their ideas in the small student-led discussion groups, called book clubs, that the program is centered around.[1] There, among peers, they relate to the literature in meaningful and powerful ways. The Book Club session ends with the class participating in a teacher-facilitated discussion called "community share." During community share, I help students connect ideas, provide closure, and support their learning with instruction. Within my classroom's Book Club program, my students read, write about, and discuss literature on a daily basis (see Raphael, Pardo, Highfield, & McMahon, 1997). I am often amazed at the depth of thinking and the level of learning evident from their response logs and student talk.

When I began teaching using the Book Club program, I was so excited about what I saw my students doing that when my principal walked through my room one morning, I invited her to stay. As she roamed, she listened to my students discuss Speare's (1983) historical fiction, *The Sign of the Beaver.* They had just read the chapter where one of the main characters, a native American named Attean, begins teaching another main character, a young settler named Matt, how to survive in the Maine wilderness. Attean has a dog named Piz Wat, which means "good for nothing." Saknis, Attean's grandfather, calls the dog stupid. My students were vividly discussing the amazing lessons Matt was learning from Attean about how to fish, trap rabbits, mark and find trails; and they were relating these lessons to what they had learned on camping trips to northern Michigan and in scouting excursions. They were also discussing dogs they knew that were, like Piz Wat, "good for nothing" and telling stories from their families and neighbors of how these dogs proved they were not the most intelligent on the block.

I saw students demonstrating their understanding of main characters and key events in the story, and making connections from what they were reading to their own lives. However, after listening several minutes, my principal commented to me that this "discussion stuff is really nice, but weren't they a little off topic?" My principal is very involved in classroom learning. She had taught fifth grade for fifteen years prior to becoming a principal. I have a great deal of respect for her professionalism and her willingness to trust my judgment in implementing new classroom instructional programs. Thus, her comment led me to question and reflect on what I was trying to achieve in my classroom.

Within my classroom community, I had established what I viewed as authentic literacy learning. Students were connecting the text to their lives by relating their own real-life stories to those of the book. Their text comprehension was evident in the topics of discussion. Further, as I listened to them talk and as I read their response logs, I thought that my students were gaining an understanding of the historical fiction they were reading. They were staying on topic for long periods of time in their writing and their discussion, and they were actively engaged in real conversations about text. Their discussions were full of multiple interpretations and varied perspectives of understanding. Their debates and discussions were issue-oriented, focusing on meaningful topics, and they were applying these ideas in new situations.

When I began implementing student-led discussion groups in my classroom, I had strong theoretical foundations that supported my choice of curriculum and related activities, and that helped me understand why I might have high expectations of my students' literacy learning: (a) social constructivist theories of learning, (b) integrated instruction, (c) reader response theory, and (d) learning communities.

First, a large influence on my thinking had stemmed from articles I had read within my graduate program about social constructivist theories (e.g., Gavelek & Raphael, 1996; Wells & Chang-Wells, 1991; Barton, 1994). I resonated with this theory's emphasis on learning as social in nature, and that language plays a foundational role in learning and development of thought. I also related to the theory's tenet that students learn within a social context where there are more knowledgeable others to help them (also see Brock & Gavelek, Chapter 4).

Second, I related to recent articles arguing for the importance of integrating the English language arts—reading, writing, speaking, listening, and thinking—and providing a variety of opportunities for students to use oral and written language (Pearson, 1994; Lipson, Valencia, Wixson, & Peters, 1993). The notion of interdisciplinary integration that Lipson and her colleagues described provided much of my impetus to connect my Book Club program to my social studies instruction.

Third, I was influenced by writings about the importance of reader response, in articles by scholars such as Rosenblatt (1991). Just as Galda (Chapter 1) and Brock and Gavelek (Chapter 4) suggest, I believe that meaning is constructed through social interactions with the reader and the text, and that readers need a variety of types of responses and purposes for responding to literature (for further discussion of reader response, also see Sipe, Chapter 3).

Fourth, I have strong beliefs about the importance of creating what scholars have described, using various terms, as types of learning communities (e.g., Rogoff, 1994; Wells & Chang-Wells, 1992). In such communities, students are active contributors to their learning and can take risks in a safe setting.

On the day of my principal's visit and comment to me about whether students were on-topic, I was conflicted. I had a lot of reasons to feel strongly that my students were successfully engaged in challenging opportunities for learning. Some of my reasons stemmed from the theoretical perspective I had developed. Other reasons stemmed from what I thought I saw happening each day. However, that day, I realized that there was a lot about discussion in classrooms that I didn't understand. My principal's innocent comment made me search within my own definition of literacy and my beliefs in socially constructed learning for answers. I found myself asking a very important question: What evidence do I have that learning is taking place?

To address this question, I began to look closely at my literacy instruction. I decided to focus on the student-led discussion groups and the students' writing in preparation for these discussions, because they provide the central focus to the learning process in Book Club. I decided to conduct a research study within my fifth-grade classroom using methods for teacher research that I had practiced during my graduate study (see Hubbard & Power, 1993).

I would focus on the role of the book club discussions—preparation for discussion and engagement within small-group book clubs—in contributing to students' story understandings, their response to the literature, and their literacy learning.

TEACHER INQUIRY ABOUT STUDENT LITERACY LEARNING: THE STUDY

I begin with a description of the context of my study, including my classroom, my literature-based reading program, and connections between my reading and social studies curricula. Second, I briefly describe the unit in which I embedded my study. Third, I discuss the nature of the evidence in the study that I believe to be important indicators of students' learning. Fourth, I present examples of evidence from my analysis that indicate learning is taking place within the literature-based reading program.

The Context

This study takes place in a rural fifth-grade classroom that I taught during 1995–1996. Typical of students throughout the school, most of my students were from lower-middle socioeconomic income levels. Forty-five percent of the elementary school population receive free or reduced lunch, and fifteen percent of the population receive special education services. The literacy instruction most of my students had experienced prior to entering my classroom typically followed what might be called "traditional" approaches. Their teachers had used commercially published reading programs. Activities associated with reading involved reading a short story and answering comprehension questions. Teacher-led discussions dominated and teachers were generally looking for a predetermined "correct" answer to the questions they posed (see Cazden, 1988).

In my classroom, as I described earlier, I use Book Club as my literature-based reading program. This involves daily reading (20–30 minutes), followed by written responses in reading logs (5–15 minutes) where students use their writing as a thinking tool. Next, students have 5–15 minutes to discuss their thinking in student-led discussion groups (i.e., book clubs), followed by teacher-facilitated community share where instruction, closure, and connections of ideas take place in a whole-class setting. While most of my students had earlier experiences with literature in some form—sometimes at home, frequently in school-related activities—student-led discussion groups were new to them.

There are many opportunities for students to engage in meaningful literacy learning in my classroom besides Book Club. I emphasize literature in a variety of settings, from reading-aloud to sustained silent reading, from formal classroom instruction to independent activities. Students have a variety of opportunities to write about their learning. They create a range of texts during writing workshop, and often their story topics are extensions of topics and issues discussed in book clubs. They also have the benefit of writing across the curriculum, which means that they write in all subject areas for a number of purposes. Drop Everything and Read (DEAR), or sustained silent reading, occurs daily. I read aloud daily from a variety of text types for a variety of purposes. Community building is a foundational core that threads all of these literacy experiences together in my classroom.

As Valencia and Lipson (Chapter 5) and Peters and Wixson (Chapter 12) describe, I find it crucial to have central themes to guide my curriculum planning, instruction, and assessment. For the past four years, I have been developing interdisciplinary units to link social studies and literacy instruction (see Highfield & Folkert, 1997). For 1995–1996, I focused my social studies and literacy learning around three central themes:

- If we learn about the past, we can positively change our future.
- The lives we know and live are a result of events that took place in the past.
- History is made up of ordinary people making extraordinary sacrifices so that we can have the privileges we enjoy today.

In planning for the year, I developed four units that linked social studies and literacy instruction around these three themes. I also had literacy units that were unrelated to the themes (e.g., a genre study of fantasy, an author study) and I had social studies units that did not involve these themes or Book Club (e.g., presidential elections, government). I begin the year with two separate units, one each in social studies and literacy, to introduce students to researching American history (the subject area mandated by the district curriculum) and to the Book Club program, respectively. In social studies, I usually begin with a study of native Americans, engaging students in research about the tribes and clans present on the North American continent prior to European landing and exploration. Students learn about sources for information, how to use text features such as the index and table of contents, how to generate inquiry questions and maintain organized notes as they gather information from different sources, and so forth. They work in small groups, in dyads, and sometimes individually, to develop reports about the topics they have chosen within the unit of study.

To introduce students to Book Club, I generally use a single chapter book for the whole class, often a contemporary realistic fiction novel such as *Last Summer with Maizon* (Woodson, 1990). My instructional goals in this unit are for my students to learn what book clubs look like and how to be an actively participating member of a book club. I include mini-lessons related to reading, writing, discussion, and group work strategies. Each day, reading aloud from a picture book about Native American legends or a related topic, I model how to write and think about literature. I write sample entries on the overhead projector, emphasizing how I used writing as a tool for thinking.

In the fall when students read the Woodson novel, they practiced the specific journal entry that I had modeled. For example, I modeled how to critique the text in terms of what the author had done well, and what I thought the author could have done to improve the book. I modeled how an event or character in the book prompted me to think about my own life, a response we called "me and the book." I modeled what I noticed about how authors developed particular characters, how authors sequenced story events, questions I wished I could ask the author, or questions that I might ask others to help clarify my confusions. In short, sometimes through a mini-lesson, sometimes through modeling, I tried to introduce students to a range of ways of responding to literature (for details of this introductory unit, see Raphael et al., 1997, pp. 55–80).

As we finished the novel, students were also completing their social studies research about Native American tribes. Students shared what they had learned by making formal presentations to their peers, thus being recognized as "experts" in their chosen areas. The next Book Club chapter book was the novel, *The Sign of the Beaver.* Throughout this Book Club unit, I encouraged students to apply what they had learned about Native Americans from their social studies research and to apply what they had learned about engaging in Book Club to make their written responses and their small-group discussions more interesting. By focusing whole-class discussions on connecting their individual responses and small-group discussions to the three broad themes for the year related to history, I provided a framework for connecting across books, across discussions, and across disciplinary units.

During the second marking period, we focused on the Revolutionary War, the founding of the United States, and the Constitution in history. The unit connecting social studies and Book Club involved students conducting a research project about the American Revolutionary War, then reading an historical fiction novel from that era. During the third marking period, the integrated unit involved studying the Civil War, followed by reading related historical fiction. During this marking period, we also studied a fantasy novel and some fantasy picture books. In the fourth marking period, we integrated social studies and Book Club through examining different aspects of American history leading up to World War II, followed by an in-depth study of World War II with research and literature extensions.

The Focus Unit

While I had collected data throughout the year, I thought it important to concentrate on a single unit as a starting point for my data analysis. I chose the unit embedded within the study of the American Civil War to explore students' learning about both literacy and history. I selected the unit since it was mid-way through the school year and students were familiar with both Book Club and with conducting research about American history. In addition, students read multiple texts within the unit, including picture books (e.g., Polacco's [1994] *Pink and Say*), informational articles from newspapers and magazines, and culminating with the reading of an historical fiction chapter book, *Charley Skedaddle* (Beatty, 1987).

What Counts as Literacy Learning?

As I considered what counts as learning within a literature-based reading program, I was influenced by a number of forces. First, there was the district curriculum guide that suggested areas my fifth-graders must learn, both about American history and about particular literacy skills such as comprehension strategies (within reading) and composition processes such as planning, drafting, and publishing. Second, I had read articles (e.g., Au, Scheu, Kawakami, & Herman, 1990) that suggested areas, such as ownership, that weren't included in my district curriculum guide, but that I felt were important (see Au & Raphael, Chapter 6). Third, I had been a part of a teacher research group that frequently discussed what was and should be taught within literature-based instruction programs such as Book Club, leading me to consider different kinds of response to literature (i.e., personal, creative, and critical). Further, as Galda (Chapter 1) and Sipe (Chapter 3) note, reading and interpreting literature involve connections between events, places, themes, and characters from the story and those from the readers' own lives. Fourth, I was influenced by articles on integrated and thematic instruction (e.g., Lipson et al., 1993) that underscore the importance of students connecting across the various texts they were reading.

Fifth, related to the writings on integrated instruction was extensive literature on the importance of intertextual connections, something I emphasized in my own teaching. In the articles I read, intertextuality was described in terms of synthesizing ideas from many text sources as writers compose (Spivey, 1991) as well as across conversations and written texts (Bloome & Bailey, 1992). I liked the image that Hartman (1992) offered of intertextuality being a prism where meaning is influenced or "refracted" by the sign system, history, reader, author, and context. In fact, Short (1992) suggests that intertextuality is a metaphor for learning and meaning-making since it captures how meaning is made through the social interactions among and between multiple readers and multiple texts. Short makes a case that research into intertextuality should not simply look at the types of connections, but should focus on how educators can create a setting where collaboration and inquiry as a basis for learning are encouraged and supported.

Together, these ideas suggest to me that for me to say that learning had occurred, I would need to have evidence that

- my students demonstrated ownership over their literacy activities;
- my students demonstrated their comprehension by connecting to other texts and others' ideas, and by extending their own background knowledge;
- my students used writing as a tool for preparing for their book club discussion, indicated understanding of how authors craft their books, and demonstrated they are facile with the different parts of a book;
- my students engaged in a range of responses to the literature they read; and
- my students were able to make effective use of the conventions of language—how our language systems (both oral and written) work.

I structured my study so that I could gather writing samples from their response logs. I took observational notes as I circulated around the room during their writing time and their discussion time. I also audio-taped discussions so that I could compare what students were self-reporting and what I was actually observing. I used transcripts of discussions and field notes. I began by analyzing the subset of these data that I had collected during the unit about the Civil War.

Analyzing Students' Writing and Discussions for Evidence of Learning

Au and Raphael (Chapter 6) discuss learning that takes place in literature-based instruction in terms of five categories: ownership, comprehension, composition, literary aspects, and language conventions. I draw on these categories as I present evidence of learning that takes place in my fifth-grade classroom.

Ownership. Ownership is an aspect of student learning that I emphasize in all areas of instruction. In literacy instruction, one of my goals is for students to demonstrate ownership in a variety of ways. For example, students may choose to read a book for fun that is connected to the theme being studied in class. They may use their writing as a thinking tool for their own purposes, or they may choose to rewrite or extend a story during process writing time.

At the conclusion of reading and discussing *Charley Skedaddle,* Natalie's written response shows ownership. She clearly values reading, has a positive attitude, enjoys reading, and shows a strong desire to share her love of reading with her family. This attitude comes through in several ways. First, in line 2, she indicates that she thinks her mother and sister would enjoy reading the book on their own. In lines 3 and 4, she suggests that her brother would not be able to read it because he doesn't "take pleasure in reading," but indicates two ways she sees helping him overcome what is, to her, a shortcoming. First, she could read to her brother (line 6); second, he could be assigned to my class in a future year so that he would be introduced to "wonderful" books (lines 7–8). Natalie writes:

1 This book was just wonderful! I love this book, as a matter of fact, I think I'll take it

2 home and read it to my mom or just have my sister read it, but I can't have my brother

3 read it cause it takes forever for him to read a 12 page book! This is because he doesn't

4 take pleasure in reading. (What I said about the 12 page book isn't true, but it sure feels

5 like it!) I love all the books you read to us. I want to take them all home and read them

6 to my brother or just have him read them. I want him to be in this class so he can read

7 all of these books cause there just so wonderful! (By the way have you noticed a strong

8 liking between me and the books.)

True to her beliefs, the following year, when Natalie discovered that her brother was not placed in my room, she came to me and asked what I could do to have him moved to my room, so that he could learn to love reading. While it was beyond my control, her follow-through and genuine interest in another's literacy learning further emphasizes Natalie's ownership and sense of agency around literacy learning.

Comprehension. I believe that comprehension is the foundation of literacy learning. As a teacher, I look for evidence in students' written responses and discussions that they have a conventional understanding of what is taking place in the story. In addition to evidence that they know the storyline, I try to push my students further to link their reading to their daily lives. In the examples that follow, I provide evidence that students used their background knowledge to make predictions about what will happen in the text, interpret characters' behaviors to make sense of what is happening in the story, and use imagery to help them understand and remember story events.

Many researchers have described how important background knowledge is to making sense of text events. In one scene near the middle of the novel, *Charley Skedaddle,* during the Battle of the Wilderness, Charley flees the battle. Confederate troops capture him the following day. Rather than send such a young drummer boy to a prison camp, an official allows Charley to escape through a flap in a tent, advising him to flee west. In another scene, the author conveyed how badly Charley wanted to return to the only home he had known, New York City. Thus, readers must sort through why—given the chance to escape and return home—Charley does not do so. In the following written response, Edie demonstrates how she uses her knowledge of geography to help her understand why Charley may not be able to return home, despite the kindness of the official. She writes:

> I don't think Charley will make it back home (to New York) because the only way to go is west and New York is North of Virginia.

Comprehension also involves understanding how characters evolve throughout a story, and what might motivate such changes. In one of his entries, Alex traces the attitude and personality changes taking place in the main character. He credits the author for her skill in conveying Charley's feelings (lines 2–3), then describes how Charley felt initially about his guardians and being a Bowery Boy (lines 4–6), and how the battle has changed his outlook or, using Alex's word, "opinion" about both New York and about himself (lines 7–9). Alex writes:

1 I thought the Battle of the Wilderness was the best chapter so far. The author did a very

2 good job of describing how like when the man died and when Charley did not feel very

3 good about himself she did good at explaining how he felt . . . I see a difference in

4 Charleys opinion. When he was in New York City he would do anything to get away

5 from Mr. Demrest and Noreen and he thought he was so cool being a Bowrey Boy, but

6 now (after the battle) he wants to go back to New York even if he has to be with Mr.

7 Demarest and Noreen and he doesn't feel very good about himself after he killed that man

8 and ran away from the army. He thinks he's a coward and nobody likes
him.

A third way in which I found students evidencing their comprehension
was through the imagery they created around particular story events. While I
discourage students from frequently drawing pictures in response to what
they've read, rather than engaging in sustained writing and other forms of
analysis, I think that pictures provide important outlets for students' thoughts.
Further, as you can see in Jay's pencil drawing (see Figure 8.1), sometimes
words are unable to capture the vividness of a readers' mental image.

Jay's picture was drawn in response to an event in *Charley Skedaddle*
when Charley finds an old woman, Jerusha, living alone in the hills of Ten-
nessee. He stays with her for a time doing odd jobs for her. One night, a
panther, or mountain lion, raids the chicken coop. The author vividly describes the incident leading Jay to use another sign symbol, art, to convey his
comprehension of the incident. In this pencil drawing, Jay shows the West
Virginia hills in the background, the cottage with a fireplace, the fence of the
chicken coop with a hole broken through where the panther got in to kill the

Figure 8.1

chickens, and the stocky nature of the animal. He accurately depicts the panther with a front twisted paw and a chicken that was not lucky enough to survive. After looking at this drawing, I had no question in my mind that Jay thoroughly comprehended both the setting, the action, and the vivid description of the incident. Further, I was convinced that his picture illustrates the maxim that, "A picture is worth a thousand words."

I saw evidence of students using both their individual written responses, as well as their peers' insights within their book club discussions, to help them comprehend the story. In their logs, they occasionally noted that an important part, or perhaps the intended purpose, of book club discussions was to help them figure out what was taking place in the story and to share their individual interpretations to learn from each other. As Tiffany suggests in one log entry:

> . . . I think it (discussion) helps me understand how the other people think the way I think. It really makes me feel very strong about the way I think. Sometimes I ask question(s and) they help me understand about what I asked.

Her entry suggests that she engages in a certain amount of self-monitoring. She indicates that at times, her peers simply help her feel even more strongly about a particular response she's had or a position she's taken; while at other times, her peers are a source of support for her when she is confused or needs some help making sense of the story. Through writing, through pictures, and through talk, my students indicated both their comprehension and their comprehension processes.

Composition. Composition entails students learning about both forms and functions of writing, and they can reveal their understanding in many ways. We study form in terms of specific text structures, features of books, sustained writing forms as well as informal writing such as occurs in response logs. We study functions of writing from conveying information to persuading readers to recording ideas. Evidence that students are learning about the forms and functions of writing abound in my classroom, in their research reports, creative writing, and response logs. Their learning is also evident in the way they talk about books and their features. I present two examples that draw on evidence from their conversations as well as their writing.

The first example illustrates how, through conversation, my students draw on their understanding of form and function as they try to understand why Charley begins to call himself Charley Skedaddle, rather than his given name, Charley Quinn. This involves their understanding that Charley has left his post; the meaning of the word, skedaddle; and Charley's own disappointment with his performance in battle. They eventually point to the book's jacket, which they understand can be used to entice the reader into the story.

Jim begins the exchange by noting that he thinks Charley is going to run home because the book cover suggests he may be a coward. This leads to discussion about whether the cowardice stems from running away from home or running away from battle. Mary draws on the back cover where she finds the word *skedaddle*, which the students realize explains Charley's use of the name.

Jim: I think he might go home cause on the front of the book it says "Is Charley really a coward?" cause he might of ran away from the war.

Mary: I don't really think

Mark: No, he's a coward because he ran away from home.

Mary: He ran away from, no, he ran away from, it says on the back that he ran away, see? (pointing to the back cover of the book on her desk)

Jim: from his home

Mary: (reading the back cover) Charley is terrified, he skedaddles away from both union and the union army.

As their conversation continues, the students note that by skedaddling away, he is showing he is a coward, and by taking the name Charley Skedaddle, he is admitting to himself that he did not behave bravely as he had earlier bragged that he would. The students are aware of the information on book jackets, as well as of the importance of conflict for moving a story forward. They have learned that conflict can involve a character against a system (as is the case in his fighting in the army) as well as internal conflict within the character (as reflected in his choice of the name, Skedaddle).

In my second example, Jake demonstrates an intertextual connection between *Charley Skedaddle* and a book he had read earlier, Collier and Collier's (1974) *My Brother Sam Is Dead.* In the latter book, Collier and Collier had used the literary convention of an epilogue to let the reader know what had happened to the characters after the events in the story had ended. Jake has critiqued the way Speare chose to end *Charley Skedaddle,* suggesting that there were too many loose ends to the story, too many questions unanswered about what happened to the characters. One comment from his longer entry draws on his preference for the way the other authors resolved their book:

. . . I think this book would of been better if it would of had an epilogue in it like in "My Brother Sam is Dead."

He applied his understanding of the function of an epilogue to a new text, and the following week wrote an epilogue during writing workshop. This served as his closure. He then volunteered to read the epilogue in the Author's Chair, leading to a lively discussion about his conclusions and his decisions to end the story the way that he chose. This sequence of events—critiquing lack of closure, suggesting an epilogue, writing one himself, and sharing it with his peers for consideration—illustrate how he drew on the literature he had read to make sense of new texts and to craft his own writing, and he participated as an active member of the writing community in sharing his writing with his classmates.

Literary Aspects.   A third area of learning crucial within a literature-based curriculum involves literary aspects, including the study of literary elements (i.e., theme, point of view, plot, setting, and characters) and response to literature (i.e., personal, creative, and critical). This knowledge is crucial so my students can better appreciate and analyze their texts and their own writing. In the examples that follow, my students provide evidence that they are learning about the literature's content and themes, about how authors craft texts, and about how, as readers, they can draw on this knowledge to help them make sense of the stories they read.

Many of the books we read are challenging for my students, complex in their structures, in the number of characters, and in their themes and issues. Alex has learned that knowing who each character is—their key traits, what motivates them—supports comprehension. Thus, he's created a one-page entry in his reading log that he can add to as the story proceeds, to help him keep track of each character who is introduced. He lists the characters' names, as well as short descriptions of traits he thinks might prove to be important as the story develops. In his map, early in his reading of *Charley Skedaddle,* he lists:

Character Map

1 Charley—is a rough boy that lives in NYC That's the only place he's ever been.

2 Jonney—By the way the author described him it sounds like he's something like

3 Sam in My Brother Sam is Dead.

4 Norine and Michael Demarest—She doesn't know what she's doing. She's

5 marrying Mr. Demarest a real jerk who totally ignores Charley and says he'll throw

6 Charley in a orphanage if he doesn't behave when they're married. Noreen is a

7 lady who works as a hat trimmer since her mother and father are dead she uses the

8 money she makes to buy food and clothes for Charley and her.

Note the features he has identified for each character. Charley is "rough" and has never left New York (line 1); Norine is naive ("doesn't know what she's doing," line 4), but kind (line 8); Mr. Demarest is a "real jerk" (lines 5–6). Notice also how he uses intertextual connections as a form of shorthand, reflected in his describing Jonney as being like Sam in another novel he had read (lines 2–3).

Another way in which characters are made memorable as students read is through imagery. Imagability is a factor that Hiebert (see Chapter 9) describes as being important to early readers. I found that imagability provides an important source of support for older readers as well. The picture of a character that students have in their minds is rarely static. Rather, the ever-changing mental image of a particular character helps them make sense of the story, relate to story events, and engage in discussion with each other. Students draw pictures, share them, and then elaborate on their descriptions. Valerie's reading log entry provides evidence that her book club group has helped her to form initial images and change those images in her mind. She writes:

1   The stuff that I realized . . . is how granny Bent really looks. I see her different

2   now. She wears overalls and has patches in them I don't think the cabbin looks different

3   in my mind now. I picture the mountain lion, or panther, or painter however you want to

4   say it well I picture it like Hobbs from Calvin and Hobbs . . .

The images shift and change in Valerie's mind, as she notes that she sees grandmother in a different way after her discussion with her peers (lines 1–2). Also, she combines what makes sense to her about Granny Bent and where Granny lives based on what others in the group have described, as well as her own sources of knowledge for developing images, including familiar cartoons (e.g., "like Hobbs from Calvin and Hobbs," lines 4–5).

Response—personal, creative, and critical—is another important area of literary aspects. My students use their reading logs as a site for engaging in response before they meet with their peers to talk about the book. This helps them prepare for discussion, but perhaps more important, gives them a chance to engage personally with the text before their own responses are influenced by their peers.

Personal response takes place when students write their impressions about books or events in books. Creative response occurs when students play with the text, extend their creative ideas into the text and "muck around" (Short, 1992) with the ideas. In the following example, Karen combines personal and creative response as she considers what might happen to Charley. She writes:

> I hope that the regiment Charley comes from doesn't find him and take him back. I wonder if someone does write a letter to Noreen and she freaks. I hope so because she might think It's her fault and not marry Michael Demarest because he's a jerk. I hope Noreen and Michael don't get married. Personally I don't think they belong together.

Sometimes a personal response emerges because something in the story reminds my students of events from their own lives or those of their friends or family. Alex had such a response toward the end of *Charley Skedaddle,* which takes place in the hills of West Virginia. He writes:

> My mom and dad know what it's like to live in the mountains because they went to college at West Virginia Mountaineers in Morgantown. They also lived in Charleston W.V. and Raleigh N.C. . . .

This simple comment provides evidence of Alex's recognition of the realism within Beatty's descriptions of the setting, since the descriptions remind him of his parents' stories of their college lives and beyond.

Critical response involves a reader stepping back to analyze the text, studying it to interpret and understand it, and judge the effectiveness of the author as storyteller. I see evidence of students' critical response in their reading logs as well as during their book club discussions. For example, Alex engages in critical response when he looks at Beatty's ability to describe scenes and events in the story:

> I thought the author did a very good job of describing how Charley felt when he first smelt clean air and when he saw the blue harbor for the first time. If I were Charley I'd be afraid of an ambush when he's on the train. I like this chapter better.

Similarly, Jim engages in critical response during his book club discussion group. He states,

> I think Charley is pretty cool. When Charley, that reminded me of my life because I always get in a lot of fights. I would, I would be going crazy if I had to go on that boat with all that gambling and all them drunken men. I like how the author really desscribed the fight and he (sic) used a lot of exciting words. This is really a cool book.

Jim explains his own ability to connect to Charley, citing the author's skill in describing a fight and complimenting the author's use of exciting words. In this way, he provides reasons for his statements that Charley "is pretty cool" and that he thinks the book is also "cool."

While I am pleased when I see evidence that my students have learned something that I have taught, I am even more satisfied when I see them transforming what I have taught in ways that they find meaningful. The next example illustrates learning as transformation. Mark demonstrates that he has learned about the literary element, point of view. He also has learned a related form of personal response where he places himself in the character's situation. Further, he has learned that he can create new ways of responding, transforming ones that I had explicitly taught or modeled.

In Chapter 3, Sipe describes the ways in which young children use humor in their response to literature. I found that, like the younger students, mine create humor for a variety of reasons. Sometimes it is invited by the texts themselves—books written to be funny. But sometimes, as in the following example, I believe my students use humor as a form of relief from the intensity and challenging nature of the themes we have been emphasizing. While they have not shied away from these themes in their discussions, they sometimes seek relief through their play with language and text, through creative response to the literature. Mark writes an entry in his reading log in response to a scene when Charley flees the Union army in the novel and hides in the dense thickets and undergrowth of the wilderness. While hiding, a rabbit, who also flees from the battle site, huddles with him until Charley pounds his fists into the ground out of fear and frustration and frightens it away. Mark writes:

> I will do a point of view of the rabbit. Hey little boy what is wrong? I wonder what is wrong with him. He probably shot someone. Well do you want to talk? Hey don't you fall on me. Ahhhhh! Now just call me "Bunny Skedaddle."

In their book club discussion groups that day Mark shares his humor with his group as they discuss this point of view (lines 1–2). He discovers that one of his book club peers, Jim, also wrote an entry from the rabbit's point of view (lines 4–7).

1 Mark: You know what I made the rabbit say? No, the rabbit's name, cause the rabbit

2   ran away too is Bunny Skedaddle.

3 Mary: Bunny Skedaddle (laughs)

4 Jim: I did a point of view of the rabbit, it says, Hey little boy, what's wrong? By the

5   way, why are you, what are you doing out here? Hello! Hello! He's not

6   listening. He's getting all mad. Fine. If you don't like me hit
           your hands on the ground,
7   you think I care? See ya.
8 Mark: Oh, I...
9   Jim: 'Cause, the bunny ran away.
10 Mary: . . . the bunny ran away.

The students engage in a brief interaction, playing with the language of the text and the themes in the story. They maintain the name, Skedaddle, that Charley had chosen, indicating that they understand that play on words. Further, they take a symbolic scene in which, like a frightened rabbit, Charley hides in the woods, and they play with it from the rabbit's point of view. They draw on their knowledge of folk tales and other stories where animals can talk. And, in doing so, they have a brief respite from—though not unrelated to—the more intense discussions about honor, courage, and self-recrimination. While some, like my principal, may interpret this as being a bit "off-task," I find that such brief escapes are rich in the evidence of how students transform learned strategies to meet their particular purposes.

Language Conventions. A fourth key curricular area is that of language conventions. Such conventions are at the heart of how we can communicate through a symbolic system such as language. As literate individuals, we count on the ordered nature of our language to support our ability to recognize words, put words together to form sentences, organize our thoughts and convey them through sustained writing, and interact with others. As Au and Raphael describe in Chapter 6, language conventions include print conventions (e.g., spelling, grammar, punctuation) and group interaction rules and organization.

I observe my students for evidence they are learning conventions for conveying ideas in print and through talk and for interacting with their peers in meaningful and supportive ways. In the following student-led discussion, Lynn's group discusses spelling issues and dialect issues that they notice while they are reading. This attention to language conventions is often expanded and extended in process writing settings. Yet, it comes up in discussions, which shows evidence that students actively and metacognitively incorporate this into their daily literacy learning. In the first example, students briefly discuss how to spell "colonel," one of the words that Lynn had recorded in her reading log as a "wonderful word," a word worth bringing to the attention of her peers:

Lynn: I wrote, um, colonel, (as a wonderful word) look at how it's
       spelled.

Mark: they write c-ol-o-nel (pronouncing each sound as he says the word)

Lynn: That's how it's really spelled.

Mary: I got

Lynn: In Mr. H's class (last year), we did that word as a spelling word.

Lynn had the word as a spelling word the previous year, remembered its unusual spelling, and thought it worth pointing out to her peers.

Later, Lynn and Alex both show evidence that they are aware of how dialect is represented by the author through her spelling. During a book club conversation, Lynn points to the book as she explains something she had in her reading log to her peers, ". . . And I wrote better'n, better'n. Look, (pointing to the book) apostrophe n." Alex notices an unusual spelling and writes a wonderful word entry in his reading log as he tries to figure out what the new spellings mean:

> I found 2 wonderful words. They are ain'tcha and git. I'm wondering
> if this is supposed to mean like get outta here and they used git in-
> stead of get in the 1860's.

I found Alex's reflection about the two words to be consistent with his over-all interest in history. He often points out to other students how historical events fit into the story line. Alex's comment suggests to me that even though he is learning particular conventions of our language as we use it today, and as used in books, he also understands that language changes over time.

CONCLUDING COMMENTS

I am grateful to my principal for being such an active instructional leader. Just as I want my students to take risks with their learning, I appreciate the environment she has created that allows me to take risks—clearly informed ones—with my own teaching. Also, just as she plays an active role in moni-toring the teaching that occurs in the school and tries to support our efforts, I wish to monitor my students' learning and support them in their efforts. My principal's visit to my classroom and her comment that simultaneously val-ued the discussion while asking me to judge its appropriateness led to my engaging in this teacher research project.

Through my research, I learned a great deal about student discussion, literature-based instruction, and what qualifies as "learning" in my fifth-grade classroom community. Taking a closer look at my students' writing and dis-cussions has led me to believe that they focus for extended periods of time on important themes and issues related to the books they are reading. They maintain their focus through their individual reading and writing and their small-group and whole-class discussions. I also saw evidence of how much my students were learning about literacy and literature through the activities that constitute my literature-based instruction. As a reflective teacher researcher, I appreciate comments and interest in the learning that is taking place my classroom. I have extended open invitations to my superintendent, assistant superintendent, and all of my colleagues to come and see for themselves the wide range of literacy learning that is taking place in room 19.

In my analysis, I saw how reading, writing, and discussion each provide essential opportunities for learning in my classroom; they serve as settings where my students can make intertextual connections that foster thought, change, and the extension of ideas. What I found to be particular interesting was the crucial role of discussion in students' literacy development and as a site for my evaluation of their literacy learning. Dyson and Freedman (1991) underscore the importance of social interaction in children's learning within the classroom and the foundational role of discussion, suggesting that "Schools can maintain order and organization, but they cannot remain halls of silence" (page 776).

ACKNOWLEDGEMENT

This chapter was prepared at the National Research Center on English Learning and Achievement (CELA), Wise Center for Educational Research (WCER), School of Education, University of Wisconsin–Madison. The Center is supported by the U.S. Department of Education Office of Educational Research and Improvement (Awared #R305A60005). However, the views expressed herein are those of the author and do not necessarily reflect the views of the department.

ENDNOTE

1. Throughout the chapter, I differentiate the Book Club program, using upper-case initial letters, from the small, student-led discussion groups or book clubs, which I refer to in lower-case letters.

REFERENCES

Au, K. H., Scheu, J. A., Kawakami, A. J., & Herman, P. A. (1990). Assessment and accountability in a whole literacy curriculum. *The Reading Teacher, 43,* 574–578.

Barton, D. (1994). *Literacy: An introduction to the ecology of written language.* Cambridge, MA: Blackwell.

Bloome, D., & Bailey, F. M. (1992). Studying language and literacy through events, particularity, and intertextuality. In R. Beach, J. L. Green, M. L. Kamil, & T. Shanahan (Eds.), *Multidisciplinary perspectives on literacy research* (pp. 181–210). Urbana, IL: National Conference on Research in English and the National Council of Teachers of English.

Cazden, C. (1988). *Classroom discourse: The language of teaching and learning.* Portsmouth, NH: Heinemann.

Dyson, A. H., & Freedman, S. W. (1991). Writing. In J. Flood, J. M. Jenson, D. Lapp, & J. R. Squire, *Handbook of research on teaching the English language arts* (pp. 754–774). New York: Macmillan.

Gavelek, J. R., & Raphael, T. E. (1996). Changing talk about text: New roles for teachers and students. *Language Arts, 73*(3), 182–192.

Goatley, V., Highfield, K., Bentley, J., Pardo, L. S., Folkert, J., Scherer, P., Raphael, T. E., & Grattan, K. (1994). Empowering teachers to be researchers: A collaborative approach. *Teacher Research: The Journal of Classroom Inquiry, 1*(2), 128–144.

Hartman, K. (1992). Intertextuality and reading: The text, the reader, the author, and the context. *Linguistics and Education, 4,* 295–311.

Highfield, K., & Folkert, J. (1997). Book Club: The content area connection. In Raphael, T. E., & McMahon, S. I. *The Book Club connection: Literacy learning and classroom talk* (pp. 286–298). New York: Teachers College Press.

Hubbard, R. S., & Power, B. M. (1993). *The art of classroom inquiry: A handbook for teacher-researchers.* Portsmouth, NH: Heinemann.

Lipson, M. Y., Valencia, S. W., Wixson, K. K., & Peters, C. W. (1993). Integration and thematic teaching: Integration to improve teaching and learning. *Language Arts, 70*(4), 252–263.

McMahon, S. I., & Raphael, T. E., with Goatley, V. J., & Pardo, L. S. (1997). *The Book Club connection: Literacy learning and classroom talk.* New York: Teachers College Press.

Pearson, P. D. (1994). Integrated language arts: Sources of controversy and seeds of consensus. In L. M. Morrow, J. K. Smith, & L. C. Wilkinson (Eds.), *Integrated language arts: Controversy to consensus* (pp. 11–31). Needham Heights, MA: Allyn and Bacon.

Raphael, T. E., & McMahon, S. I. (1994). "Book Club": An alternative framework for reading instruction. *The Reading Teacher, 48*(2), 102–118.

Raphael, T. E., Pardo, L. S., Highfield, K., & McMahon, S. I. (1997). *Book Club: A literature-based curriculum.* Littleton, MA: Small Planet Communication, Inc.

Rogoff, B. (1994). Developing understanding of the idea of communities of learners. *Mind, Culture, and Activity, 1*(4), 209–229.

Rosenblatt, L. M., (1991). Literature-S.O.S.! *Language Arts, 68*(6), 444–448.

Short, K. (1992). Researching intertextuality within collaborative classroom learning environments. *Linguistics and Education, 4,* 313–333.

Spivey, N. N. (1981). Discourse synthesis: Questions/answers. In K. S. Jongsma (Ed.), *Questions and Answers Column. The Reading Teacher,* 702–703.

Wells, G., & Chang-Wells, G. L. (1992). *Constructing knowledge together.* Portsmouth, NH: Heinemann Educational Books.

CHILDREN'S BOOKS CITED

Beatty, P. (1987). *Charley Skedaddle.* New York: Troll.

Collier, J. L., & Collier, C. (1974). *My brother Sam is dead.* Lancaster, PA: Four Winds Publishing.

Polacco, P. (1994). *Pink and Say.* New York: The Putnam Publishing Group.

Speare, E. (1983). *The sign of the beaver.* New York: Bantam Doubleday Dell Publishing Group.

Woodson, J. (1990). *Last summer with Maizon.* New York: Dell.

Chapter 9

Selecting Texts for Beginning Reading Instruction

●————————●

Elfrieda H. Hiebert, University of Michigan

Walking into Mrs. Grattan's first-grade classroom, visitors can't help but notice that literature pervades the room (Grattan, 1997). On the south wall are tall bookcases filled with I-Can-Read books such as *Frog and Toad Are Friends* (Lobel, 1970), books created by children over the years, books that follow a character such as Arthur (Brown, 1993), and outstanding picture books, ranging from fairly easy reads such as Fox's (1988) *Hattie and the Fox* to more complex stories such as McCully's (1991) *Mirette on the High Wire.* Along the back of the room are more bookcases, again filled with books. On top of each bookcase are books grouped by different themes and topics (see Valencia & Lipson, Chapter 5), invitingly displayed. By the north wall, under the windows, are plastic tubs and crates, again filled with different kinds of books. Further, student anthologies from a popular basal reading program are in a nearby set of shelves. Clearly, Mrs. Grattan values and uses literature as a foundation for literacy instruction. But, Mrs. Grattan and other first grade teachers (see Chapter 6 for a description of Mrs. Araki's classroom) face some particularly difficult decisions once they've elected to move away from the "graded" reading materials of the basal reading program to building a program around trade books.

Teachers such as Mrs. Grattan and Mrs. Araki want their students to love literature, to understand the stories they read and hear, and to engage in reading and response to interesting stories, compelling nonfiction, and informational storybooks (Hiebert & Raphael, 1997), but this creates dilemmas. First, while teachers readily can identify compelling stories to read to children, it is more challenging to identify high-quality literature that young children can read, at least at what has been termed an "instructional level." That is, with support, young children could read and make sense of the text. What can and should students be able to read independently? What are the features of these books? Second, while teachers want to use "real" literature from the body of published texts written by recognized children's authors, these are not written with literacy instruction in mind. Thus, they may present challenges to young readers (e.g., finding print in the midst of an illustration, understanding left-right progression when the author may be playing with text placement), making it difficult to practice literacy skills they are learning. Third, our field has justifiably—but rapidly—moved away from relatively limited readability formulas that determined text difficulty using only a few factors (e.g., word frequency, sentence length). Yet, nothing has replaced these formulas to guide text selection.

How can teachers of young children make informed choices about literature to use within their reading programs? What books should teachers select for students to read on their own? Which ones serve important purposes for teachers to read aloud? What kind of books provide the practice students need for becoming fluent readers? What of the tension between wanting to have students read from high-quality literature while, at the same time, ensuring that they practice those word recognition skills that are fundamental to successful reading? To begin to answer these questions, my colleagues and I observed in classrooms and interviewed children (Fisher & Hiebert, 1990; Hagerty & Hiebert, 1989; Hiebert, Liu, Levin, Huxley, & Chung, 1995). The teachers in these classrooms were using literature to teach reading, and the students I focused most closely on were those who struggled the most in learning to read. What I found was that, while many of these struggling readers enjoy listening to books read aloud, they have not made much progress toward independent reading and writing.

I read the research literature—much of it written from perspectives of cognitive psychology and emergent literacy—about early readers and early literacy instruction. I then made connections between what I was reading and what I was observing among young readers and writers. Together, the readings and the research helped me develop a theoretical framework that can serve as a useful guide for teachers' decision-making about text selection, as well as a guide for future research by classroom and university researchers.

A unifying theme throughout the framework is that texts can serve as "scaffolds" for students' learning. The metaphor of a scaffold has been used often in the research literature to describe features that, like a building's scaffold, provide *temporary, adjustable support* to young learners (Wood, Bruner, & Ross, 1976). Scaffolds in texts can come from many different features: pictures, the frequency of the words that are used, the patterns of the words, and so forth. In this chapter, I describe different perspectives literacy educators and researchers have held about text scaffolds for beginning readers. Second, I present the components of a model of how these scaffolds work together to support beginning reading. Third, I present a set of guidelines for teachers who are seeking ways to support beginning readers' acquisition of independent reading skills—skills that include interest and engagement in the ideas of texts.

PERSPECTIVES OF TEXT SCAFFOLDS FOR BEGINNING READERS

Why don't we have more guidelines today for selecting literature appropriate for different aspects of the literature-based instructional program for beginning readers? The answer to this question lies in the kinds of beginning reading materials that long dominated in the United States.

High-Frequency and Phonetically Regular Words as a Basis for Text Selection and Creation

For most of this century, literature was not used in the early reading texts that were used to instruct American children. Instead, texts for beginning readers were developed to feature one of the following:

- high-frequency words (Elson & Gray, 1930; Thorndike, 1921) such as *and, the, of,* and *or.*
- phonetically regular words (Bloomfield & Barnhart, 1961; Chall, 1967/1982; Flesch, 1957) such as *cat, hat, rat, sat, bat.*

Generations of American school children learned to read with texts that emphasized high-frequency words, such as prepositions, articles, and conjunctions (e.g., *of, the, and*) that serve critical functions in sentences. Texts of this type were based on suggestions from educational psychologists such as Thorndike (1921) and Gray (Elston & Gray, 1930), who helped create the early Scott-Foresman basal readers. For decades, these early programs were updated, but philosophically remained unchanged.

Selections with high-frequency words dominated the children's collection of stories in the basal readers. The story, "Tiny" (Rider, 1986) is illustrative of these texts and reflects a somewhat "modern" version that might still be found in today's classrooms. Other than the name of the main character (i.e., Tiny), 18 high-frequency words are combined to create a story about two children who need to capture an escaped baby pig. The scene in which the children solve the problem by scattering food to allure Tiny back into the pen is captured by, "I have it! Now we will get Tiny. Tiny will want to come" (p. 23). As is typical, little of the story is conveyed through the language of the text.

In the 1950s and 1960s, phonetically regular words were suggested as the basis for the texts of early reading instruction (Bloomfield & Barnhart,

1961; Chall, 1967/1982; Flesch, 1957). Developers of reading programs based on word regularity followed similar procedures as in the past. They created contrived texts to highlight a word's feature. For example, in the text, *The Bad Fan* (Rasmussen & Goldberg, 1964), a set of characters named Dad, Nan, and Dan engage in a series of actions that involve a fan. The denouement of the passage is expressed as "Dad had a bad fan." As was typical, the text conveys little of the story, instead focusing on the phoneme /an/. While such texts were neither used universally in American schools nor produced strong evidence that more children learned to read at higher levels as a result of their use (Bond & Dykstra, 1967), phonetically regular texts continue to be presented as a panacea for American reading problems (Adams, Bereiter, Hirshberg, Anderson, & Bernier, 1995).

Texts based on high-frequency words dominated instructional materials and assessments through readability formulas. The presence of words on high-frequency word lists was one of the factors used to establish the ease or difficulty of texts in most readability formulas (Klare, 1984). To ensure that a text was viewed to be readable, adjustments would have been of the following type (from a current favorite, Henkes's (1996) *Lilly's Purple Plastic Purse*): An uncommon word such as "permitted" might be substituted with a high-frequency word such as "let," "creations" with "things," or "jaunty" with "happy." In the mid-1980s, a number of researchers analyzed the effects of such changes in texts on children's comprehension (e.g., Beck, McKeown, Omanson, & Pople, 1984; Brennan, Bridge, & Winograd, 1986). They showed that children were able to understand original stories more successfully than the rewritten "easier" ones. The original stories had structures that fit the expectations of readers regarding stories. The original stories also had descriptions and actions that were memorable for readers and made sense. This research helped set the stage for shifting the focus away from "words used" "to literary merit." However, this new criterion has presented new challenges for beginning reading instruction.

Literary Quality as the Basis for Text Selection

With the publication of *Becoming a Nation of Readers* (Anderson, Hiebert, Scott, & Wilkinson, 1985), the findings on the possible problems of contrived texts for meaningful reading were shared with literacy educators beyond the research community. This message resonated with what teachers had observed as they taught young children, and educators at many levels shared the belief that different books were needed. They turned to trade books—written by authors for children's pleasure and learning, not for school instruction.

However, there were few guidelines for making decisions about what kinds of stories within the realm of high-quality literature could be used to support students' literacy learning. Moreover, concerns about "basalizing" the literature and ruining the literary experience were raised. Despite these concerns, high-quality literature became the norm for teaching literacy to students of all ages and levels of readers. For example, in California, trade books had been mandated in the California English/Language Arts Framework Committee (1987); in Texas, through the Texas Education Agency (1990). Because of the influence of these large, state-adoption states, basal reading programs replaced contrived text with literature selections. For example, in the series in which the story, Tiny, appeared, a new story featuring a pig was included. This selection, *If I Had a Pig* (Inkpen, 1988), uses a predictable pattern, narrated by a child describing a fanciful set of events that he and his pet pig might do: make a house, paint pictures, have fights, and so forth until it is time to "tell him a story and take him to bed."

Initial studies such as that by Hiebert et al. (1995) indicate that unless children have a substantial foundation in emergent literacy at the beginning of first grade, they struggle when literary quality is the sole or primary criterion for selecting passages. At the end of first grade, about 45 percent of the children in literature-based classrooms were not able to read trade books that were less difficult than *If I Had a Pig*. There are just too many unknown words with complex features for those children who are not already competent readers to learn. These findings contributed to my focus on features of texts that could potentially scaffold beginning readers' literacy learning. Further, I was interested in how particular features of text that support independent reading skills could be balanced with literary merit.

A FRAMEWORK FOR TEXT SELECTION

In today's polarized and politicized debate about beginning reading instruction, there are striking differences in views of what constitutes effective early reading instruction (Honig, 1996). Some argue the importance of returning to phonetically regular texts to support students' phonemic awareness and understanding of the written code (Adams et al., 1995). While young children do need to learn such skills, engaging literature—rather than the highly controlled contrived texts—invites children to reread, a primary way to learn about the relationship between oral and written language. Further, compelling literature invites children to study the language system (see Sipe, Chapter 3). Children are motivated by the messages in books with intriguing content such as Say's (1993) *Grandfather's Journey*; by what they can learn from informational books such as Yabuuchi's (1981) *Whose Baby Is This?* where they can learn the names of baby animals; and by encountering familiar characters and issues when they read Brown's series of books about Arthur and his friends and family. Finally, they can be entertained by the rhythmic nature and humor in *Hattie and the Fox* (Fox, 1988).

However, not all texts with literary merit designed for young readers are equally helpful in early literacy instruction. How do teachers select books? How should publishers and professional groups make recommendations? Which of the thousands and thousands of trade books will be the material for study? In this section, I lay the foundations for a framework that supports selections of texts for teaching beginning readers and writers.

This framework for text selection is based on a model of beginning reading processes. Text selection has to happen in relationship to the strategies and skills that young readers are acquiring in the moment, and those that they are moving toward learning. Thus, decisions about texts are based in an understanding of what children are learning, how they learn it, and the text features that can provide support during this process. To capture a comprehensive view of reading acquisition, I believe that educators must turn to the contributions of several paradigms—paradigms that are frequently juxtaposed (Stanovich, 1990).

The contributions of both emergent literacy and social constructivist perspectives (see also Hiebert & Raphael, 1997) are crucial because they emphasize linguistic and social processes that had been ignored previously. Emergent literacy perspectives recognize the importance of linguistic understandings that children bring to the task of reading (Brown, 1973). They recognize the role of writing in reading acquisition, as well as the critical role of authentic functions over a focus emphasizing form (Dyson, 1993). Social constructivist perspectives emphasize teacher scaffolding through language and activity, arguing for the importance of dialogue in children's construction of reading and writing tasks and the meanings of the texts (Vygotsky, 1962). Both emergent literacy and social constructivist perspectives underscore the centrality of meaningful and engaging text in early literacy learning. Unfortunately, neither provides guidance for determining which texts can be beneficial for students of varying literacy competence and experience.

Perspectives from cognitive psychology are also critical in this view because of their emphasis on cognitive processing with respect to beginning reading (see Adams, 1990; Juel, 1991). Thus, I draw on the contributions of cognitive psychology for helping determine appropriate texts for teaching youngsters to read, with the caveat that the texts be used in authentic and meaningful activities involving dialogue between teacher and students and among students, as suggested by those from social constructivist and emergent literacy perspectives. I discuss issues related to what research tells us about:

- the amount of text read,
- the structures and patterns of whole text, and
- the words within the text.

Amount of text relates to the importance of automaticity—practice leading to fluent reading without having to use up conscious attention to processing strategies. Structures of whole text relates to successful readers' competence in drawing on multiple sources of text information. Words within the text relates to proficient readers' underlying knowledge of important distinctions within our language system. I believe that these three constructs—among many within cognitive psychological perspectives—are critical to creating early reading experiences for young learners.

Amounts of Texts in Early Literacy Programs

Expert readers are automatic in applying their skills. Research suggests that many American students' problems in learning to read are due to a lack of automaticity, not a lack of fundamental skills (Campbell & Ashworth, 1995). To apply knowledge automatically requires experience with numerous texts, measured in both the amount of time that children spent reading in classrooms (Fisher & Berliner, 1985), and in the amount of text that is provided within reading programs.

The Issue. In reading instruction within the United States, we have paid little attention to the amount of reading that we require of beginning readers. It is not uncommon to find a single page of text in a reading program surrounded with a full day or two of related activities. In fact, incredible variation exists in the amount of text with which children have interacted before coming to school (Adams, 1990). Some children have extensive home text experiences while others' text experiences have been confined to kindergarten and preschool sessions. For children whose text experiences are first concentrated in the classroom, opportunities to see many different texts are essential to understanding the purposes and nature of literacy. How successful children are when literature is used as the primary source for beginning reading instruction may well be attributed to the amount of text provided, not simply the texts' characteristics.

What We Have Learned from Research. In the research I have surveyed, remarkably little is known about the amount of text needed to support early literacy instruction, especially for those students who do not have extensive reading and writing experiences prior to school. Further, in my own research, I found that I ended up raising more questions than I answered. For example:

- Does all of the text need to be sequenced carefully?
- How do texts with different characteristics contribute to children's experiences?
- Is there a particular percentage of text that needs to be easily accessible to beginning readers while other texts within a program can be

Table 9.1

Critical Features in Texts for Beginning Readers*

Characteristic	Components	Evaluation Criteria
CHARACTERISTICS OF TEXTS		
Predictability	• Size of predictable unit	— Small predictable unit (3–5 words) — Sizable unit (6–10 words) — Large unit (11 to 15 or more words) — No predictable unit
	• Proportion of text accounted for by predictable unit	— Very high 3/4 or more — High 1/2 to 2/3 — Moderate 1/4 to 1/3 — Low Less than 1/4
Contextual	• Familiarity of concepts	— Very familiar — Familiar — Somewhat familiar — Not common
	• Usefulness of illustrations in identifying key words	— Very useful — Useful — Somewhat useful — Not useful
Word Density	• Number of distinct words	— Count of distinct or different words
	• Ratio of distinct to total words	— Number of all words is divided by the number of distinct words
CHARACTERISTICS OF DISTINCT WORDS		
Decodability	• Of the distinct words in text, proportion of words with a V-C rime is:	— Very high 3 of 5 — High 2 of 5 — Moderate 1 of 5 — Low Less than 1 of 5
High-Frequency	• Of distinct words in text, proportion of words that are 20 most frequent words in written English is:	— Very high 3 of 10 — High 2 of 10 — Moderate 1 of 10 — Low Less than 1 of 10

*This table is a modified version of one that appears in: E. H. Hiebert & T. E. Raphael (1997). *Early literacy instruction.* Fort Worth, TX: Harcourt Brace College Publishers, p. 114. Used with permission of the authors and publisher.

terns inconsistent, and the syntactic and semantic contexts ambiguous, as is the case with "Tiny." The whimsical pig in *If I Had a Pig* and the child who is narrating the story are more memorable and engaging than "Tiny" and its two unnamed owners will ever be. But, no matter how much interest children have in a passage, attention to 57 different words can be overwhelming for beginning readers. Vocabulary density means that children cannot consistently apply their growing strategies related to high-frequency words and common rimes. In all likelihood, the teacher will read aloud the book and children will distinguish few, if any, words from it.

Because word learning is a function of numerous factors, it is highly unlikely that precise formulas dictating the number of unique words that beginning readers can successfully process at particular points in their development will or can ever be identified. Some unique words have easily accessible patterns. Other words hold interest for children and are highly imagable or recognizable from the illustrations. While the issue is complex, understanding the range of whole text features that influence word learning can help make text selection less arbitrary.

The Nature of Words within a Text

Research by cognitive psychologists and linguists highlights the rules our language follows—albeit, not always perfectly. Successful learners know critical features of the systems that make up language, including the sounds represented by the symbols, the order in which words appear in a sentence, and the affixes that convey meaning when added to a word. However, proficient readers do not cite the rules, nor do they explicitly apply a rule when encountering an unfamiliar word. Rather, they use their knowledge through analogies (Cunningham, 1992).

The Issues. Whatever the words children are learning—*sat, bat, cat, hat* or *you, to, the, from, have,* or *play, plays, playing, played, playful*—early theories of learning suggested having students repeat words they were shown until they could produce the word accurately (e.g., using flash cards). Today, we continue to recognize that repetitive methods are quite helpful when learning words that have less than perfect sound-symbol connections (e.g., *have, the*). However, for many other words, proficient readers draw on rules as they play out in both words and in morphemic units such as inflected endings, prefixes, and suffixes.

What We Have Learned from Research. How might the materials at the earliest levels support children's early acquisition of word recognition strategies? As I described in the opening section of the chapter, this research has examined: (a) phonetically regular words and (b) high-frequency words.

Phonetically Regular Words. Reviews of children's reading acquisition report a similar pattern: Children benefit from information about the consistent patterns within written words (Adams, 1990; Anderson et al., 1985; Bond & Dykstra, 1967). Once youngsters grasp the relationship between sounds and written symbols, they can read words that, when decoded, they understand because the words are familiar; they are part of their oral vocabulary. Once children are facile with common and consistent letter-sound patterns, they can be introduced to the morphemic patterns of English. For example, a group of words with a common morpheme—*play, playing, played, playful, player*—will be read first on the basis of its common letter-sound pattern and the shared meaning of the different forms of the word understood subsequently.

Early reading can be supported using texts where common and consistent letter-sound patterns of English are made visible. However, when all the words are selected for consistency, texts run into problems, as illustrated in the earlier example of "The Bad Fan." Surprisingly, there isn't much research informing teachers about the best balance between words with the target letter-sound patterns and other words in the text. In my preliminary framework, I focus on the presence of particular patterns within words, based on the following lines of research.

First, Juel and Roper-Schneider's (1985) work indicates that children apply their phonics strategies more consistently when the texts that they are reading have many examples of these patterns. Their line of work suggests that if children are learning about simple vowel patterns—a typical point of departure in American reading instruction—texts should contain at least a modicum of words with these patterns. But, which ones should be used?

Wylie and Durrell's (1970) research helps determine which patterns might be used. They found that 37 different rimes (i.e., patterns) account for 500 words that occur in primary-level text, though their frequencies vary markedly (Solso & Juel, 1980). In related research (Juel & Solso, 1981), there is evidence that young readers benefit from repeated exposures to different words using the same pattern (e.g., *bat, cat, hat, mat, flat*) than seeing the same word repeatedly (e.g., *hat*). Thus, instead of the perspective reflected in "The Bad Fan," readers would be better off if a text contained various iterations of a rime rather than six iterations of a single word like *rat*. Moreover, it would make sense to emphasize the most common rimes.

Young children begin to develop a "metacognitive stance" toward their reading—engaging strategically in trying to decode words—when a high portion of words in their stories are decodable (e.g., contain a familiar V-C rime). Strategic approaches to decoding words can be enhanced when young children are taught to generalize from the simplest patterns they are learning. Later in their program of instruction, rimes are introduced with more complex vowel representations such as the V-C-e (ride) and V-V-C (meat). Words with these patterns and from the earlier taught patterns (V-C rimes) should be considered in selecting text.

High-frequency Words. For learning high-frequency words, early educational psychologists were on the right track, expecting beginning readers to learn specific focus words at particular points in their reading development. Martin and Hiebert (1997) demonstrated that initially struggling readers who became successful readers during first grade knew few words by midyear but, once they had acquired a core group of high-frequency words, they progressed rapidly in their word recognition skills. The key is that they learned a small group of such words first, then built from that experience to learn other high-frequency and phonetically regular words much more quickly than occurred in their first smaller set.

Ironically, while the initial researchers in this area were right in expecting beginning readers to memorize a subset of high-frequency words from a common list, such as the Dolch 220 Basic Sight Words, they were wrong to simply divide up the words into subset lists of 40 to 50 words each that were to be learned by children sequentially. The magnitude of such lists is overwhelming to the beginning reader, and the neat division into relatively equal lists assumes an incremental learning process. In Table 9.1, notice that the difficulty of a text for beginning readers is based on the presence of words among the 20 most frequent words in written English (Carroll, Davies, & Richman, 1971). Acquiring these words will be a challenge for many beginning readers. But once this proficiency is gained, children will move more quickly in learning other words.

GUIDELINES FOR SELECTING TEXTS

What does the information in this chapter mean for teachers such as Mrs. Grattan, whose classroom I described at the beginning of the chapter? We don't yet have all of the answers about elements of texts that assist beginning readers in becoming independent readers. As teachers and researchers study particular choices of materials and effects of these choices on children's reading acquisition, many more descriptions and guidelines will be available. But there are guidelines available now—from the practices of effective teachers.

Because of the long-standing use of readability formulas in selecting and designing beginning reading texts, I believe it necessary to preface the description of guidelines by contrasting the meanings of "guideline" and "formula." A guideline is "a standard or principle by which to make a judgment or determine a policy or course of action" (Guralnik, 1979, p. 621). By contrast, a formula is "a rule or method for doing something, especially when conventional and used or repeated without thought" (Guralnik, 1979, p. 549). In the past, formulas were applied to texts. A text was described as "1.4 grade equivalent" or "1.7 grade equivalent" in difficulty. Texts were manipulated so that the elements that made them harder or easier were adjusted to fit the formula. I have already discussed the manner in which this manipulation distorted the language of the text for children—and subsequently their ease in reading it. The application of formulas also disregarded the role of readers' knowledge and engagement in reading. Further, the role of instructional supports from teacher and peers was left out of the text selection process. No matter how much more insight educators gain on the text features that support particular processes in beginning readers, there can never be formulas that precisely match a reader and a text. Children are sufficiently different in what they know about the world and about written language that selecting text will never be an exact science. Guidelines such as the four that follow, however, can support teachers and publishers in making the best possible selections of text for beginning readers.

- Instructional texts need to be chosen to highlight features that promote particular processes for particular beginning readers.

In presenting the framework for text features, I stated that the source for the model lies in beginning reading processes. To reiterate: Text selection has to happen in relationship to the strategies and skills that young readers are acquiring in the moment, and those that they are moving toward learning. Features of the framework in Table 9.1 such as phonetically regular words or high-frequency words relate to aspects of written language. To make meaning from texts, readers need to be skillful with these aspects of text. Since children need to attend to particular high-frequency words, this means that the same group of words needs to be in many of the texts that children see. In the framework in Table 9.1, I have suggested that these high-frequency words initially come from the 20 most frequent words in written English (*the, of, and, a, to, in, is, you, that, it, he, for, was, on, are, as, with, his, they, at*). Since children are learning to extend the "rime" in phonetically regular words, this means that they need to be exemplars of common and consistent patterns. As presented in Table 9.1, the most common and consistent patterns for the children at the very earliest stages of reading instruction are those that have a V-C rime such as *bat, cat, hat, rat, fat, sat* as well as *bad, mad, sad.*

The guideline to emphasize the 20 most frequent words and words with V-C rimes is well and good. But there are many books with these features. After all, the 20 most frequent words, by definition, appear often in books for young children, as do words with common patterns (i.e., V-C rimes). Let me illustrate the different choices that teachers have with two texts that have been offered as appropriate for beginning readers. One is Deming's *Who Is*

Tapping at My Window?, which is the first passage in a literature-based program (Pikulski, Cooper, Durr et al., 1993); the other is Wildsmith's (1982) *Cat on the Mat,* a text that is frequently offered as appropriate for beginning readers while maintaining literary quality (Cullinan & Galda, 1994).

In *Who Is Tapping at My Window?,* there are five V-C rimes represented: at (*cat, rat*), ap (*tapping*), og (*dog, frog*), ox (*ox, fox*), en (*hen, wren*). Except for *tapping,* which occurs twice in the text, each word occurs once. Of the 112 words in the text, 10 words or 9 percent of the text offer beginning readers opportunities to attend to or apply knowledge about V-C rimes. In *Cat on the Mat,* two V-C rimes are represented: at (*cat, sat, mat*) and og (*dog*). The appearances of these words are: *cat* (2), *sat* (6), *mat* (6), and *dog* (1). Out of 40 words in the entire text, 15 or 38 percent give children occasion to attend to or apply knowledge about V-C rimes.

A similar analysis can be conducted with the presence of high-frequency words. There are three words from the top 20 list in *Who Is Tapping at My Window?: the* (15), *is* (3), and *it* (1). Out of the 112 words in the text, 19 or 17 percent expose children to the most frequent words in written English. In *Cat on the Mat,* there are two words from the top 20 list: *the* (12) and *on* (6). Out of 40 words, 18 or 45 percent give beginning readers exposure to the most-frequent words. For children who are at the very beginning stages of reading, these two texts provide contrasting opportunities to attend to and apply knowledge of phonetically regular and high-frequency words.

- Features of a text that may distract beginning readers from attending to and applying key skills and strategies need to be considered in selecting texts for instruction.

A teacher may find that a text has some of the information that he or she wishes to emphasize with a group of children. But the attention of beginning readers can easily be distracted from this information by other aspects of a text. Peterson (1991) proposes that unique placement of text or print types, such as the text *Klippity Klop* (Emberley, 1974) can confuse beginning readers. While factors such as text placement or print type need to be considered, two common obstacles are text that is too dense or long and text that has unfamiliar concepts.

I turn again to the two texts, *Who Is Tapping at My Window?* and *Cat on the Mat,* to demonstrate this guideline. When a text has more than 100 words, as *Who Is Tapping at My Window?* has (112 words altogether), the instances of high-frequency and phonetically regular words can be difficult for beginning readers to find. Children whose book experiences have been negligible may be struggling to figure out what the squiggles on the page are all about, much less attending to the differentiations between "og" in *frog* and "ox" in *fox.* Of the 28 unique words in *Who Is Tapping at My Window?,* there are 3 high-frequency words that fit the criterion in Table 9.1 and 8 phonetically regular words. That means that, among the 112 words in the text, another 17 unique words need to be pointed out to children.

By contrast, 50 percent of the 10 words in *Cat on the Mat* pertain to the content that a teacher might emphasize at the beginning of children's reading acquisition. Of the other five, four can be easily identified through pictures. The final word—*sssstpppt!*—represents the sound that the cat makes to scare the other animals off the mat.

The familiarity of the content in *Cat on the Mat* demonstrates a second way in which children's attention can be directed to the critical content, rather than distracted from it. All of the animals—cat, dog, goat, cow, and elephant—are easily identifiable from the pictures and are common to games and materials for young children. While *Who Is Tapping at My Window?* is also about animals, some of the animals—especially wren, cony, loon, and ox—are not common ones to children. Even after a discussion about what these animals are, children will not automatically make the association when they see the picture in subsequent visits to the text. While texts should be a means whereby children's world knowledge is expanded (Hiebert & Raphael, 1997), texts that are used for beginning reading instruction—especially during the very earliest lessons—should require less explanation than a text such as this.

- The scaffolds of illustrations and predictable syntax should be varied, even at the earliest stages of reading acquisition.

Clear and salient illustrations of the key concepts in a book are a primary means whereby children are "invited" into books. The repeated phrases and episodes of predictable books are a second scaffold that allows children who are new readers to understand what reading is all about. However, possibly because of the powerful contributions of illustrations, they may potentially be overused. Children with few print strategies may rely on the illustrations, rather than text features, to decode and verify words (Samuels, 1970). Beginning readers may well be sharpening their auditory and memory skills, but not acquiring word recognition skills.

Even at the very earliest stages, children need to see a variety of texts. A varied diet of text in which features other than the predictable text are "exaggerated" allows children to apply their emerging word recognition strategies. For example, some texts might emphasize V-C rimes (and over time, other rimes) in the manner that Dr. Seuss (1960) did with *Green Eggs and Ham*. Other texts might exaggerate high-frequency words in the manner that Minarik did so successfully with her Little Bear books.

To turn once more to the texts that I have been using to demonstrate these guidelines, the literature-based program that begins with *Who Is Tap-*

ping at My Window? provides only one text without a predictable pattern for the first six weeks of reading instruction. Any diet that emphasizes only one feature—as the texts based only on high-frequency words, such as "Tiny," and those based only on phonetically regular words, such as *The Bad Fan*— does not give beginning readers sufficient opportunities to apply their knowledge. So, too, a diet based on only predictable text can create problems.

- It takes children who have had few prior book experiences numerous experiences with texts to focus on critical features and to remember them.

The difference among beginning readers in prior experiences with texts is substantial. These prior experiences become apparent quickly in a first-grade classroom. The children who have had 1,000 or more hours of lapreading at home or in preschools (Adams, 1990) often become conventional readers within the first few months of first grade. They have seen enough texts that an introductory story such as *Who Is Tapping at My Window?* may be challenging but sufficiently familiar in style and form that the difficulty of the text does not deter them from learning to read.

Children with few book experiences are often measured by the same yardstick. Their teachers are reluctant to involve them with new texts because they haven't learned the words in texts such as *Who Is Tapping at My Window?*—an expectation that is fostered when a text such as this is the primary reading material for an entire week of instruction. But seeing many different texts was precisely the way in which successful early readers learned to associate oral and written language, to understand the functions and forms of written language, and to distinguish the language of books from typical speech. Even though some children may not be able to visibly learn the words in particular books, they require exposure to many different books if they are to grasp fundamental concepts that underlie word recognition (Juel, 1991).

In programs where children with few prior text experiences learn to read well, the number of books that children encounter before becoming conventional readers may be as many as 100 or more (Martin & Hiebert, 1997). These texts have characteristics like those of *Cat on the Mat* rather than *Who Is Tapping at My Window?* in terms of the number of unique words and the presence of phonetically regular and high-frequency words. Children are guided in tracking print and attending to particular words in the text. They practice writing words they have seen in the text. Teachers have expectations about their learning and attention to print. However, learning to read is not viewed to be rigidly sequenced, with children required to master elements of one text before moving to the next. Teachers in these programs recognize that children need to be involved in many texts to understand what reading is all about.

CONCLUDING COMMENTS

We want future generations to enjoy literature, to read widely, and to draw
on text to make informed decisions in the democratic society in which they
live. We want them to be excited about books and avid readers of all types of
literature and nonfiction. But, none of this will occur if they do not learn to
read. It is a major responsibility of teachers in the earliest grades to invite
their young children into literacy events and activities, and to provide lessons that support their learning (Hiebert & Raphael, 1997). One important
source for enhancing children's experiences with texts within literacy lessons as well as in their independent reading is the support that the texts themselves provide. Through an understanding of the nature of the support and
knowing the needs of their students, teachers can develop workable and worthwhile literature-based reading programs.

REFERENCES

Adams, M. J. (1990). *Beginning to read: Thinking and learning about print.*
   Cambridge, MA: MIT Press.
Adams, M. J., Bereiter, C., Hirshberg, J., Anderson, V., & Bernier, S. A.
   (1995). *Framework for effective teaching. Grade 1: Thinking and learn-
   ing about print, Teacher's guide, Part A.* Chicago, IL: Open Court.
Anderson, R. C., Hiebert, E. H., Scott, J., & Wilkinson, I. A. G. (1985).
   Becoming a nation of readers. Champaign-Urbana, IL: Center for the
   Study of Reading & The National Academy of Education.
Beck, I. L., McKeown, M., Omanson, R., & Pople, M. (1984). Improving the
   comprehensibility of stories: The effects of revisions that improve co-
   herence. *Reading Research Quarterly, 19,* 263–277.
Bloomfield, L., & Barnhart, C. L. (1961). *Let's read: A linguistic approach.*
   Detroit, MI: Wayne State University Press.
Bond, G., & Dykstra, R. (1967). The cooperative research program in first-
   grade reading instruction. *Reading Research Quarterly, 2,* 5–142.
Brennan, A., Bridge, C., & Winograd, P. (1986). The effects of structural
   variation on children's recall of basal reader stories. *Reading Research
   Quarterly, 21,* 91–104.
Bridge, C. (1986). Predictable books for beginning readers and writers. In
   M. R. Sampson (Ed.), *The pursuit of literacy: Early reading and writing*
   (pp. 81–96). Dubuque, IA: Kendall/Hunt.
Brown, R. (1973). *A first language.* Cambridge, MA: Harvard University
   Press.

California English/Language Arts Committee (1987). *English-Language Arts Framework for California Public Schools* (Kindergarten through Grade Twelve). Sacramento, CA: California Department of Education.

Campbell, J. R., & Ashworth, K. P. (Eds.) (1995). *A synthesis of data from NAEP's 1992 Integrated Reading Performance Record at Grade 4.* Washington, DC: Office of Educational Research & Improvement, U.S. Department of Education.

Carroll, J. B., Davies, P., & Richman, B. (1971). *Word frequency book.* Boston: Houghton Mifflin.

Chall, J. S. (1982). *Learning to read: The great debate* (2nd ed.). New York: McGraw-Hill. (Original work published 1967).

Cullinan, B., & Galda, L. (1994). *Literature and the child* (3rd ed.). Fort Worth, TX: Harcourt Brace College Publishers.

Cunningham, P. M. (1992). What kinds of phonics instruction will we have? In C. Kinzer & D. Leu (Eds.), *Literacy research, theory, and practice: Views from many perspectives* (pp. 17–32). Chicago, IL: National Reading Conference, Inc.

Dyson, A. H. (1993). *Social worlds of children learning to write in an urban primary school.* New York: Teachers College Press.

Elson, W. H., & Gray, W. S. (1930). *Elson basic readers.* Chicago, IL: Scott, Foresman.

Fisher, C. W., & Berliner, D. C. (1985). *Perspectives on instructional time.* New York: Longman.

Fisher, C. W., & Hiebert, E. H. (1990). Characteristics of tasks in two literacy programs. *Elementary School Journal, 91,* 6–13.

Flesch, R. (1957). *Why Johnny can't read.* New York: Random House.

Grattan, K. W. (1997). They can do it too!: Book club with first and second graders. In S. I. McMahon and T. E. Raphael with V. J. Goatley and L. S. Pardo (Eds.), *The book club connection: Literacy learning and classroom talk* (pp. 267–283). New York: Teachers College Press & International Reading Association.

Guralnik, D. B. (1979). *Webster's New World Dictionary* (2nd ed.). New York: Williams Collins.

Hagerty, P., & Hiebert, E. H. (1989). Students' comprehension, writing, and perceptions in two approaches to literacy instruction. In S. McCormick & J. Zutell (Eds.), *Cognitive and social perspectives for literacy research and instruction* (38th Yearbook of the National Reading Conference), pp. 453–460. Chicago, IL: NRC.

Hiebert, E. H., & Raphael, T. E. (1997). *Early literacy instruction.* Fort Worth, TX: Harcourt Brace College Publishers.

Hiebert, E. H., Colt, J. M., Catto, S., & Gury, E. (1992). Reading and writing of first-grade students in a restructured Chapter 1 program. *American Educational Research Journal, 29,* 545–572.

Hiebert, E. H., Liu, G., Levin, L., Huxley, A., & Chung, K. (November 1995). *First graders reading the new first-grade readers.* Presented at the annual meeting of the National Reading Conference, New Orleans, LA.

Holdaway, D. (1979). *The foundations of literacy.* Sydney: Ashton Scholastic.

Honig, B. (1996). *How should we teach our children to read? A balanced approach.* Sacramento, CA: California Department of Education.

Juel, C. (1991). Beginning reading. In R. Barr, M. L. Kamil, P. B. Mosenthal, & P. D. Pearson (Eds.), *Handbook of reading research* (pp. 759–788). New York: Longman.

Juel, C., & Roper-Schneider, D. (1985). The influence of basal readers on first grade reading. *Reading Research Quarterly, 20,* 134–152.

Juel, C., & Solso, R. L. (1981). The role of orthographic redundancy, versatility, and spelling-sound correspondences in word identification. In M. L. Kamil (Ed.), *Directions in reading: Research and instruction* (30th Yearbook of the National Reading Conference), (pp. 74–92). Rochester, NY: National Reading Conference.

Klare, G. (1984). Readability. In P. D. Pearson, R. Barr, M. L. Kamil, & P. Mosenthal (Eds.), *Handbook of reading research* (Vol. 1). New York: Longman.

Martin, B., & Brogan, P. (1971). *Teacher's guide to the instant readers.* New York: Holt, Rinehart, & Winston.

Martin, L. A., & Hiebert, E. H. (April 1997). *Becoming literate in school: Examining the profiles of first-grade readers in Chapter 1.* Paper presented at the annual meeting of the American Educational Research Association, Chicago, IL.

Paivio, A. (1968). A factor-analytic study of word attributes and learning. *Journal of Verbal Learning and Verbal Behavior, 7,* 41–48.

Peterson, B. (1991). Selecting books for beginning readers: Children's literature suitable for young readers. In D. E. DeFord, C. A. Lyons, & G. S. Pinnell (Eds.), *Bridges to literacy: Learning from reading recovery* (pp. 119–147). Portsmouth, NH: Heinemann.

Pikulski, J. J., Cooper, J. D., Durr, W. K., et al. (1993). *The literature experience.* Boston: Houghton Mifflin.

Rasmussen, D., & Goldberg, L. (1964). *The Bad Fan* (Level A, Basic Reading Series). Chicago: Science Research Associates.

Rider, N. F. (1986). Tiny. In W. K. Durr, J. J. Pikulski, et al. (Eds.), *Bells.* Boston: Houghton Mifflin.

Rumelhart, D. E. (1977). Toward an interactive model of reading. In S. Dornic (Ed.), *Attention and performance* VI (pp. 573–603). Hillsdale, NJ: Lawrence Erlbaum Associates.

Samuels, S. J. (1970). Effects of pictures on learning to read, comprehension and attitudes. *Review of Educational Research, 40,* 397–408.

Smith, N. B. (1934/1965). *American reading instruction.* Newark, DE: International Reading Association.

Solso, R. L., & Juel, C. L. (1980). Positional frequency and versatility of bigrams for two- through nine-letter English words. *Behavior Research Methods and Instrumentation, 12,* 297–343.

Stanovich, K. (1990). A call for an end of the paradigm wars in reading research. *Journal of Reading Behavior, 22,* 221–231.

Stein, N. L., & Glenn, C. G. (1979). An analysis of story comprehension in elementary children. In R. Freedle (Ed.), *New directions in discourse processing* (pp. 53–120). Norwood, NJ: Ablex.

Stickney, J. (1885). *A primer.* Boston: Ginn and Company.

Sulzby, E. (1985). Children's emergent reading of favorite storybooks: A developmental study. *Reading Research Quarterly, 20,* 458–481.

Texas Education Agency (1990). Proclamation of the State Board of Education advertisings for bids on textbooks (Proclomation 68). Austin, TX: Texas Education Agency.

Thorndike, E. L. (1921). *The teacher's word book.* New York: Columbia University Press.

van der Veur, B. (1975). Imagery rating of 1,000 frequently used words. *Journal of Educational Psychology, 67,* 44–56.

Vygotsky, L. S. (1962). *Thought and language.* Cambridge, MA: MIT Press.

Wood, B., Bruner, J. S., & Ross, G. (1976). The role of tutoring in problem solving. *Journal of Child Psychology and Psychiatry, 17,* 89–100.

Wylie, R. E., & Durrell, D. D. (1970). Teaching vowels through phonograms. *Elementary English 47,* 787–791.

CHILDREN'S BOOKS CITED

Brown, M. (1993). *Arthur's family vacation.* Boston: Little, Brown.

Deming, A. G. (1988). *Who is tapping at my window?* Illus. M. Wellington. New York: Dutton.

Emberley, E. (1974). *Klippity klop.* New York: Little, Brown.

Fox, M. (1988). *Hattie and the fox.* Illus. P. Mullins. New York: Bradbury.

Henkes, K. (1996). *Lilly's purple plastic purse.* New York: Greenwillow Books.

Inkpen, M. (1988). *If I had a pig.* New York: Macmillan Children's Books.

Krauss, R. (1945). *The carrot seed.* New York: Harper.

Lobel, A. (1970). *Frog and toad are friends.* New York: HarperCollins.

Martin, B. (1967). *Brown bear, brown bear, what do you see?* New York: Henry Holt.

McCully, E. A. (1992). *Mirette on the high wire.* New York: Putnam.

Minarik, E. H. (1957). *Little bear.* New York: Harper.

Moss, L. (1995). *Zin! zin! zin!: A violin.* New York: Simon & Schuster.

Say, A. (1993). *Grandfather's journey.* Boston: Houghton Mifflin.

Seuss, Dr. (1960). *Green eggs and ham.* New York: Beginner Books, Random House.

Wildsmith, B. (1982). *Cat on a mat.* Oxford: Oxford University Press.

Yabuuchi, M. (1981). *Whose baby is this?* New York: Philomel Books.

Chapter 10

Criteria for Selecting Literature in Upper Elementary Grades

●——————●

Laura S. Pardo, Silver Burdett & Ginn

Teachers using literature-based instruction face many decisions as they strive to bring literacy learning into their elementary classrooms. As Galda suggested in Chapter 1, perhaps one of the most difficult and frequently visited decisions is that of literature selection. Classroom teachers must decide what books to use for what purposes, and quite often these decisions can directly impact the amounts and kinds of student learning. How do teachers determine what books to select to create opportunities for increased learning? In this chapter, I explore the criteria I used in my fourth- and fifth-grade classrooms as I selected literature that I hoped my students would enjoy and learn from, and that would meet our literacy learning goals.

THE CONTEXT

I taught for 14 years, the last six of which I taught fourth or fifth grade. I first taught middle school mathematics for six years, and was fairly traditional in both my methods of instruction and assessment practices. Beginning my master's degree in reading instruction coincided with a move to elementary school teaching—first in second grade, then in third grade, and finally in upper grades. It was at this point in my career that I started to think about the instruction in my classroom. As I read, discussed and thought about literacy learning, I began to question some of my previous assumptions about how children learn. Further, I became involved in several literacy projects and began to think of myself as a teacher researcher. During the last eight years I became increasingly interested in classroom research, and particularly in my own growth and reflection upon my teaching (see Pardo, 1996, 1997).

Within the context of reflective teaching, I examined many issues within my classroom. One of these issues was literature-based instruction, growing out of my work on the Book Club Project (see McMahon & Raphael, with

Goatley & Pardo, 1997). Book Club is a program focused on student-led discussion groups, within the context of reading and responding to real literature. Through Book Club and reflective teaching I studied issues such as grouping students (Pardo & Raphael, 1994; Pardo, 1996, 1997), promoting talk in student-led response groups (Pardo, 1997), and literature selection (Pardo, 1995, 1996). This chapter stems from my own reflections and decisions within this framework.

Students in my classroom were involved in many types of literacy activities. Book Club was the reading program, as well as an important part of my social studies instruction. I did this by using historical fiction books, primarily, and by organizing instruction around units of American history. My students also engaged in other literacy activities throughout the day, including the sustained, silent reading program, Drop Everything and Read (DEAR); bi-weekly book reports; writing workshop; focus journals; and writing during content area study such as in social studies and science. There were many issues related to both instruction and assessment that arose for me as my role as a teacher researcher grew, but because literature formed the foundation of my language arts instruction, issues surrounding literature selection caused me to reflect upon and develop my decision-making processes first (see Pardo, 1997, for a full discussion of reflection within my teacher research activities).

As I began to consider the criteria involved in choosing literature, I was able to identify several issues that were important to address in order to select literature that would best benefit students. After discussing these issues, I turn to some of the specific decisions I made concerning literature selection as I look at a particular year and then a specific unit of study from one fifth-grade classroom.

THE ISSUES

I have found three issues to be critical in selecting literature for upper elementary grade students: (a) identifying themes around which to organize literature selection and related instruction; (b) finding books with the greatest potential for discussion among students; and (c) determining the balance between providing students with choice and yet maintaining enough common thematic elements to facilitate discussion across the books.

Identifying Themes for Organizing Literature Selection and Instruction

For years, teachers have organized their instruction into units or topics of study. Recently, however, educational researchers have explored the idea of thematic instruction (see Lipson, Valencia, Wixson, & Peters, 1993; Pearson,

1995; Valencia & Lipson, Chapter 5; Peters & Wixson, Chapter 12). As I began to read and talk with colleagues about thematic instruction, I became aware of how limiting my prior beliefs had been. Like many teachers, I had equated topics and themes, but I now realize there is a critical distinction between the terms (see, also, Valencia & Lipson, Chapter 5). Topics are units of study that revolve around a noun (such as "spiders," "the Civil War," or "the environment") or an idea (such as "friendship," "death" or "family"). Much of my previous instruction had been centered around these topical units. Now, however, I see a theme as a big idea that I want students to think about. For example, "It is important to develop human relationships" is a theme, while "friendships" is a topic. A theme should cause children to think. A theme could be made up of several units, each offering additional ways to approach and develop the theme. During the course of the school year, I may teach many units across many content areas, but only one or two may fit under the big themes or megathemes (see Valencia & Lipson, Chapter 5) that I used during the course of the school year. As I thought about all of this I began to see how the two ideas—themes and topical units—could and should work together. Conceptual understanding of this came fairly easily, although implementing the practice within my fifth-grade classroom was much more difficult.

The first thing I grappled with was the idea of total inclusion of all content areas. I tried to come up with a wonderful, all encompassing theme that I could build my entire curriculum around. Needless to say, this was not possible, and I began to question whether it was even a good idea. I came to realize I could not integrate everything, and I had to make choices about the content areas and curricular objectives I most wanted to teach through thematic instruction, and then work from that point. I made instructional choices that would be easy to implement, meaningful to students, and appropriate to my curricular goals. My goal the first year was to maintain one theme, with hopes that in future years I could add units to this theme, or add another theme. As I selected my first theme, I did so knowing I would have to monitor and revise it as my planning for instruction and selecting of literature continued.

Once I had a beginning theme, I had to determine which units I wanted to use to develop this theme with students. Selecting units the first year was difficult, but I tried to keep several things in mind. First, I wanted the connections to the theme to be clearly evident to students in the literature and content. Looking at units of study with this in mind changed the way I selected units. Second, I did not want to lose all the work I had already done to build topical units, so I incorporated some of the units I had used previously. I did change the focus of some existing units to better promote the theme I had selected. Third, I decided to focus on one or two main content areas (language arts and social studies) and teach the other content areas in the manner of my previous instruction. And finally, I knew this was a learning process, and so reminded myself that, as with any new endeavor, it would take time, patience and adaptation.

I also thought about an issue that had been gaining popularity in math and science education for some time, the idea that "less is more" (Willis, 1995). In other words, it is better to teach a few things in-depth and cover them well, than to cover many things in a haphazard and shallow way. This idea seemed to make sense as I thought about thematic instruction. If I were to select several units within one theme, my students would have the greatest opportunities for success within that theme, because I could provide quality instruction and sufficient time for students to make connections. I felt secure in my selection of a theme and connecting units, and ready to move to the next part of the process—selecting literature to support my teaching of these units.

I began by putting together lists of books for each of the units I had selected within my theme. I put titles of picture books, novels, expository/ nonfiction books, magazines, and CD ROM materials on this list. I combined the titles from books previously used in my classroom with recommendations from colleagues, books found in the library, lists from teaching journals (such as *The Reading Teacher* or *Language Arts*), and titles from the Internet. I then identified the purposes for which I needed specific books and looked for titles to meet each purpose.

Finding Books with the Greatest Potential to Encourage Discussion Among Students

As I looked at the list of books I had identified for each unit, I decided to put my goals for Book Club foremost. I used my prior experiences with Book Club to think about the purposes for literature. Discussion is a key component of Book Club, and I felt that children's conversations centered around the books would help them make thematic connections. Therefore, I began to look at the list of books in light of their potential for promoting discussion. I knew from my prior experiences with Book Club that some books led to better discussions than others. For example, during a unit in which we read Coerr's (1977) *Sadako and the Thousand Paper Cranes,* my students shared conversations about the unfairness of war. They discussed how Sadako was going to die of leukemia from the radiation of the atom bomb, and how she had only been a baby when the bombing occurred. Their conversations were furthered after I read aloud *Faithful Elephants* (Tsuchiya, 1988), a picture book depicting events in a Tokyo zoo during World War II. This book added fuel to their fiery discussion of the unfairness of war and the randomness of war's events.

In contrast, when this same class read Dahl's (1961) *James and the Giant Peach,* discussions were not nearly as rich. The students had fun with the book and enjoyed its humor and absurdity. However, they remarked that it didn't feel as though it was a book worth spending Book Club time discussing. They noted that it didn't have enough "meat" to discuss.

For my research, I had maintained a teacher journal, as well as some tapes and transcripts of students' discussions and writing in response to the books they had read. By reviewing my notes and doing some analyses of the writing and conversations, I developed a list of criteria for judging a book's potential for discussion. I looked for commonalties in the books that had led to interesting and lively discussions and that had engaged students' interest beyond the time when they had actually read the book (e.g., in the context of later books or other parts of the school day). My criteria include books that:

- present big ideas or themes,
- reflect real issues,
- describe the condition of humanity,
- contain mature content, and
- can be considered controversial.

Books with these features had led to the best discussion among my students in the past. Therefore, I used these criteria to narrow the list of titles I had selected to develop the unit and theme connection. I drew upon my experiences with previous fifth-grade students as I thought about familiar books. In order to know if these books met the criteria, I had to read many of them again.

In addition to selecting literature for Book Club, I had several other purposes for literature selection. For example, I chose books to read aloud, for content study, and for a themed classroom library. I chose books of various genres including expository texts, picture books, and historical fiction. By beginning with the entire list of titles that would help develop the theme, using the criteria for books with high potential for discussion, and considering the various purposes for which I would need additional books, I was able to narrow the list to a manageable size and match books to their specific purposes.

Balancing Student Choice and Common Thematic Elements

As a literature-based teacher, I had been aware of the research findings on the importance of providing students with choice when selecting literature (see Routman, 1988; Short, 1992; Swift 1993). This research found that children were more likely to choose to read, and read with increased comprehension, if they had a choice in the books they read. I knew too from my own teaching experiences and classroom-based research that students have a wide range of reading interests and choose many genres and styles when selecting books from the library and for DEAR. However, I wrestled with the following dilemma: How could I provide my students with choices in their literature selection for Book Club instruction, and yet make sure those books were from the list I had identified for developing theme and content? My students considered many criteria when freely choosing books, but it was not realistic to assume they would choose books within a particular theme, and with the greatest potential for discussion.

For these reasons I decided to constrain the literature selection for Book Club in the units I identified to help develop my theme. I continued to encourage students' choice of books in other areas of the curriculum within my classroom. For example, students selected their own books for the bi-weekly book reports, for DEAR, and their weekly library book. Within Book Club, I incorporated choice by allowing students to meet with their book club peers at places they chose in the room, rather than requiring them to sit at their desks. I ensured that students had choices daily about how they responded in the reading logs. I also knew that my students could choose the topics and points to be discussed in Book Club.

I then turned to choice in terms of book selection. I wanted only to use those books that met the criteria for a worthwhile Book Club discussion. Further, the books I included on my list had to be available in multiple copies, as well as grade level and developmentally appropriate. Within these constraints, I identified two ways of providing choice that worked quite well. First, I developed multi-title Book Club units. From among several titles that fit a particular theme, students could select their first, second, and third choices. In addition, I asked them to list two people they would like to have in their Book Club groups. I then grouped students so that they had some combination of selected text and peers for their Book Clubs.

Second, I built in student choice when I used a single title unit. I conveyed to students the genre that we would be reading, and listed several titles that I would be able to obtain for Book Club. The class then voted on the book they would like to read. For example, after I read aloud from *James and the Giant Peach,* we discussed the fantasy genre and decided that we would enjoy reading another fantasy book. I compiled a list of appropriate fantasy stories, including *Tuck Everlasting* (Babbitt, 1980), *A Wrinkle in Time* (L'Engle, 1962), *From the Mixed-up Files of Mrs. Basil E. Frankweiler* (Konigsburg, 1967) and *George Washington's Socks* (Woodruff, 1991). From this list I held a brief "book sale" and allowed students to vote. In this way, I controlled the factors important to me (i.e., discussion potential, availability, appropriateness, theme development), while allowing my students to have choice.

Similarly, a third way I provided choice was to open the selection at the unit level, since many themes can be explored with more than one title and with books of more than one genre. Thus, in some cases, I would let students choose from different genres—biography, historical fiction, or fantasy—with a theme-related title in mind for each of the possibilities. Students picked the genre and associated book to read.

A CLOSER LOOK

After struggling with the three issues discussed above, I began creating thematic instruction and identifying relevant literature. In the remainder of this chapter, I focus on the development of theme during one school year and the corresponding units used to build that theme. I then look closely at one unit and its selection of literature. Much adjusting, monitoring, and revising took place throughout the year, and in each successive year the themes evolved and changed based on my teacher research and reflections.

Developing the Theme

As a fifth-grade teacher, I had been teaching American history through the use of historical fiction and the Book Club. Since I wanted to maintain both Book Club and the social studies link, I began my search for a theme by looking at my plan for instruction for social studies from the previous school year (see Figure 10.1). As I looked across issues and themes I had identified, I tried to look for some commonality. I saw several recurring themes (i.e., issues of prejudice, war, friendships). Because I wanted to identify a big idea that I could phrase as a sentence, I decided also to consider my science curriculum and the units I usually taught as part of science. I felt fairly confused at this point until I finally focused my attention on a Book Club unit about survival. I recalled that this unit had been popular with students in the past, and I saw how I could move several of the social studies themes in that direction as well as a science unit. Therefore, I decided to focus on this "big idea" or theme: "Survival requires adaptation."

Identifying the Units to Accompany the Theme

In selecting units to accompany my chosen theme of "Survival requires adaptation," I tried to keep in mind several issues. I wanted to use units I had previously taught and felt comfortable with, on topics that my students had some prior knowledge of and had enjoyed in the past. I knew I wanted to keep the survival unit with Gary Paulsen's (1987) *Hatchet* and now had to

Figure 10.1 1993/94 Social Studies/Book Club Unit Plan

Integration of Social Studies and Book Club Plan for 1993–94 School Year							
Date of unit	September/ October	October/ November	December	January	February/ March	March/ April	May
Unit topic	Native Americans	Exploration-Colonization	The American Revolution	Survival	The Civil War	World War II	Fantasy
Book Club Literature	*Sing Down the Moon* –O'Dell	*Sign of the Beaver* –Speare	*The Fighting Ground* –Avi	*Hatchet* –Paulsen	*Charley Skedaddle* –Beatty	*Sadako and the Thousand Paper Cranes* –Coerr	*Tuck Everlasting* –Babbitt
Themes/ issues	prejudice, slavery, cultural heritage awareness	persecution, freedom, new beginnings, friendships	war, death, patriotism, loyalty, growing up	elements of self and survival, self-esteem and confidence	war, death, slavery, prejudice, friendship, loyalty	war, death, prejudice, friendships, family	immortality, everlasting life, death

Pardo, 1995

decide what other units to use. As I reflected on this theme, many aspects of American history that I usually taught came to mind, even though I had not identified survival as a theme or issue in prior years. I began to look at how some of the units might reflect my selection of theme: *Native Americans* and their relocation and survival due to the arrival of the "white man," *The Pilgrims and Colonization* as the European settlers had to survive in a new land, *The American Revolution* and the establishment of government as a new country forged forward, and *The Civil War* as a nation struggled to remain unified. In science I could see further connections: *Adaptations* of living things to the environment and each other, *Weather* and its effects on humans and how we combat it, and *The Human Body* as we adapt ourselves to new foods and environmental factors.

With this in mind and recognizing a multitude of associated choices, I decided for the first year to use a total of four units: the survival unit, two units from social studies, and one from science. I selected topics of *Native Americans* and *The Civil War* from my social studies curriculum and *Adaptations* from my science curriculum. I felt these three units would help children develop and understand the theme. The order in which I taught the topical units related to the theme was: (1) *Native Americans,* (2) *Adaptation,* (3) *Survival in the Wilderness,* and (4) *The Civil War* (see Figure 10.2). I contin-

Figure 10.2 Year-long Theme/Unit Plan

Theme: Survival Requires Adaptation

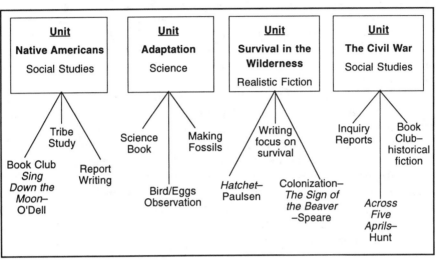

ued to teach other social studies and science units, but these were the units I specifically used to teach the theme "Survival requires adaptation."

The Civil War Unit: An Illustration

In the remainder of this chapter, I discuss the Civil War unit. I organize the discussion around planning for instruction, identifying activities to support instruction, and literature selected as the foundation for the unit. This discussion offers a glimpse into the complexity of literature selection in a real classroom. Identifying the various purposes for literature and then the specific titles to meet those purposes involves intricate planning and monitoring.

The Civil War unit was taught during late April and May of the school year with my 23 fifth-grade students. The school was one of thirty-four elementary buildings within an urban school district in the Midwest. The class showed diversity in ethnicity, academic ability, and socioeconomic status.

Planning for Instruction. As I planned the unit about the Civil War, my primary goal was continued development of the theme, "Survival requires adaptation." However, I had several other curricular goals in mind as well (see Figure 10.3). First, I wanted my students to develop content understanding about the people and issues involved in the Civil War and its surrounding years, as set forth in our district's social studies curriculum. Related to this, I wanted to extend our work within social studies, examining how our country developed. Second, I wanted my students to look at point of view from a literary standpoint as we examined books representing different perspectives during the war. Often students understand only the point of view of the North, as most stories, both oral and written, are told from a Northern perspective. Also, my students and I live in the northern part of the United States. I wanted students to think about how the point of view of the story affects the meanings they create and to be able to sympathize with others of a different viewpoint or perspective.

Third, I wanted my students to make intertextual links between various books about the Civil War. I decided to select several novels set during this time period and wanted the children to connect issues and big ideas across the books. Fourth, I wanted my students to improve the quality of their written and oral responses during the course of Book Club and to be self-evaluative of these processes. And finally, I wanted students to plan for and monitor their own learning and understanding. I wanted to prepare my fifth graders for middle school, as well as help them to reflect on the learning they had been involved in throughout the school year.

The chart seen in Figure 10.3 is a visual representation of the way I outlined the unit. This chart guided my instruction and sequencing of the unit, and also served as the introductory lesson to the unit. I used this chart on an overhead with students as part of the fifth objective, to model my planning process and help them begin to think about monitoring their own learning. As I thought further about the five goals for instruction embedded within the theme I had chosen, I realized I had to select many pieces of literature for many different purposes, as I explain in the following section.

Figure 10.3

Civil War Unit Plan

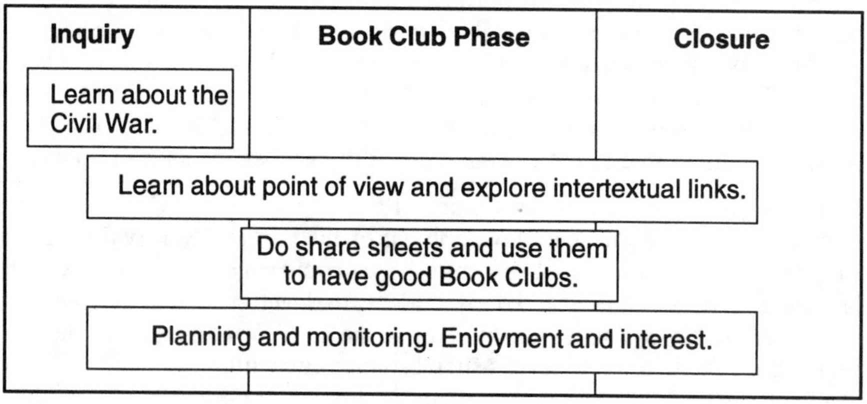

Inquiry	Book Club Phase	Closure
Learn about the Civil War.		
Learn about point of view and explore intertextual links.		
	Do share sheets and use them to have good Book Clubs.	
Planning and monitoring. Enjoyment and interest.		

Activities to Support Instruction.   As illustrated in Figure 10.3, the plan had three phases. It began with a 2–3-week inquiry phase in which students gathered content information about the Civil War. This was followed by a 2–3-week Book Club phase in which students read and responded to historical fiction. The final phase of the unit was a 2–3-day closure phase. I also read aloud during the entire length of the unit, and students viewed the film, *The Blue and the Gray.* I planned activities within each phase, which helped determine the purposes for which literature was needed.

I had several goals for the inquiry portion of the unit. I wanted to elicit from my students the information they already knew about the Civil War, add to that existing information, and connect the two in order to build strong background knowledge before beginning the Book Club phase. I planned several charts (i.e., a modification of KWL introduced by Ogle, 1986; Inquiry or I-Charts, discussed in Hoffman, 1992; timelines) to record and monitor information throughout the unit (see Figure 10.4 for a complete list of activities). I also modeled the inquiry process: identifying a question worthy of study, gathering information to help answer that question, drafting an answer, and presenting the information to the class. Within these activities, several purposes for literature selection were evident. We needed books that contained content information about many aspects of the Civil War, in a wide range of reading and interest levels. I also needed one expository text in multiple copies to model how to gather and organize information gained from such books.

Further, during the Book Club phase I knew I wanted the students to read historical fiction that would present a range of viewpoints and perspectives about the war. I knew that I wanted to provide students with some choices about the book they would read and that I wanted the books to be appropriate for theme development as well as reading level. I also wanted to maintain several more classroom charts to help us track the novels and to help connect the stories by issues and related big ideas. I wanted to connect the Book Club phase to the inquiry phase by continuing to read aloud a novel and to add to the charts begun in the first phase.

Finally, during the closure phase, I wanted to provide multiple opportunities for my students to synthesize the information learned. I wanted to bring the theme into the discussion and hoped to find a contemporary piece of literature to help the children with this synthesis. As I thought about these varied purposes for literature selection, it was obvious that I not only needed many books, but I also needed to think carefully about each book in light of the purpose I wanted it to serve.

Selection of Literature.   Since I had taught the content of the Civil War several times before, and since a wealth of children's books exists on this topic, I found the search for the "right" titles overwhelming. However, I asked col-

was too difficult for most of my fifth-grade students to read independently and therefore they would be unlikely to read it on their own. I planned to use the book to model intertextuality. I did this by keeping a class chart of the characters, issues, and point of view evident in the story.

This chart served two purposes. First, the chart helped us monitor events that spanned a long time, thus creating a timeline of sorts of the Civil War era. Second, the chart provided students with a way to think about the novel they would be reading for their Book Clubs later on. For example, we read in *Across Five Aprils* about Eb, cousin of the main character Jethro. Eb had enlisted in the army, but as a result of tough conditions and lack of food, had deserted. We listed desertion as an issue on our chart and discussed the idea. Many of us were able to see Eb's point of view, as well as that of the U.S. Army. When we began reading our novels, the group that read Beatty's *Turn Homeward Hannalee* (1984) was able to bring the rest of the class into their novel more easily because of the previous discussion of desertion. In Beatty's novel, Davey has come home on furlough from the war, but must return to battle. His sister, Hannalee, is unsure and confused about this. But Davey tells her he can't desert, that if he does he'll be branded on the forehead with a "D", by a red hot iron. Because students had discussed desertion earlier, the rest of the class was able to understand and relate to the novel, although they weren't reading it in their group. Further connections were possible later in the unit when the students viewed the video of *The Blue and the Gray* and witnessed a deserter being branded.

For the inquiry phase, I selected numerous titles (see Figure 10.5) that I felt would provide a wide range of information about the Civil War era. I tried to pick both picture books as well as expository novels. We also used our social studies textbook, encyclopedias, and other reference materials, CD-ROM and World Wide Web information, and newspaper accounts. I placed all of these materials together in the classroom for children to use for their inquiry reports. The students were free to check them out for home use and to use them during the school day as well.

For Book Club I chose four novels that presented a wide range of perspectives held during the Civil War. *Shades of Gray* by Carolyn Reeder (1989) takes place in the South after the war. Will, the main character has been orphaned due to the war and he goes to live with his uncle. Will's uncle chose to remain neutral during the war, a situation that becomes an issue for Will and the heart of the story. *Turn Homeward Hannalee* by Patricia Beatty (1984) tells the story of young Hannalee and her brother. The two children live and work in a Southern factory, making uniforms for the Confederate soldiers. When the Union army invades and burns the factory down, the children are captured, taken to the North, and sold as house servants. The story unfolds around the children's journey to return home.

Beatty's (1992) book *Who Comes With Cannons?* tells the story of young Truth, a Quaker, whose family's home becomes a stop on the Underground Railroad during the war. When one of Truth's cousins is wounded and placed in a prison hospital by the Union soldiers, she uses the Underground Railroad to travel north and rescue her cousin. And finally Reit's (1988) *Behind Rebel Lines* is the story of Emma Thompson, a Michigan woman who disguises herself as a man to join the Union army. She becomes a spy for the North and adopts several more disguises as she goes "behind rebel lines." This set of books presented a wide and interesting array of perspectives and locations. The books also encouraged intertextual links and provided ample opportunities for oral and written response as the children continued to develop the theme, "Survival requires adaptation."

To enhance the theme, I also chose several picture books to read aloud. In my search for good books, I had encountered many wonderful picture books and decided to include them for students' enjoyment. To encourage viewing literacy, including critical thinking and connection making, students viewed the video, *The Blue and the Gray.* To model and support students through this process, I used a structured note-taking think sheet (see Figure 10.6). I also provided students with time to respond personally to the video in a manner consistent with Book Club. Further, I compiled a classroom set of books that children could read during DEAR or as time and interest permitted. This library was composed of both fiction and nonfiction, picture books and novels, in a wide range of reading levels. I wanted to provide my students with many opportunities for intertextual connections as well as content learning.

Finally, for the closure phase, I decided to read Eve Bunting's (1994) *Smoky Night,* which focuses on the Los Angeles riots. I wanted my students not only to synthesize information about the Civil War and its impact on our theme, but to draw connections to recent times and their own lives. I wanted to bring closure not only to this unit but to the year-long theme as well.

This description of thematic instruction provides teachers with much to consider. Foremost, it demonstrates that literature selection can be an overwhelming task. As Figure 10.5 illustrates, one unit can include many titles. The process described here was successful for this fifth-grade class for many reasons, but a vitally important one is that the books were selected according to specific criteria (to meet thematic goals, to promote discussion, and with some student choice) and to meet specific and varied purposes (for content learning, for reading and responding, and for synthesis). In short, regardless of the amount of thought and planning, without the selection of appropriate and effective literature, a unit cannot succeed. However, it is also true that in all good instruction, planning and monitoring are crucial.

Figure 10.6. Note-Taking Think Sheet for Writing of *The Blue and The Gray*

Notes from *The Blue and the Gray*

Date	Two Things I Learned Today	Retelling

The Unit Concludes. As the end of the Civil War unit approached, I was encouraged to hear students making intertextual links across the novels read. I also witnessed an understanding of the theme as students wrote final synthesis papers connecting the Civil War to the book *Smoky Night*. Below are several excerpts my students wrote in their final synthesis papers, when asked what they had learned. Spelling and other language conventions are presented as they appeared in the students' unedited writing.

- ... If we learned everything we wouldn't have Roits or wars. We could talk it out ensted of wars. . . . Lenny
- . . . Violence is not as sweet as violin music. Violence is something we should have stopped by now. . . . Derek
- . . . it is not right to die over your arguments to a group of people that like to do things different than you and some people like you. . . . Katrina
- . . . I think we should learn from history that killing each other is wrong and so is rasicm. . . . Ricardo
- . . . to help us learn the treatment of other human beings and how aufull we treat each other. Like the riots in Los Angelos . . . we nead to treat each other like we are soposed to. . . . Charles
- . . . should have taught the government to make laws that were fair for everyone and not just one part of the country. . . . Meg
- . . . we should know that everyone is equal no matter what their color is or what religion they are. We should know not to hate people from our own country, because it will tear us apart. . . . Julianne

As I read these papers and listened to students' powerful discussions, I became convinced that the time and energy spent on literature selection for The Civil War unit were crucial in achieving my goals, as well as continuing students' movement toward theme understanding.

CONCLUDING COMMENT

Literature selection is so much more than just picking books from the shelves of a classroom or school library. Teachers in today's busy classrooms face enormous decisions that impact their instruction and their children's learning. As a teacher researcher, I prefer to identify areas of study that have immediate relevance for my teaching and that are foundational to how I approach the enactment of the literacy curriculum. Through observing my students as they talked about the books they read, writing reflections about what I was seeing in my classroom, and analyzing students' learning from and responses to literature, I built my understanding of the role of literature within my instruction and its potential for students' literacy and content learning. As I struggled with issues related to selecting high-quality, interesting, relevant, and engaging literature, I found that I could impact both my instruction and my students' learning in major ways. Many wonderful texts engaged my students as readers and thinkers across a wide range of content areas, as well as across genres and authors. My research helped channel my thinking so that I could identify relevant criteria for selecting books and, with confidence, create appropriate instructional activities around the literature.

REFERENCES

Hoffman, J. V. (1992). Critical reading/Thinking across the curriculum: Using I-charts to support learning. *Language Arts, 69*(2), 121–127.

Lipson, M. Y., Valencia, S. W., Wixson, K. K., & Peters, C. W. (1993). Integration and thematic teaching: Integration to improve teaching and learning. *Language Arts, 70,* 252–263.

McMahon, S. I., Raphael, T. E. with Goatley, V. J. & Pardo, L. S. (1997). *The Book Club connection: Literacy learning and classroom talk.* New York: Teachers College Press.

Ogle, D. M. (1986). K-W-L: A Teaching model that develops active reading of expository text. *The Reading Teacher, 39*(6), 564–570.

Pardo, L. S. (1994). *Accommodating diversity in the elementary classroom: A look at literature-based instruction in an inner city school.* Paper presented at the annual meeting of the National Reading Conference, San Antonio, TX.

Pardo, L. S. (1995). A fifth grade teacher's perspective on literature selection. In K. H. Au & T. E. Raphael (Co-chairs), *Everything you always wanted to know about literature-based instruction: Texts, organization, instruction, and assessment.* Institute presented at the annual meeting of the International Reading Association, Anaheim, CA.

Pardo, L. S. (1996). Becoming a reflective teacher: One teacher's journey on the road to reflective teaching. *Michigan Reading Journal, 29*(4), 28–36.

Pardo, L. S. (1996). Thematic instruction with upper elementary students: Linking literature and social studies. In K. H. Au & T. E. Raphael (Co-chairs), *A closer look at literature-based instruction: Promoting students talk about books.* Institute presented at the annual meeting of the International Reading Association, New Orleans, LA.

Pardo, L. S. (1997). Reflective teaching for continuing development of book club. In S. I. McMahon, T. E. Raphael, with V. G. Goatley, & L. S. Pardo, *The Book Club connection: Literacy learning and classroom talk.* New York: Teachers College Press.

Pearson, P. D. (1994). Integrated language arts: Sources of controversy and seeds of consensus. In L. M. Morrow, J. K. Smith, & L. C. Wilkinson (Eds.), *Integrated language arts: Controversy to consensus* (pp. 11–31). Boston: Allyn & Bacon.

Routman, R. (1988). *Transitions: From literature to literacy.* Portsmouth, NH: Heinemann Educational Books.

Short, K. (1992). The literature circles project. In K. Jongsma (Chair), *Understanding and enhancing literature discussion in elementary classrooms.* Symposium presented at the annual meeting of the National Reading Conference, San Antonio, TX.

Swift, K. (1993). Try reading workshop in your classroom. *The Reading Teacher, 46*(5), 366–371.

Valencia, S. (1995). *Thematic teaching in the reading program.* Paper presented at the annual meeting of the International Reading Association, Anaheim, CA.

Willis, S. (1995). Reinventing science education: Reformers promote hands-on, inquiry-based learning. *Association for Supervision and Curriculum Development,* Curriculum Update, Summer 1995.

CHILDREN'S BOOKS CITED

Allen, T. B. (1992). *The blue and the gray.* Washington DC: National Geographic Society.

Babbitt, N. (1975). *Tuck everlasting.* New York: Farrar, Straus & Giroux.

Bakeless, K., & Bakeless, J. (1973). *Confederate spy stories.* Philadelphia: J.B. Lippincott.

Beatty, P. (1987). *Charley Skedaddle.* New York: Troll.

Beatty, P. (1984). *Turn homeward Hannalee.* New York: Troll Associates.

Beatty, P. (1992). *Who comes with cannons?* New York: Scholastic, Inc.

Bunting, E. (1994). *Smoky night.* Illustrated by David Diaz. Orlando, FL: Harcourt Brace.

Coerr, E. (1977). *Sadako and the thousand paper cranes.* New York: Putnam.

Dahl, R. (1961). *James and the giant peach.* New York: Puffin.

Davidson, M. (1968). *Frederick Douglass fights for freedom.* New York: Scholastic.

Donovan, F. R. (1964). *Ironclads of the Civil War.* New York: American Heritage.

Everett, G. (1993). *John Brown: One man against slavery.* Illustrated by J. Lawrence. New York: Rizzoli.

Freedman, R. (1987). *Lincoln: A photobiography.* New York: Houghton Mifflin.

Gauch, P. L. (1975). *Thunder at Gettysburg.* Illustrated by S. Gammell. New York: Dell.

Hamilton, V. (1993). *Many thousand gone: African Americans from slavery to freedom.* Illustrated by L. & D. Dillon. New York: Alfred A. Knopf.

Haskins, J. (1993). *Get on board: The story of the underground railroad.* New York: Scholastic.

Hopkinson, D. (1993). *Sweet Clara and the freedom quilt.* Illustrated by J. Ransome. New York: Dragonfly Books.

Hunt, I. (1964). *Across five Aprils.* New York: Berkley Books.

Kiliam, M. (1995). The war between the capitals. In *The Chicago Tribune,* Travel section, 12, Sunday, April 2, 1995.

Konigsburg, E. L. (1967). *From the mixed-up files of Mrs. Basil E. Frankweiler.* New York: Atheneum.

L'Engle, M. (1962). *A wrinkle in time.* New York: Dell.

Levine, E. (1988). *. . . If you traveled on the Underground Railroad.* Illustrated by L. Johnson. New York: Scholastic.

Lunn, J. (1981). *The root cellar.* New York: Puffin.

Meltzer, M. (Ed.) (1993). *Lincoln: In his own words.* San Diego: Harcourt Brace.

Microsoft Encarta. (1993). *Civil War, American (Bibliography).* Funk & Wagnalls.

Murphy, J. (1990). *The boys' war: Confederate and Union soldiers talk about the Civil War.* Boston: Houghton Mifflin.

O'Dell, S. (1970). *Sing down the Moon.* New York: Dell.

Polacco, P. (1994). *Pink and Say.* New York: Philomel Books.

Paulsen, G. (1987). *Hatchet.* New York, Puffin Books.

Ray, D. (1991). *Behind the blue and gray: The soldier's life in the Civil War.* New York: Scholastic.

Reeder, C. (1989). *Shades of gray.* New York: Avon Books.

Reit, S. (1988). *Behind rebel lines.* Orlando, FL: Harcourt Brace.

Richards, K. (1992). *The Gettysburg Address.* Chicago: Children's Press.

Ringgold, F. (1992). *Aunt Harriet's underground railroad in the sky.* New York: Crown Publishing.

Smith, C. C. (1993). *1863: The crucial year: A sourcebook on the Civil War.* Brookfield, CT: Millbrook Press.

Speare, E. (1983). *The sign of the beaver.* Boston: Houghton Mifflin.

Sterling, D. (1954). *Freedom train: The story of Harriet Tubman.* New York: Doubleday.

Tsuchiya, Y. (1988). *Faithful elephants.* Boston: Houghton Mifflin.

Wade, L. R. (1991). *Andersonville: A Civil War tragedy.* Vero Beach, FL: Rourke Enterprises.

Ward, G. C. (1991). *Famous battles of the Civil War.* 100 card set. Glen Allen, VA: Tuff Stuff, Inc.

Winter, J. (1988). *Follow the drinking gourd.* New York: Alfred A. Knopf.

Woodruff, E. (1991). *George Washington's socks.* New York: Scholastic.

Chapter II

Assessment in Literature-Based Reading Programs: Have We Kept Our Promises?

Tanja Bisesi, Devon Brenner, Mary McVee,
P. David Pearson, and *Loukia K. Sarroub*[1]
Michigan State University

We have made incredible progress, both conceptually and practically, in the development of literacy assessment tools that appropriately reflect the goals and activities of literature-based reading programs. This progress, however, has not come without obstacles, many of which have not yet been (and may never be) fully negotiated. The purpose of this chapter is to provide an overview of the "promises" we as a literacy assessment community have made to ourselves, as we implement new forms of assessment for new purposes, and to critically evaluate our progress toward keeping those promises. We begin by briefly describing recent shifts in literacy instruction that have prompted us to make a set of promises for better literacy assessment. Second, we lay out the implicit promises we have made to ourselves as we have worked to develop alternative assessment tools and procedures and judge how well these promises have been kept. Finally, we address dilemmas that we will continue to face as we develop new literacy assessment tools and implement them for new purposes.

AN HISTORICAL LOOK AT
LITERACY INSTRUCTION AND ASSESSMENT

To fully appreciate and effectively evaluate progress made and challenges still faced by those who engage in the development of literacy assessments, it is important to situate our discussion in an historical context. Thus, in this section, we begin with a description of shifts in literacy instruction, including a portrait of a classroom in which these shifts have been implemented. We also discuss the challenges to traditional assessment practices presented by these shifts in literacy instruction, challenges that have prompted us to promise ourselves better literacy assessment and to develop an array of alternative assessment tools.

Shifts in Literacy Instruction

The views that we hold concerning what it means to be literate shape the way we teach and assess our students' literacy. Within the last 50 years there has been a shift in the beliefs of the literacy education community, not only in terms of what it means to be a literate individual, but also in how students learn and should best be taught (Langer, 1991). These changes in basic assumptions about literacy, knowledge, teaching, and learning are represented in changes in literacy education, including the recent literature-based instruction movement. At least four specific shifts accompanying this movement have had an influence on the way we think about assessing literacy growth and achievement and are reflected in the following instructional portrait: (a) emphasis on personal response, (b) appreciation of social and cultural aspects of literacy, (c) recognition of the fundamental and interrelated nature of language, and (d) concern for the meaningfulness of materials and tasks.

A Portrait of Current Practice. June is an exemplary, fifth-grade, literature-based reading teacher. Her classroom represents the best of what literature-based reading instruction has to offer in terms of instruction, curriculum, and assessment. In particular, when you walk into her classroom you see students engaging in the kinds of complex, meaningful activities that you would hope to see when visiting a literature-based classroom. Students are reading good literature (e.g., *Hatchet* by Paulsen, 1987; *Number the Stars* by Lowry, 1989) silently and in groups, responding to the literature in written journals, and using these journal responses as a tool for talking about the literature in student-led, small-group and teacher-guided, whole-class discussions. June does not limit her instruction to literacy conventions (e.g., how to decode print; how to talk about books). She also creates opportunities for students to develop comprehension strategies (e.g., summarizing, sequencing, predicting), and provides instruction on literary elements (e.g., genre, text structure), as well as models for responding personally (e.g., "how does this relate to my own life?"), creatively (e.g., "I would change the end of the story to this . . ."), and critically (e.g., "I wonder why the author wrote the book this way?") so that students develop rich interpretations of the literature they read. Further, June uses a portfolio assessment system, including student-generated artifacts (i.e., journal entries, discussion tape/transcripts, journal and discussion self-assessments) and tools that she has created (e.g., anecdotal notes, discussion and journal checklists) to report student strengths and weaknesses and growth to parents, to guide and help students reflect on their own learning, to aid her in instructional planning, and to demonstrate curriculum effectiveness to her administrator. June's classroom, while exemplary rather than typical, illustrates the shifts in literacy instruction we have experienced as a field.

Emphasis on Personal Response. The constructive and personal nature of literacy has been emphasized in literature-based instruction and is instantiated in the tasks (e.g., journal writing) and goals (e.g., personal response) of June's daily instruction. Comprehension instruction of the 1980s concerned itself with the constructive processes involved in textual understanding, and remains a focus (e.g., comprehension strategy goals) of literature-based teachers like June. Its goal, on the one hand, was to help students effectively "get," through activation or building of background, what was "in" the text, the author's message. Literature-based instruction, on the other hand, draws on reader response theories of textual understanding (Langer, 1990; Rosenblatt, 1991) that stress the transactional nature of reading, including what readers bring to the text as well as what they take from it. Instruction based on reader response theory also highlights the evolutionary and personal nature of interpretation, as the reader takes different stances on the text and responds both aesthetically and efferently. This orientation is reflected in June's use of journal writing and discussion as windows on student personal response as well as her direct instruction on a variety of ways to personally respond to text (e.g., "What do I like about the story and why?" "How does this relate to my own life?").

Appreciation of Social and Cultural Aspects of Literacy. With an increasing awareness of the social and cultural diversity of the student population has come a greater appreciation of the sociocultural aspects of literacy. Literature-based curriculum developers (e.g., Raphael, Pardo, Highfield, & McMahon, 1997) have begun to draw on the ideas of Vygotsky (1978) in an attempt to celebrate and cultivate these aspects of literacy. Literature-based programs grounded in a sociocultural perspective assume that knowledge is socially constructed within the context of collaborative, meaningful activities (Brock & Gavelek, Chapter 4). While the comprehension instruction of the recent past (e.g., Pearson & Fielding, 1991) attempted to help students get the author's message and make accurate inferences through the use of specific strategies such as KWL (Ogle, 1986), socially-oriented literature-based instruction provides students with multiple opportunities to demonstrate, internalize, and transform their knowledge and understandings through social interaction with their teacher and peers. These kinds of opportunities for socially-based knowledge construction are clearly demonstrated in our description of June's classroom. For example, June relies heavily on small-group and whole-class discussions as contexts for students to construct diverse and multiple interpretations of text.

Recognition of the Fundamental and Interrelated Nature of Language. Recently developed literature-based programs (e.g., Raphael et al., 1997; Au, Carroll, & Scheu, 1997) have almost universally recognized the fundamental and interrelated nature of language. While comprehension instruction of the past decade focused primarily on reading and writing and the ways in which each could be used to support the other, literature-based instruction targets oral language processes (e.g., speaking, listening) as a means of constructing text-based understanding and interpretations, as well as supporting written literacy processes. Thus, from the perspective of literature-based instruction, oral and written language promote the development of each other as they both contribute to new forms of thought and learning (Wells & Chang-Wells, 1992). Again, this perspective is reflected in June's instruction, as she has students read texts, write about their thoughts, and share ideas in the context of oral discussion.

Concern for Meaningfulness of Materials and Tasks. The use of "real" literature within the context of meaningful literacy activity has become a staple of literature-based literacy instruction. While comprehension instruction of the past decade stressed the constructive nature of reading, as does literature-based instruction, it relied almost exclusively on contrived textual materials or excerpts from complete literary works to constrain the students' reading task and help them develop effective comprehension strategies. Building on comprehension instruction's constructive nature, which drew on cognitive approaches to literacy (e.g., schema theory) in order to equip students with strategies (e.g., drawing on background knowledge) for understanding texts more effectively, literature-based instruction also promotes having students engage in holistic (e.g., reading a whole novel), meaningful (e.g., talking to peers about books read) literacy activity. These activities, where the teacher (or a peer) provides an appropriate level of assistance or scaffolding, help the student to make sense of text in complex and diverse ways (e.g., from multiple perspectives) rather than relying on a predictable or contrived text structure to provide the support. June's instruction, described above, reflects this concern for meaningfulness, as she has students read complete pieces of interesting literature and supports (along with peers) their evolving understandings.

Challenges to Traditional Assessment Practices

While beliefs about literacy learning and instruction have changed in the ways previously described, the principles and methods that shape the way we assess students' literacy have remained relatively unchanged. Many of the challenges to traditional assessments such as standardized tests have arisen from the fact that these assessments do not align well with literature-based literacy curricula (see Bisesi & Raphael, in press).

Standardized tests tend to tap isolated, low-level skills in decontextualized contexts (Haladyna, Nolan, & Haas, 1991; Shepard, 1989), rather than the complex understandings, personal responses, or intertextual interpretations constructed during meaningful literacy activities. They do not reflect the tasks or texts, such as trade books, used within the context of literature-based instruction. These tests have led students to focus on performance over learning, and they have caused teachers to focus on tested skills rather than their beliefs about literacy (Paris, Calfee, Filby, Hiebert, Pearson, Valencia, & Wolf, 1992; Shepard, 1989). The narrowing of curricula, to focus on the isolated and low-level skills caused by high-stakes standardized testing, is not consistent with the interactive, social, holistic aspects of literature-based instruction. What is uncertain is whether *any* form of multiple-choice, standardized assessment can ever support the goals and principles underlying literature-based reading. Indeed, the most serious attempts to build multiple-choice formats to meet such goals, the statewide assessments in Michigan and Illinois (Valencia, Wixson, Peters, & Pearson, 1989), have met with incredible resistance and criticism from literature-based reading advocates.

In addition to serious problems with curriculum misalignment, conventional tests have been taken to task for a variety of other sins of omission or commission. Tests don't respect the cultural nature of language and literacy (García & Pearson, 1994). They have a long history of negative impact on minorities, with some forms of bias being more blatant, and some more insidious (García & Pearson, 1994). With an emphasis on secrecy and the isolation of individuals during testing, tests have ignored the social aspects of literacy learning (Pearson, DeStefano, & García, in press). With their focus on objectivity and machine-scoring, tests remove the very individuals most responsible for making decisions, the teachers, from the evaluation process.

As we became aware of these challenges to standardized tests (e.g., Paris, Lawton, Turner, & Roth, 1991; Shepard, 1989), we developed an awareness of the need for appropriate, alternative approaches for thinking about, examining, and evaluating students' learning (e.g., Paris, Calfee, Filby, Hiebert, Pearson, Valencia, & Wolf, 1992; Au et al., 1990; Valencia, 1990). This concern prompted us, as a profession, to make a set of promises to ourselves, our students, and our constituents as we went about the business of developing assessments more appropriate to our curriculum and our information needs in the 1990s. In the remainder of this chapter, we discuss these promises and evaluate how well we have kept them.

PROMISES

The set of promises involved authenticity, instructional validity, openness, diversity, client-centeredness, and imaginative assessments.

Authenticity

First was the promise of authenticity. We promised to build assessments grounded in real-world literacy activities and tasks, rather than invented out of psychometric convenience. Our new assessments would have the look and feel of the real thing. Students would read real texts, like the trade books used in June's classroom, not short snippets contrived by item writers to provide lots of tricky distracters or opaque items focusing on obscure details of the text. Instead of selecting the line or words in a snippet that illustrate correct grammar, diction, vocabulary, punctuation, or spelling to demonstrate their knowledge of composition, students would demonstrate both their writing prowess and control over conventions by writing real essays, stories, and reflections, with plenty of time to complete the steps in the writing process—activities emphasized in literature-based classrooms like June's.

Authenticity is complicated. The most important question is the source of the standard for authenticity. If authenticity is determined by comparing a task to a curriculum, then given a separate skills, decontextualized curriculum, many of the decontextualized, specific-skill, multiple-choice items of standardized tests might well meet the authenticity standard. However, if authenticity comes from the uses of literacy in everyday life, or from the concepts of literacy that underlie the curriculum in process writing and literature-based reading, then only performance tasks and work samples in portfolios are likely to meet the authenticity standard. Authenticity is *not* identical to curricular validity. In fact, for an assessment task to meet the authenticity criterion, it must come from a curriculum that is itself grounded in the authentic uses of literacy outside of school settings. This authenticity was illustrated in the portrait of June's instruction, as she encouraged students to discuss the books they read and use their writing as a tool to support their discussions.

How well have we kept the promise of authenticity? Tolerably well, we think. The proliferation of articles and books about portfolio projects in schools throughout the English-speaking world is quite amazing. Our own work in schools in Michigan suggests that an increasing number of schools are moving rapidly to a central role for portfolios, at least for classroom use. Increasingly, multi-draft papers, response journals, and essays reflecting on one's progress in reading and writing are being included in portfolios. And at least a few states, such as Vermont, Kentucky, and Maryland, have developed elaborate portfolio or performance assessment systems for statewide assessment and school accountability schemes.

On the negative side, portfolios and performance assessments are often seen as auxiliary to the "real" assessment system of standardized tests and grading practices. Rarely are they used as a part of the grading process in schools. In fact, some educators disparage the use of portfolios for grading on the grounds that it somehow makes the experience less valuable, in terms of ownership and reflection, for students. Subjecting student work and reflection to scoring rubrics or point values seems to "sully" the whole process (e.g., Tierney et al., 1991). We find ourselves in a dilemma. We are worried about the negative impact of connecting high stakes (grades and scores) to portfolios. Yet by failing to do so, we may insure a marginalized role for portfolios in the overall assessment picture. At the large-scale level, we note that many states (e.g., California, Wisconsin, and Indiana) have either reversed or abandoned performance assessment systems in response to concerns about expense, time, and intrusiveness.

Instructional Validity

Second was the promise of *instructional validity.* To say that an assessment possesses instructional validity is to say that it both reflects and promotes good instructional practices. The first requirement of instructional validity is to build assessments derived from best practice—not just any old instructional practice, but best practice—or what we as a profession point to when we say, this is exemplary (an example of this kind of exemplary practice is reflected in our portrait of June described earlier in this chapter). A second requirement of instructional validity is that the assessments lead to good instructional practice; teachers who use the assessments will end up exposing students to first-rate instruction. A third requirement of instructional validity that follows from the previous requirements is that assessments will no longer put teachers at odds with their better judgment. As tests have assumed increasingly high stakes for individual students, teachers, or schools, teachers have experienced internal conflict. Many feel compelled to put their instructional programs on hold in order to get students ready to take tests so foreign to their normal curriculum that special preparation is necessary.

To say that we have promised to worry about instructional validity is to say that we have promised to evaluate the validity of tests in terms of their consequences, their *consequential validity,* for students, teachers, and schools (Messick, 1989; Linn, Baker, & Dunbar, 1993). Literacy assessments should result in decisions that propel students into activities that are optimally suited to helping them become more accomplished readers and writers, such as June's literacy portfolios, which encourage students to be self-reflective readers and writers. All too often, we fear, as a consequence of participating in examinations, students are guided into inappropriate or counterproductive activities, such as practicing the skill of filling out bubble sheets. According to this criterion of consequences, such assessments would be judged invalid.

How have we fared on this promise? Again, moderately well. With the rapid spread of portfolios and performance assessments, accompanied by their use by teachers in making curricular decisions for classes and instructional decisions for individual students, more students than ever before are gaining access to challenging, engaging, curricular tasks, like those that are part of June's curriculum. These tasks involve lots of reading, writing, drama, and discussions prompted by the need to find a diverse array of artifacts to represent student growth and accomplishment. Unfortunately, these positive developments are only part of the picture. We still hear all too many accounts of schools and teachers who feel compelled to spend hours and hours preparing students to take high-stakes performance assessments that will result in published scores for the schools and consequences (such as diploma endorsement) for students. We even hear stories of classrooms in which students and teachers find themselves "packing to the portfolio" (i.e., creating items specifically to enhance the appearance of the portfolio) rather than "teaching to the test." If and where this occurs, it is strong evidence of the insidious power that we, as a society and a school culture, accord to assessments of any and all stripes when we require them to serve high-stakes functions in our society.

Openness

Promising "openness" in our assessment systems means that teachers, students, and parents are privy to the principles and standards underlying the assessment systems that affect students' lives and academic well-being. Assessment can be viewed as a process of making claims about knowledge (Wiggins, 1993). Students, teachers, and parents should have the opportunity to understand (and even influence) the implicit and explicit criteria underlying knowledge claims made in the classroom and in the larger school setting. Consequently, openness incorporates the prior knowledge of all experiences and tasks that teachers and students have in their collective possession (Wiggins, 1993). In addition, openness requires clarity in the explication of standards and criteria that teachers use to make judgments about students' work. In turn, the need for clarity suggests that dialogue among students and teachers about standards should become a central part of the assessment process. Such as is the case in June's classroom when she negotiates with students target performance criteria for journal writing and discussions. In other words, tests and test experiences can no longer be the "secret" journeys that students dread to make because of intimidation and fear of the unexpected. Instead, dialogue and common exploration can render the whole process, including the knowledge requirements and the standards for mastery, transparent. Students and teachers, by having the opportunity to be open about evaluation and assessment procedures and criteria, can easily draw connections between curriculum and assessments derived from it. Openness, then, allows for individual as well as collective opportunities to claim a genuine understanding both of knowledge and the ways that students can claim that knowledge for themselves.

Openness also means being open to self-examination. Related to this is the issue of accessibility. If the assessment system is not open to both self-examination and public scrutiny, people who can negotiate the system (figure out the rules on their own) are automatically privileged. Those who cannot negotiate the system tend to use compensatory strategies with short-term positive effects and find themselves falling behind; they are then tracked differently from those who can effectively negotiate the system. It is also worthwhile to note another side of openness. Lack of secrecy also makes teachers and students vulnerable to public scrutiny. Standardized tests, for example, expedite the process of large-scale evaluation because they are rather uncomplicated and can "travel" across a range of teaching philosophies and styles (which may mean simply that they are equally as irrelevant to the goals of many philosophies and styles). Performance-based assessments, on the other hand, are often co-constructed by teachers and students (and even parents) and may raise the specter of subjectivity (a positivist assumption that has been imported into the constructivist paradigm). The complicated implicit and explicit agreements embedded in performance assessment can be difficult for teachers or the public to penetrate. One teacher we worked with told us that she could implement the portfolio, for example, as the only means of assessment if she "put herself in her classroom with her students and did not pay attention to outside pressures" (Sarroub, Pearson, Dykema, Lloyd, 1996; p. 13). In other words, the challenge we face in being open is to balance our need to create accountable systems of evaluation that are clear to the public with our desire to acknowledge and respect the perspectives and decisions teachers and students make.

Progress on this promise is mixed. In our attempts to be more "open" in the examination of student work, we have shifted our focus from standardized, multiple-choice assessments to alternative forms such as performance-based assessments. Because measures are derived from actual performance, performance-based assessments are more "open" (and perhaps valid) because students have more opportunities to reflect on and be engaged in their work. In addition, the widespread use of rubrics, especially rubrics that are published and widely shared in advance of actual assessments, provides everyone with access to the apparent standards for mastery. For example, one teacher we worked with showed us his eighth-grade students' papers in which his students focused on four criteria in their writing: content, voice/creativity, form, and mechanics (Sarroub, Pearson, Dykema, & Lloyd, 1996). By utilizing this rubric, the students were able to openly negotiate and reflect on ways to meet the writing standards in their classroom. However, many problems existed. First, it was not always apparent just how "clearly" the rubrics conveyed a portrait of mastery. In other words, a good rubric evolved from a teacher's examination of many aspects of students' work over time, such that both the teacher and the student had a clear understanding of the relative difference in mastery between, for example, a 3.5 and a 4.0. This process, however, was a difficult one to navigate, as teachers and students tried out new types of assignments and changed their curricula.

Second, as suggested by Linn, Baker, and Dunbar, "serious validation of alternative assessments needs to include evidence regarding the intended and unintended consequences, the degree to which performance on specific assessment tasks transfers to other situations, including everyday performance, and the fairness of the assessments" (1991, p. 20). In other words, reconciling internal (classroom-based) and external (outside of the classroom domain in which we are currently working) means of accountability is crucial, especially if assessments are to reflect curricular and societal goals. We must be open to the possibility that it is not obvious whether internal or external means of accountability are more open. In fact, students complain all the time about what it is exactly that the teacher expects of them. Hence, the jury is still out on our promise of openness; we need more reflexive, critical examination of current tools before we can make any definitive pronouncements.

Diversity

Even before literacy and teacher educators began to consider the role of assessment in literature-based programs, researchers and those concerned with the education of diverse students had begun to call for assessments that were not biased in favor of mainstream students. Traditional assessments such as standardized tests as well as more specialized measures such as IQ tests, it was argued, were biased toward students with high levels of proficiency in English and knowledge of Anglo mainstream culture. In response, some proposed culture-free or culture-fair testing, while others proposed changes in how tests were norm-referenced, and yet others advocated testing in the student's first language.

As these and other suggestions surfaced, various drawbacks also became apparent. For example, culture-free and culture-fair tests did not eliminate the correlation between IQ performance and socioeconomic status and also had lower predictive validity than traditional standardized tests; changing the way tests were norm-referenced was found to be expensive and problematic because tests could not be compared to the general population; and testing in students' first languages was also found to be problematic because it is difficult to determine which language is dominant for the student and it is extremely difficult for a test to reflect the multiple ways language is used

(García & Pearson, 1994). Yet in spite of these and other difficulties that have arisen, we promised ourselves that our new assessments would value and more accurately and fairly assess the knowledge of students from diverse economic, racial, and linguistic backgrounds. Toward this end, authentic, contextualized assessments have been proposed as alternatives to standardized, formalized measures, and progress has been made in designing various tools such as portfolios, rubrics, standards, anecdotal records, essay exams, and the like. Thus, there are more options available to educators. Viewed from this perspective, we may even conclude that we have fulfilled our promise.

We must be careful, however, not to assume that the availability of such alternatives is a solution in itself, for little research exists to demonstrate that such measures are truly more reflective of what students with diverse linguistic and cultural backgrounds know and can do (Madaus, 1994). At a national level, research that has been done around various performance-based tests, such as the National Assessment of Educational Progress (NAEP), still indicates significant achievement differences between ethnic and linguistic minorities and their Anglo counterparts (Linn, Baker, Dunbar, 1991; NAEP, 1994). At the local level, there is little documentation that explores the implementation and sustained use of alternative assessments with students from diverse cultural, economic, and linguistic backgrounds, although there are a few notable exceptions.

Central Park East Secondary School and International High School are among those schools that have successfully restructured to include portfolio assessment as an integral and successful component in the curriculum (Darling-Hammond, Ancess, & Falk, 1995). These successful examples indicate that performance-based assessment can provide an equitable accounting of what students from diverse cultural and linguistic backgrounds have learned. We must keep in mind, however, that performance assessment is not the only issue that precipitated success in these school settings, as many other factors also came into play as these schools were restructured. While results from particular schools are encouraging and provide a model for future reform, the promise that alternative assessments are more equitable must continue to be viewed from a critical stance at both the local and national level.

From a practical standpoint, and as exemplified by Central Park East Secondary School and International High School, the use of innovative assessments requires innovative thinking by teachers, administrators, and policy makers. To fulfill the promise, teachers, administrators, and policy makers must have the knowledge and resources to implement alternative assessments. In part, this means that teacher educators and researchers interested in assessment must provide resources, support, feedback, and documentation for those who are willing to implement alternative assessments. It also means that we will need to commit ourselves to valuing alternative assessments so that high-stakes decisions within schools reflect these changes.

We must acknowledge that implementing and sustaining alternative assessments with learners from diverse backgrounds will not help those learners unless we also work to develop a reflective stance among key participants—parents, students, teachers, administrators, and policy makers. This is of particular importance for teachers because, while the student population has continued to increase in linguistic and ethnic diversity, the teaching force has remained predominantly Anglo, female, and middle class. Thus, it is not only necessary to develop and implement alternative assessments, but to facilitate teachers' understanding and reflection by considering questions such as the following: What are the benefits and pitfalls of alternative assessments? Are alternative assessments less biased toward linguistic and ethnic minorities? Do they allow students to draw on their cultural and linguistic strengths? What are the practical concerns teachers must consider when implementing and sustaining such alternatives? Only after we have fully explored these and other related questions will we be able to fully evaluate our progress toward creating assessments that value ethnic and linguistic diversity.

Client-Centeredness

As our beliefs about the nature of literacy learning and instruction and the nature of assessment changed, so did our commitment to the clients of assessment. We vowed that our new assessments would be more client-centered and provide valuable information to all audiences: students, teachers, families, administrators, and policy makers. In the past, the assessments that mattered were designed for and focused on the needs of administrators and program decision makers (Abruscato, 1993). Alternative assessments, we vowed, would provide new and more important information to teachers, students, and parents. In this section, we talk about the various clients for assessment and the ways that alternative assessments have attempted to meet their needs.

Teachers need information that helps them describe what their students can do, that allows them to discover and recreate the kinds of experiences that help children learn, that encourages them to modify and refine their teaching practices, and that facilitates their communication with students about both expectations and accomplishments. Traditional high-stakes assessments, such as report cards and test scores, often do not provide such information. On-going classroom activities have the potential to provide information about progress on important curricular goals, especially when they are supported by the ancillary tools of alternative assessment: reflection, collaboration, rubrics, and portfolio collections.

Students need assessments that allow them to reflect upon their learning, to gauge their progress, and to set future goals for learning (IRA/NCTE standards, 1994). All of this can take place when the act of performing the assessment itself causes students to think actively and reflect on their own learning. In June's classroom, for example, students reflect on their growth and accomplishment as they collect, write about, and share their portfolio artifacts.

Teachers can also help students to understand their own learning progress and to set learning goals by conducting assessments that serve students' needs as well as their own. As teachers collect and think about the artifacts they need to understand their students and their own teaching, they can share what they learn with students. Rather than telling students "how they did" on a task, teachers can share their assessment tools—such as benchmarks and rubrics—and their interpretations with students in order to assist students in evaluating their own efforts and making decisions about their future learning. In June's classroom, for example, June regularly scores her students' portfolios according to a set of target benchmarks, and shares those benchmarks and scores with students, talking with them at length about just how and why she assigned the score she did.

Parents are often most interested in information that lets them understand their own child's progress. Traditionally, parents have been provided with test scores, letter grades, and unannotated work samples. Alternative assessments often provide parents with unfamiliar kinds of data, including student and teacher reflections on growth and accomplishment and information about the process, as well as the products, of assessment. While teachers are working to provide parents with richer, more detailed descriptions of student learning, parents often continue to ask for data that allows them to make comparisons between students. When faced with such questions, teachers reluctant to make comparisons can help parents understand just how their child "stacks up" against predetermined and preset benchmarks, rather than against other students. Teachers can share with parents their standards for learning. They can help parents have a sense of the typical or a sense of the ways that standards and expectations grow and change across time and across grade levels.

Have we met these promises? It isn't clear at this point that assessments are being used consistently in ways that meet the needs of students, teachers, and parents. Gillespie, Ford, Gillespie and Leavall (1996), for example, raise concerns about portfolio assessment, including concerns that teachers may tend to focus on management and collection rather than reflection and learning, and that portfolios may lead to less, rather than more, conversation with teachers.

However, new kinds of assessments and new attitudes toward assessments have the potential for serving these three types of clients (Bisesi, 1997).

Teachers have begun to add their voices to the assessment milieu and have become actively involved in developing and creating alternative assessments for use in their own classrooms (Wiggins, 1993). The documents that arise naturally out of sound instructional practices (e.g., written journals, responses to literature, performances) have taken on new significance as artifacts for assessment. Increasingly, teachers, students, and parents pore over these artifacts to create portfolios that reflect the learning that has taken place (e.g., Graves & Sunstein, 1992; Educators in Connecticut's Pomperaug Regional School District 15, 1996). The process of creating these collections has been as valuable as the information that arises out of them.

Parents, teachers, and students are grouped together here in part because the emphasis on these assessment audiences has increased, but also because all of these clients, in their own ways, needs thick description of students' learning and accomplishment. Administrators and policy makers need, or at least request, aggregated data, which often takes the form of scores averaged across students, classrooms, or schools. But even though administrators continue to feel the need for numbers and scores, the assessments that lead up to those scores are changing. Teachers and administrators in several states (e.g., Vermont, Kentucky, California, Maryland) have worked together to provide both individual and aggregate scores that arise from portfolios or performance assessments. These assessments have the potential of providing results that support instruction and also permit policy analysis, thus simultaneously supplying valuable information not only to administrators but to teachers, students, and parents. It is possible that the same tools that teachers, parents, and students reflect on could be consistently and concisely used to provide information to audiences outside the classroom. While there are inherent difficulties in exporting classroom-based assessments (Pearson, DeStefano, & García, in press), both in maintaining the richness of information and in preserving worthwhile instructional activities, this process holds great potential for all the clients of assessment.

Imaginative, "Break-the-Mold" Assessments

Standardized, limited-response tests, including large-scale norm-referenced as well as curriculum-oriented criterion-referenced tests, have been the touchstone of educational assessment for several decades. While these tests have come to serve the purposes of school administrators and policy makers quite well, providing a simple measure of achievement across large numbers of students and a degree of fairness with their standardized "level playing field" administration and scoring, they have become increasingly limited in helping teachers, students, and even parents understand the complexities of curriculum, instruction, and student learning (Bisesi, 1997; Farr, 1992). New forms of assessment came to us with the potential not only to provide information that would allow us to monitor student academic progress, but also help teachers to teach better and students to learn more effectively.

Given this potential, we promised ourselves to develop new, imaginative, "break-the-mold" assessments that we did not assume or require to resemble or even correlate highly with conventional assessments. We started to ask ourselves questions such as, "What would literacy assessments look like if we put the emphasis on literacy rather than assessment?" "What would these assessments look like if reading theory rather than psychometric theory were the driving force behind their development?"

The process of literacy teaching and learning, as it is conceptualized both theoretically and in today's literature-based classrooms, is awesome and complex. In literature-based classrooms students engage in a range of purposeful and interrelated language arts activities including reading, writing, and talking about good literature and trade books, as instantiated in June's instruction described earlier in this chapter. Students interpret and reinterpret the texts they read in written forms and through discussion with both teacher and peers. These rich activities, within which students are making sense of text, require rich and imaginative assessment tools, in order to provide information that reflects the range of student learning taking place (e.g., Wiggins, 1993; Resnick & Resnick, 1985).

Our promise for "break-the-mold" assessments, not limited to the standardized test models of the past, has been relatively well kept. The assessment literature is full of accounts of attempts, on both a large-scale (e.g., NAEP; Vermont; Kentucky) and classroom-oriented level (Bisesi, 1995; Graves & Sunstein, 1992; Tierney et al., 1991), to create portfolios and performance assessments that apply new methods of collecting (e.g., Bisesi & Raphael, 1996; Au et al., 1990) and interpreting information about literacy teaching and learning (e.g., Moss, 1996; Delandshere & Petrosky, 1994) and new standards for judging the validity of our methods (e.g., Moss, 1992; Messick, 1989). We must, however, craft our assessments carefully to ensure that the focus remains on curriculum and not on the "test." While some researchers have advocated driving curriculum/instruction in directions we want it to go by creating and implementing "good" assessments (Resnick & Resnick, 1985), we have to take care not to design innovative assessments that lead curriculum too far off track. Thus, we should look to curriculum for our lead in developing break-the-mold assessments.

ONGOING DILEMMAS

We have talked about the ways that the field of assessment has responded to changes in literacy instruction and about criticism of more traditional assessments. Not all of the promised innovations have materialized yet. But the promises of authenticity, validity, respect for diversity, imagination, and client-centeredness continue to be ideals that parents, teachers, administrators, and students strive for as they continue to reflect on and articulate their assessment needs. Even if we could fulfill our promises by expanding the tools and the range of evidence for assessing students, we still would not reach a fully satisfying outcome, for a set of dilemmas would remain. These dilemmas are not unique to alternative assessments; rather they are inherent in any act of assessment. We highlight four that are as important as they are elusive: (1) feasibility, (2) fairness, (3) purpose, and (4) values.

Feasibility

Feasibility of assessments concern their benefit-to-cost (in terms of time and money) ratio. While traditional, standardized tests are cost effective, they have imposed on the instructional and learning time of teachers and students, without benefiting the teaching and learning taking place in literature-based classrooms. New assessments promise to provide more meaningful information about teaching and learning, while intruding less on (or even enhancing) the everyday literacy activity taking place in the classroom. Because portfolios draw on documents generated during the course of instruction, assessment information is directly relevant to decisions about teaching and learning. Furthermore, assessments are more feasible for teachers to implement in their classrooms and school buildings (e.g., Au et al., 1990).

Nevertheless, using instructionally related documents can place a burden on teachers and schools, a burden that only time and effort can carry. First, standards for evaluating documents must be clearly defined through extensive negotiation and consensus building to avoid later disagreements and disappointment. These standards are frequently laid out in the form of rubrics to simplify the process of evaluating student work (e.g., Bisesi, 1996). Second, because interjudge reliability is often low for artifacts scored using rubrics, the number of artifacts in a portfolio collection will need to be relatively high in order to ensure adequate representation of performance.

Fairness

Fairness, being as equitable as possible to all who must live with tests, has long been touted as an ideal, a standard, of all good assessments. It is fairness that drives us to "treat everyone equally." But equitable treatment is an elusive goal, and when we attempt to ensure it, we often end up victims of a conspiracy of our own good intentions. The problem is that any time we use one criterion (e.g., everyone answers the same questions under the same conditions) to establish "equity," then some individuals, those who would have benefited from a different criterion of "sameness," are marginalized. Falling victim to our own good intentions is all the more serious and all the more likely with respect to matters of cultural and linguistic diversity.

In discussing issues of equity, it is common for us to use metaphors of equality, such as a level playing field or a common yardstick. Yet, the one-size-fits-all approach is likely to perpetuate the differences in academic performance that we commonly find in indices such as dropout rates, scores on college entrance tests, and national standards attainment. Put differently, the level playing field approach establishes one kind of equity (they all did the same task under the same conditions) while allowing other kinds of equity (e.g., the opportunity to perform familiar tasks in familiar contexts or the opportunity to put one's best foot forward) to vary dramatically. Ironically, in the few documented instances in which we have used assessment tools that recognize, acknowledge, and value diversity, we get a very different and more positive picture of students' capabilities (see the earlier section on diversity).

If we want to establish an alternative type of equity, an equity in which all students get the opportunity to put their "best-foot-forward" or "show their stuff," then other options may be necessary. The best-foot-forward metaphor for equity would lead us toward *choice* as a primary tool for achieving equity: choice of passages to read, questions to answer, prompts to write to, projects to complete, or even sociolinguistic contexts in which to work. In principle, this would not seem to be a problem within a performance assessment milieu; performance assessment, particularly portfolios, ought to allow—even champion—diverse ways of solving problems, accomplishing tasks, and meeting standards.

Even staying within the logic of the level-playing-field metaphor, other options are available. If we use the framework of dynamic assessment, we change the task for ourselves as teachers and our students. We end up asking ourselves how much support is needed to help particular students accomplish a specified goal or level of achievement. In this instance, instead of leveling opportunity, we are leveling achievement and allowing the type and amount of scaffolding provided to vary. Consider the revolution that might occur if choice and scaffolding rather than standardization drove our quest for equity. We would have a very different concept of assessment, not to mention a very different concept of curriculum.

Purpose

As Farr (1992) so astutely pointed out, different assessment audiences need different kinds of assessment information. Unfortunately, there is often a tension among the needs of different assessment constituencies. While administrators and other policy makers tend to need aggregated, standardized test score data in order to make decisions about curricular programs or educational policy, and teachers and students need instructionally relevant information to guide curriculum, instruction, and learning in the classroom, parents want information concerning how their individual child is performing relative to classroom standards and his or her peer group (Bisesi, 1997). Sometimes the needs of more powerful constituencies (e.g., administrators' and policy makers' need for standardized test information) subvert the needs of less powerful constituencies (e.g., the need of students and teachers to be held accountable for instruction and learning relevant to literature-based reading programs).

Unless we come to terms with the fact that different assessment audiences need and deserve different kinds of assessment information, the dilemma of conflicting assessment purposes will continue to plague the implementation of alternative assessments. We must respect the unique needs of all assessment audiences and work to build assessment systems that ensure that all groups concerned get the assessment information they want and need (Bisesi, 1997). Furthermore, it is critical that we not fall into the trap of relying on only a single source of information (e.g., standardized tests) to make important decisions about curriculum and instruction (in place in literature-based reading classrooms) in order to avoid undervaluing the complexity of learning we want to encourage.

Values

Literature-based programs are meant to do much more than help students learn to decode text. As they interact with texts and each other, children are meant to become critical, problem-solving users of language. As the authors of the *International Reading Association/National Council of Teachers of English Standards for the English Language Arts* (1994) state, "Our aim is to ensure that all students develop the literacy skills they need to succeed in school, in the workplace, and in the various domains of life" (p. B). All of the other aims of literacy education, from personal response to literature to multiple ways of representing and sharing interpretations of text, eventually link back to helping students grow the literacy skills they need for success in their lives. And because of this link, our final dilemma will never disappear.

While we all hope for successful lives for our students as they use their literacy skills, we cannot ever agree about just what it means to be successful. Defining success, like defining any other benchmark of accomplishment, is an inherently value-laden action. Success might be financial, it might be emotional, it might be intellectual. This discussion of the value-ladenness dilemma provides a convenient and appropriate place to end our discussion of promises and problems. Differences in values color every aspect of the assessment of student learning in literature-based classrooms. The setting of goals, the choosing of evidence, the interpretation of artifacts, all ultimately depend upon teachers' values and their goals for teaching and learning. It is perhaps because assessment is so value-laden that the promises we have made—promises for authenticity, instructional validity, diversity, openness, client-centeredness, and imagination—have been so difficult, and so important, to keep.

CONCLUDING COMMENT

In conclusion, we as a literacy assessment community have come a long way toward keeping our promises to create alternative assessments that are authentic, instructionally valid, innovative, open, client-centered and respectful of the ethnic, cultural, and linguistic diversity of students making up current literature-based reading classrooms. And while we have kept some of the promises to a greater degree (e.g., the promise for break-the-mold assessments) than others (e.g., the promise for assessments that respect diversity), we must remain committed to these promises, as well as to the ongoing dilemmas of feasibility, fairness, purpose, and values, as we continue to design and implement alternative assessments for use in literature-based reading classrooms.

ENDNOTE

1. Authorship order was determined by attributing first author status to the individual that we, collectively, decided had made the greatest contribution to the overall effort. The second through the fifth authors, we determined, contributed equally to the process, so we listed their names alphabetically.

REFERENCES

Abruscato, J. (1993). Early results and tentative implications from the Vermont Portfolio Project. *Phi Delta Kappan, 474–477.*

Afflerbach, P. P., & Johnston, P. H. (1993). Writing language arts report cards: Eleven teachers' conflicts of knowing and communicating. *The Elementary School Journal, 94*(1), 72–74.

Au, K. H., Scheu, J. A., Kawakami, A. J., & Herman, P. A. (1990). Assessment and accountability in a whole literacy curriculum. *The Reading Teacher, 43,* 574–578.

Bisesi, T. (1997). *Exploring the value of a performance-based assessment: A social validity analysis.* East Lansing, MI: Unpublished dissertation, Michigan State University.

Bisesi, T. L. (1996). Upper-elementary students' written responses to text: A holistic scoring rubric for evaluating journal entries. In D. J. Leu, C. K. Kinzer, & K. A. Hinchman (Eds.), *Literacies for the 21st century: Research and practice* (pp. 76–87). Chicago, IL: National Reading Conference.

Bisesi, T. L., & Raphael, T. E. (1997). Assessment research in the Book Club program. In S. McMahon & T. Raphael (Eds.), *The Book Club project: Exploring literature-based reading instruction* (pp. 184–204). New York: Teachers College Press.

Darling-Hammond, L., Ancess, J., & Falk, B. (1995). *Authentic assessment in action: Studies of schools and students at work.* New York: Teachers College Press.

Delandshere, G., & Petrosky, A. (1994). Capturing teachers' knowledge: Performance assessment and post-structuralism. *Educational Researcher, 23*(5), 11–18.

Educators in Connecticut's Pomperaug Regional School District 15 (1996). *A teacher's guide to performance based learning and assessment.* Alexandria, VA: Association for Supervision and Curriculum Development.

Farr, R. (1992). Putting it all together: Solving the reading assessment puzzle. *The Reading Teacher, 46*(1), 26–37.

García, G. E., & Pearson, P. D. (1994). Assessment and diversity. In L. Darling-Hammond (Ed.), *Review of research in education* (Vol. 20) (pp. 337–391). Washington, DC: American Educational Research Association.

Gillespie, C., Ford, K., Gillespie, R., & Leavall, A. (1991). Portfolio assessment: Some questions, some answers, some recommendations. *Journal of Adolescent and Adult Literacy, 39*(6), 480–491.

Graves, D., & Sunstein, B. (1992). *Portfolio portraits.* Portsmouth, NH: Heinemann.

Haladyna, R., Nolan, S. B., & Haas, N. (1991). Raising standardized achievement tests scores and the origins of test score pollution. *Educational Researcher, 20*(5), 2–7.

International Reading Association/National Council of Teachers of English (1994). *Professional summary: Standards for the English language arts.* Urbana, IL: National Council of Teachers of English.

Langer, J. A. (1990). Understanding literature. *Language Arts, 67,* 812–816.

Linn, R. L., Baker, E. L., & Dunbar, S. B. (1991). Complex, performance-based assessment: Expectations and validation criteria. *Educational Researcher, 20,* 15–21.

Madaus, G. F. (1994). A technological and historical consideration of equity issues associated with proposals to change the nation's testing policy. *Harvard Educational Review, 64*(1), 76–95.

Messick, S. (1989). Validity. In R. L. Linn (Ed.), *Educational measurement* (3rd ed., pp. 13–103). Washington, DC: American Council on Education and National Council on Measurement in Education.

Moss, P. (1996). Enlarging the dialogue in educational measurement: Voices from interpretive research traditions. *Educational Researcher, 25*(1), 20–28, 43.

Moss, P. (1992). Validity in educational measurement. *Review of Educational Research, 62*(3), 229–258.

National Assessment of Educational Progress (1994). *1994 Reading Report Card for the Nation and the States.* Washington DC: National Center for Educational Statistics.

Ogle, D. M. (1986). K-W-L: A teaching model that develops active reading of expository text. *The Reading Teacher, 39*(6), 564–570.

Paris, S., Lawton, T., Turner, J., & Roth, J. (1991). A developmental perspective on standardized achievement testing. *Educational Researcher, 20*(5), 12–20.

Paris, S., Calfee, R., Filby, N., Hiebert, E., Pearson, P. D., Valencia, S., & Wolf, K. (1992). A framework for authentic literacy assessment. *The Reading Teacher, 46*(2), 88–98.

Pearson, P. D., DeStefano, L., & Garciá, G. E. (in press). Dilemmas in reading assessment. In C. Harrison & T. Salinger (Eds.), *Assessing reading 1: Theory and practice.* London: Routledge.

Pearson, P. D., & Fielding, L. (1991). Comprehension instruction. In R. Barr, M. L. Kamil, P. Mosenthal, & P. D. Pearson (Eds.), *Handbook of reading research* (pp. 819–860). New York: Longman.

Raphael, T. E., Pardo, L. S., Highfield, K., & McMahon, S. I. (1997). *Book Club: A literature-based curriculum.* Newton, MA: Small Planet Communications.

Resnick, D., & Resnick, L. (1985). Standards, curriculum, and performance: A historical and comparative perspective. *Educational Researcher,* 5–20.

Rosenblatt, L. M. (1991). Literary theory. In J. Flood, J. M. Jensen, D. Lapp, & J. R. Squire (Eds.), *Handbook of research on teaching the English language arts* (pp. 57–62). New York: Macmillan.

Sarroub, L. K., Pearson, P. D., Dykema, C., & Lloyd, R. (1996, December). When portfolios become part of the grading process: A case study in a junior high setting. Paper presented at the annual meeting of the National Reading Conference, Charleston, SC.

Shepard, L. (1989). Why we need better assessments. *Educational Leadership, 46*(7), 4–9.

Tierney, R. J., Carter, M. A., & Desai, L. E. (1991). *Portfolio assessment in the reading-writing classroom.* Norwood, MA: Christopher-Gordon.

Valencia, S. (1990). A portfolio approach to classroom reading assessment: The whys, whats, and hows. *The Reading Teacher,* 338–340.

Valencia, S., Wixson, K., Peters, C., & Pearson, P. D. (1989). Theory and practice in statewide reading assessment: Closing the gap. *Educational Leadership, 47*(7), 57–63.

Vygotsky, L. (1978). *Mind in society: The development of higher psychological processes.* Cambridge: Harvard University Press.

Wells, G., & Chang-Wells, L. (1992). *Constructing meaning together.* Portsmouth, NH: Heinemann Educational Books.

Wiggins, G. P. (1993). *Assessing student performance: Exploring the purpose and limits of testing.* San Francisco: Jossey-Bass Publishers.

CHILDREN'S BOOKS CITED

Lowry, L. (1989). *Number the stars.* South Holland, IL: Yearling Books.

Paulsen, G. (1987). *Hatchet.* New York: Puffin Books.

Chapter 12

Aligning Curriculum, Instruction, and Assessment in Literature-Based Approaches

●————————●

Charles W. Peters, Oakland Schools
Karen K. Wixson, University of Michigan

A basic premise of this chapter is that the alignment of instruction and assessment is largely dependent on the curriculum; that is, on what is being taught. While alignment between instruction and assessment has been a long-standing problem in literacy education, the move to literature-based instruction has made the problems even more visible. Literature-based instruction does not emphasize uniform objectives, instructional materials, and tests that characterize mastery models of instruction. Thus, teachers moving away from traditional instructional materials toward trade materials and process approaches (e.g., writer's workshop) find few guidelines for determining *what* is important to teach. Teachers who continue using published programs find that these, too, have shifted toward literature-based approaches and, as a result, now offer an array of instructional choices. The result is more innovation and variation in methods and process, but little coherence and sometimes little substance, in what is taught across grade levels within districts or among classes at a particular grade level. This situation presents substantial challenges to identifying appropriate assessment methods for informing instruction and evaluating student progress.

CURRENT STATUS

How do teachers using literature-based approaches decide what to teach? Beliefs about English language arts (ELA) curriculum and other factors (e.g., materials, students' and teachers' interest) all contribute to teachers' decision-making. Since decisions about what to teach play such an important role in the alignment of instruction and assessment, it helps to understand their bases.

Curriculum Models

Teacher's beliefs—implicit or explicit—about what should be taught play an important role in determining the English language arts curriculum. Three models of the curriculum have prevailed at least since 1980: mastery, cultural heritage, and process (Mandel, 1980; Farrell, 1991).

According to Farrell (1991), the mastery model is closely associated with competency assessment, instructional objectives, and basic skills learning. In the form described by scholars such as B. Bloom (1981), students experience carefully controlled, sequenced learning activities until mastery of the skill/knowledge is exhibited. Then they are allowed to proceed to other skills. Although the mastery model makes goals for student learning explicit, these goals are often fragmented and decontextualized from the more holistic knowledge and processes we would like students to acquire. As Gehrke, Knapp, and Sirotnik (1992) note, today's language arts educators generally do not speak from the mastery model point of view. Instead, this model is expressed more in practice and through curriculum materials and textbooks.

The cultural heritage model looks to the traditionally accepted canon for literature of enduring worth that embodies the values and great ideas of the larger culture as the basis for English language arts instruction. In preference to identifying specific works to be taught at a given grade or level, proponents of the heritage model often recommend that teachers make choices from within the corpus based on their knowledge of their students' needs. Adler (1982), H. Bloom (1994), Hirsch (1987), Cheney (1987), and Ravitch and Finn (1987) are among the more prominent advocates of the heritage model. Although the cultural heritage model makes the curriculum content clear, this content is often treated as ideas or facts that need to be transmitted to the student, rather than examined by students from a variety of perspectives.

The process model is considered the most student-centered and is especially concerned with the way each individual constructs knowledge from experience. Scholars working from this model see language use as developmental, encourage creativity and writing from an early age, and focus on students' understanding of the relationship between the writer's intent and the reader's response. Although the process model makes clear the students' role as active participants in their own learning, it provides little guidance about *what* it is students should be processing. Rosenblatt (1938), Britton (1972), and Moffett and Wagner (1983) are considered among the primary spokespersons for the process model, which provides much of the basis for integrated, literature-based instruction.

To be sure, new models continue to arise. For example, some have moved into a realm of curriculum as inquiry and conversation (e.g., Applebee, 1996; Harste, 1994). No new models, however, have taken hold the way mastery, heritage, and process models have in the past. This is apparent from an examination of current state and national standards in English language arts, which often reflect one or more of these models. Although many teachers characterize their instruction as integrated, literature-based, or both, it is unlikely that any single model can accurately describe what takes place in the classroom (Farrell, 1991). Most teachers' instructional activities incorporate practices associated with more than one curriculum model.

Aside from personal beliefs embedded in one or more models of curriculum, there are a host of other factors that affect teachers' decisions about what to teach. For example, some teachers are influenced by accessibility—what's in the textbook or what resources are readily available. Others are influenced by what they find interesting and what they believe will be interesting to their students. Evidence of this comes from examining teachers' practices in using thematic units as part of their integrated, literature-based instruction.

Thematic Instruction

In 1992–93, we and our colleagues sent a survey regarding practices associated with thematic instruction to six teachers from each of the 50 states: three State Council members from the International Reading Association and three members of the National Council of Teachers of English who subscribe to the journal *Language Arts* (Valencia, Lipson, Peters, & Wixson, 1994). We received responses from 125 of the 300 individuals who were sent the survey: forty K–2 teachers, thirty-seven 3–6 teachers, thirteen middle school teachers, seventeen special reading teachers, and eighteen others.

Of those who responded, almost 90 percent reported that they devoted a part of their instructional time to teaching in thematic or integrated units. Only about 25 percent of the teachers at all levels spent all their time teaching themes. However, approximately 70 percent of the teachers spent at least three-fourths of their time teaching this way. When asked how they chose the topics for their thematic units, teachers at K–2 levels indicated that they relied first on student interest (40 percent), followed closely by attention to broad curricular concerns and materials (32 percent). At both upper elementary (grades 3–6) and middle school levels, teachers' decisions were based primarily on a combination of broad curricular concerns and instructional materials (52 percent, and 43 percent, respectively), followed by student interest (21 percent in each case).

In a related effort, we selected four teachers from grades 2–5 on the basis of their reputations as exemplary teachers employing thematic units (Wixson, Davis, Hodson, & Spitulnik, 1994). Each teacher was observed and interviewed at least twice and case studies were developed. The findings support the idea that literature-based teachers often decide what to teach on the basis of their beliefs about English language arts curriculum, broad curricular concerns, and student and teacher interest. For example, Ms. Benning's curricular goals emphasized learning how to learn, developing problem-solving skills, and learning through experience. She also wanted to instill a love of reading and writing in each student and to help them see themselves as readers and writers. Her instruction focused on writer's workshop and literature-based activities in connection with thematic units.

Ms. Benning believed a teacher could develop thematic units based on any topic and that although there were not any "bad themes," the most effective were topics that interested the teacher. At the time of our observation, the theme underway was "Art and Artists." Ms. Benning's underlying goal for the unit was that the students view art as a form of communication in the same way writing is a means of expression. In addition, she wanted her students to see art as a process, just as they saw writing as a process. Activities from this unit included: (1) a discussion about what the color blue is; (2) reading and discussing poetry and literature about different colors; (3) studying and discussing work by artists such as Henri Matisse and Mary Cassatt; (4) hands-on experience mixing primary colors and using different media such as watercolors; (5) writing descriptions about art experiences (e.g., mixing food color and water); and (6) creating color wheels. As with the other teachers we observed, it appeared to us that the activities were only loosely connected to the goals of the unit (see also Valencia & Lipson, Chapter 5).

Similarly, Ms. Simpson described her teaching as "whole language" which, in her view, required "starting where the kids are, literature-based instruction . . . and skills instruction taught through students' writing." Her global language arts outcomes included synthesis and analysis of texts; use of evidence to support a position; awareness of characters and themes in literature; and student responsibility for reading, writing, and discussion tasks.

Ms. Simpson's use of themes involved all areas of the language arts and emphasized student involvement in the learning process. She drew on several sources in selecting particular themes for study. First, during an interview, she stated that one "idea source" for developing thematic language arts units included "something that I find interesting." Second, the unit on Africa—underway at the time of this observation—had been chosen, in part, because she was looking for a theme that addressed a specific social studies curriculum requirement. Other factors she described as influencing her selection of the unit about Africa involved: (a) children reading literature "about children their own age, and involving problems that they, themselves, might have," (b) "to introduce students to great literature" as reflected in her collection of African folk tales, and (c) to use "a wonderful Ishangi play being performed" locally as a culminating field trip. She described her intended outcomes as including "student awareness and appreciation for African-American history and culture." Thus, she considered her interest, the literature she wanted students to read, connections to other curricular areas, and opportune events such as the play she mentioned.

As a central activity of the Africa unit, each student read one of four novels and engaged in a variety of activities to reinforce and extend their understanding. Other activities connected with the Africa theme included reading African folk tales, making *tepe* cloths depicting characters and scenes from these tales, and Ms. Simpson reading from Mildred D. Taylor's (1991) *Roll of Thunder, Hear My Cry.* The culminating activity involved groups representing all four novels discussing and reporting back to the class on "What would happen if the main characters from the four novels got together and talked?" Despite the many interesting activities associated with this unit, we saw little depth of learning and connection among the activities other than their being superficially related to the study of Africa.

Within the context of literature-based instruction, many advocate thematic instruction as a means of promoting more meaningful, in-depth teaching and learning. The descriptions of units and unit activities provided by the respondents to the survey and case studies of exemplary teachers suggest that this is an unlikely outcome of current practice with regard to thematic instruction. We think that one possible explanation is an overemphasis on process and an underemphasis on the importance of ideas or content in current models of English language arts curriculum.

An examination of the mastery, heritage, and process models reveals that they all lack attention to content in the form of ideas that are relevant to the world outside the classroom. The mastery model focuses primarily on skills and strategies, but provides no direction about the content to which these skills and strategies should be applied. The heritage model focuses on a narrow set of materials, which do not—in and of themselves—constitute content. Similarly, the process model provides few clues to content—that is, What are the students listening to? What should they be speaking and writing about? And what are they reading?

As Valencia and Lipson (Chapter 5) also observe, often, the result of current teaching through themes is attention to trivial content in the form of units on topics such as "Buttons," "Chocolate," or "Clocks." Furthermore, even when unit topics are more substantive, as we found in the case studies by Wixson et al. (1994), the activities are often loosely related to the content, and do not help students see connections either among the language arts or between the language arts and other subject areas. It is primarily through the grappling with "big ideas" in literature and other texts that students seek deeper and richer understandings and demonstrate the thoughtful and skillful use of language.

To improve the quality of English language arts teaching and learning, we need curricula with an emphasis on *content* in the form of important ideas from literature and other texts combined with attention to the *processes* of reading, writing, listening, speaking, and viewing. The content standards and benchmarks we helped develop in Michigan (Wixson, Peters, & Potter, 1996) through the Michigan English Language Arts Framework (MELAF) project provide the basis for such a curriculum and will be discussed further in later sections of this chapter. The national standards in English language arts (Standards for the English Language Arts, 1996) developed by the National Council of Teachers of English (NCTE) and the International Reading Association (IRA) also represent a content-process approach.

CONTENT AND PROCESS AS THE BASIS FOR ASSESSMENT IN LITERATURE-BASED INSTRUCTION

The view of content we present in this chapter is consistent with the one described by Suhor (1988); that is, content focuses on what is to be processed, specifically the ideas to which skills and strategies will be applied. This view of content differs from many traditional views (e.g., the heritage model) in that it acknowledges a wide range of literature and includes nonprint media, as well as the student's store of personal experience. Ideas are the content of the English language arts—not skills, processes, or materials (Peters, 1994). The processes involved in reading, writing, listening, speaking, and viewing are the tools that support students as they explore language, experiment with voice, conduct research and inquiry, construct meaning, examine diverse perspectives, craft a response or write poetry, and critique ideas. The process focus in the curriculum provides the tools that foster a deeper understanding of the ideas and issues that flow from the content.

Attention to content can promote alignment between what is learned and how it is assessed and taught. When we are clear about the powerful ideas we want students to understand and to develop their perspective about, we have a stronger basis for evaluating the appropriateness of our instructional activities and for developing assessments (Perkins, 1993). By their nature, powerful ideas are integrative and help students form deeper and richer understandings. By doing so, they can avoid fragmented and disconnected learning. Powerful ideas provide the substance that enables students to engage in the higher-order thinking that results in new knowledge, as well as creative applications of knowledge. In this context, higher-order thinking challenges the student to interpret, analyze, and manipulate information, because questions and problems that emanate from the connection among powerful ideas cannot be resolved through the routine application of previously learned knowledge. It is this application of powerful ideas to new contexts that is the heart of authentic assessment (Peters, 1991).

AN EXAMPLE

One example of an English language arts curriculum framework that combines content and process is the Michigan English Language Arts Framework (MELAF) (Wixson, Peters, & Potter, 1996). At the center of this framework are ten content standards that define the content and process of English Language Arts (see Figure 12.1). For example, the content standards labeled "Literature," "Depth of Understanding," and "Ideas in Action" all focus on understanding and using powerful ideas. Depth of understanding is necessary for the application of knowledge and allows students to move beyond superficial understandings by connecting content to the larger contexts within the student's life. Through such connections, students are in a position to put their ideas into action, because powerful ideas provide links to the world beyond the classroom.

Other content standards focus more on the process aspects of the curriculum such as "Voice," "Genre and Craft of Language," and "Skills and Strategies." Benchmarks clarify what students are to know and be able to do at four developmental levels: early elementary, later elementary, middle school, and high school (see Figure 12.2 for example).

There is a clearly identified content to these curriculum standards and benchmarks and it is centered on powerful ideas. The standards and benchmarks also integrate the processes of reading, writing, speaking, listening, and viewing so they become tools for understanding the ideas. We continue with the example of thematic instruction as a means of illustrating how such a content-process model facilitates the alignment of assessment and instruction.

Thematic Instruction

When content is an important part of the ELA curriculum, planning for thematic instruction begins by identifying the powerful ideas that are important for students to know. Decisions about what is to be learned then provide the basis for decisions about instruction and assessment. For example, Cheryl Elsworth, a fourth-grade teacher in Waterford, Michigan, developed a unit using this approach around the topic of change.[1] When she began planning her unit she started by asking, "What is it about change I want students to understand?" Since Ms. Elsworth wanted to connect the topic of change to a social studies unit on communities, she decided to focus on community change. As Ms. Elsworth thought about it more, she realized that she wanted her students to understand how their own community has changed over the years.

The combination of big ideas around community and change led to the development of a thematic statement for Ms. Elsworth's unit. Powerful ideas or concepts are too abstract and broad by themselves, so it helps to transform them into a statement that focuses on meaningful and worthwhile learning experiences connected to the world outside the classroom (see also, Valencia

Figure 12.1

MELAF
ENGLISH LANGUAGE ARTS
CONTENT STANDARDS

	In grades K–12, the English language arts standards will ensure that all students have opportunities to engage successfully in discovering, creating, and analyzing spoken, written, electronic, and visual texts which reflect multiple perspectives and diverse communities. All students will:
Meaning and Communication	1. focus on meaning and communication as they listen, speak, view, read, and write in personal, social, occupational, and civic contexts;
Language	2. use the English language effectively in informal situations within schools, communities, and work-places by building upon an understanding of their own and other language patterns;
Literature	3. interact with a wide variety of classic and contemporary literature and other texts to seek information, ideas, enjoyment, and understanding of their individuality, our common humanity, and the rich diversity in our society;
Voice	4. view themselves as effective speakers and writers and demonstrate their expressive abilities by creating oral, written, and visual texts that engage their audiences;
Skills and Processes	5. demonstrate, monitor, and reflect upon the skills and processes used to communicate through listening, speaking, viewing, reading, and writing;
Genre and Craft of Language	6. explore and use the characteristics of different types of texts, aesthetic elements, and mechanics—including text structure, figurative and descriptive language, spelling, punctuation, and grammar—to construct and convey meaning;
Depth of Understanding	7. demonstrate understanding of the complexity of enduring issues and recurring problems by making connections and generating themes within and across texts;
Ideas in Action	8. apply knowledge, ideas, and issues drawn from texts to their lives and the lives of others;
Inquiry and Research	9. define and investigate important issues and problems using a variety of resources, including technology, to explore and create texts; and
Critical Standards	10. develop and apply personal, shared, and academic criteria for the enjoyment, appreciation, and evaluation of their own and others' oral, written, and visual texts.

Figure 12.2

IDEAS IN ACTION

Content Standard 8: All students will apply knowledge, ideas, and issues drawn from texts to their lives and the lives of others.			
Early Elementary	**Later Elementary**	**Middle School**	**High School**
1. Make connections between key ideas in literature and other texts and their own lives.	1. Identify how their own experiences influence their understanding of key ideas in literature and other texts.	1. Analyze themes and central ideas in literature and other texts in relation to issues in their own lives.	1. Use themes and central ideas in literature and other texts to generate solutions to problems and formulate perspectives on issues in their own lives.
2. Demonstrate their developing literacy by using text to enhance their daily lives. Examples include reading with a parent, discussing favorite text, writing to a friend or relative about an experience, and creating a visual representation of an important idea.	2. Combine skills to reveal their strengthening literacy. Examples include writing and illustrating a text, reading and then orally analyzing text, and listening to and then summarizing a presentation.	2. Perform the daily functions of a literate individual. Examples include acquiring information from multiple sources and then evaluating, organizing, and communicating it in various context.	2. Function as literate individuals in varied context within their lives in and beyond the classroom. Examples include using text resources while thinking creatively, making decisions, solving problems, and reasoning in complex situations.
3. Use oral, visual, and written texts to identify and explore school and community issues and problems, and discuss how one individual or group can make a difference. An example is responding orally, artistically, or in writing about an issue or problem they have studied and/or experienced.	3. Use oral, visual, and written texts to research how individuals have had an impact on people in their community and nation. An example is creating texts to inform others about school or community issues and problems.	3. Use oral, visual, and written texts to identify and research issues of importance that confront adolescents, their community, nation, and world. An example is using research findings to create texts that persuade others to take a particular position or to alter their course of action with regard to a particular school/community issue or problem.	3. Utilize the persuasive power of text as an instrument of change in their community, nation, and world. An example is identifying a community issue and designing an authentic project using oral, visual, and written texts to promote social action.

Michigan Curriculum Framework

& Lipson, Chapter 5). To accomplish this, a thematic statement must establish a clear purpose for learning, help students connect powerful ideas to authentic learning situations, and be issue-oriented. This means there are no predetermined answers or solutions. Nor can the issues or questions be adequately addressed with single words, short phrases, or memorized information. Furthermore, thematic statements mitigate against overly broad topics that typically serve as "blackholes" or "magnets" for large quantities of fragmented information. Units with thematic statements derived from powerful ideas encourage teachers to abandon the role of "knowledge transmitter" and instead assume the role of "inquiry facilitator" (Peters, 1994).

For Ms. Elsworth's unit the thematic statement was:

> People have a responsibility to consider the rights of others when making community change.

Once she developed a thematic statement, the topic moved from an abstract idea of community change to a more concrete notion of what she wanted students to learn about community change. The thematic statement was sufficiently challenging to stimulate reflective inquiry by referring to an authentic problem—one actually faced by many communities. In fact, their own community was struggling with issues of how best to deal with change. Good thematic statements such as Ms. Elsworth's are not created for academic purposes only. Rather, they are designed to deal with issues and problems that persist over time and place. Because of their enduring nature, the themes invite students to engage in the meaningful and worthwhile pursuit of knowledge (Brophy, Onosko & Newmann, 1994).

Ms. Elsworth also developed a set of focus questions to accompany the thematic statement and assist the students in their unit study. The focus questions come directly from the thematic statement. They narrow the thematic statement by making it more concrete. The purpose of the focus questions is to center students' attention on an authentic problem or issue identified by the thematic statement. For this unit the focus questions were:

- How do we balance community interests and individual interests?
- Who is harmed by change?
- Who benefits from change?
- Who determines whether change is beneficial?
- What standards or criteria can we use to determine responsible community change?

Designing the Performance Assessments

The next phase of development involved designing a performance demonstration. This phase is crucial since it helps teachers make explicit for themselves where the unit is headed, the end point of the unit. With the goals in mind, it becomes possible to develop relevant instructional activities and intermediary assessment tasks. When Ms. Elsworth began designing the performance demonstration, she kept two points in mind. First, she wanted the performance demonstration to provide evidence of students' in-depth understanding relative to the thematic statement. Second, she wanted it to offer authentic evidence of knowing.

For guidance in developing the performance demonstration, Ms. Elsworth turned to the benchmarks, because they provide specific direction for the type of reading, writing, listening, speaking, and viewing students should engage in at a particular developmental level. From the Waterford ELA curriculum—based on the MELAF content standards and benchmarks—Ms. Elsworth selected the following benchmarks:

- Students gather and analyze relevant information;
- Students assess the power and consistency of competing arguments; and
- Students make reasoned decisions that include the consideration of competing values embedded in alternative points of view.

As Ms. Elsworth thought about her performance demonstration in relation to the thematic statement, the benchmarks became crucial in guiding her decision making. She drew on the benchmarks as she determined relevant evidence of student understanding for both the powerful ideas embedded within the thematic statement and the benchmarks critical to the curriculum.

To make sure that she did not omit important benchmarks or repeat ones she had covered previously, Ms. Elsworth used a Curriculum Planning Matrix to determine her coverage of the curriculum (see Figure 12.3).

She placed a check in every box that the performance demonstration covered. She did this for both the performance demonstration and the instructional activities. At the end of the year she then had a record of the content standards and benchmarks she had taught. This was an important step because, with literature-based instruction, it can be difficult to determine what portions of the curriculum have been taught and learned. Often, the books and other resources become the primary focus, rather than a means for understanding and applying the "big ideas" they portray. We cannot be

Figure 12.3

Curriculum Planning Matrix

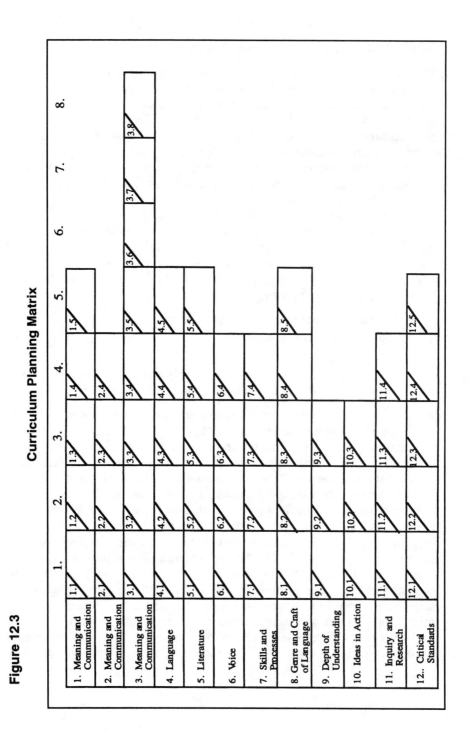

confident that the curriculum is being advanced solely because we use quality literature. The Curriculum Planning Matrix is a tool for ensuring that important elements in the curriculum are not neglected.

Once the benchmarks had been identified, Ms. Elsworth designed a performance demonstration that asked students to assume the role of a community planner. In that role they were expected to demonstrate their ability to access, process, organize, and interpret information regarding changes that had occurred in their community. The performance demonstration contained three components: (1) an individual plan for community change, (2) a group collaborative plan for community change, and (3) a personal reflection on students' own individual growth.

The first component of the performance demonstration required students to develop an individual plan that included recommendations for the future of his or her self-selected topic (e.g., new school, new restaurant, recreational facility) and to describe how his or her recommendations fit the criteria for responsible community change. Students' recommendations were to be based on the criteria for responsible change they developed as a result of a thoughtful analysis of the thematic statement. Throughout the unit, students developed criteria in response to the variety of perspectives on community change presented in the literature they read.

In developing their written responses, Ms. Elsworth asked her students to consider the following focus questions:

- What is the proposed change?
- What effects will the change have on the community?
- Who is affected by the change?
- Who will see the changes as positive and negative and why?

This portion of the performance demonstration was important because it asked students to take a position on the thematic statement—to evaluate and apply their position on the importance of considering the rights of others when investigating the need for community change. This is what we mean when we describe authentic assessment. Ms. Elsworth required students to take powerful ideas from the literature they read and apply them to a new context, a context with value beyond school. However, one important question remains: What does a quality performance look like?

To address the issue of quality, as well as alignment, Ms. Elsworth once again turned to the content standards and benchmarks for help. She developed a rubric or scoring guide that reflected the content and process demands of this component of the performance demonstration. The content portion of the rubric focused on the student's ability to:

(a) demonstrate a clear and informed understanding of a thematic statement by synthesizing and drawing insightful generalizations from a variety of literature and other texts that represent various perspectives;

(b) represent accurately the views of the selected texts; and

(c) use key concepts that demonstrate in-depth understanding of the thematic statement.

The process portion of the rubric focused on the student's ability to:

(a) use effective organizational structure, without over-reliance on form, in order to convincingly persuade readers;

(b) present a clear position;

(c) produce original insights, personal connections, and examples related to a position on the thematic statement; and

(d) use conventions consistent with grade level benchmarks.

We present the complete rubric in Figure 12.4.

The use of rubrics that are closely aligned with the curriculum are important for several reasons. First, they explicitly define what quality work represents. In the rubric presented in Figure 12.4, a four is considered quality work. Second, rubrics help students understand the expectations of the performance; these are not left to speculation. Third, when rubrics are developed by groups of teachers within a building, the definition of a quality performance remains consistent across teachers and classrooms. Fourth, when the rubric is based upon a common curriculum, the concept of growth across time—especially across several years—is easier to define. The concept of growth is based upon the curriculum and not left solely to individual preferences.

The second component of the performance demonstration required a group presentation. Once students completed their individual plans, they were assigned to a group. Each student presented his or her individual plan to the group and then the group decided which plan was the best candidate for their group presentation. The group then modified the plan to fit their collective understanding of responsible community change. There were several requirements groups were expected to meet: a presentation no longer than 10 minutes; all group members must take part; and the group chooses the mode(s) of presentation (e.g., video, charts and graphs, photographs, skit, music/dance, game).

An interesting change took place as Ms. Elsworth was planning the group presentation portion of the performance demonstration. When she examined the Curriculum Planning Matrix (Figure 12.3), she discovered that the listening and speaking benchmarks had been overlooked. To rectify this oversight she added the following benchmarks: (1) the use of focused oral inquiry to

Figure 12.4

Persuasive Writing Rubric

Content	Demonstrates a clear and informed understanding of a thematic statement drawn from complex texts by synthesizing and drawing insightful generalizations from a variety of texts and perspectives. • Uses a minimum of 4 texts representing a variety of perspectives in order to provide strong support for stated position • Accurately represents the views of selected texts • Uses key concepts that demonstrate in-depth understanding of the thematic statement	Demonstrates an understanding of a thematic statement drawn from complex texts by synthesizing and drawing generalizations from a variety of texts and perspectives. • Uses a minimum of 4 texts representing a variety of perspectives in order to provide strong support for stated position • Accurately represents the views of selected texts • Uses some key concepts that demonstrate in-depth understanding of the thematic statement.	Demonstrates a limited understanding of a thematic statement drawn from complex texts by synthesizing and drawing limited generalizations from a variety of texts and perspectives. • Uses a minimum of 3 texts representing a variety of perspectives to provide support for stated position • Occasionally misrepresents the views of text • Uses key concepts but does not demonstrates adequate understanding	Demonstrates little or no understanding drawn from complex texts of a thematic statement with minimal ability to synthesize or draw generalizations from a variety of texts and perspectives. • Uses 2 or fewer texts representing a variety of perspectives to provide limited support for stated position • Usually misrepresents the views of texts • Uses no key concepts and demonstrates limited understanding
Form	Uses effective organizational structure, without over reliance on form, in order to convincingly persuade readers. • Presents a clear position • Crafts an introduction that invites the reader in • Supports position with at least 3 strong examples. Uses a format appropriate for identified audience • Anticipates and counters potential arguments • Employs transitions in order to move readers easily through text • Concludes with a satisfying resolution	Uses effective organizational structure with appropriate organizational form in order to persuade readers. • Presents a clear position • Crafts an interesting introduction • Supports position with at least 2 appropriate examples but may contain some extraneous details. Uses a format appropriate for an identified audience • Develops a conclusion	Attempts to organize ideas into an appropriate form to persuade readers. • Presents a somewhat developed position • Attempts development of beginning, middle, and ending but the piece lacks an overall sense of wholeness • Supports position on thematic statement with at least 1 example but may include some examples that are extraneous	Organization is lacking or arbitrary • Presents a position with little or no development • Has no clear beginning, middle or end • Uses no examples to support position
Voice	Produces original insights, personal connections and examples related to position on the thematic statement. Sustains the reader's attention.	Describes insights, personal connections and examples related to position on thematic statements. Sustains the reader's attention.	Describes few personal insights, connections and examples related to position on thematic statement.	Identifies no personal insights, connections or examples related to position on thematic statement.
Conventions See ELA curriculum, grade level benchmarks	Uses conventions consistent with curriculum grade level benchmarks where errors are rare and do not interfere with the reader's understanding.	Uses conventions consistent with curriculum grade level benchmarks where some errors may distract but do not seriously interfere with the reader's understanding.	Uses some conventions consistent with grade level benchmarks but frequent errors tend to make the reader's understanding difficult.	Uses few conventions consistent with grade level benchmarks. Numerous errors severely interfere with the reader's understanding.

produce meaningful structured oral messages, and (2) the evaluation of genre, speaker's craft, and conventions of the communication process to convey ideas and perspectives for a specified purpose and audience. To assess these benchmarks, she added an interview that asked students about the data they collected, the process they used to get to the final presentation, and their personal reflections on how well they thought the process worked. By closely monitoring her planning, Ms. Elsworth was able to avoid omitting important elements of the curriculum and add them while they were still meaningful within the context of the instructional unit. If curriculum coverage is an important goal in literature-based instruction, then teachers need to monitor which components they explicitly teach and assess. Again, Ms. Elsworth designed a rubric that defined the quality expectations for the group performance drawing from the appropriate benchmarks.

The third component of the performance demonstration was a one-page reflection by the students in which they described their individual growth in relation to community change. Students used their journals as their source of evidence for documenting personal change. Though journals are used widely in today's schools, this was not the main reason Ms. Elsworth decided to use them in the assessment. Rather, she felt they provided a unique source of evidence for students to measure their depth of understanding. By keeping dated journal entries that tracked their thinking about the big ideas embedded within the thematic statement, students could examine their developing understanding and determine whether their own views had changed.

The performance demonstration for Ms. Elsworth's unit was determined by both the content and process demands of the curriculum and highlighted throughout the unit. Ms. Elsworth's unit required that students: (a) apply key ideas and themes derived from multiple texts representing a balance of perspectives and (b) formulate personal views on persisting issues and problems drawn from multiple texts. She asked her students to take a position on what responsible community change involved and create a persuasive essay. She chose this vehicle since it provided a good way to offer evidence that students understood the content in a manner consistent with what was called for in the benchmarks. That is, the persuasive essay made sense in the context of the thematic unit of study and the goals of the unit; it was not simply an arbitrary activity within the overall English language arts curriculum.

A content-process curriculum provides the parameters for decisions about assessment. While individual teachers have a variety of options, the choices must take place within the boundaries of the curriculum. With this type of performance demonstration, students apply their understanding to authentic content in the form of problems or issues specifically linked to the benchmarks. Assessment focused in this manner is neither fragmented nor decontextualized.

Aligning Instruction

With her performance demonstration in place, Ms. Elsworth returned to the benchmarks to identify the ones her students must know to be successful with the unit. Again, she used the Curriculum Planning Matrix as a guide. As she "unpacked" the content and process demands embedded in the performance demonstration, Ms. Elsworth matched them with curriculum benchmarks. She did this by brainstorming a list of all the necessary enabling content knowledge and processing skills required to produce a quality performance. Once the enabling benchmarks were identified, she developed an instructional plan and a sequence she thought provided the appropriate instructional scaffolding. Best instructional practice needs a context and it is the alignment between curriculum and assessment that provides the context.

An important part of her instructional plan was modeling how good readers extract complex ideas from literary texts that present multiple perspectives on the thematic statement. One activity Ms. Elsworth designed to guide students through this process is the summary graphic organizer displayed in Figure 12.5. She used this to reveal her students' competencies in organizing, synthesizing, interpreting, explaining, and evaluating complex information related to the thematic statement. The graphic organizer initially focused on students' identification of key ideas and supporting ideas in the selection, then asked them to connect these ideas to the thematic statement.

Ms. Elsworth also used the summary graphic organizer as a tool for providing evidence of student growth in reading comprehension. The rubric she designed for summarization (see Figure 12.6) was not only consistent with the benchmarks, but also addressed the issue of quality performance.

The content portion of the rubric required students to accurately identify key concepts related to the theme in a single text, link essential key ideas to the theme, and provide multiple examples that elaborate on the meaning of the theme and key ideas. The process portion of the rubric required students to synthesize the theme, key ideas, and examples into a cohesive whole; convey meaning through effective sentence structure and precise wording; and use a variety of compound and complex sentences with correct use of conjunctions and punctuation. Together, the summary graphic organizer activity and the rubric for summarization created a seamless web among curriculum, instruction, and assessment.

Since the benchmarks call for multiple texts with multiple perspectives, Ms. Elsworth selected texts that were a combination of print, oral, and visual materials representing different perspectives on responsible community change. To assure that the materials presented a balanced perspective, she used a number of criteria. Once again, the criteria came from the thematic statement and the content standards and benchmarks and included some of

Figure 12.5   **Organizer for Summary**

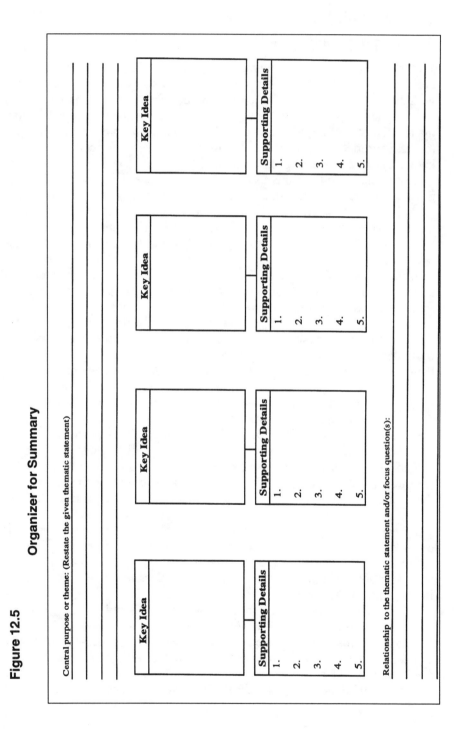

Figure 12.6

Summary Writing Rubric

	4	3	2	1
Content	• Accurately identifies key ideas related to the theme in a single text • Links essential key ideas to the theme • Provides multiple examples that elaborate on the meaning of the theme and key ideas • Accurately represents information presented in the text • Successfully summarizes key ideas and central purpose of text	• Accurately identifies key ideas related to the theme in a single text • Links most essential key ideas to the theme • Provides some examples to elaborate on the meaning of the theme and key ideas • Accurately represents information presented in the text • Paraphrases key ideas and theme of text	• Vaguely identifies the key ideas related to the theme in a single text • Links some key ideas to the theme • Provides few examples to elaborate on the meaning of the theme and key ideas • Represents the ideas presented in text with few misconceptions • Restates and includes extraneous, insignificant examples	• Does not identify the key ideas related to the theme in text • Unable to relate key ideas to theme • Unable to provide examples in order to elaborate on meaning of the theme and key ideas • Presents numerous misconceptions about the ideas represented text • Unable to differentiate theme and key examples from insignificant and extraneous
Form	• Synthesizes theme, key ideas and examples into a cohesive whole • Conveys meaning through effective sentence structure and precise wording • Theme receives greater attention than supporting key ideas or examples in ways that enhance the reader's understanding	• Synthesizes theme, key ideas and examples into a cohesive whole although some extraneous examples may be present • Conveys meaning through various sentence structure and word choice • A clear distinction is shown between the theme and supporting ideas or examples	• Attempts organization around theme, key ideas and examples although ideas may not be well connected • Conveys meaning through basic sentence structure with limited vocabulary • Little distinction is shown between central purpose or theme and supporting key ideas or examples	• Little organization is evident • Awkward sentence structure and inadequate vocabulary seriously interferes with understanding • No distinction is shown between theme and supporting key ideas and examples
Conventions It is assumed that students will have control of conventions previously taught (See ELA curriculum)	• Uses the following conventions with rare errors that do not interfere with the reader's understanding — Transitional words between paragraphs — A variety of compound, complete sentences with correct use of conjunctions and punctuation	• Makes minimal errors with the following conventions that do not seriously interfere with the reader's understanding — Transitional words between paragraphs — A variety of compound, complex sentences with correct use of conjunctions and punctuation	• Frequent errors with the following conventions make the reader's understanding difficult — Transitional words between paragraphs — A variety of compound, complex sentences with correct use of conjunctions and punctuation	• Numerous errors with the following conventions severely interfere with the reader's understanding — Transitional words between paragraphs — A variety of compound, complex sentences with correct use of conjunctions and punctuation

the following. The literature must (1) represent classic and contemporary texts, (2) reflect multiple genre, (3) represent differing points of view on the thematic statement, and (4) represent a wide range of diverse perspectives (e.g., cultural, region, age, gender). Books Ms. Elsworth used included:

- *The Great Kapok Tree* (Lynne Cherry, 1990), a contemporary tale that presents the point of view of animals that live in the Amazon rain forest,

- *Keepers of the Earth* (Joseph Bruchac & Michael Caduto, 1989), a classic collection of poems and legends that present community change from the perspective of the Native Americans,

- *Riverkeeper* (George Ancona, 1990), an informational text that profiles a man's attempt to protect the Hudson River, and

- *Window* (Jeannie Baker, 1991), a picture book that examines community change from the perspective of what goes on outside a window in one house.

Each book presents information on the thematic statement that reflects different genres, points of view, and perspectives.

We believe that when literature-based instruction is guided by attention to powerful ideas that are embedded within the content and process demands of the curriculum, teacher planning becomes more systematic, the curriculum is aligned with assessment, and best practice has a context. When these elements are in place, students and teachers see deeper and richer learning based on the application of knowledge that has value beyond the classroom. Literature-based instruction guided by these considerations allows students to move beyond superficial understanding by connecting content to larger contexts within the student's life.

CONCLUSIONS AND IMPLICATIONS

It is clear by now that we believe curriculum to be at the heart of the alignment issue in literature-based instruction and assessment. Curriculum that focuses almost exclusively on processes, as in many literature-based approaches to instruction, does not provide sufficient guidance for decision-making about which methods, materials, and assessments are most appropriate in a particular instructional context. Curriculum that focuses heavily on literary works does not provide sufficient guidance about what the focus of instruction should be. As a result, decisions about what to teach are often made in highly individualistic ways. These decisions are often based primarily on the interests of students and teachers, familiarity with particular methods, and/or the availability of resources, with little attention given to the coherence of information across classes and grade levels, to issues of depth and breadth, or to coverage and growth.

We believe that a curriculum model that combines content and process—such as the one implied by the Michigan standards and benchmarks or the NCTE/IRA standards—can go a long way toward reducing the lack of alignment and coherence often observed with literature-based approaches to instruction. According to this view, the domain of English language arts is composed of both the *processes* of listening, speaking, reading, writing, and viewing, and the *content* of the oral, visual, and written texts that promotes connections with other disciplines as well as the world outside the classroom. Insights from the significant ideas, concepts, cultural perspectives, and moral questions in literature and other texts help us shape our personal vision of the world; understand our own cultural, linguistic, and literary heritages; and value the diversity and commonalties of local, state, national, and world communities.

A content-process view of English language arts curriculum, such as the one we have described, provides a basis for decisions about methods, materials, and assessments. With an emphasis on deep understanding of powerful ideas and issues that represent diverse perspectives, the conversation about what to teach does not begin with "What skills or methods do I use?", but instead with "What do I expect students to know and be able to do?" The question is not whether a literature-based approach is preferable to a skills-based approach or a basal series, but rather,

- What content do I expect students to know?
- How do I provide evidence that they have learned what I have taught?
- What is the most appropriate instruction?
- How does what I have taught link with what others are teaching at the same grade level as well as other grade levels?

Literature circles or collections of stories, plays, novels, and poems do not make a curriculum. They become tools or the means used to foster deeper understanding of powerful ideas and issues. Once we can agree on what we want students to know and how to document their understanding, we can decide on valid ways to get there.

We believe there are many benefits to students from a content-process approach to English language arts curriculum, instruction, and assessment. First, and foremost, their instruction is about something important that can be applied to their lives outside of school. Second, this approach promotes deeper and richer understanding of important ideas and issues and provides multiple opportunities to develop complex, higher-order processing skills in the areas of listening, speaking, reading, writing, and viewing. Third, there can be greater continuity to student learning across the grade levels. Finally, students learn to be independent learners by setting goals, making choices, evaluating themselves and their work, and reflecting on their progress.

In our view, literature-based instruction does not mean "anything goes." As many other chapters in this volume have argued (e.g., Sipe, Chapter 3; Au & Raphael, Chapter 6; Denyer & Florio-Ruane, Chapter 7), there is substantial content to be learned in a literature-based reading program. We need guidelines such as Michigan's standards and benchmarks that address both the content and process of English language arts curriculum, instruction, and assessment (see Casteel, Roop, & Schiller, 1996; Fleischer, Koch, Lewis, & Roop, 1996). Many object to the idea of standards as too prescriptive. Others argue that curriculum should be generated solely from teacher and student interests. We are arguing for a middle ground that provides guidelines specific enough to serve as the basis for decision making, but general enough to allow flexibility and choice in decision making. We see standards and benchmarks as invitations to conversations about what students should know and be able to do and what constitutes evidence that they have achieved agreed-upon goals. It is through these conversations that we are most likely to achieve the alignment of curriculum, instruction, and assessment and the coherence across grade levels that we desire.

ENDNOTE

1. Ms. Elsworth's unit is a modification of a unit originally developed by Liz Smith, another Waterford fourth-grade teacher. Others who contributed to the unit were Julie Casteel and Marilyn Wendt. They are district resource consultants for Waterford School District.

REFERENCES

Adler, M. (1982). *The paideia proposal: An educational manifesto.* New York: Macmillan.

Applebee, A. N. (1996). *Curriculum as conversation.* Chicago: University of Chicago Press.

Bloom, B. (1981). *All our children learning.* New York: McGraw-Hill.

Bloom, H. (1994). *The western canon: The books and school of the ages.* New York: Harcourt Brace Publishers.

Britton, J. (1972). *Language and learning.* Harmondsworth, Middlesex, England: Penguin Books. (First published by Allen Lane, The Penguin Press, 1970).

Brophy, J. (1992). Probing the subleties of subject matter teaching. *Educational Leadership, 49*(7), 4–8.

Casteel, J., Roop, L., & Schiller, L. (1996). "No such thing as an expert": Learning to live with standards in the classroom. *Language Arts, 73,* 30–35.

Cheney, L. V. (1987). *American memory: A report on the humanities in the nation's public schools.* Washington, DC: U.S. Government Printing Office.

Farrell, E. J. (1991). Instructional models for English language arts, K–12. In J. Flood, J. M. Jensen, D. Lapp, & J. R. Squire (Eds.), *Handbook of research on teaching the English language arts* (pp. 63–84). New York: Macmillan.

Fleischer, C., Koch, R., Lewis, J., & Roop, L. (1996). Learning to walk it, not just talk it: Standards and Michigan's demonstration sites. *Language Arts, 73,* 36–43.

Gehrke, N. J., Knapp, M. S., & Sirotnik, K. A. (1992). In search of the school curriculum. In G. Grant (Ed.), *Review of research in education* (Vol. 18) (pp. 51–110). Washington, DC: AERA.

Harste, J. C. (1994). Literacy as curricular conversations about knowledge, inquiry, and morality. In R. R. Ruddell, M. R. Ruddell, & H. Singer (Eds.), *Theoretical models and processes of reading* (4th ed.) (pp.1222–1242). Newark, DE: International Reading Association.

Hirsch, E. D., Jr. (1987). *Cultural literacy: What every American needs to know.* Boston: Houghton Mifflin.

Mandel, B. J. (Ed.) (1980). *Three language arts curriculum models: Pre-kindergarten through college.* Urbana, IL: National Council of Teachers of English.

Moffett, J., & and Wagner, B. J. (1983). *Student-centered language arts and reading, K–12: A handbook for teachers* (3rd ed.). Boston: Houghton Mifflin.

Newmann, F. M. (1991). Linking restructuring to authentic student achievement. *Phi Delta Kappan, 72*(6), 458–463.

Onosko, J. J., & Newmann, F. M. (1994). Creating more thoughtful learning environments. In J. N. Manieri & C. C. Black (Eds.), *Creating powerful thinking in teachers and students: Diverse perspectives* (pp. 27–49). New York: Hartcourt Brace.

Perkins, D. P. (1993). Teaching for understanding. *American Educator, 17*(3), 8, 28–35.

Peters, C. W. (1991). You can't have authentic assessment without authentic content. *Reading Teacher, 44*(8), 590–591.

Peters, C. W. (1994). Making connections to American literature. In B. Honig and N. Peterson (Eds.), *What's a teacher to do? New curricula for new standards* [Vol. 2, English Language Arts]. Washington DC: National Center on Education and the Economy.

Ravitch, D., & Finn, C. E., Jr. (1987). *What do our 17-year-olds know? A report on the first national assessment of history and literature.* New York: Harper & Row.

Rosenblatt, L. M. (1938). *Literature as exploration.* New York: Appleton-Century. (New York: Noble & Noble, 1968 [rev. ed.]; London: Heinemann, 1970 [3rd ed.]; New York: Noble & Noble, 1976 [rev. ed.]; New York: Modern Language Association, 1983 [4th ed.]).

Standards for the English language arts. (1996). National Council of Teachers of English and the International Reading Association, Newark, DE.

Suhor, C. (1988). Content and process in the English curriculum. In R. S. Brandt (Ed.), *Content of the curriculum* (pp. 31–52). Alexandria, VA: Association for Supervision and Curriculum Development.

Valencia, S. W., Lipson, M. Y., Peters, C. W., & Wixson, K. K. (1994, April). A national survey of practices in thematic/integrated language arts instruction. In S. Florio-Ruane (Chair), *Thematic/integrated language arts instruction: From theory to practice.* Symposium conducted at the annual meeting of the American Educational Research Association, New Orleans.

Wixson, K., Davis, J., Hodson, L., & Spitulnik, J. (1994, April). Case studies of thematic/integrated language arts instruction in the classroom. In S. Florio-Ruane (Chair), *Thematic/integrated language arts instruction: From theory to practice.* Symposium conducted at the annual meeting of the American Educational Research Association, New Orleans.

Wixson, K. K., Peters, C. W., & Potter, S. A. (1996). The case for integrated standards in English language arts. *Language Arts, 73,* 20–29.

CHILDREN'S BOOKS CITED

Ancona, G. (1990). *Riverkeeper.* New York: Macmillan.

Baker, J. (1991). *Window.* New York: Greenwillow.

Bruchac, J., & Caduto, M. (1989). *Keepers of the earth: Native American stories and environmental activities for children.* Illus. J. K. Fadden & C. Wood. Golden, CO: Fulcrum.

Cherry, L. (1992). *The great Kapok tree: A tale of the Amazon rain forest.* San Diego: Harcourt.

Taylor, M. (1976). *Roll of thunder, hear my cry.* New York: Dial.

Chapter 13

"My Spark Is a Little Brighter for Teaching Reading This Year": A Fifth-grade Teacher's Quest to Improve Assessment in Her Integrated Literature-based Program

●————————●

Susan I. McMahon, University of Wisconsin–Madison

Jacqueline Wells teaches fifth grade in an elementary school located in the middle of a small town in central Wisconsin. She had been teaching for six years when I first began observing her class and working with her to modify her assessment practices. She began teaching reading the way so many of us did, using the district-mandated basal series with an occasional unit built around a novel. With each novel she noticed that her students seemed more engaged with the texts and the responses they evoked; yet, her district's requirement caused her to continue her practice with limited use of novels. When she accepted a teaching position at her current school, she learned that all the teachers used trade books for reading instruction. Jacqueline found this to be an exciting opportunity since, for the first time, she had access to classroom sets of many novels. At the same time, this seemed to provide "almost too much freedom" because she did not know exactly what to teach with the novels. Later, she described her response to her use of the new materials as "basalizing" the trade books because her needs for evaluation led her to constructing questions and worksheets to help her assess students' comprehension and to develop higher-order thinking.

During the summer of 1995, Jacqueline entered the Master's program at the University of Wisconsin–Madison. As a student enrolled in my course, she heard Laura Pardo discuss Book Club, a literature-based reading program (McMahon & Raphael, 1997). Laura's description of her own efforts with a literature-based program encouraged Jacqueline to continue to make modifications in her own instruction. These changes included a movement away from more traditional assessment measures and the inclusion of integrated language arts and social studies curricula. As the year progressed, Jacqueline was becoming more and more comfortable with the instructional aspect of her program, but, like other teachers trying to implement a literature-based program (e.g., Scharer, 1992), she continued to struggle with assessment. This effort to include trade books with an integrated curriculum led her to ask me for some support as she made further adjustments in both her instruction and assessment. We discussed this late that fall semester and I agreed to visit her classroom and work with her to design appropriate assessment measures for her students. This chapter is based on our work together.

"AUTHENTIC ASSESSMENT": IDENTIFYING ISSUES OF CONCERN

Many educators (see Bisesi et al., Chapter 11) are reconsidering the relationship between instruction and assessment, revealing several issues that make changing practices difficult. As Jacqueline and I worked to establish a plan, we considered what others had already written and identified those issues she felt she was then grappling with. One issue was the lack of a unified vision for making changes in existing assessment measures (Cizer, 1995; Johnston, 1987; Stiggins, 1995). Jacqueline's district, like many others, was in a process of change, but the result was the inclusion of a variety of state- and district-mandated measures. Thus, Jacqueline expressed a need to develop a larger plan that integrated her classroom-based assessments with her instruction and curriculum, as well as helped her provide instruction that facilitated her students' efforts to do well on the other evaluation tools in the district.

Another issue for Jacqueline was the tension she felt between her assessment of students' literacy development based on her observational and classroom materials and the students' scores on more standardized measures (Wixson, Valencia, & Lipson, 1994). She believed the classroom-based measures were more accurate since there were multiple examples of students' work upon which to make an evaluation, but the other scores appeared to have more emphasis in her district. Because these measures were not always congruent, she questioned her own knowledge. This is not uncommon; others have also noted the lack of teacher preparation in assessing children's literacy growth (Johnston, 1987; Schafer, 1993), which often results in errors in interpretation (MacGinitie, 1993). Jacqueline's teaching experience and knowledge of her students led her to believe her evaluations were accurate, but she wanted more "proven" methods for supporting them.

Jacqueline's third issue was one Stiggins (1995) also identified as a concern for many educators—the extreme complexity in trying to develop performance-based measures, particularly given the district's emphasis on standardized tests. She felt she was taking an extreme risk in trying to make changes that her district might or might not appreciate.

Finally, as Darling-Hammond (1991) noted, Jacqueline believed that her students did not have sufficient opportunities to talk about what they knew. She wanted to provide more occasions for students to discuss and write about what they were thinking. Such discourse could facilitate her own assessment of their learning.

SCHOOL READING GOALS: INITIATING A PLAN FOR ASSESSING A LITERATURE-BASED PROGRAM

With Jacqueline's issues clearly identified, we began as others have suggested (Highfield & Folkert, 1997; Pardo, 1997; Paris, Calfee, Filby, Hiebert, Pearson, & Valencia, 1992) by analyzing the district's goals for the reading program and developing a framework so that we could begin to design a plan for (a) collecting evidence of student growth, (b) evaluating this evidence, and (c) interpreting and using the data (Figure 13.1).

These provided us a way of articulating some of the many goals that were inherent within Jacqueline's program. For example, she had consistently focused on the district's goals, such as having students express, develop, support, and/or change their opinions about what they had read (see # 7). However, she noted that assessing student growth in such areas was a problem for her with the existing measures. Therefore, we identified several of these goals to emphasize during the next unit. Both books to be included, *Let the Hurricane Roar* (Lane, 1945) and *Prairie Songs* (Conrad, 1985), were set in the Midwest during pioneer America, each dealt with causal relationships, and each presented implicit information related to the climax. We decided that helping students make inferences (#8), draw conclusions (#9), and identify cause and effect (#11) were strategies students needed to begin working on. Further, Jacqueline wanted to continue on their development of opinions (#7), their ability to paraphrase and summarize (#10), and their vocabulary development (# 3), so we added these to the list. Thus, consulting the district's goals provided us with a long list of attributes in literacy development for her to work on. While this was helpful, we did not stop with these because Jacqueline also wanted her students to (a) respond personally to the events represented in the texts, (b) connect what they were reading in fiction to the events and ideas they had just studied during their social studies unit, and (c) write in Standard English. Therefore, her final list included both goals from the district and ones she identified for her students. Once we had identified the key goals for the unit, we began to develop daily lesson plans and assignments that addressed each of these. Two examples help illustrate this: one related to students' journal writing, the other to their oral discussions.

Figure 13.1

READING STRATEGIES AND BEHAVIORS CHECKLIST

NAME OF STUDENT:	TEACHER:		GRADE:
Strategic Reading Skills and Behaviors Checklist—Grade 5	DATE: Working on	DATE: Secure	Comments
1. Student will demonstrate an active interest in reading and will choose to read independently for enjoyment and information.			
2. Student will use written resources appropriate for their purpose.			
3. Student will use a variety of skills to aid the recognition of unfamiliar words.			
4. Student will use appropriate reading strategies to monitor comprehension.			
5. Student will identify and distinguish between main ideas and supporting details.			
6. Student will recognize and use figurative language.			
7. Student will express, develop, support, and/or change opinions about what she/he has read.			
8. Student will be able to make inferences after reading material.			
9. Student will draw conclusions from material read.			
10. Student will summarize/paraphrase what she/he has read.			
11. Student will identify cause and effect.			
12. Student will integrate new vocabulary in a variety of contexts.			

JOURNALS: HELPING STUDENTS FOCUS ON QUALITY RESPONSE

One issue that Jacqueline wanted to address specifically was the quality of the responses students included within their logs. While their previous log entries provided her with glimpses into their thinking, she felt they lacked development. She was not sure how to help students understand her goals for them, begin to establish their own literacy goals, or evaluate their own journal writing. Our process included three stages: (a) identifying students' existing writing patterns, (b) planning instruction based on these patterns, and (c) implementing instruction and assessment related to these patterns.

Identifying Students' Existing Writing Patterns

Having identified the literacy goals for the unit, we decided to examine students' entries from previous units (1) to substantiate Jacqueline's assessment of the current status of their writing, (2) to establish an instructional beginning, and (3) to identify some specific examples to share with students so they could see the range of possible responses. Rereading prior log entries from *Bridge to Terabithia* (Paterson, 1977) revealed the variety of student writing within the class:

- limited response revealing few personal reactions or opinions
- summarized text events with little or no personal response or opinion
- inconsistent quality
- some personal reactions or opinions, but lacking elaboration

Some students had provided very **limited responses** that did not display their ability to express, support, and/or change their opinions. Often, students expressed an opinion with little specific detail and therefore represented their position without offering any development. Bob's response about "good sportsmanship" is a good example of this. He wrote, "Good sportsmanship is so no fights or anything else happens. Bad sportsmanship is when you're being bad." Even though Bob gave one example of what he thinks is good, he defined "bad sportsmanship" with the same term, not revealing much about his thinking. Further, he made no effort to connect his thinking with the text the class had just read or with his own experience.

The second emerging pattern was that some students constructed **summaries** of text events without personal connections or elaborations. Will's log reflects this consistently. For example, in one entry he wrote about gift giving. He began by describing his feelings when receiving a present, then elaborated by summarizing key events in the chapter. "Well Jess gave Leslie a puppy (and) she was very happy and she gave Jess a box of water coler paints and Jesse was happy too. That's how this chapter is like gift giving." While Will's written explanation is more elaborate than Bob's, it is primarily a summary of events in the text without connections to his experience. Even though Jacqueline wanted students to strengthen their ability to summarize, she also wanted them to understand when summaries were appropriate. In this instance, a summary was not suitable because the stated goal for this log entry was for students to demonstrate how they were connecting personally with the text and to express their opinions about text events. Will's entries often began with an effort to make a personal connection but then shifted to a summary.

Another pattern that emerged as we analyzed students' prior log entries was that they were **inconsistent**. Sometimes students wrote vague entries, while at other times they wrote more extended responses. Samantha's log serves as a good example of this. When responding to the concept of good sportsmanship, she wrote, "I think that good sportsmanship is good but if you have bad sportsmanship you shouldn't play." Such writing reveals little about Samantha's thinking; however, a later entry was closer to what Jacqueline had been looking for. "I think that if you want to give somebody a gift go for it, because you could light up a persons day and make them very happy like when Jess and Leslie exchanged gifts." In this entry Samantha responded with her opinion on gift giving, then briefly related it to an event in the text.

A fourth pattern demonstrated by an analysis of the logs was that some students consistently elected to write more extended entries, but their responses **lacked opinions or personal connections**. For example, when writing about good sportsmanship, Rebecka expressed the following: "Good sportsmanship is you don't cry or get mad because you lost. If you win, you don't say they are not good at something and you say good try or you did a good job." Also, when responding to the exchange of gifts in Chapter 6, she wrote, "Jess and Leslie gave each other presents. I think it's nice to give presents, but you don't always have to give them. It is who you are inside that counts." Rebecka's written responses revealed some of her thinking related to the book but were lacking in providing the depth of personal connections or strong opinions about events in the text.

Analysis of the students' prior log entries revealed problems students had meeting the district's goals. In addition to these limitations, Jacqueline's insight helped her see how one of her instructional practices might have been contributing to students' difficulty with meeting the goal of expressing personal responses.

When Jacqueline first began making the shift from a basal-driven program to a more literature-based approach, two issues loomed in her thinking about how to incorporate journals into her program. First, she wanted to help her students make the adjustment from the text materials that provided specific guidelines and that were often used with basals to the more open format of reading logs. Second, Jacqueline realized that she was not yet ready to release control to the students. That is, she was not then ready to let them decide what to write about in their logs. However, as Jacqueline reread their entries as part of the analysis, she became critical of her use of the same prompts for the entire class because she began to see that the prompt may have been inhibiting students' abilities to make personal connections or express their developing opinions. She then remembered hand-outs from her Master's class the previous summer that demonstrated the variety of options Laura Pardo provided her classes. While offering students choices, these prompts also provided them some direction. With these as guides, Jacqueline decided to begin providing students more choices when responding in their logs.

With a new awareness of what additional instruction students needed and how changing the prompts might foster greater flexibility in student thinking, we were prepared to move to the next step—planning instruction. Together, we began to brainstorm how to provide instruction that enabled students to discuss, analyze, and understand their prior entries in light of the district's and their own goals. As already mentioned, Jacqueline believed that students would benefit from having opportunities to discuss what they knew (Darling-Hammond, 1991). Further, she wanted them to assume ownership and control over their own literacy development, so including them in the process was essential to this end (See Wong-Kam, Chapter 14).

Planning Instruction Based on Students' Writing Patterns

As Jacqueline and I discussed how to begin providing students with instruction to improve their journal entries, I shared with her how Julie Folkert and Sara Bean had integrated their writing instruction and assessment in Book Club, a literature-based reading program (Folkert & Bean, 1997). Julie and Sara had faced a similar situation since they, too, wanted their students to write more extended, personal responses to texts and to be willing to adopt and support a position related to events in the text. To this end, they developed "targets" along with their students for their journal entries. Jacqueline liked this approach, so we began discussing how we might implement this in her classroom.

Since we had already analyzed students' prior entries, we had a strong sense of the range within the class. We decided that the best approach might be for Jacqueline to type three examples from different students' prior logs. One of these would be very weak; another, one of the strongest; and the third, somewhere in between. Since students in Jacqueline's class were familiar with peer editing during process writing, she was confident they understood how to be critical analysts of a text without being personally mean or faultfinding. Further, we decided that a second approach used with Book Club (McMahon, 1997) should also be incorporated into the discussion. That is, for all discussions of their work, Jacqueline began by asking students to find what an individual had done well, then move to what could be improved. This balance contributed to a more positive class discussion since it stressed that everyone was doing something well and all could improve. No one was in a static situation. Three different entries provided a range of possibilities, without representing an embodiment of perfection or failure.

In deciding the order of the entries, Jacqueline anticipated that students could more easily identify the qualities of the best and weakest than they could distinguish criteria for the one in the middle range, so she decided to begin with the entry that was the strongest of the three. She led a discussion with students, exploring the strengths the entry revealed and the areas for improvement. She then moved to the weakest sample entry, following the same pattern, and ended with the one representing qualities someplace in the middle. Once the class had fully discussed all three entries, they developed a rubric both they and she would use to assess their progress in writing their logs (see Figure 13.2). Through this process, students (1) became more explicitly aware of Jacqueline's expectations for their log entries, (2) had a voice in developing the measure, and (3) created a tool with which they could assess their own growth.

Implementing Instruction and Assessment Related to These Patterns

Once the class had developed the rubric, Jacqueline continued to remind them of her expectations. Further, she modified her prompts to provide more options for students. After the children had had some time to work on their writing, she asked them to reread their entries for *Bridge to Terabithia* and, using their rubric, assess their own writing and set their own goals for improvement. The students' responses revealed how well they were understanding this process.

As with the previous activity, Jacqueline asked students to identify their strengths, areas to work on, and their plans for improvement. Students' answers revealed to Jacqueline that they were focusing on form (spelling, sentence structure, paragraphing), quantity of writing, and the time devoted to completing their entries. Three students' evaluations demonstrate their emphases well.

Bob's reaction was brief. "The best thing about my journal is spelling and paragraphs. Sometimes there werent very many sentences, More sen-

Figure 13.2

Journal Rubric

Name: _____   Date: _____

	Legendary	A-Ha! That's it! "5"	Getting There "3"	Still Work-ing "1"
PROMPT		• Good description and explanation of prompt. • Gives examples and details by using words directly from the book. • Also includes page numbers.	• Includes more information about the prompt and book with more "umph." • Uses some details but could elaborate more.	• Doesn't tell much about what is happening. • Needs more detail.
ORGANIZA-TION		• The journal entry makes sense. • Uses paragraphs appropriately with several sentences.	• Most of the sentences make sense. • Writes a paragraph with at least five sentences.	• Difficult for the reader to understand what is meant. • Writes four or fewer sentences. • Needs more information.
PERSONAL CONNEC-TIONS		• Relates the story to self or tells how the reader feels about the book.	• Personal connection could be made clearer for the reader.	• Missing a personal connection to own life or to another book read.
MECHANICS		• Uses correct spelling and punctuation	• Has few spelling and punctuation mistakes.	• Needs to work on spelling and punctuation.

Self Assessment:

I think I did the best on:

I think I worked the hardest on:

I could have done better on:

tences or paragraphs in a sentence." Will wrote a longer entry than Bob's but without specificity. "The best thing about my B.T. (*Bridge to Terabithia*) journal was in chapter nine because I felt I did a good job on it. The worst thing about my B.T. journal is in chapter seven I felt I needed to do a better job on it. My goals to improve my journal are to not rush to take my time and write better." Rebecka's entry demonstrated that she seemed to understand how to improve her entries to meet the goals the class discussed. "My best thing about my B.T. journal was my spelling. The worst thing about my B.T. journal was that I didn't give examples from a time in my life. One goal I have is to put more detail in this journal than in the B.T. journal." This range of answers provided Jacqueline a basis upon which to provide further instruction. For example, even though she wanted students to work on appropriate language usage, she did not want them to focus on form at the expense of substance. In addition, she was hopeful that, by asking students to identify their own goals, they would begin assuming responsibility for writing better entries in their journals.

After several days in which students responded in their logs to their reading of *Let the Hurricane Roar*, Jacqueline began an ongoing process of asking students to use the rubric to evaluate their current entries against their own goals and plan how they would improve upon them. At the same time, she continued instruction on how to provide details supporting opinions and on how to elaborate personal responses. The student's final log entries, in which Jacqueline asked them to explain (a) what they liked best about the book, (b) what could have been better, and (c) whether they would recommend the book to a friend, demonstrate their growth over this time period.

Bob's previous entries provided limited information, with few details or evidence of his personal reactions to a text. After a few weeks of instruction and practice, though, Bob was beginning to provide more detail: "The best part I liked about this book was when David got home because it was real neat to hear that David finally got home. I think they could have told more about David and his job. I'd recommend this book because it's real adventurers and it's in the pioneer days."

Will's earlier entries were primarily summaries; however, after some instruction and practice, he no longer resorted to reiterating text events. "The thing I liked best about the book was when the Svenson's came. Well, because they were nice and helped David and Molly a lot. The starting of the book could of been better because it was kind of boring but it got better. I would recommend this book because it tells the life of two pioneers and is very interesting in the middle of the book." While Will's entry could still benefit from more specific details, it demonstrated his progress in elaborating his opinion instead of restating text events.

During the previous units, Samantha's log entries had been inconsistent in quality. After instruction focusing her attention on this, however, her entries were becoming more consistent. That is, her entries demonstrated that she was steadily making connections between the text and her personal experiences, stating her beliefs, and critiquing the book. At the same time, she still needed to work on providing details. "The thing I liked best was the end when David came back. The thing that I thought could have been better was that the auther could have explaned better who was talking. I would recommend this book because it was fun to hear all of the adventures Molly has."

Rebecka's earlier log entries represented those that gave some glimpse into her thinking but needed further development. Her final entry demonstrated that she was beginning to grow in this area. "The thing I liked best about this book was when she got the cow and when the wolves came because I think she deserved the cow and I liked the wolves because it was exiting and a little scary. The thing that could be better was they could tell what happened to Mr. Gray and what happed after David came and what they did. I would recommend this book because it was exceting and they put a lot of detail in the book."

As these four examples demonstrate, most of Jacqueline's students made progress toward her goals for their log entries even within a short period of time. In fact, she and I analyzed selected entries from their logs for *Let the Hurricane Roar* and found that of the fifteen students, ten had improved their log entries, three had remained about the same, and two seemed to be writing slightly less engaged responses. Like many educators, Jacqueline began to consider how to meet the needs of the five students who had not seemed to make any progress, while still supporting the growth of the other students as well.

The progress of the majority of students in Jacqueline's class resulted from

- explicit instruction about Jacqueline's expectations
- the instructional use of examples from students' logs
- students' contributions to the rubric
- students' identification of their own goals
- time for students to analyze their own entries
- time to practice
- the close connections between instruction and assessment

These four final entries from *Let the Hurricane Roar* also reveal that students still needed additional time with this process to develop the types of entries that both Jacqueline and the students had set as a goal to be met by the end of the year. With this specific knowledge and concrete examples of students' work, she had a solid basis upon which to continue instruction that would foster critical readers and writers.

DISCUSSION: CAPTURING AND ASSESSING ORAL TALK

Each day, Jacqueline had students meet in small, student-led groups to discuss the books they were reading. As they talked, she circulated among them, noting discussion topics and problems. She suspected that even though there were times when groups engaged in meaningful conversations, there were other occasions during which students simply read from their logs or engaged in discourse that did not result in greater understandings. Thus, Jacqueline wanted a way to assess what students discussed and evaluate this in terms of her literacy goals.

Unlike the task of trying to understand students' written work, attempting to assess and evaluate their oral conversations about texts was more complicated. First, while there were the district curriculum guides for reading and writing, there was no such document related to students' oral discussions associated with reading. Second, unlike the log entries, their discussions did not leave a concrete document for close examination. While students talked, Jacqueline circulated, noting discussion topics, problems, and issues that engaged the group. However, other than her notes, there remained no record of the conversation, so it appeared that students could not analyze their contributions to the group in the same ways they could by referring to their written log entries. As with the assessment of their writing, however, my previous experiences with Book Club helped us with this problem.

As part of our research the first year or two of Book Club, we taped and transcribed students' discussions and used the transcripts for instructional purposes (McMahon, 1997). I explained this process to Jacqueline and presented the option of using some of these transcripts as a beginning for analysis and instruction. Not only did this idea appeal to her, but she also decided to tape and transcribe her groups.

Analysis of Other Students' Talk

As we began to focus students' attention on talk as well as writing, I led class discussions, initiating student conversations with a set of transcripts from a group of Book Club students. Each of Jacqueline's groups had a transcript of the same group but from a different day during the same unit on historical fiction. Together, the transcripts represented a range of quality. I explained that we would be doing a type of Reader's Theater in which they would read the transcripts aloud in a small group, then discuss the strengths and areas for improvement that they identified for the group. After this, they would read the transcript before the class and lead a discussion about the group's interactions. Since Jacqueline had followed a similar format when they evaluated their log entries, students adjusted quickly to the idea of analyzing oral conversations. As a first stage of analysis of oral talk, this provided students a framework with which to critique their own discussions. By using other students' discussion groups, the class felt safe in evaluating oral talk. Further, this process reinforced the one we had initiated with their log entries. This process took a few days to complete, but when we had finished, students were ready to move on to analyses of their own talk.

Analyses of Their Own Talk

While we were discussing the transcripts from another classroom, the reading program continued as normal. That is, they continued to read, write about, and discuss a book. As they talked, Jacqueline taped their discussions and transcribed them for instructional use. Once these were completed and duplicated, we analyzed them to identify existing strengths and limitations across the class. As we read the transcripts, we found exactly what she had observed as she monitored student talk. That is, even though some groups sustained engaging discussions for a time, many students either read from their logs or seemed unable to maintain such conversations. Like issues related to their written work, these problems surfaced to varying degrees. The following transcripts demonstrate the two main problems most clearly.

Round Robin Turn-Taking. One problem students had in their groups was determining the order of speakers. This was also a common problem we had with students participating initially in Book Club (McMahon, 1997). A common classroom practice for helping students establish turn-taking is to suggest they go in a predetermined order, such as going around the circle. While this facilitates an orderly procedure, it does not foster the best climate for engaging conversations (McMahon, 1996). The following section of transcript demonstrates how this group has mastered this technique to the extent that no one interrupts another or changes the order. In this particular unit, Jacqueline had created a log entry format that she hoped would provide students more options for writing and discussion (see Figure 13.3). In this group, the boys decided not only to respond by going around their circle, but also by limiting their talk to their responses to the listed options.

Robert: Okay, my connection to social studies and the Civil War: I was learning about the Civil War and as the war went on in *Shades of Gray,* um, ah, Matt, no not Matt, Will was learning about it too and the war went on.

/ /

Samuel: Um, connections to social studies: I thought, ah, his father because his father died in the Civil War and so did his two brothers.

Figure 13.3

Log Entry for Civil War Unit

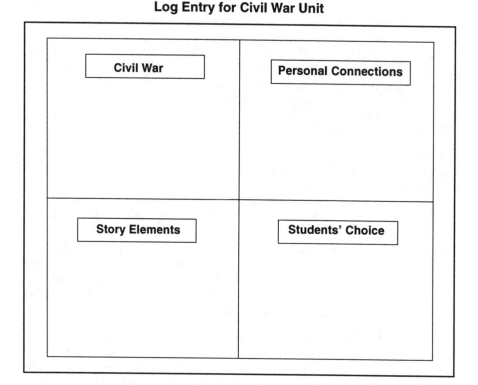

Mark: I thought . . . Why it was connected to the Civil War in that way because the confederates came and took the things from the uncle's farm.

Robert: Personal connection between this book and me was: He was a boy and I was. We both, wait / / I know how he feels about having to do little work, to do little work and then have to suddenly do lots more.

/ /

Samuel: Mine is, ah, when I went over to stay at my aunt's house, I had to go over there too, when my parents went on vacation.

Mark: Mmm. I've also had to go to my grandparents' house alone, but I didn't have to stay there.

/ /

Robert: All right, plot. The plot was, I thought the plot was, the setting, um, the country at Ross's house.

Samuel: I found, ah, he was living, his new home was, ah, a small house with a porch. It had a summer kitchen, ah, and had a hen house and a barn with a garden patch.

Mark: I think the setting was when they were on the road and at their grandparents' house.

Robert: Okay, we're done.

Clearly, this group is not "engaged" in a discussion at all since there is no interaction, only "telling." While this pattern represents what Jacqueline saw as an extreme example, it also served as an excellent illustration for instructional purposes.

A Lack of Substance. A second problem Jacqueline observed was that students interacted about procedural issues instead of topics prompted by reading the books. The following transcript, taped about the same time as the previous one, demonstrated how one student, Dan, could keep the group from interacting because of his preoccupation with the most recent section of the book his peers had read.

Dan: What's the last thing that happened in you guy's chapter?

Jim: I read 5.

Dan: What was the last thing that happened? What are you on Tony? Wait, you're on 5. What are you on?

Tony: 7

Dan: Okay, I'm on 9.

Jim: The last thing that happened in chapter 6 was . . .

Tony: I thought you were on 5.

Jim: Oh, 5, yeah. Well, um, Brady and his friend Range were in, they were in a wagon type thing. And there was a slave [hunter . . .

Dan: [Oh! Can [I talk?

Jim: [slave catcher and, um, he had a hound dog and Mr. McKain was trying to run out of town, out of the place because he didn't want him there.

Dan: Yeah. Have you read chapter 6?

Jim: No.

Dan: Okay what was the last word in your book?

Jim: In my book?

Dan: No, in chapter 5.

Jim: Um, the last word in chapter 5 is . . .

Dan: Maybe that will help us 'cause there's one part I don't know if I'm supposed to say or not.

Jim: Drover Hill.

Dan: Let me see. Okay, he hadn't set out to do it, but, oh, he just made the scarecrow?

Jim: Yeah, he made it look just like Drover Hull.

Dan: Oh, that's where we are?

Reading this section of the transcript revealed how one member could keep the group from discussing topics related to their reading. As with the other transcript, this one provided a clear example for instructional purposes.

As previously mentioned, Jacqueline had already observed these two problems as she circulated among the groups while they talked. However, the transcripts provided her with clear illustrations from the students' own discussions to help them comprehend how these issues were preventing them from engaging in meaningful discussions. More meaningful discussions would not only enable them to clarify their interpretations of the texts, but would also be more engaging. Therefore, she needed to provide further instruction on the interactional patterns she wanted them to adopt and on the topics they could discuss so that their discussion groups would be more interesting and informative. These related directly to the district's reading goals.

With a clearer sense of the issues she needed to address explicitly, Jacqueline was prepared to provide instruction on how students should interact in their small groups. As with the instruction using transcripts from another class, she began by giving students copies of a transcript, asking them to prepare a type of Reader's Theater, and sharing with the class what the group had done well and what they could improve. The main difference was that, this time, they knew they were analyzing discussions occurring within their own class. Jacqueline reminded them that their goal was to be helpful to others by analyzing the *talk,* not criticizing individuals. Further, as the class analyzed their own book discussions, Jacqueline helped them focus on the district's goals and the group's interactional patterns. For example, as students read through transcripts of their own groups, they looked for how well they expressed opinions and the means of supporting their ideas, as well as noting who participated, how well group members interacted with one another, and how they entered the conversation.

As a result of this instruction, student groups became more engaged in conversations related to ideas presented in the texts. At times, they still resorted to more structured forms of turn-taking or struggled with ways to express their opinions and responses if they differed from those of other members of the group. However, Jacqueline continued to enlist their help in assessing their talk, identifying strengths as well as areas to improve, and implementing plans for improvement. As the year progressed, their oral discourse became more engaging, more interesting for them, and, more important, more revealing about their developing sophistication in responding to texts.

COLLABORATIVE WORK FACILITATED JACQUELINE'S ASSESSMENT OF HER PROGRAM

At the end of the school year, Jacqueline and I looked back to evaluate the success of our efforts to modify her assessment of her integrated literature-based reading program. In general, we found that she had been successful in many ways. For her, the true measure was the improvement she saw in students' writing, in the discussions, and in their increased engagement in reading. While this might have been sufficient, we also reviewed some of the ideas others have articulated related to assessment reform. These demonstrated to us that Jacqueline's efforts were successful in many ways.

First, Jacqueline's conclusions were much like those of the teachers in Scharer's (1992) study. That is, like them, she built on students' needs and redefined her criteria for making decisions about grading. At the same time, unlike them, she did not become less concerned with satisfying the district's course of study. Instead, she found ways of aligning students' literacy needs and interests with the district's goals. This was more satisfactory for her as a teacher since it helped her cope with the tensions created by trying to resist district mandates. Further, she believed that the district's goals were valid and that students would benefit if she could find ways of helping them achieve them.

Another benefit that arose from Jacqueline's changes in her assessment practices was that her program was becoming more aligned with critical dimensions of literacy (Paris et al., 1992). That is, students were becoming increasingly engaged with the texts they were reading and those they were writing. They grew in their understanding of literacy and began assuming ownership over their own growth. They began collaborating in small groups to foster greater understanding and construct meaning. Finally, students began to make connections between the events portrayed in non-fiction texts and the issues and events they were studying in social studies. As a result, Jacqueline's class became increasingly more interactive as they constructed meanings and developed their own metacognitive awareness of their growth as critical readers and writers.

A third benefit was that Jacqueline was able to construct performance-based measures that were valid means of assessing students' growth. Stiggins (1995) notes that "sound assessments" (a) arise from and serve clear purposes, (b) reflect clear and appropriate achievement targets, (c) rely on proper methods, (d) sample student achievement appropriately, and (e) control for bias and distortion. As we reviewed these points, we were pleased to note that we had met all but the final category. While all the other characteristics made sense for Jacqueline's class, trying to control for bias and distortion seemed incongruent with her intent to align the district's mandates, her goals, and students' needs. As Wolf (1993) noted, day-to-day assessment needs to be meaningful for the teacher. Through her careful analysis of her students' prior and current work, the district's mandates, and her own literacy goals for the students, she created "informed" assessment measures (Wolf, 1993). Further, she met another criteria of clearly articulating her goals and criteria for success to the students (Hiebert, Valencia, & Afflerbach, 1993). She reached her conclusions about students' achievement based on patterns she detected, appropriate adjustments in classroom procedures, listening to students and others who were knowledgeable about literacy development, choosing measures that were aligned with instruction, empowering her students, and connecting instruction to assessment (Johnston, 1987). Thus, neither of us were concerned with Stiggins's final category, controlling for bias, since all of Jacqueline's decisions were grounded in thoughtful analysis and careful implementation of new practices and procedures in her classroom.

CONCLUDING COMMENT

Since she is a thoughtful, reflective teacher, Jacqueline began her efforts to improve her practice the day she began teaching. Therefore, our work together was just one small period of time framed within a life's professional work. She continues to reflect on her program and how to improve it so that her students will become more critical readers and writers. As this chapter has tried to describe, all learning is a process that requires time and practice. Jacqueline described herself as a life-long learner and appears to enjoy the process. At the end of the school year, I asked her how she personally felt about her success. A large smile filled her face as she exclaimed, "My spark is a little brighter for teaching reading this year." Clearly, her students are fortunate to have a teacher who is not only committed to improving her practice in ways that meet their needs, but also pleased to have been able to do so.

REFERENCES

Cizer, G. J. (1995). The big picture in assessment and who ought to have it. *Phi Delta Kappan, 77,* 246–249.

Darling-Hammond, L. (1991). The implications of testing policy for quality and equality. *Phi Delta Kappan, 73,* 220–225.

Folkert, J., & Bean, S. (1997). A portfolio approach to Book Club assessment: Navigating instruction and monitoring student growth. In S. I. McMahon & T. E. Raphael (Eds.), *The Book Club connection: Literacy learning and classroom talk* (pp. 301–319). New York: Teachers College Press.

Highfield, K., & Folkert, J. (1997). Book Club: The content area connection. In S. I. McMahon & T. E. Raphael (Eds.), *The Book Club connection: Literacy learning and classroom talk* (pp. 286–298). New York: Teachers College Press.

Johnston, P. (1987). Teachers as evaluation experts. *The Reading Teacher, 40*(8), 744–748.

MacGinitie, W. H. (1993). Some limits of assessment. *Journal of Reading, 36,* 556–560.

McMahon, S. I. (1997). Book Clubs: Contexts for students to lead their own discussions. In S. I. McMahon, & T. E. Raphael (Eds.), *The Book Club connection: Literacy learning and classroom talk* (pp. 89–106). New York: Teachers College Press.

McMahon, S. I. (1996). Guiding student-led discussion groups. In L. B. Gambrell & J. F. Almasi (Eds.), *Creating classroom cultures that foster discussion, interpretation, and comprehension of text.* (pp. 224–227). Newark, DE: International Reading Association.

McMahon, S. I., & Raphael, T. E. (Eds.) (1997). *The Book Club connection: Literacy learning and classroom talk.* New York: Teachers College Press.

Pardo, L. S. (1997). Reflective teaching for continuing development of Book Club. In S. I. McMahon, & T. E. Raphael (Eds.), *The Book Club connection: Literacy learning and classroom talk* (pp. 227–247). New York: Teachers College Press.

Paris, S. G., Calfee, R. C., Filby, N., Hiebert, E. H., Pearson, P. D., Valencia, S. W., & Wolf, K. P. (1992). A framework for authentic literacy. *The Reading Teacher, 46,* 88–98.

Schafer, W. D. (1993). Assessment literacy for teachers. *Theory into Practice, 32*(2), 118.

Scharer, P. L. (1992). Tensions between numbers and knowing: A study of changes in assessment during implementation of literature-based reading instruction. In N. D. Padak, T. V. Rasinski, & J. Logan (Eds.), *Literacy research and practice: Foundations for the year 2000.* Year of College Reading Association.

Stiggins, R. J. (1995). Assessment literature for the 21st century. *Phi Delta Kappan, 77*(3), 238–245.

Wixson, K. K., Valencia, S. W., & Lipson, M. Y. (1994). Issues in literacy assessment: Facing the realities of internal and external assessment. *Journal of Reading Behavior, 26,* 315–337.

CHILDREN'S BOOKS CITED

Conrad, P. (1985). *Prairie songs*. New York: Harper & Row.
Lane, R. W. (1945). *Let the hurricane roar*. New York: Longmans, Green.
Paterson, K. (1977). *Bridge to Terabithia*. New York: Harper Trophy.

Chapter 14

Sharing Responsibility for Assessment and Evaluation with Our Students

●────────●

Jo Ann Wong-Kam, Punahou School

It was in the mid-1980s that I began using novels as the basis for reading instruction in my fourth-grade classroom. Living through Julie's experience as she fled her home for the open tundra in *Julie of the Wolves* (George, 1972) or escaping underground with *Mrs. Frisby and the Rats of NIMH* (O'Brien, 1971) excited my students more than any stories I had taught from a basal series. I now realize that as I opened my classroom to literature, I was changing more than just the reading material. I was changing the way I looked at reading. Reading was no longer a simple act of comprehension and decoding. With the use of literature, reading had the power to change lives. I believe in the way Eeds and Hudelson (1995) describe literature use in classrooms:

> Literature is a way of making sense of our experiences; it is a way of figuring out the world. . . . Literature provides us opportunities to enter into the lives of others in order to illuminate our own existence and to struggle with the what and why of it. We use literature to interpret ourselves. (p. 2)

Those connections between story and our lives are what make literature-based instruction so powerful.

A related change in my instructional practice has been to encourage students to seek out each other's interpretations through discussion while actively constructing their own meaning. I no longer hold the teacher's manual with the preselected questions and responses. Instead, I invite students to share their questions and responses, listening to how they make sense of events and characters. I may add a question or thought to nudge further exploration of connections, themes, or symbolism, or to clarify a confusing sequence of events. My intent, however, is not to control but to encourage

305

talk. In literature-based instruction, the role of teachers and students is to support one another in building understandings of "what it means to be human beings, living in this diverse and increasingly divided world" (Eeds & Hudelson, 1995, p. 3).

In opening up discussions to the students, I realized that I needed to provide them with more choice in selecting the literature they would read and discuss. While I chose a few literature selections for small-group and class discussions, I encouraged students to seek out books that interested them. Students valued these choices and shared the insights from their self-selected reading during literature circles. These individual presentations often sparked the interest of other students. As a result, popular books were passed around the class. In short, I found that students flourished as readers when they took the responsibility for choosing the literature they would read and for sharing their responses to the literature.

QUESTIONING TYPICAL ASSESSMENT PRACTICES

As I changed my instructional practices based on my beliefs about choice and responsibility, I no longer felt comfortable with the assessment and evaluation system I was using. I didn't feel I could be the sole evaluator in the classroom, bearing the responsibility for looking at students' work and deciding what it reflected about their learning. By making those decisions, I took the ownership of learning away from my students. To become lifelong learners, the students needed to be able to set their own goals and make plans about how to achieve those goals. To improve their own learning, they had to see assessment and evaluation as means of informing themselves about their progress toward meeting their goals.

I realized that I needed to bring the same principles of student choice and responsibility, incorporated in literature-based instruction, into my assessment and evaluation procedures. That would mean:

- Students would actively participate in the assessment and evaluation process. They would look at what they were able to do, compare that to what they wanted to achieve, then plan what they needed to do next. Having discussions with the teacher and other students about their work would help them construct a richer understanding of themselves and their learning.

- Teachers and fellow students would support the learner who was struggling to understand what she had learned. Students might not always reach their goals, but the feeling of failure could be reduced by speaking with others about the challenge and receiving encouragement about how to proceed.

- Students would have choice in selecting the evidence that showed what they were learning. Students were the only ones who could fully explain what a piece of work represented, since they had created it.

- Students would find connections between what was assessed and evaluated and their own lives, so learning became meaningful.

- Students would learn to ask themselves questions. What am I trying to achieve? Why is it important to me? What am I trying to show about myself?

In this chapter, I share my work as a teacher of third- and fifth-grade students to honor these principles in my assessment and evaluation practices. First, I discuss how I helped students to set goals and make plans. By helping students set goals for their own learning, I shared the responsibility for assessment with them. Second, I explore my role as a teacher in connecting instruction to the goals students had set. I knew that I needed to support students in reaching their goals, so I tried to bring the curriculum closer to students' needs. Third, I describe how I guided my students to collect the evidence they needed to show how well they had succeeded in meeting their goals. This evidence was placed in progress folios. Fourth, I look at how the students and I evaluated their achievements, as shown by the evidence in their progress folios. While I considered students' self-evaluations to be important, I also felt students needed to know about my expectations for their performance, so I developed rubrics or descriptors of quality. Finally, I discuss three-way conferences, in which students shared their achievements with their parents (Davies, Cameron, Politano, Davies, & Gregory, 1992). The three-way conferences helped parents to become active participants in supporting students' pursuit of their goals.

SETTING GOALS AND MAKING PLANS

Others in this volume (Peters & Wixson Chapter 12; McMahon, Chapter 13) emphasize goal setting based on standards established at the national, state, and district levels. My approach to goal setting was somewhat different, in that I emphasized goals established by the students themeselves, under my guidance. I believe that the connection between instruction and evaluation begins when students identify goals for improving their learning. But how does a teacher help students to understand goals? I have found it works well to ask students, "What do good readers do?" When I organize their responses in a web, I can determine what the students understand about reading and the skills they need to be successful readers. Using the students' own words in listing ideas keeps the chart and information at their level of understanding.

As indicated in the good reader chart shown in Figure 14.1, my class of third graders had many ideas about good readers. For example, they knew that good readers had certain word reading skills, such as sounding out hard words and reading smoothly with expression. They also knew that good readers read with understanding because they can summarize what they read and make connections to other books and to experiences in their lives. They also were aware of certain attitudes and habits of good readers, such as spending time reading and reading a variety of books.

Figure 14.1

Good Reader Chart, third grade class

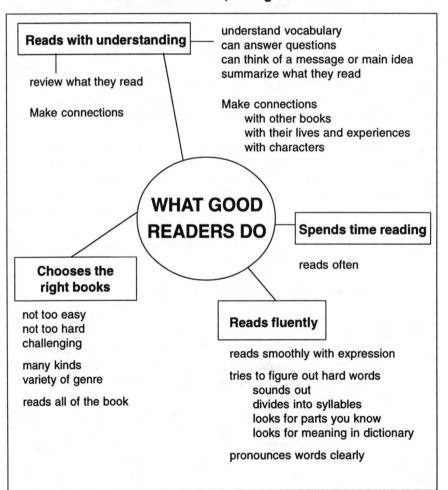

After the good reader chart had been created, I had students look it over to choose one thing they could do to help themselves become better readers. The item chosen became their reading goal for the term. Popular choices for goals were spending more time reading, reading more books, and reading harder books. These responses showed me that my students understood that one learns to read by reading, and that one gets better at reading by doing more reading.

I know that I had an influence on students' choices, because they were aware of the value I placed on time spent reading and reading a variety of literature. We had a classroom library that was well-stocked with many kinds of books—mysteries, folk tales, nonfiction, scary stories, and humorous works, among others. We received the local newspaper and copies of *Sports Illustrated for Kids, Cricket*, and *National Geographic World*. Our daily schedule included time for me to read aloud, as well as time for students to read their own selections silently. Book talks were a regular part of our morning circle time. In other words, students were presented with numerous opportunities to engage in reading on many levels and on many topics, depending on their own interests.

My students had goals, but what good are goals without plans of action to accomplish them? I learned from Jane Hansen (1992) and her work with the Manchester Project to ask students, "What would you like to learn to do to become a better reader?" and then "How do you intend to do that?" This second question guides students toward understanding that they have a better chance of achieving their goals if they identify the steps needed to get there.

The following examples of planning come from the fifth-grade class I taught last year. Kendall was a poor reader. On a self-evaluation sheet filled out at the end of the second quarter, he wrote, "I still need to improve on my reading. Sometimes I don't understand what I read." He set the goals of reading more books and of trying to understand what he was reading. In the conference when we discussed the self-evaluation sheet, I asked Kendall about his plan for reaching his goals. He said he would set a regular time to read each night. Kendall said that keeping a reading log would help him to keep track of his progress toward his goal of reading more. (As part of their regular routine, I had the students keep a reading log including title, date, and number of pages read.) Because I knew that reading was difficult for Kendall, I assumed some of the responsibility for setting up a plan of action. To support Kendall in his goal of trying to understand what he was reading, I told him we would get together to discuss his reading. He said that would help. Kendall followed through by spending time in daily individual reading conferences with me. Kendall's writing about his goals and plans is shown in Figure 14.2.

Figure 14.2

Name: Kendall

Challenges:

I still need to improve on my reading. Sometimes I don't understand what I read.

Goals and plans for next term:

Read more books and try to understand what I read.

    Set a regular time to read each night.
    Record what I read on my reading log.

- -

Name: Stephanie

Challenges:

My challenges are spelling because I have a hard time remembering words. Reading is hard because I can't read very fluently.

Goals and plans for next term:

My gooals are to read more books and to spell harder words correctly.

    Read with dad every night.
    Circle words that don't look right, use a dictionary

Stephanie, another fifth grader, wanted to "read more books" so she could become a fluent reader (see Figure 14.2). She read slowly, often word by word, at times leaving out punctuation, and this labored reading affected her ability to understand what she was reading. I could see the importance of fluency as a goal for Stephanie. She talked about using reading logs to keep track of her reading. I asked Stephanie how she would be working on reading more fluently. She said that she would read with her dad every night. I told her that I would meet with her during reading workshop to give her some individual help. She thought that would be very helpful.

While Kendall and Stephanie were both reading below grade level, they identified different needs. Kendall wanted to understand what he was reading, while Stephanie wanted to read more fluently. Meeting these needs would certainly improve the quality of their reading. In conferring with these two students, I had the opportunity to support their plans of action by letting them know that I would provide them with individual instruction.

These goal-setting and planning procedures serve to support students as they take ownership of their learning. Students are given choices about what will help them to improve as readers. Together, the student and the teacher set up a structure or plan to achieve the goal. Parents, teachers, and at times other students provide encouragement and assistance as the plans are followed during the semester.

Creating a classroom environment to support the goal-setting process takes time. As students are involved in the reading workshop, I observe and take notes on how they are doing as they work to improve their reading skills. I often share my observations with students. For example, after a literature circle discussion on *The Matchlock Gun* (Edmonds, 1990) with two fifth grade struggling readers, I remarked, "Well, I can see that you are both working on your goal of understanding what you read, because you shared good ideas in our discussion today." We went on to discuss how "good ideas" are those that begin with an accurate reading of the text but extend to the reader's own interpretation. When students go to the library to borrow books, I might comment about how their choice of books is helping them to work toward the goal of reading a variety of books. Periodically we have a class discussion about goals, and the students talk about how they are progressing. In this way, students who have similar goals can share ideas.

Another way I keep students focused is to post the goals on their desks or work folders. I also give parents copies of the goals so they can help their children be successful. Following these procedures requires a great deal of my time at the beginning of the year. Gradually, as students learn to follow their plans to achieve goals, they take more responsibility (and I take less) for monitoring this process. The students slowly develop an understanding of how their daily work and activities are connected to improvements in learning. This is the connection between instruction and assessment that I am trying to achieve.

There are times when the students are not successful in meeting their goals. At these moments we sit down together and talk honestly about what made the goal difficult to meet. Was it too hard? Did they need more time? Did they need more help? Taren was a fifth grader who had difficulty paying attention in class. During discussions, she often played with something in her desk, daydreamed, or lay down on the carpet. She recognized that "I have a problem with sitting up and paying attention." Her goal was written as "I will work on sitting up and paying attention more so I can do better."

It took Taren and me almost the whole year to find the right plan of action to help her achieve her goal. We did some rearranging of seats, moving her desk toward the front of the room so that she would be near the teacher during lessons. We worked on eye contact, and she and I would make sure to focus on each other during discussions so her attention wouldn't wander. When I met with her mother, we talked about Taren's bed time and if getting more sleep would make it easier for Taren to concentrate. I was able to provide feedback about improvements I noticed in Taren's work due to better focusing. Her level of participation in class activities increased as she gained confidence, and she developed better relationships with peers. It took the support of her peers, as well as her parents and me, to help Taren meet her goal.

THE TEACHER'S ROLE: CONNECTING INSTRUCTION TO STUDENT GOALS

At first glance, teachers may think it unmanageable for each student to have individual goals for becoming a better reader. In the case of my third grade classroom, the process was made manageable because students selected three main goals for reading. These goals, taken from the good reader chart shown in Figure 14.1, focused on (a) making good reading choices, (b) improving word reading skills, and (c) developing better reading habits. Although the students had chosen to focus on these three, I decided that I would emphasize a balance of good reading behaviors, including those not selected by students. In this way, I could continue to improve students' skills and strategies in areas of both strength and weakness. It was interesting to note that many of the areas the students identified as weaknesses were the same ones I had noted in my observations. As seen in the examples of Kendall and Stephanie, discussed earlier, the students were able to show me that they had insights about their own strengths and weaknesses as readers and that they wanted help in improving.

The way I set up my reading workshop time enables me to provide students with opportunities to work on reaching their goals. In my 90-minute period for language arts, I devote 20–30 minutes to silent reading. During this time I meet with students in individual reading conferences, help students select books, and also monitor the class to make sure that everyone has space for uninterrupted reading. Students spend the next 60 minutes working on various literature study activities, such as reading the literature, meeting for small-group literature discussions with me, or responding in writing to the literature. I usually divide the class into three groups, and I meet daily with each group for a 20-minute literature discussion. My role in these discussions is to enrich the students' experience with the literature, by facilitating talk about the characters, events, and other ideas in the text and by helping students draw connections to other literature or to their own experiences.

In the reading workshop, since students select their own materials for reading, it is easy for them to work on their goals of "reading a variety of books" or "reading harder books." In my third-grade classroom, Corinne read stories about Henry and Mudge by Rylant (e.g., *Henry and Mudge and the Forever Sea*, 1989), right next to Keith, who had the *Great Brain* book series (Fitzgerald, 1967) piled on his desk. Sydney read about interesting insects next to Lyanne, who was reading books by Laura Ingalls Wilder.

During literature discussions I emphasize comprehension and meaningful connections to literature to support the progress of students who want to improve their understanding of what they read. I teach students how to write responses to texts, create webs of important ideas, draw sketches of key events, role-play different characters, and develop summaries of text information. During our morning circle time, students informally share the books they are reading. Students who have read the same book add their impressions to the talk. For example, when Nicollette shared Dahl's (1966) *The Magic Finger*, students mentioned other books by the same author. I told them that it was wonderful that we had read books by the same author. I asked if they would recommend that others also read his books. Kyle said yes, while noting that Dahl's writing is different because his stories take place in England. I asked him to explain what he meant. Kyle noted how in some books the characters stopped for tea or mentioned the queen of England. Others told about how Dahl used hard words in his books, or even nonsense words, as in *The BFG* (1982). In these discussions, I tried to show the students how much reading was valued in our class.

In setting up a classroom where shared responsibility for evaluation is expected, I give students the opportunity to evaluate and rate their own work. Students freely discuss what they feel good about and what is not easy for them. I often stop and hold brief discussions about "how things are going" to let students talk about what they understand and what they are unsure of. Then I develop mini-lessons for small groups or provide students with individual assistance to improve the quality of their work.

Kalani, a third grader, had turned in a response that consisted of retelling the events in *Smoky Night* by Eve Bunting (1994). I asked him if he thought his response showed good thinking. When he replied yes, we talked about how good readers don't just retell but also share their thoughts about what they have read. Kalani then said that the story reminded him of how easy it is to be afraid of people before you get to know them. He recalled what it was like when he was in kindergarten, when he didn't know anyone and was afraid to talk to people. I asked Kalani to add these thoughts to his piece, to show his good thinking. From this and similar incidents, I learned that my students wanted to improve as readers but needed to be shown exactly what was expected of them.

COLLECTING EVIDENCE:
SHOWING WHAT WE HAVE LEARNED

Throughout the year, my students are involved in rich language activities that help them develop reading and writing skills. Literature responses, other written pieces, projects, and artwork are all saved and stored so they can be brought out for re-examination when report cards are due. All of this material is gathered for the purpose of creating progress folios.

Progress folios are a form of authentic assessment developed by Anne Davies and Colleen Politano (1994). They describe how to use a large booklet to hold samples of student work in a particular area of student learning (for example, science, art, or reading). For each reporting period, students select a representative sample of work to show what they have learned. Each sample is glued next to the sample from the previous reporting period. In this way, direct comparisons can be made between the student's past and present performance. Figure 14.3 shows the format of a progress folio. This format met my purpose of displaying progress over time and allows students and their parents to see improvements in the quality of work.

Figure 14.3

Format of a Progress Folio

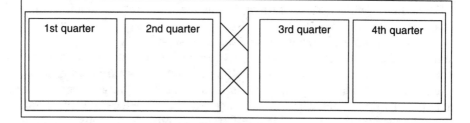

I extended the approach used by Davies and Politano by having students attach their reflections to the work sample. After students have selected a sample of work representing their learning in a particular subject, they write a reflection about what the sample shows about them as a reader, writer, or mathematician. Figure 14.4 shows a blank reflection form and Kaleo's reflection on his reading. The evidence he chose, his reading log, and his reading response show that he is reading more. He enjoyed reading biographies because they were not "fake" books. He notes that he reads with better understanding and has learned to attack unfamiliar words by breaking them into parts. As you can see, the form for the reflection sheet provides students with a way of starting their sentences, while leaving the content of the reflection to their own discretion.

Figure 14.4

This piece is an example of . . .

I want you to notice . . .

Date: Signature:

This piece is an example of . . .   *my reading*

I want you to notice . . .   *That I am reading more and writing better responds but I don't like to read fake books I like biography. Now I read with more under standing. I try to sound out hard words by breaking it apart*

Date: **nov**   Signature: *Haleo*

I follow a certain procedure in introducing students to the idea of progress folios. About two weeks before the end of each term, I gather the students together to review what we have accomplished in our reading workshop. I ask the students to bring out all their stored work, so they can look back over their accomplishments. The students are often surprised and proud to see that they have completed so much work. As they look at earlier pieces, they smile at the mistakes they used to make.

We enjoy reminiscing about the wonderful stories and projects created, but we also have serious questions to address. How do we show what we have learned? What does our work say about us as readers? What do we want to show about ourselves and what we have learned to do? What do we want others to notice about our progress? This evaluation process gives students the opportunity to reflect upon themselves as learners and to recognize their accomplishments. It also opens doors for continued learning, as students ask themselves, "What's next? What other challenges do I need to overcome to become a better reader? Where do I go from here?"

As the students evaluate their work, I am doing evaluations of my own. I look for strengths shown and for steps students have taken. At this point I do not focus on students' weaknesses. I find it particularly interesting that, at first, students can only see the problems they have had, their weaknesses, what they couldn't do. Somehow, they have gotten the idea that formal reports on progress are always associated with the negative, with what they aren't good at. They have the impression that parents and teachers only want to talk about their areas of difficulty, not their accomplishments. This deficit model of reporting is part of the traditional teacher-controlled curriculum and evaluation system.

Because I have made the shift to the paradigm of student-centered learning and shared evaluation, I am more interested in what students can already do and in how I can help them tackle the challenges they face. Having a variety of evidence helps students to show the many ways they learn. There may be written responses to literature, art work completed to show an important character or moment in the novel, or reading logs to show reading habits. Students may choose a copy of a page or the cover of a book, enjoyed or struggled over, to include as evidence of their progress as readers.

The reason that my students can choose evidence of their growth as readers is because I have given them choices for responding to literature. Students' individual strengths are difficult to see if they have all filled in the same question-answer form, workbook page, or structured response form. Open-ended activities and performance assessments give us the best picture of an individual's learning. These approaches give us the chance to send parents the message, and to remind ourselves, that each child is unique and equally magnificent.

In a literature-based classroom with new forms of assessment, students need to learn that it is all right to show their mistakes. Students usually select their best work to show that they are doing well. I try to point out that they may want to include pieces showing their struggles, and not just their best work, so they can demonstrate their improvement as readers. "You mean we can do that?" is their usual reply. As a teacher, I have to help students understand that we all make mistakes, and that it is from our mistakes that we learn and improve. Being able to recognize and then correct mistakes is an important part of self-evaluation. I want students to see that the challenges they face can become their goals for the next term.

After students have selected the work to be included in their progress folios, they take out their goal sheets to see if the work samples they have selected provide evidence of progress toward the goals they set for themselves. If the samples do not match the goals, students return to their collection of work to seek other samples. If students cannot find any suitable work, I have the opportunity to discuss with them why such evidence is unavailable. Did the student forget the goal? Did she fail to achieve the goal? Is some other type of evidence needed, beyond written or printed matter? How could the student show what she learned? What did she plan to do? By helping students solve this problem, I support them in taking responsibility not only for their learning and but for the documentation of their learning.

I cover several curriculum areas in the progress folios, so I need to give students lots of time to select evidence and to evaluate their work. I have the students spend one day on selecting evidence and preparing self-evaluations for reading, another day on writing, and still other days on mathematics and social studies. This allows the students time to focus clearly on each area and its special strength or challenges.

I believe that teachers who undertake the portfolio process for the first time should divide the school year into about four periods, about equal in length, for collecting evidence and writing evaluations. At the beginning of the year, as I am showing the students how to select evidence, I conduct a 45-minute lesson for each subject area to be included in the progress folio. During these lessons, we spend the first 15 minutes in a whole-class discussion, talking about the kinds of work we did in that subject during the past quarter. For reading, we talk about literature studies, silent reading, book projects, and the reading logs. I help the students understand that these activities have given us the evidence of our growth as readers, and we discuss the work that can show we met our goals. During the remaining 30 minutes of the lesson, I ask the students to go over their completed work to find the samples they want to include and write their reflections on these samples.

For another four or five days, I use the language arts periods for teacher-student conferences. During this time we go over the progress folios and discuss what they show about the students' learning. These conferences help prepare the students for the three-way conferences with parents to follow. Each student conference lasts about 15–20 minutes, and I have to find ways to fit conferences into my daily schedule. For example, I may meet with one or two students before and after school or during recess. I may lengthen silent reading time or have the students work on independent activities during the reading workshop, so I will have more time for conferences.

As you can tell, I commit a lot of time to helping students take responsibility for their own learning. However, as we repeat the process each quarter, the students need less teacher supervision and guidance in selecting evidence and writing reflections. The students soon get a sense of the progress folios as an ongoing process. They tell me about work just completed that they want to include in their progress folios the next time. By the end of the year, the students can explain their strengths and their goals for the next quarter.

My goal is to have students show the progress made in their learning over the course of a school year. I want evidence of all their efforts—successes as well as challenges—as they struggle to improve as learners. I want the work samples to be concrete evidence of the results of my teaching and my students' learning, not simply collections of student work. My concern for the quality of the progress folios is shared by my students. As the year progresses, students develop a deep sense of ownership for their progress folios and become highly selective about what they want to see documented on each page.

EVALUATING ACHIEVEMENTS: SELF-EVALUATION, TEACHER EXPECTATIONS, AND RUBRICS

In the beginning I did not find it easy to teach students to evaluate their own achievements. The task of evaluation has usually been the responsibility of teachers, because we believed that students did not have the knowledge, or could not be trusted, to review their own work. In sharing responsibility for evaluation with students, teachers have to be willing to listen to children's voices and to value their perspectives.

In teaching self-evaluation, I use a number of different approaches with students. First, I talk to the whole class about reflecting on their learning. I pose questions such as: What was easy about what you did? What was hard for you? What could you do next time to make it better or easier for yourself? What kind of help do you need? At the beginning of the year, this type of guided reflection is needed to help model the thinking behind self-evaluation. For instance, at the end of a study of Caldecott books with my third graders, we sat together as a class to discuss how they had done on their written responses. I had asked the students to write a simple summary of the story and share their feelings about what they had read. The students all liked reading the books and looking at the beautiful illustrations. But some said they had a hard time writing a summary of the story. They found that they were retelling the story. I told the students we could work on making judgments about what was important in the story and so should be included in a summary.

Second, I continue the discussion with individual students, sometimes in interviews and sometimes using written reflections. I respond to the students' comments by praising the steps they have taken and showing support for their concerns. Often, it takes time and practice for students to know themselves and their work well enough to write a clear and accurate description of their accomplishments. I assist students in this process by referring to the good reader chart. I pose questions such as the following: "What are some things that you can do well as a reader? Do you spend time reading? Do you know how to choose the right books to read? Do you read with understanding? How fluently do you read?" By prompting the students with descriptions of what good readers do, I help them begin to talk about themselves as readers. They give responses such as "I read often and I can read smoothly with expression. I need help finding books that are just right for me. I can think of a main idea or message in what I read."

At the end of the year, when I look over the range of student reflections, I notice that their later writing is much more detailed and specific. Here are two reflections that Kaleo, a fifth-grade student, attached to the reading samples in his progress folio:

9/20:   This piece is an example of a reading response to War with Grandpa. I want you to notice that it is a very good book.

3/18:   This piece is an example of my reading (response to *Sing Down the Moon*). I want you to notice that this is very hard but I got better. I could read for a longer time and read longer books but sometimes I get lazy because it is very hard. I think understanding is hard. At first in Sing Down the Moon I could not understand the characters but it got better and I liked it.

At the beginning of the year, Kaleo had little to say about himself as a reader. As he gained experience in evaluating his own efforts, he was able to tell what he was doing better and what was still hard for him.

I hold individual conferences with my students to go over the work they have selected as evidence and their written reflections. I nudge students to think more deeply about certain areas of their performance. I ask, "What made you think of that? What does that show about you?" During the first conferences, students often give responses such as "This is hard to explain" or "I don't know." They have never had to explain themselves before or think about why they did things a certain way. They have not been accountable for talking about their learning and what they are going to do to improve. With practice and support, the process of reflecting about their learning and articulating their ideas, verbally and in writing, becomes easier for students. Gradually, they take greater risks in sharing their frustrations and needs.

Third, I share my expectations with students, so they can incorporate these expectations into their self-evaluations. I remember many times during my own schooling when I had to try to guess what the teacher wanted so I could get a good grade. It wasn't the learning but pleasing the teacher that mattered. If students are to participate in evaluation, they need to know the criteria.

In my classroom, the good reader charts illustrate the criteria to some degree, but I think students need something even more concrete and tangible by which to judge their work. This is the reason that I involve students with rubrics. According to Hart (1994), "a rubric is an established set of criteria used for scoring or rating students' tests, portfolios, or performances" (p. 70). Rubrics help the teacher and students to be clear about the characteristics that cause a piece of work to be rated poor, good, or exceptional. When students understand rubrics, they can evaluate the quality of their work for themselves, and they gain ideas about what they must do to improve.

Rubrics or quality standards for performance are most effective with students when stated in language they can understand. An example of stating rubrics in students' language can be seen in the work of the science teacher at our school. She uses rubrics to evaluate the students' science reports. In her explanation to the students, she compares a science report to a hamburger. If you just have a plain hamburger and bun, you have a basic meal. However, the hamburger is tastier if you add some ketchup and pickles to it. An even better hamburger would have lettuce, cheese, onions, and a sesame seed bun. The science teacher asks students what kind of science report they plan to turn in. Will their work compare to a basic, to a slightly enhanced, or to a deluxe hamburger? She goes on to discuss the specific features that allow a science report to meet the criteria for minimum performance, for good performance, and for exceptional performance. Discussions such as this help students know that they need to look for specific features in their work, see what is missing, and strive to improve. Without such discussions to make criteria clear, students are forced to resort to guesswork about what is expected.

I am still working on the rubrics that define the reading performance I expect of my third graders. In particular, I am experimenting with the language that best communicates my ideas to students. Figure 14.5 shows the rubrics that I am currently using with my third graders. Two qualities I look for are *comprehension*—understands what is read from the book, and *response*—makes connections between story and understanding of self and life. These qualities build on Rosenblatt's (1991) ideas about reader response theory and efferent and aesthetic stances. I want to give students the opportunity to respond to literature from a personal, "lived through" perspective, as well as to recall specific information and events from their reading.

Figure 14.5

Evaluating Reading

	1—some thinking	3—good thinking	5—excellent thinking
Comprehension understands what is read from the book	Retells most story events	Summarizes story by explaining main ideas and details	Links ideas, characters, information and events to show how they are related in the story.
Response makes connecting between story and understanding of self and life.	Makes a personal response to story; tells what they liked or didn't like	Connects story to own ideas and experiences; tells how they feel and gives reasons	Connects story to a theme, lessons. Gives own interpretation, opinion of story and explains thinking.

Evaluating Writing

	1—some thinking	3—good thinking	5—excellent thinking
Content expresses ideas clearly -develops ideas well -orgnaized	limited information; doesn't have a clear main idea or focus; confusing to read	has a main idea and is easy to under- stand, but could be developed more to show great understanding	has a clear message; message is supported with details; shows excellent under- standing of topic
Style enhances writing with interesting detail and vocabulary	only few details; some interesting vocabulary	some interesting details and good description using some good vocabulary	very expressive piece which captures readers interest; uses specific vocabulary and has memorable language & sentences
Mechanics and spelling	errors in spelling, punctuation, capitalization making it hard to read	most spelling is correct; tried to use paragraphs; most punctuation and capitals is correct	good spelling, accurate punctua- tion and para- graphs; may use a variety of punctuation.

I use a numerical scale so that I have a clear idea of the students' progress. I selected a five-point scale beause I could see beginning, middle, and end points corresponding to the numbers 1, 3, and 5. Level 1 reflected limited depth of thought, while Level 3 was the expected level of performance where students were able to summarize the important ideas in the text and make connections to their own experiences. Level 5 performance requires understanding relationships between characters and events and also means the reader can construct a theme and explain her thinking clearly with examples from the literature. Level 2 represents a transition where students are moving beyond retelling and beginning to identify important ideas and events in the story. Similarly, Level 4 represents the transition where students are moving beyond summary writing into critiques and interpretation. While I want all my students to reach Level 5, I know it may take more than one year to achieve this goal. The scale allows me to chart improvement, even little steps forward.

Ideally, I want students to generate the rubrics and to struggle with what constitutes rigorous learning and quality performance. I believe that turning the process of developing rubrics over to students helps them take more responsibility for their achievements. In reality, I find that students are not able to create sound rubrics at the beginning of the school year. Rubrics generated by students at that point tend to omit many features of successful reading performance, because students are not yet aware of these features. As the year goes on, students gain a fuller picture of reading in a literature-based program, have a better understanding of my expectations for performance, and are gradually able to participate in the process of developing rubrics. To help students identify features of work that meet or exceed expectations, I share examples of good work and ask students what qualities they notice in the pieces. They are used to seeing the rubrics up on the classroom wall, but this time I ask them to try to tell me in their own words what makes good work.

THREE-WAY CONFERENCES: SHARING WHAT WE HAVE LEARNED

Once the evaluation process described above is complete, the students and I have a clear and detailed picture of their development as readers and writers. We are now ready to share what we know with a very important audience: the parents. This sharing takes place through a three-way conference.

Parent-teacher conferences are typically viewed as a time for adults to discuss what students can and cannot do. Typically, parents relay some of the content of the conference to their child. Sometimes parents compliment the child on her work, but at other times they punish the child on the basis of the teacher's remarks and tell the child to try harder. As one of my students said of these conferences, "It wasn't fair. I don't know what my teacher said, and my parents came home and yelled at me."

When I decided to share responsibility for assessment with my students, I realized this also meant sharing the responsibility for reporting to parents. I couldn't give students a voice in deciding upon their own learning goals, have them focus their energy on meeting those goals and documenting their own progress, but then tell them, "Now I will report about how you are doing to your parents." It made sense to have students report on their progress to their parents, rather than reporting to parents myself. For this to happen, I had to prepare my students to conduct three-way conferences.

Three-way conferences involve the student, parents, and teacher. A three-way conference differs from a student-led conference in which the student does most of the talking with the parents and the teacher joins in at the end. In a three-way conference, the student, parents, and teacher are present throughout. In three-way conferences students do most of the sharing, but I can still give them support in the process, especially during the first conference with their parents. Although I don't interrupt their sharing, the students know that I will help them answer difficult questions and provide added information for their parents.

To be successful, three-way conferences require thoughtful preparation. I meet with my students individually prior to the conferences. At these meetings the students present their progress folio to me and discuss areas in which they feel they did well and areas in which they feel they need further help. They also discuss how their needs can be turned into goals. I share my own evaluation, comparing it to the reflections students have made about their learning. The students and I often agree on the strengths and challenges, due to our constant talks about expectations and criteria, my continual modeling of the reflection process, and my responses to the students' assignments.

When the student and I disagree about performance in a given area, we review further evidence to gain a more accurate understanding of what was accomplished. I find it helpful to review a variety of work products, since students have different strengths as learners. For example, some students can express ideas during literature discussions but are not able to write these same ideas in a literature response or essay. Others can show a greater depth of understanding in art than in discussions or written work.

During the teacher-student meetings, both parties may use a form to record important ideas and issues to be discussed during the three-way conference. The form used by students is shown in Figure 14.6 (Davies et al., 1992), while the form for teachers is presented in Figure 14.7. In the student form, students are given assistance in preparing their thoughts about their strengths, two areas of need, evidence to support their strengths and needs, and goals for the next term. On the teacher form there are spaces for the teacher to prepare notes and later add parent comments made during the conference. Because a limited amount of time is allotted for each three-way conference, I want to make sure that time is used wisely and that parents have the opportunity to take an active part in the discussion. Conference time can be put to good use if students practice for the conference and refer to notes. My third-

Figure 14.6

THREE-WAY CONFERENCE GUIDE FOR STUDENTS

Name: Lori

Date: 11/12/96

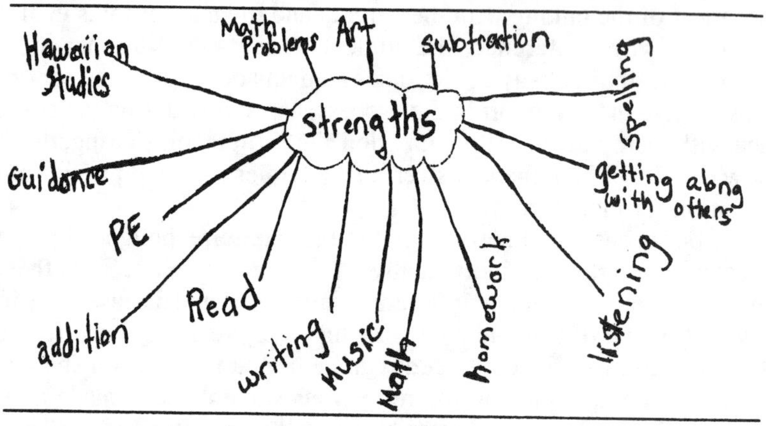

strengths: Hawaiian Studies, Math Problems, Art, subtraction, Spelling, getting along with others, listening, homework, Math, Music, writing, Read, addition, PE, Guidance

Two things I need to improve...
Write longer stories and add more detail.
Think of different ways to figure out problems

Things to show...
Reading, writing, Math, Hawaiian Studies,

My next term goal is...
To talk louder!!! when I'm sharing my presentation, or speaking in front of the class

Figure 7, page 37, "Conference Guide for Students."
From *Together is Better* by Davies/Cameron/Politano/Gregory © Peguis Publishers, 1992.
This page may be reproduced for classroom use.
Printed with permission.

Figure 14.7
Three-Way Conference Guide for Teachers

Student's Name	Date
Strengths	Challenges
Notes for the Conference	Additional Notes
Goal Action Plan Student will . . .	Goal Action Plan Student will . . .
Teacher will . . .	Parent will . . .
Other Notes	

AKK '95

grade students find it helpful to practice their conferences with classmates. This provides them with one more opportunity to gain confidence in their presentations.

Before the three-way conferences, I send out a letter (see Figure 14.8) informing parents about how the time will be structured. Parents are seldom accustomed to having their child at these conferences, and they expect to rely on the teacher to tell them everything they need to know. They may be leery about how honestly their children will present themselves. Will they only share the positive? What about the problems? Doesn't the teacher know best? Parents also are unaccustomed to responding to their child about specific work with the teacher present. In short, a three-way conference requires both parents, as well as students, to think and act in new ways.

My role is to serve as a facilitator of the discussion and to encourage open and honest dialogue. I keep the tone positive, especially when the discussion is moving toward "child bashing." I help parents understand that, if we highlight the strengths, the student will be better able to deal with the challenges.

Figure 14.8

News from Room 304
April 6, 1997

Dear Parents,

This is what you can expect when you attend the parent(s)/teacher/student conference on _____ at _____.

- You and your child will have time to look over his or her collection of work and the classroom displays.
- You and your child will then meet with me to discuss your childs strengths, any concerns, and set new learning goals for the next quarter.
- Your child will take an active part in the conference. There will be opportunities for you to ask questions, make comments, or express concerns.
- If you have any questions you wish to discuss privately with me, there will be a few minutes at the end of the conference for you to do so.

We believe that this three-way conference is one important way to support student learning. We look forward to meeting with you.

Sincerely,

Jo Ann Wong-Kam
Grade 3 teacher

Before the conference itself begins, students take parents on a tour of the classroom, informing them about the topics we are currently studying, learning areas, and activities. Then we meet at the conference table, with the student seated between the parents and the teacher. The students have their progress folio and notes, and they begin the conference by sharing these materials. Parents are free to ask about anything that isn't clear. I help students as needed and offer my perspective when students are finished. Together, we set goals and plans of action, and parents have a concrete sense of what they can expect in the future. At the end of the conference, students take their progress folios home for parents to review at their leisure. I send home a feedback form so parents can share their response to the conference and progress folio with me.

I have found that all three parties—the parents, the student, and the teacher—gain from three-way conferences. Due to the careful preparation by students and teacher for the conference, parents are genuinely impressed by what they hear. Their comments often run along the following lines: "I didn't know my child could talk about himself that way." "I know now that she really does know what is going on in school." Parents leave with positive feelings about their children and the concrete plans of action for improving weak areas. I notice a distinct difference from previous years, when the parents of successful students felt content, while the parents of struggling students felt frustrated, not knowing what else to do but tell their children to be good and try harder. With the three-way conferences, all parents have a clear picture of their children's progress and of the areas in which they can help their children.

Students tell me they are nervous at the beginning but relax as they see their parents responding positively to their honesty and openness. The students like speaking for themselves and having evidence to demonstrate their progress. They are glad to have a choice about what to work on next.

As a teacher, I feel a burden has been lifted from my shoulders. I have never been comfortable being the expert about a child's learning. Motivation and attitude have a great influence on learning, and I used to be unsure about how to help students to assume more responsibility. I didn't think that this could be accomplished through extrinsic rewards, such as good work charts or grades. I knew that lasting learning would come only when the work and evaluation were meaningful to the students. Working together with my students freed me to be a better teacher, supporter, and cheerleader for them. My goal is to help each child succeed, and with shared responsibility for evaluation I finally feel I am accomplishing my goal. Three-way conferences seem like a win-win situation for all.

CONCLUDING COMMENTS: WHAT I HAVE LEARNED

Through literature-based instruction, I changed the way I looked at reading. Given this change, I also had to open my eyes to look at evaluation differently. I have come to a number of conclusions about successful evaluation in a literature-based classroom.

First, the evaluation process requires active student involvement in all phases. The process begins by involving students in setting goals for their own learning and in making plans to achieve these goals. Students are involved in collecting evidence of their progress and in reflecting upon and evaluating their progress as readers and writers. They are even involved in reporting their progress to their parents. The Chinese have a saying, "I do, I understand." Students do not learn to understand themselves by listening to what others say about them. They develop a better sense of self through careful examination of and reflection about their accomplishments and the steps taken to bring these accomplishments about. Selecting work samples and writing self-evaluations is hard work, because students need to look closely at themselves. Sometimes they don't like what they see, and they need to take responsibility for making changes. Clearly, this approach of putting students at the center of the evaluation process is a radical departure from traditional forms of evaluation, which rely on teacher judgment or on commercially developed tests.

Second, the role of the teacher is to provide students with the direct, continuous support they need to share in the responsibility for their own evaluation. Self-evaluation does not just happen but is the result of a great deal of teacher planning and active teaching. Teachers must model the process and guide students every step of the way, through whole-class lessons and small-group and individual conferences. Teachers must be clear about their criteria for quality work and help students to internalize these criteria. Considerable time must be committed to the process, over the entire school year, if students are to take ownership of the process. Teachers create the climate for risk-taking and collaboration, but the support of classmates is also important. Students are reassured by knowing that the whole class is working toward the same goal of becoming better readers.

Third, the logistics of the evaluation process can be quite complex. Teachers must develop clear procedures for involving students in all the steps of the evaluation process. Procedures must be clear because students will often have had little or no previous experience with self-evaluation. There must be procedures for setting goals and making plans, for collecting evidence and having students review the evidence, for having students reflect upon their work and prepare written evaluations, and for organizing the evidence and written reflections in progress folios. Finally, there must be procedures for students to follow in planning for and conducting three-way conferences. Teachers should realize that the development of all these procedures is a trial-and-error process, and that it may take several years before the evaluation system is running smoothly.

Finally, if they are to take ownership of the evaluation process, students must have the freedom to make choices. In literature-based classrooms, students make choices about what they read and how they respond. Similarly, in evaluation, students should make choices about the goals they want to achieve and about the evidence they submit to represent their learning. Through observation and analysis of these choices, teachers begin to see each student as unique. With this new vision of evaluation, we can teach the child rather than the curriculum.

Note: The work with children detailed in this chapter occurred while I was a teacher at Kamehameha Schools, working with Hawaiian and part-Hawaiian students.

REFERENCES

Davies, A., Cameron, C., Politano, C., & Gregory, K. (1992). *Together is better: Collaborative assessment, evaluation and reporting.* Winnipeg, Canada: Peguis Publishers.

Davies, A., & Politano, C. (1994). *Multiage and more.* Winnipeg, Canada: Peguis Publishers.

Eeds, M., & Hudelson, S. (1995). Literature as foundation for personal and classroom life. *Primary Voices, 3(2),* 2–7.

Hansen, J. (1992). Student evaluations bring reading and writing together. *The Reading Teacher, 46 (2),* 100–105.

Hart, D. (1994). *Authentic assessment: A handbook for educators.* Menlo Park, CA: Addison-Wesley.

Rosenblatt, L. (1991). Literature-S.O.S.! *Language Arts 68 (6),* 444–448.

CHILDREN'S BOOKS CITED

Bunting, E. (1994). *Smoky night.* San Diego, CA: Harcourt.

Dahl, R. (1982). *The BFG.* New York: Viking Penguin.

Dahl, R. (1966). *The magic finger.* New York: Harper & Row.

Edmonds, W. D. (1990). *The matchlock gun.* New York: Troll.

Fitzgerald, J. D. (1967). *The great brain.* New York: Dial.

George, J. C. (1972). *Julie of the wolves.* New York: Harper & Row.

O'Brien, R. C. (1971). *Mrs. Frisby and the rats of NIMH.* New York: Atheneum.

Rylant, C. (1989). *Henry and Mudge and the forever sea.* New York: Bradbury.

Essays on the Future of
Literature-Based Instruction

●────────●

Eight prominent figures in the field of language arts were asked to prepare brief essays on the future of literature-based instruction. In formulating their predictions and recommendations, these experts drew upon their experiences as researchers, classroom teachers, teacher educators, and readers.

Essay I

Literature as a Core Component of the Elementary Literacy Program

●————————————●

Sean A. Walmsley, State University of New York at Albany

Five years ago, in an article in *Language Arts*, I reflected on the state of elementary literature instruction (Walmsley, 1992). Drawing on research of my own and others on children's literary experiences, curriculum work in elementary schools, and a survey of elementary classroom teachers, specialists, librarians, and administrators, I made the following observations:

- elementary schools didn't have either an instructional philosophy for the teaching of literature or a well-developed practical scheme for integrating it within the elementary curriculum;
- the teaching of literature in elementary schools wasn't well-coordinated across the grade levels, often resulting in a poor balance of authors, genres, and topics (the lack of continuity from elementary to middle to high school was particularly noticeable);
- literature seemed to be used primarily to teach reading skills and for fun and enjoyment;
- the respective roles of classroom teachers and school librarians wasn't worked out, resulting in quite a bit of tension between the two groups of professionals;
- poorer readers were generally exposed to less literature than better readers.

In the five years since writing that article, I have continued to conduct research on children's literary experiences (e.g., Walmsley, Rosenthal, & Whipple, 1996), and I've worked directly with elementary schools, helping them reform their language arts programs. In the past few months, I have spent time in over 100 K–2 classrooms in upstate New York. As I reflect on these recent encounters with children, teachers, and schools, I can see that some aspects of literature instruction have remained pretty much the same, while others have changed quite substantially.

WHAT'S STAYED THE SAME

I haven't seen much progress in coordinating the teaching of literature across the grades (other than reserving specific books for particular grade levels), or relating it directly to the teaching of reading and writing skills. Of course there are exceptions—some schools have seen this as an important issue and have been actively working on it. But in the majority of elementary schools where I've been recently, reading and literature are quite distinct components of the language arts program.

Reading literature to children seems to have become institutionalized in most elementary schools, thank goodness, although I wish it was used more for pedagogical purposes than relaxation after recess or gym. So has independent reading time, although it often doesn't last very long, and is easily squeezed out in a busy week. Guided reading of full-length books is a common sight in classrooms, but so are cutesy activities based on these books, and lots of commercial dittos that have children answer literal questions and color things in.

WHAT'S CHANGED

The most obvious change is in the basal reading series. Their primary focus is still the teaching of reading skills, but the stories used to teach these skills are no longer written-for-the-text pieces, but mostly real literature—and, unlike the extracts found in earlier basals, much of it is full-length, even in the upper elementary grades. I find it significant, however, that basals treat the literature—authentic though it may be—as merely vehicles for reading skill development. They also treat themes in the same way—to teach reading skills, not as vehicles for enlarging children's knowledge of the world. But this is largely how teachers seem to view literature, and basals rarely stray far from their clients.

The other big change I've noticed is how literature instruction is organized. Although traditional reading groups are still in evidence in the early grades, increasingly elementary teachers are teaching literature as a whole-class activity, with a single book—clearly a reaction to criticism of grouping children by reading ability. Whole-class literature instruction is difficult at best, but with the ever-widening range of children's literacy abilities (caused by children entering school with inadequate preschool literacy experiences, reduced retention rates, and more "included" children in the regular classroom), it's a pedagogy that will frustrate even the most experienced teacher—

how can she possibly meet such a wide range of interests, background knowledge, and literacy skills with a single book? Luckily, there are alternatives available, all involving small groups of children reading literature—"grand conversations" (Peterson & Eeds, 1990), "literature circles" (Daniels, 1994; Samway & Whang, 1995) and "literature focus units" (Moss, 1996). Teachers who have been trying to teach a single book to the whole class will find welcome relief in these alternative approaches.

The biggest change isn't about literature instruction directly. It's the current hysteria about whole language and phonics. Unfortunately, the teaching of literature in elementary school is assumed to be a whole language activity. I have already seen schools sharply reduce literature instruction and increase whole-class phonics teaching. This says something about how they viewed the role of literature in nurturing children's literacy development in the first place. I have also noticed how many schools in New York State, facing less-than-perfect scores on the now public "report cards," have abandoned even well-developed literature-based programs, and re-instituted mandatory use of basal reading series. (The irony here is that within two years, New York's new fourth-grade literacy examination will test children's knowledge of fiction, nonfiction and poetry, using extended writing as a primary assessment tool. To prepare for this examination, schools will need strong literature-based language arts programs, starting in kindergarten.) Although the tensions between school librarians and classroom teachers are still evident in many elementary schools, what I've seen recently is library aides replacing full-time school librarians.

My colleagues (Guice & Allington, 1994) have also noticed how poorly stocked many elementary school libraries are, especially in schools with high numbers of children at-risk for literacy failure. I don't know if these are signs that schools don't think that having a good supply of books is necessary to the successful teaching of literature, or if they've decided to stock classroom rather than school libraries, or if it's simply a sign of declining school budgets. Certainly my fieldnotes are full of comments about how out of date the library holdings are; and I haven't seen much evidence that the collections have moved from library to classroom. Most teachers I know spend a great deal of their own money—and all their points from the book clubs—on buying books for their classroom literature program.

WHITHER LITERATURE INSTRUCTION?

I'm not very good at predicting the future of anything, and so I'm not going to speculate on where I think literature instruction will be in the next five or ten years. My hunch is that it will be very different in a small number of elementary schools, and won't be much different from what it is now in most schools. Educational reform crawls along at a snail's pace. But I think there are some things we can do to further the cause of literature-based approaches, and to stave off threats to its existence. Here's my to-do list:

- articulate the role of literature in the literacy program, clearly and simply;
- build literature right into the language arts goals for elementary school and make sure it's on the report card;
- keep track of children's book reading (books read aloud to them, books read with them, and books read independently by them);
- ensure that when testing children's decoding skills, they are examined within the context of reading real literature;
- broaden our definition of what counts as literature, and how a good reader is defined;
- get to know children as readers, individually.

Let me briefly explain what I mean by each of these.

Articulating the Role of Literature in the Literacy Program

We need to better articulate for the field what role literature plays in the development of literacy in the early years. Advocates of phonics have done a much better job of putting their views before the public than have advocates of literature-based instruction. When we do try to articulate what we stand for, we clothe it in language that is so convoluted and full of jargon (e.g., IRA/NCTE Standards, 1996) that all we communicate is an inability to express ourselves.

Building Literature Right into the Language Arts Goals and Report Card

In most schools, literature is something you do as part of a program whose aims are the development of reading and writing skills. It doesn't seem to be a goal in its own right. Look at a typical elementary school report card, and you'll see what I mean (see Figure 1).

If the only place that literature is specifically mentioned in the report card is as a vehicle for effective writing, then why should we be surprised that literature plays such a small role in the elementary language arts program? Contrast this to a set of goals for reading I've been developing with teachers in Carmel School District (Carmel, NY) (see Figure 2).

The role played by literature in these reading standards is substantial; it's an integral part of the reading component of the language arts curricu-

Figure 1

Extract from a Typical Elementary School Report Card

Area Marking Period:	1	2	3
READING/LANGUAGE ARTS			
1. Recognizes words.			
2. Understands what is read.			
3. Uses sounds to attack words.			
4. Reads well orally.			
5. Uses context clues.			
6. Reads independently.			
7. Written work —journal —practice book —worksheets			
8. Responds to literature through effective writing.			
9. Organizes ideas in writing.			
10. Uses proper sentence structure.			
11. Grammar skills.			
12. Capitalization & punctuation.			
PENMANSHIP			
1. Writes neatly.			
2. Forms letters correctly.			
SPELLING			
1. Tests.			

lum. You'll see in these standards a commitment to children reading widely and deeply, and for pleasure, as well as having the strategies necessary for silent and oral reading. Each of these goals is to be assessed three times a year, so that teachers know where children are in their literacy development. It's the only way we know of to ensure that all our expectations are followed through in the classroom.

Keeping Track of Children's Book Reading

Most elementary schools support the idea that children should read a lot of books, but rarely do they keep track of what children have read, except for

Figure 2

Independent Reader Standards
(Carmel School District, Carmel, NY)

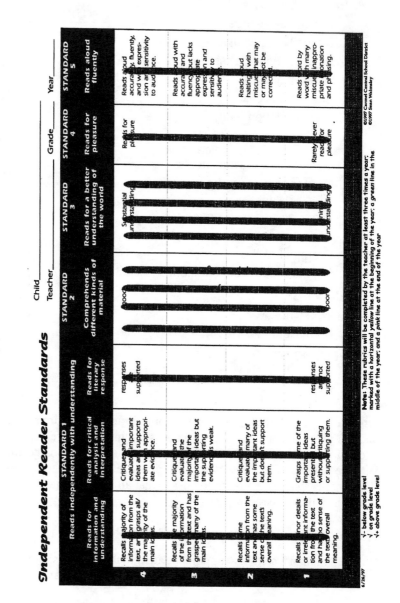

competitive purposes (e.g., Book-It). Keeping track of the literature that children have heard read, what they've read as guided or shared reading, and what they've read independently is a sure way to ensure that literature remains at the core of the language arts program. Once children can read independently, they can easily keep track of their reading on their own.

In kindergarten and first grade, there are so many books that are read to children—my wife, Bonnie, reads about 500 books to her kindergartners in a typical year (Walmsley, Camp, & Walmsley, 1992)—that it's difficult to write them all down. But we've found that keeping a class chart of the books read aloud (children can write the titles and help decide the genres), is a constant reminder of both the amount and kind of books read on a daily basis. And the chart, prominently displayed, reminds everyone of how important literature is to the program. We should celebrate the child's first book read independently (i.e., not a book that's been read to the child, or one whose text or illustrations are so predictable that little actual decoding has transpired), and begin an independent reading log with that book as its first entry.

Testing Children's Decoding Skills in Real Literature

Even in the best literature-based programs, there are children who may need quite explicit instruction to help them become independent decoders of text; we shouldn't assume that all children will become independent readers without such assistance. On the other hand, the true test of successful decoding instruction is not whether a child can read a list of nonsense syllables (although it may be useful as assessment during instruction), but whether she can read meaningful connected text, i.e., a real book. We shouldn't hesitate to temporarily divert a child from a literature-based approach if she needs decoding instruction, but we need to assess her progress relative to real reading, and restore her to a literature-based approach as soon as possible. Sometimes I think we lose sight of the whole purpose of teaching children to read, which is that they can and will read real books and other authentic written material. Reading real material isn't just the goal, it's a critical component of the experience and instruction needed to learn how to read.

Broadening Our Definition of Literature, and of Good Readers

Finally, we need to pay attention to how we define literature and literary understanding, and what it means to be a good reader. In several studies (Walmsley, Fielding, & Spiro, 1990; Walmsley, Rosenthal, & Whipple, 1996; Rosenthal, 1997), we have noticed that being a good reader from a literary perspective and being a good reader from a school's perspective aren't the same things at all. Good literary readers read a lot, enter the texts they read, grapple with the underlying themes, and engage with the characters and the stories. Good school readers don't necessarily read a lot, nor do they necessarily enter the texts, but they are very successful in doing the tasks assigned to them by teachers, which typically don't require much beyond literal recall of what's been read. Again and again in our studies, we've found that many of the children whom the school regards and defines as the weakest readers are among the most thoughtful readers from a literary point of view. And vice versa—some of the "best" readers from the school's perspective are the weakest readers from a literary point of view. Rosenthal (1997) has also shown that if we broaden our definition of literature to include books and films significant to the children's peer culture, and engage them in discussions about their experiences with these works, we'll find that many children display a far greater literary and cognitive understanding than is revealed in classroom discussions of standard literary works.

Get to Know Children as Readers, Individually

One of the things that has struck us in our research is how different children are as book readers. As far as literature is concerned, the more you know children's reading habits, interests, and styles, the more you realize their uniqueness as readers. With large classes and a busy schedule, teachers can't interact with children with the same intensity that we have been able to in our research studies, but any effort to get to know individual children as readers will be well worthwhile. How about a one-on-one conversation with each child once a month or so, to learn about what he's been reading and what understandings he's taking from these books? Even this brief conversation will reveal important insights about children as readers.

How to transform elementary literature teaching to acknowledge and nurture individual children's literary understandings, and to reconcile the different notions of what it means to be a good reader is a challenge we haven't really engaged in elementary schools. In the current back-to-decoding climate, this might seem an impossible task. Yet for those of us who see literature as the proper content and purpose of the reading program, it's something we simply have to press forward with, and hope our colleagues will eventually see that literature isn't just the *end*, but a very large component of the *means* for promoting genuine literacy among elementary school children.

REFERENCES

Daniels, H. (1994). *Literature circles: Voice and choice in the student-centered classroom*. York, ME: Stenhouse Publishers.

Guice, S., & Allington, R. L. (1994). Using literature in reading programs. *The School Administrator,* June, 41.

International Reading Association/National Council of Teachers of English (1996). *Standards for the English Language Arts*. Newark, DE: International Reading Association.

Moss, J. F. (1996). *Teaching literature in the elementary school: A thematic approach*. Norwood, MA: Christopher-Gordon Publishers.

Peterson, R., & Eeds, M. (1990). *Grand conversations*. New York: Scholastic, Inc.

Rosenthal, I. (1997). *Sixth graders' interpretative thinking about texts significant to their peer culture*. Unpublished Ph.D. Dissertation, State University of New York at Albany, NY.

Samway, K. D., & Whang, G. (1995). *Literature study circles in a multicultural classroom*. York, ME: Stenhouse Publishers.

Walmsley, B. D., Camp, A.-M., & Walmsley, S. A. (1992). *Teaching kindergarten: A theme-centered curriculum*. Portsmouth, NH: Heinemann.

Walmsley, S. A. (1992). Reflections on the state of elementary literature instruction. *Language Arts, 69,* 508–514.

Walmsley, S. A., Fielding, L. F., & Spiro, R. (1990). *The literary experiences of second graders*. Paper presented at the annual meeting of the American Educational Research Association, Boston, MA.

Walmsley, S. A., Rosenthal, I., & Whipple, M. (1996). *In betwixt and between: Tracking the literary development of students from fifth to seventh grade*. Albany, NY: Center for the Learning and Teaching of Literature.

Essay 2

The Best and the Worst of Times

●————————●

Kathy Short, University of Arizona

"It was the best of times and it was the worst of times." This cliche immediately came to my mind as I thought about the future of literature in the curriculum. It is the best of times because so many educators are bringing children and books together in ever more powerful ways. This work is part of a long process of gradually uncovering new potentials and understandings for children's explorations of literature. It is also the worst of times as schools experience a backlash against literature-based curriculum and a call to return to isolated skills instruction, especially for young readers.

Given the current context, I see many possible scenarios for the role of literature in the classroom, only some of which give me optimism. The political context brings forth one set of scenarios that reflect a restricted and narrowing role for literature in the curriculum. In contrast, the educational context foretells an increasingly transforming role for literature in classrooms based around an inquiry perspective on teaching, learning, and researching. In the following sections, I will explore these two contexts and the scenarios they suggest.

THE WORST OF TIMES

Just a few years ago, educators who valued the role that literature plays in children's lives and learning were riding a wave of success (Smith, 1997). Libraries, bookstores, and classrooms were filled with more books and higher-quality books than ever before. Children's literature was replacing basal readers and subject area textbooks on the shelves of many classrooms. Teachers no longer saw literature just as a way to teach reading. Literature was woven into children's inquiry about mathematics, science, and social studies. Most important, literature was coming to be valued as a way of knowing about the world and children's own lives.

Books, articles, conferences, and workshops on literature-based curriculum dotted the landscapes of teachers' lives. A new journal, *The New Advocate*, was launched with fanfare in 1987 because of its focus on extending the conversations about children's literature and teaching. Increasingly greater numbers of articles and books were published by teachers who wrote about the ways their work with literature was transforming their thinking about children and schools. Everyone was talking about literature and its potentials for changing curriculum and children's lives.

The world looks very different now as the field reconsiders the role of literature and repeated attacks are made on any approach that appears innovative. In California, once the vanguard for literature-based approaches, these approaches have now been declared failures and the cause of falling test scores (Freeman, Freeman, & Fennacy, 1997). The pendulum has swung and politicians call for a return to systematic, intense phonics instruction. The new answer to literacy problems is "balanced" reading instruction—which Honig (1996) interprets as starting with phonemic awareness lessons, followed by phonics lessons and reading from "decodable" texts, and then (and only then) the introduction of literature and reading for meaning.

The future in this political context is grim. Literature will be banished into the upper grades—but only if students have become "proficient" readers according to standardized tests. Students will again be subjected to the isolated "skill and drill" boot camps that so many of us remember from our own days as students and our early teaching experiences. Their reading materials will consist of endless, and mindless, renditions of "the cat sat on the mat." Teachers will use "teacher proof" scripts, such as Success for All, which tell them what to say and do at all times. Teacher educators will return to teaching reading methods as a set of procedures separate from meaningful reading of literature.

Even within this grim scenario, however, things won't quite go back to what they were before. Huck (1996) notes that while the individualized reading movement was dealt a major blow by Rudolph Flesch's (1955) *Why Johnny Can't Read*, the movement had a lasting effect through the "recognition that children could be active in their own learning and would seek, self-select and pace themselves. Children became excited about reading and read widely. And teachers learned to appreciate what good stories could do to turn children on to reading" (p. 2).

These recognitions have become even stronger and others have been added through recent explorations. Educators at all levels and from very different theoretical perspectives believe that literature should be available in all classrooms as a daily, integral part of children's school experiences. While literature may be withdrawn from "reading instruction," I believe that teachers will find ways to weave powerful experiences with books throughout the rest of the school day. We also understand so much more about the importance of dialogue and story and these understandings will have a lasting effect on instruction.

Another important recognition that teachers bring is that of themselves as professional decision-makers. The literature-based movement was led by teachers with strong backgrounds in reading process, literary theory, and curriculum (Smith, 1997). These teachers developed their own theories of learning and reading to guide them in the classroom. They no longer need basal readers to control the lesson, the literature, and the meanings children make of their reading (Hade, 1994). In fact, they explicitly reject this control and the ways in which basal readers, including those labeled "literature anthologies," continue to be based in a system of controlling instruction and a belief that reading is composed of decoding and encoding skills.

This group of teachers will resist programmed, isolated instruction. Because of their strong theoretical and curricular base, they will transform the mandates and materials that are handed to them. The surface structures of their classrooms may appear to change as a survival mechanism, but the deep structure of their teaching will remain the same.

Of course, many educators at universities and schools who jumped on the bandwagon of literature-based instruction did so without any real understanding of literature, story, dialogue, or the reading process. These educators relied on activities handed to them by consultants and basal companies. They will most likely continue to follow the current mandates and return to isolated skill instruction. Literature-based instruction was never a transformation of teaching and curriculum for them, but an activity to add to their already existing basal curriculum. The only real change will be adding phonics drills to replace or supplement literature activities.

Many of these educators are thoughtful teachers who plan carefully and care deeply about their students. However, they lack the theoretical and curricular understandings they need to construct effective learning environments with their students. The failure of literature-based instruction in their classrooms indicates the failure of the educational system to give teachers time for professional development and research into the nature of reading and the role of literature in their classrooms (Freeman, Freeman, & Fennacy, 1997; Routman, 1996; Smith, 1997).

THE BEST OF TIMES

Within the context of this political backlash stands exciting research, theory, and practice aimed at bringing literature and children together in increasingly transforming ways. Teachers and teacher educators continue to push their understandings by building on previous work to explore new potentials and possibilities, especially in inquiry, dialogue, and learning about the reading process.

One significant shift is from literature-based curriculum to inquiry-based curriculum. Inquiry is a philosophical stance that highlights learners having time to search for the questions that are significant in their lives and to systematically investigate those questions. Learners are problem-posers as well as problem-solvers within a democratic learning environment. Teachers don't just build curriculum from students but negotiate curriculum with students (Short & Harste, 1996).

In an inquiry-based classroom, inquiry itself, not the subject areas or literature, become the heart of the curriculum. Instead of dividing the day into different subject areas or organizing theme units around subject area activities, the subject areas become tools and perspectives that learners use to explore their inquiry focus. Literature is a way of knowing that is woven throughout the inquiry process—a perspective that influences the questions that become compelling for students and the understandings they construct about those questions. Literature doesn't stand alone but is part of many other experiences and resources that surround students' learning.

If all of learning is inquiry, then reading is inquiry. Students read to inquire about their world and their lives. Inquiry is not a value-free process but one that involves taking multiple, critical perspectives on life. Reading and dialoging about literature allows students to interrogate their views of the world and try on new perspectives.

Much of the previous work on literature discussion groups focused on getting these groups organized and students engaged in some kind of productive talk about literature (Short & Pierce, 1990). Now the stakes are higher. Not just any talk will do. Teachers are interested in in-depth, thoughtful discussions about books in which students explore literary and political significance (Smith, 1997). The dialogue in these groups has taken on a strong political tone as students critically examine the ways they and others live their lives. The teacher's role is not to impose a particular critical perspective, but to establish learning contexts in which students confront a range of perspectives and are encouraged to dialogue about those perspectives.

This work has the potential of transforming students' lives and thinking. Instead of producing adults who expect that their thinking will be controlled by those in authority, this dialogue could lead to adults who expect to thoughtfully participate in the decisions that affect their lives. There is much we don't yet understand about how to create democratic environments that support this kind of critical thinking, but children's dialogue about literature will undoubtedly play an essential role.

If reading is inquiry, then learning about language and how the reading process functions is also an inquiry process. It is clear that many educators made the mistake of assuming that immersing students in lots of books would be enough to support them in becoming proficient readers. Educators seemed to have only two options—either do nothing with reading instruction or develop skill sheets for each piece of literature.

The current backlash has been a painful reminder that the future depends on teachers having solid understandings of the reading process. Using these understandings, they can find ways to work at reading instruction throughout the day. Some of this instruction will arise out of students' ongoing inquiries and the materials they need to read as part of these inquiries. Other times, the inquiry will be about the reading process as students and teachers puzzle out the kinds of strategies and knowledge about reading students need to become proficient readers.

SO, WHAT'S NEXT?

Literature does appear to be here to stay in classrooms and schools, no matter what happens to the phonics pendulum. Books will continue to be present in classrooms and to be integrated into the curriculum. In most classrooms, however, that curriculum will be an eclectic one that shifts according to the public mood and the current set of teacher manuals. Teachers and students will operate under opposing and contradictory views of the reading process and literature at different times of the day.

In a few classrooms and schools, teachers will continue to seek out the potentials offered by integrating literature into an inquiry curriculum. They will explore their understandings of reading as an inquiry process and the ways in which story and dialogue can provide critical perspectives on students' worlds and lives. As informed, articulate professionals, they will remain in control of their classrooms and will push their theoretical boundaries.

For a more positive and broadly based future scenario than this one, ongoing focused professional development is essential. Time for teachers to think, read, dialogue, and research will have to become part of how we "do school" at all levels of university and school life. This dialogue is essential in supporting teachers in becoming knowledgeable, informed professionals who are in control of their classrooms. It is also essential in supporting teachers in becoming articulate about their beliefs and practices so they can respond to political pressures and engage in wider public debates about education.

It's clear that this dialogue must occur in ever-widening circles within and outside of the school context if long-term change is to occur. One of the major mistakes many educators made as they worked to bring literature and process-centered approaches into the classroom was that parents and community members were excluded from the conversations. Just as we have worked to develop more collaborative approaches with students, so must we now open up those approaches to include parents, administrators, and the broader community. Together we need to examine the complexity of life in schools instead of trying to find simple solutions to complex problems.

REFERENCES

Flesch, R. (1955). *Why Johnny can't read.* New York: Harper and Row.

Freeman, Y., Freeman, D., & Fennacy, J. (1996). California's reading revolution: What happened. *The New Advocate, 10*(1), 31–47.

Hade, D. (1994). Aiding and abetting the basalization of children's literature. *The New Advocate, 7*(1), 29–44.

Honig, B. (1996). *How should we teach our children to read?* San Francisco: Far West Laboratory.

Huck, C. (1996). Literature-based reading programs: A retrospective. *The New Advocate, 9*(1), 23–33.

Routman, R. (1996). *Literacy at the crossroads.* Portsmouth, NH: Heinemann.

Short, K., & Harste, J., with C. Burke. (1996). *Creating classrooms for authors and inquirers.* Portsmouth, NH: Heinemann.

Short, K., & Pierce, K. (Eds). (1990). *Talking about books.* Portsmouth, NH: Heinemann.

Smith, K. (1996). A retrospective from the classroom: One teacher's view. *The New Advocate, 10*(1), 15–30.

Essay 3

Addressing the Needs of a Diverse Society

●————————————●

Robert Rueda, University of Southern California

Although diversity has always been a feature of American public schools, it is only recently that theories underlying educational practice have begun to consider the ramifications of this diversity. As the following paragraphs suggest, this move to recognize diversity may be due to the accelerated diversification of the nation as a whole and the resulting "spillover" into classrooms. When considered together with the increasing levels of literacy required to secure employment and negotiate everyday life, it can be argued that the job that schools and teachers are being asked to do has changed significantly. Not only is the job more difficult, it increasingly involves diverse groups of students with various cultural traditions and languages. Moreover, this diversity is often accompanied by fewer resources. A brief peek at these changes, in the case of language minority students, is informative as a context for examining issues related to literature-based instruction in future years.

LANGUAGE MINORITY STUDENTS AND SCHOOL ACHIEVEMENT

Recent demographic trends present an astounding picture of change in the nation as a whole and more specifically in the schools. For example, population counts from the 1990 census indicate that the Latino population[1] is the fastest growing of the nation's large ethnic minority groups. The population increased by 53 percent between 1980 and 1990, while the total population increased by only 9 percent (U.S. Department of Commerce, Bureau of the Census, 1991). Schools have seen a parallel change. From 1985 to 1993, for example, the LEP (limited English proficient) population increased at an average 9.2 percent per year, while the overall student population increased by about one percent annually. The 2,736,000 LEP students enrolled during the 1992 school year comprised about 5.7 percent of the total student population (Henderson et al., 1994). Most of these students are young: more than two-thirds are in grades K–6, and the largest number (about three out of four) of these limited English speaking students speak Spanish. In 1993, 2 out of 10 students attending public schools in central cities of metropolitan areas were Hispanic (Henderson et al., 1994). Disturbingly, in the face of increasing diversity, poverty is rising. In 1993, 39 percent of Latino children compared to 16 percent of white children lived in families with an income level below the poverty line (Fromboluti, 1994).

At the same time as schools are becoming more diverse, and more of these students experience poverty, achievement levels show declines. Across the nation, for example, NAEP data indicate that there were declines in average reading proficiency from 1992 to 1994 for Hispanic students in grade 4 as well as in grade 12. Average reading proficiency was found to be related to the number of different types of reading materials, to parents' education, to the amount of television watching, and free pleasure reading, all factors normally more favorable for middle- and upper-class children. As early as age 9, differences between Latino and white students emerge in reading as well as in math and science (U.S. Department of Education, National Center for Educational Statistics, 1996).

Given this changing context, and the new demands being placed on schools, what are the implications for literature-based instruction and the field of literacy education in general? This will be explored in the remainder of this essay beginning with the theories guiding practice.

THEORIES OF LEARNING, DEVELOPMENT, AND DIVERSITY

The move to literature-based instruction from traditional basal reading approaches can be traced at least in part to changes in prevailing theories of not only the nature of literacy but of learning in general. In many ways, psychology has been especially important as a foundation for reading and literacy research and theory, especially the constructivist orientation of cognitive psychology. Traditional basal materials, often emphasizing a passive learner role, simply did not lend themselves to the meaning-making processes of active learners emphasized in constructivist approaches. Literature, on the other hand, provides a more meaningful and coherent vehicle for embedding literacy learning activities.

More recently, sociocultural perspectives have been increasingly visible in literacy theory and practice, either alone (Dixon-Krauss, 1996) or in combination with cognitive orientations (Lipson & Wixson, 1997). This sociocultural perspective has emphasized the social and cultural bases of cognition, learning, and development, including those processes thought to underlie language and literacy. The connection of meaningful literature to everyday life, as well as the affordance of a social context for discussion and personal response, has furthered the use of literacy in instructional practice.

An interesting task, and something which is likely to define an important strand of future work in the field, will be to make sense of the contributions of each of these perspectives. Cognitive psychologists, for example, will increasingly struggle with issues such as trying to integrate notions of social context and cultural considerations into prevailing views of learning and thinking (Marshall, 1996). Social constructivists, on the other hand, will struggle with integrating the insights of the cognitive tradition and will struggle with ways of documenting the outcomes of instructional practices in ways that satisfy traditional educational constituencies. It is likely that increasingly diverse classrooms will help drive this process—the nature of the population will continue to provide challenges to theories and methods developed for the most part without concern for important learner characteristics. Interestingly, these challenges are true even of the body of knowledge developed to address language differences, such as the literature on bilingual education. While much of the research in this area was developed under the assumption of one majority and one minority language context, classrooms in large urban settings are increasingly populated by several different language groups. As the theories that guide the use of literature in the classroom continue to develop, and insights into the learning process progress, it can be expected that the ways in which literature is used will continue to develop as well.

ADDRESSING DIVERSITY THROUGH MULTICULTURAL LITERATURE

In dealing with diversity, schools face a dual challenge. First, there is the issue of how to accommodate cultural differences in the classroom. Second, there is the issue of how to equalize the intellectual content of the curriculum for students with different languages, cultural traditions, and abilities. An important development in the future of literacy-based instruction might be its increasing use as a vehicle to address these needs.

Discussions of cultural differences and diversity often seem to reflect a view of culture as stable and patterned values, beliefs, and standards that help individuals make sense of the world. This view is evident in multicultural training programs that seek to familiarize participants with the "cultural characteristics" of a given group or groups, with the goal of increasing multicultural awareness, promoting positive interactions, reducing cultural conflicts in the classroom, and so on. However, researchers increasingly argue that cultural traditions and practices are in fact dynamic and changing, created and re-created on an ongoing basis in various contexts. That is, these dynamic patterns are learned and negotiated on an ongoing basis (Mehan, Lintz, Okamoto, & Will, 1994). Given this view of cultural differences, many schools are searching for ways of becoming culturally responsive to the various students often found within the same classroom.

At the same time that schools struggle to become more culturally responsive, they face another significant challenge. Simply stated, schools are not socially neutral places. Wealthy students, for example, often get a more academically challenging curriculum than working-class children. In addition, when students are working-class and from culturally diverse groups, or when their first language is not English, there is more of a tendency to reduce the intellectual content of the curriculum, or to concentrate on only rudimentary literacy skills (Oakes, 1986).

Fortunately, the use of trade books, especially trade books with a multicultural emphasis, provides a vehicle for addressing these needs in the context of literacy instruction. In recognition of the fact that different individuals have different interests, both students and teachers select and respond to topics and materials. These materials then provide the social organization for multiple, lively contexts for creating meaning. They not only facilitate prolonged discussions of texts by students, but provide increased opportunities to draw on students' interests and developing understandings. In addition, book selection can include texts that enable teachers to help students use their own experiences and knowledge in making meaning, and in connecting to other texts and experiences. Clearly, there is a greater role for literature-based instruction as a tool for addressing cultural diversity and varying needs in the classroom. A positive future development would be the increased integration of literature, especially well-written multicultural literature, in all classrooms.

A FINAL NOTE: POLITICS AND EDUCATIONAL CONCERNS

As a final consideration, it can be argued that education is increasingly political. There are many cases where classrooms have become the focal point for power struggles of various constituents. One trend is clear: the public is more involved in public education than ever before. This is especially important in a system of public education that is taxpayer-supported. Given this situation, it is critical that the man on the street understand the basis for the type of instruction argued for in this volume. It is often significantly different from what many adults experienced in their own educational histories. Sometimes the theoretical rationale, methods, and goals are not readily comprehensible to the those without a basic understanding of recent developments in theory and practice. In fact, in the worst case, these "new" approaches are counter-intuitive and may be seen as diversions in the process of assuring proficiency in "basic" skills. Recent events in California surrounding the phonic-whole language struggle, for example, or the struggle to adopt performance-based assessments, illustrate the extent to which these issues can become obstacles to educational practice.

This state of affairs should be of extreme concern to all those involved in literacy instruction. Unfortunately, academics exist in a culture that does not value dissemination to those who are not academics, that is, the public. The most highly valued dissemination activities are those aimed at elite academic audiences. However, if the trend is toward linking classrooms and conducting educational research in a way that is meaningful to teachers and students, is to continue, this cultural norm will have to change. Literacy educators will of necessity need to target dissemination of all types to the public and other constituents. If literacy-based instruction and similar pedagogies are to play a prominent role in the future of literacy instruction, those in the field will have to be increasingly sensitive to the needs of audiences traditionally ignored. The promise of this approach, especially in an increasingly diverse context, suggests that this course of action requires serious consideration.

ENDNOTE

1. Latino is sometimes preferred over the term Hispanic, although many authors use the terms interchangeably. This group represents an aggregation of several distinct national origin subgroups: Mexican, Puerto Rican, Cuban, Central and South American, and other Hispanics. Mexican origin persons constitute about two-thirds of this group (Chapa & Valencia, 1993).

REFERENCES

Chapa, J., & Valencia, R. R. (1993). Latino population growth, demographic characteristics, and education stagnation: An examination of recent trends. *Hispanic Journal of Behavioral Sciences, 15*(2), 165–187.

Dixson-Krauss, L. (1996). *Vygotsky in the classroom: Mediated literacy instruction and assessment.* White Plains, NY: Longman.

Fromboluti, C. S. (1994). *Mini-digest of education statistics.* Washington, DC: U.S. Department of Education. Office of Educational Research and Improvement. National Center for Education Statistics.

Henderson, A., et al. (1994). *Summary of the bilingual education state education agency program survey of states' limited English proficient persons and available educational services 1992–1993.* Arlington, VA: Development Associates, Inc.

Lipson, M. Y., & Wixson, K. K. (1997). *Assessment and instruction of reading and writing disability: An interactive approach*. White Plains, NY: Longman.

Marshall, H. H. (Ed.). (1996). Recent and emerging theoretical frameworks for research on classroom learning: Contributions and limitations [Special issue]. *Educational Psychologist, 31*(3/4).

McMahon, S. I., & Raphael, T. E. (1993). Effective use of trade books: why and how? *The leadership letters: Issues and trends in reading and language arts*. Boston, MA: Silver Burdett Ginn.

Mehan, H., Lintz, A., Okamoto, D., & Will, J. (1994). Ethnographic studies of multicultural education in classrooms and schools. In J. Banks & C. McGee Banks (Eds.), *Handbook of research on multicultural education* (pp. 129–144). New York: Macmillan.

Oakes, J. (1986). Tracking, inequality, and the rhetoric of school reform: Why schools don't change. *Journal of Education, 168*, 61–80.

U.S. Department of Commerce, Bureau of the Census. (1991). *The Hispanic population of the United States: March 1990*. (Current Population Reports, Series P-25, No. 995). Washington, DC: U.S. Government Printing Office.

U.S. Department of Education, National Center for Education Statistics. (1996). *National assessment of educational progress, 1994 reading report card for the nation and the states*. Washington, DC: U.S. Government Printing Office.

Essay 4

The Literature Makes the Difference

•————————•

Barbara J. Diamond, Eastern Michigan University

As a child I was an avid reader, even though the stories I read in school were about "other people." I vividly remember a gnawing discontent because *all* of the stories I read were about children and families that looked nothing like me, set in communities that looked nothing like mine. Even the stories we read in the basal readers rendered me invisible, in the bland, sterile world of Dick and Jane. It was as if I were intruding somehow, always on the outside, longing to be drawn into the story. I knew that my Black family and I had stories to tell—of my fabulous tenth birthday party, the family festivities, food, and animated conversation that abounded when my favorite Uncle came to visit, and an adventurous family trip to New York when my sister got lost at Coney Island! I remember thinking, other children would find my stories funny and intriguing, certainly more exciting and colorful than "See Dick. See Jane.!" As I grew older, I began to wonder and question, "Why am I excluded?"

Fortunately, my father, a dedicated science teacher and graduate of Morehouse, the college of Martin Luther King, often read stories of famous African Americans. Stories of Booker T. Washington and George Washington Carver were commonplace in my home, even though the books that they came from were much too advanced for me to read. My mother, also a teacher, made proud recountings of the life of Marian Anderson, the noted African American contralto, a time of pride and reflections. While there were no children's stories about African Americans that I could read, I was able to hear stories about people that made me proud. For my parents, unlike many other African American parents, knew the importance of literature, particularly culturally relevant literature in the making of a reader.

The journey has been a long one, from the days of my youth when basals and children's books excluded people of color, to the diversity contained in the books of today. A whole series of events has occurred since reading was characterized by "Dick and Jane" and "exclusive" children's literature—literature that left out and misrepresented people of color. Among the most important was the modern civil rights movement through which the social consciousness of a nation was raised.

Importantly, Larrick's article (1965) in the *Saturday Review* was published in the midst of the triumph and turmoil of the civil rights movement, and notified the rest of the world about a truth that people of color already knew: that the "All White World of Children's Books" was indeed a reality. Larrick discovered that of the 5,206 books published in 1962 through 1964, a mere 6.7 percent included African Americans in their plot or their illustrations. Similarly, in 1976, a committee of Asian American book reviewers formed the Asian American Children's Book Project under the Council for Interracial Books for Children (Aoki, 1992). This group evaluated children's books in which one or more central characters were Asian Pacific Americans and found only 66 books contained Asian Pacific Americans (of the more than 3,900–5,000 children's books published in the United States each year) (Aoki, 1992). With the impetus of reports like these, during the decades of the 1960s and 1970s, the world of children's literature slowly began to change. It became more representative of the population of the United States, and provided all children an opportunity to feel validated and included.

While publishers of basal readers were being urged to alter their materials (Anderson, Osborn, & Tierney 1984), it was the literature-based movement that brought literature into the school, and eventually exposed more children to the diversity of people, values, and beliefs. The literature-based reading program, rooted in the whole language movement, was in full swing (Cullinan, 1987) in the mid-to-late 1980s. In fact, on May 9, 1986, the State Superintendent of Public Instruction in California launched the California Reading Initiative, a model designed to address illiteracy, semiliteracy, and aliteracy. The strategy was implemented to both improve reading instruction and to provide students access to good books. Other states began to adopt similar initiatives. Scholars began to advocate literature in reading programs and research support grew for the movement (Alexander, 1987).

Unfortunately, the proponents of the literature-based movement never clearly articulated a plan for incorporating the roots of literacy, the beginning-to-read strategies for the early grades, into the movement (Honig, 1995). Moreover, teachers were often asked to implement literature-based programs with virtually no input and little or no staff development (Hoffman, McCarthey, Abbott, Christian, Corman, Curry, Dressman, Elliott, Matherne, & Stahle, 1994). Consequently, a little more than a decade later, test scores of California students are said to have plummeted, there is a nationwide backlash against the literature-based movement (Alexander, 1987), and the future of literature-based reading remains in doubt.

For all students, but particularly students of color, the possibility that the imperiled literature-based reading movement could be reversed is unsettling. As we look toward the future, the literature in literature-based instruction (and the children who benefit from it) are the most powerful reasons to keep the movement alive. For unlike my school experiences, a generation of students has begun to discover the pleasure and excitement of reading about people like themselves. Puerto Rican students, for example, are able to experience personal affirmation as they read about people of similar lifestyles and linguistic backgrounds, because of a trend of literature that is slowly emerging about the Puerto Rican community (Nieto, 1992). Native American students, who have been blatantly misrepresented in children's literature, and who often are unable to locate texts and stories that are free from stereotypes, are beginning to find selections in the poetry and folklore genre (Norton, 1991). These selections, in particular, sensitively and insightfully portray Native American lifestyles and the rich oral tradition of the culture.

European-American students also need continued exposure to literature-based instruction. While they typically read literature that reflects their own life experiences, values, and perspectives, until literature was systematically included in reading instruction, European-American students had limited or no opportunities to read about groups different from themselves. In fact, reading from only one perspective has, on the one hand, developed some students who have pride in their culture, and rightfully so, but on the other hand, have little knowledge, understanding, and appreciation for the cultures of others. Importantly, as students have been afforded opportunities to read literature from diverse cultures, they have reported, as one child noted, "that it's like going on an interesting journey into different, uncharted lands." Or as another student shared, "it really helps you understand your own culture better" (Diamond & Moore, 1995).

In addition to opportunities to read about students of diverse backgrounds, the literature in literature-based programs challenges students to explore issues of social justice. Some educators and parents suggest that schools exclude literature that has themes of social justice and other social issues, in order to protect children from conflict and confusion. However, it has been documented that children at a very early age have a strong concept of fairness and justice (Banks, 1992; Pang, 1991). Because justice is a cornerstone of our democracy, children can explore this value, with literature as a catalyst, and relate it to themes such as immigration, homelessness, and racism.

As these issues become more prominent in our society, literature can become a natural vehicle not only to teach the basic skills of reading, but to help students understand social change and their role in this change. For example, a white pre-student teacher in my elementary reading course, which is taught on-site in a large city, wrote in her journal that one African American student revealed to her that he thought all white people belonged to the Ku Klux Klan. Astonished and perplexed, she repeatedly assured the student that this was not the case, citing personal examples of many white people who were outraged by the KKK and who actually sought opportunities to help Blacks. However, it wasn't until she read with the class the story poem, *Follow the Drinking Gourd* by Jeannette Winter (1988), and discussed the underground railroad, that the student began to understand that there were white people, even 200 years ago, who fought for racial justice and against oppression and racism. They continued to dialogue and read other books about how change in race relations has occurred and the continuing challenges that need to be faced.

In the April 21, 1997 edition of *USA Today,* it was reported that immigration figures for 1996 rose 116,000 over the previous year, an increase of 9 percent. Children who read and write stories and factual accounts of the lives of people who immigrate to this country learn about conflict and dilemmas that both the immigrants and U. S. citizens face. They learn at an early age to appropriately face complex issues, identify and clarify their values, and reflectively make moral choices.

Among the new realities that American educators must face, as we speed toward the new millennium, is that demographic, social, technological, and linguistic changes are not going to reverse themselves. The country will never be as it was in the past. All educators, but especially literacy educators, must view their roles in teaching children to read and write as opportunities to not only help them break the alphabetic code and read words, but to use these words to read "the world." Children are capable of acquiring skills of decoding *and* acquiring skills of critical thinking about current issues, of engaging in storymapping and engaging in complex decision making.

But what about skills? Although literature is at the core of literature-based instruction, proponents generally support skill development within the context of good literature. In fact, teachers have shared their views about how this can be done. Thelma, a teacher and friend who teaches in an urban district, was very excited about her new literature-based basal anthology, saying, "I would never go back to the traditional basals. My children have changed completely. Now when I say it's time for reading, students immediately take out their books and begin to read. Even the 'high-tension' kids are involved. They view reading as a pleasure. They have something real and important that they can read and write and talk about." I questioned her further, because I knew of her belief that students need to focus on special skills. She continued. "Oh, I include the skills!! I know which skills they need and I incorporate them into their reading on a regular basis. For some students I give them a special time for concentrated instruction and practice." Although Thelma, a veteran teacher, is adept at incorporating skills into her program, other less able teachers need support. For literature-based instruction to be sustained, that support must be forthcoming.

Educators are thus faced with how to effect lasting and meaningful change. We know from lessons learned in the past that curriculum and pedagogy are not simple devices to be picked up and manipulated. Rather, in order for change to occur, educators and researchers must thoughtfully consider the source and nature of factors that prohibit effective change. I argue that the problem lies not in weaknesses inherent in literature-based reading instruction, but in how we support teachers who are called on to implement this type of instruction. In order to successfully institutionalize literature-based instruction, we must fundamentally reorient teachers, helping them to make this major transformation. In my experiences with teachers in our multicultural literature-based program (Diamond & Moore, 1995), we found that the degree to which support was provided for teachers by their districts was directly related to the degree of success they experienced in implementing the program. What this meant was that teachers needed time to (1) learn the fundamentals of the literature-based program, (2) become actively engaged in a "learning by doing" process, and (3) have support in their classrooms through demonstration lessons and co-teaching as they engaged a new curriculum and gained new pedagogical skills.

Through professional development programs, often collaboratively developed between university and local school districts, teachers can begin to develop implementation skills. Whether the program uses a literature-based basal anthology or a program structured around trade books identified by the teacher or a curriculum committee, one of the fundamental and critical aspects of the program is knowledge of the literature and how it can be used in instruction. In our program, teachers were given five full inservice days a year over a period of three years (rotating grade levels each year) to learn all aspects of the program and infuse their ideas and students' needs into the program. In this way they took ownership (Diamond & Moore, 1995).

While this type of professional development is costly, the costs are small when compared to costs incurred by districts who vacillate between one reading approach and another. More importantly, when we consider the costs to children who are denied access to quality, authentic, culturally relevant literature and the other benefits of a literature-based program, the costs pale by comparison.

When I think back on my early days and my life as a reader, I believe that I have come full circle, from a reader struggling to find meaning in what I read, to a teacher of those who would be teachers. As I teach my students, I share with them my excitement about the wide range of literature that is a critical part of literature-based instruction. I enthusiastically support them in using literature in their instruction so that their students of the future will be both readers of words and readers of ideas. Literature-based reading instruction offers them this opportunity.

REFERENCES

Alexander, F. (1987). The California reading initiative. In B. Cullinan (Ed.), *Children's literature in the reading program* (pp. 149–155). Newark, DE: International Reading Association.

Anderson, R., Osborn, J., & Tierney, R. (1984). *Learning to read in American schools: Basal readers and content tests.* Hillsdale, NJ: Lawrence Erlbaum.

Aoki, E. (1992). Turning the page: Asian Pacific American literature. In V. Harris (Ed.), *Teaching multicultural literature in grades K–8* (pp. 109–135). Norwood, MA: Christopher-Gordon.

Cullinan, B. E. (1987). *Children's literature in the reading program.* Newark, DE: International Reading Association.

Diamond, B., & Moore, M. (1995). *Multicultural literacy: Mirroring the reality of the classroom.* New York: Longman.

Hoffman, J. V., McCarthey, S. J., Abbott, J., Christian, C., Corman, L., Curry, C., Dressman, M., Elliott, B., Matherne, D., & Stahle, D. (1994). So what's new in the new basal readers: A focus on first grade. *Journal of Reading Behavior, 26,* 47–73.

Honig, B. (1995). *How should we teach our children to read? A balanced approach.* San Francisco: Far West Laboratory.

Larrick, N. (1965). The all-white world of children's books. *Saturday Review, 48,* 63–65, 84–85.

MacCann, D. (1992). Native Americans in books for the young. In V. Harris (Ed.), *Teaching multicultural literature in grades K–8* (pp. 137–153). Norwood, MA: Christopher-Gordon.

Nieto, S. (1992). We have stories to tell: A case study of Puerto Ricans in children's books. In V. Harris (Ed.), *Teaching multicultural literature in grades K–8* (pp. 171–201). Norwood, MA: Christopher-Gordon.

Norton, D. (1991). *Through the eyes of a child: An introduction to children's literature.* New York: Merrill.

Pang, V. (1991). Teaching children about social issues. In C. Sleeter (Ed.), *Empowerment through multicultural education* (pp. 179–197). Albany: State University of New York Press.

Polacco, P. (1990). *Babushka's doll.* New York: Simon & Schuster.

Winter, J. (1988). *Follow the drinking gourd.* New York: Knopf.

Essay 5

Preserving What Is Most Vital

●————————●

Barbara M. Taylor, University of Minnesota

As evidenced by the insightful chapters in this book, we have come a long way in the last ten years in incorporating literature into the elementary reading program. Having children read and discuss a number of intact, authentic children's books during the school year is a regular occurrence in elementary classrooms around the country. Today parents come to the fall curriculum night expecting to learn which books from children's literature will be covered during the year as part of the reading class. An elementary reading program would no longer seem complete unless literature circles, in which groups of children or the whole class discuss the same book, were interspersed throughout the year.

As someone who teaches courses in children's literature for preservice elementary teachers, I am personally pleased with the growth in use of children's literature in the elementary curriculum over the years. At the same time, as I write this essay in 1997, I am concerned about the growing backlash against "whole language" (Routman, 1996) and the movement within states toward high-stakes testing in reading (Wolk, 1997). I see these pressures causing the reading instruction pendulum to swing toward more systematic decoding and comprehension instruction and away from literature study. I am not concerned about increases in decoding and comprehension instruction if these are based on documented need and sound practices. We know that many children need systematic decoding instruction to learn to read (Adams, 1990). We know that many children need to improve in reading comprehension, especially in the area of informational text (Campbell, Donahue, Reese, & Phillips, 1996). However, I am concerned that the pendulum may swing too far, as often seems to be the case in K–12 education. I am concerned that children may have insufficient opportunities to enjoy and learn from literature as we move toward a less literature-based elementary reading program in the near future.

My plea, then, in writing this essay is to encourage teachers to continue to preserve what is most vital in literature circles in the elementary classroom. What is most vital? I would argue that experiencing and sharing aesthetic responses to literature are the most important things for children to engage in when they read intact books together in the classroom. As Rosenblatt (1991) has so eloquently explained, an aesthetic stance toward a text means reading with attention to what one is "experiencing, thinking, and feeling during the reading" (Rosenblatt, 1991, p. 444). Rosenblatt argues that this is the primary stance we should use when reading literature. It is through the aesthetic responses we have to literature that we experience, learn and, in literature circles, share what it means to be human.

Rosenblatt (1991) points out that teachers need to be clear about the difference between aesthetic and efferent reading. Too often, teachers have directed children, perhaps unknowingly, toward an efferent stance toward literature (Cox & Zarrillo, 1993; Sebesta, Monson, & Senn, 1995). An efferent stance involves reading to carry away information to perform a task (Rosenblatt, 1991; Sebesta, Monson, & Senn, 1995). Teachers are encouraging an efferent stance to literature as they ask children to find vocabulary words in their novel, write answers to comprehension questions, produce a character map, write a plot summary, or critique a book. While these may be useful educational tasks, they should not be the primary reason children read and share stories they have read. Literacy analysis and criticism may be useful for English majors, but this is not what children need to focus on when they engage in literature circles.

Instead, children need to be encouraged by their teachers to recognize and appreciate the aesthetic responses they have to stories and novels they are reading in school. How did a character make you feel? What did you like about the story and why? What does the story have to say to you about your own life? Through questions like these teachers are helping children become aware of their aesthetic responses to literature. By focusing on an aesthetic stance to reading literature, teachers will help children experience the joy of reading. As teachers engage children in reading and discussing books, they must hold on to the notion that the joy of reading comes from the aesthetic responses readers have while reading.

On a related note, teachers need to help children experience the pleasure of expressing their feelings and ideas pertaining to aesthetic response in literature circle discussions. By talking about a story from an aesthetic stance, children can become more aware of their personal ideas, feelings, and reactions to the story. However, to do this effectively children need to grow in their ability to participate in discussions that are meaningful to them.

Teacher-led discussions of books may fall flat in terms of children sharing their aesthetic responses because the children do not get engaged or do not sense the teacher is really looking for authentic conversation. Or, a teacher, reading from an adult perspective, may not know what aspects of a story particularly appeal to, excite, or intrigue children. Although skillful teacher-led discussions of books certainly can stimulate aesthetic response, children also need to learn how to lead their own literature circle discussions. Children may express themselves more freely and may be more likely to discuss what matters most to them in the books they are reading together when they are in control of their own discussions. Raphael and McMahon (1994) offer excellent research-based suggestions for helping children learn to lead their own discussions in literature circles. Roser and Martinez (1995) and Cullinan (1993) also present excellent ideas for engaging students in book discussions, as do many of the chapters in the present volume.

To have meaningful literature circle discussions, children need to know how to discuss. Teaching children the art of discussion may be a neglected aspect of the language arts curriculum in the elementary classroom today. Granted, teachers have children discuss stories, and many teach their pupils how to engage in student-led discussions. However, teachers may not do enough to help students improve in their ability to effectively participate in discussions. Except for reminders such as "Don't interrupt" or "Be sure to give others a chance," teachers may have children get better at discussions simply by participating in discussions. Teachers may tend to "take what they get" from their students in terms of the quality and level of participation in discussions about books.

I would contend that in addition to helping children express their thoughts and feelings about books, teachers need to explicitly help children grow in their ability to listen to and respond to what others are saying, to learn how to negotiate turn-taking, to gain confidence in their ability to express their ideas, and to speak clearly and with sufficient elaboration so others can understand. Teachers need to model for children how to participate in authentic conversations about books and to help them evaluate their progress as a group after they have engaged in book conversations.

As this century is drawing to a close and teachers sense that the reading instruction pendulum is pulling them toward an increased focus on decoding and comprehension lessons, they will find they have less time for literature study. Teachers may have to cut out some of the skill work often connected to reading books. I would recommend cutting activities such as finding words in the dictionary and writing definitions, writing papers to compare and/or contrast the characters in two books, making story maps, or summarizing chapters. At all costs, however, teachers should hold on to independent reading time in which children read literature they want to read, literature that will naturally evoke in them aesthetic response. Equally important, teachers should preserve literature circle discussions in which students have the opportunity to engage in authentic, exciting, meaningful conversations about books they have read together. It is through these latter activities that children will become the lifelong readers we want them to be.

REFERENCES

Adams, M. J. (1990). *Beginning to read: Thinking and learning about print.* Cambridge, MA: MIT Press.

Campbell, J. R., Donahue, P. L., Reese, C. M., & Phillips, G. W. (1996). *NAEP 1994 reading report card for the nation and the states.* Washington, DC: Office of Educational Research and Improvement, U.S. Department of Education.

Cox, C., & Zarillo, J. (1993). Teaching with literature in the elementary school: A qualitative study applying Rosenblatt's transactional theory. Paper presented at the annual meeting of the American Educational Research Association.

Cullinan, B. E. (1993). *Children's voices: Talk in the classroom.* Newark, DE: International Reading Association.

Raphael, T. E., & McMahon, S. I. (1994). Book Club: An alternative framework for reading instruction. *The Reading Teacher, 48,* 102–116.

Rosenblatt, L. M. (1991). Literature-S.O.S.! *Language Art, 68,* 444–448.

Roser, N. L., & Martinez, M. G. (Eds.). (1995). *Book talk and beyond: Children and teachers respond to literature.* Newark, DE: International Reading Association.

Routman, R. (1996). *Literacy at the crossroads: Critical talk about reading, writing, and other teaching dilemmas.* Portsmouth, NH: Heinemann.

Sebesta, S. L., Monson, D. L., & Senn, H. D. (1995). A hierarchy to assess reader response. *Journal of Reading, 38,* 444–450.

Wolk, R. (Ed.). (1997). Quality counts: An *Education Week*/Pew Charitable Trusts special report on the condition of education in the 50 states. Washington, DC: *Education Week.*

Essay 6

Discussion of Text for Understanding

●————————●

Margaret G. McKeown, University of Pittsburgh

My perspective is based on a cognitive view of text-processing in which the key to interacting with text is to obtain meaning, to make sense of what it offers—in a word, understanding. I believe that reading is a constructive process in which the reader interacts with print, assigning meaning to what is read by connecting ideas together and integrating that with prior knowledge (see, for example, Beck & Carpenter, 1986; Just & Carpenter, 1987; Chiesi, Spilich, & Voss, 1979).

Coming to place a premium on understanding arose from my reaction to observing great numbers of young students respond to their texts without understanding. These observations were based on studies in which students were given a text to read and asked to recall it (Beck, McKeown, Sinatra, & Loxterman, 1991; McKeown & Beck, 1990). Too often these retellings bore little resemblance to the ideas and events depicted in the text, such as saying that the Indians won freedom from the British during the Revolutionary War. These students seemed to deal with the text in a distant, cursory way. Their goal seemed to be to get something—anything—from the encounter with the text as quickly as possible and not look back to consider the coherence or reasonableness of the information they grabbed onto.

Similar issues arise in students' experiences with literature. Granted, the demands and purposes for reading literature and reading expository text (e.g., in textbooks) are different. For example, literature experiences are generally seen as more pleasurable and more personal, and these characteristics are often exactly what teachers want to capture in incorporating literature into their instruction. Yet the personal meaning and pleasure that arise will be very shallow if students deal with the texts in a cursory way.

As my colleagues and I considered how to counter a shallow approach to text in a way that would encourage dealing with the text toward building understanding, we conceived of the problem as having a cognitive and an affective component. The cognitive one was that the students did not approach the text as something potentially meaningful to be worked with toward understanding. The affective part was that the students seemed to feel that if they did expend some effort trying to understand the text, and especially if that effort was not totally successful, then it indicated that they lacked particular abilities. That is, not to try is not to fail.

Our solution to trying to orient students toward understanding began with taking them through text, probing frequently as to what was said and what that meant, and why such information would be presented. As we worked with students in trying to develop a new orientation, we noticed that the probes that seemed most effective included a reference to the author: "What's the author trying to say?" "Why would the author tell us that?" "What does the author mean by that?" Bringing the author in so explicitly seemed to be valuable in addressing the affective part of the equation as well. It helped students to see that reading is a process of dealing with what someone else has created, and working through that to figure out what that person is trying to get across (Beck, McKeown, Worthy, Sandora, & Kucan, 1996; McKeown, Beck, & Sandora, 1996).

Approaching discussion of text as building meaning by "questioning the author" stands in contrast to the traditional way that text is handled in classrooms, the IRE—initiation (the teacher's), response (a student's—brief!), evaluation (the teacher's). An IRE discussion basically means that the teacher asks questions and students provide the answers the teacher expects. Thus, the IRE focuses students on isolated pieces of information, one at a time—both one student at a time and one piece of information at a time. There is little opportunity for putting things together, at least for the students. The cognitive work and thinking is all handled by the teacher. The teacher has a mental outline of what the "discussion" will be like, and the students' role is to fill in occasional blanks along the way.

Consider, for example, the following excerpt of a discussion about a story the class has just read:

Teacher: His horse ran away. What kind of luck is that?

Student: Bad luck

Teacher: But then what happened next?

Student: His horse came back

Teacher: It came back and brought lots of other horses with it. So his bad luck turned to good?

Student: Yes

In the IRE, as the above exchange illustrates, students' thinking is kept to a minimum. The IRE pattern is based on a rather limited view of comprehension that assumes that a student's reiteration of what was in the text indicates understanding.

Another approach to discussion that also stands in contrast to the IRE involves holding the reader's response to the text as primary. In a reader-response orientation—such as those described in Sipe (Chapter 3) and Brock and Gavelek (Chapter 4), what is read is evoked as a lived event and the reading is a lived-through experience (Rosenblatt, 1982). The focus is on taking personal meaning from reading.

The notion of authentic, personally meaningful talk about text has great appeal for educators who are trying to revamp instructional approaches away from the perspective of discussion as giving the right answers from the text. Energetic teachers develop visions of discussion in their mind's eye and strive to create engaging experiences with literature for students (see, for example, Villaume, Worden, Williams, Hopkins, & Rosenblatt, 1994). Students are invited to form their own views and express their opinions. Such open forums can be lively, stimulating, and rewarding.

Yet, despite the availability of such refreshing concepts of discussion, the IRE pattern continues to dominate classrooms. Citations of the IRE's dominance appear in the mid-1960s (Bellack, Kliebard, Hyman, & Smith, 1966; Guszak, 1967), continue through the 1970s and 1980s (Mehan, 1979; Cazden, 1986; O'Flahavan, Hartman, & Pearson, 1988), and still proliferate in the 1990s (Almasi, 1995; Alvermann, O'Brien, & Dillon, 1990; Barr & Dreeben, 1991).

One reason the IRE is still so prevalent may be that it is not easy to make the vision of authentic, stimulating discussion match reality. For example, Villaume et al. (1994) talk of initiating discussion with general prompts such as "what is important to you about this book?" (p. 482) and finding that it led to students each addressing a different topic. They did not develop ideas and talk to each other. Also, when the focus is on students' personal reactions, there is a tendency to require little of the students in terms of accounting for the ideas in a text. Yet, as students express what they took from a text, misunderstandings of text ideas or events can be revealed, and it is hard for a teacher to know how to handle them without returning to the IRE role of asking and telling.

A meaning-building orientation offers a way to move the talk away from a close rendition of the words in the text while keeping some fidelity to the ideas expressed. A meaning-building orientation does not preclude readers responding to text in emotional or personal ways. The orientations of reader response and of cognitive meaning-building have important common ground in seeking to engage readers, to galvanize their attention to text and the reading process. In a meaning-building orientation, students are invited to react to literature, but not in an idiosyncratic way that may leave little room for peers or teacher to join in. Rather they are invited to respond in a way that can start a conversation, exposing views and ideas for challenge, elaboration, and refinement. Since the goal is to build meaning together, the teacher has recourse to asking for clarification or further reflection on what was expressed without feeling as though he or she is interfering in someone's personal construction. As ideas are exposed and grappled with in conversation, connections emerge and "brick by brick" understanding is built. A coherent goal is reached, collaboratively.

This kind of collaborative grappling with ideas is indeed what Isabel Beck and I and our colleagues found to result from classroom implementations of a cognitive meaning-building approach to text discussion (Beck et al., 1996; McKeown, Beck, & Sandora, 1996). From work with five teachers and about 120 fourth- and fifth-grade students over three years, we found that the approach, Questioning the Author, led to significant changes in classroom discourse about text. Teacher questions, student responses, and teacher responses to students all became more meaning-oriented. Teachers were more likely to ask why something happened or why certain information was presented and how it related to other information in a text rather than asking for a replay of the information. Teachers' responses to students were more likely to extend the conversation rather than evaluating or merely repeating what the students said. Teachers often rephrased a comment to emphasize certain aspects or turned back to students for elaboration of the ideas that a student presented.

Students were more likely to phrase their contributions in their own language, going beyond verbatim responses nearly 90 percent of the time. Student responses showed more integration of prior knowledge, hypothesizing solutions to problems, or extrapolating consequences about what they were reading. Students were much more active participants in Questioning the Author discussions, doing between two and three times as much talking as before, and teachers did proportionally less talking. Students were also much more likely to initiate their own questions and comments in Questioning the Author. Interactions between students also increased, as students expressed agreement or disagreement with each other's ideas, responded to each other's questions, and explicitly built on ideas that other students had presented.

If text-based discussion is to become a productive and sustained classroom activity—not something teachers try once and dismiss, or pull out occasionally for novelty—then it is crucial that students be held accountable for what they express about text. As readers share their views, their motivations for them also need to be made public. The key is to strive for some grounding, creating the kind of talk that stretches students' thinking and their ability to form, articulate, and support their views. I argue that the kind of grounding that calls a reader to apply effort to make sense of a text is a critical ability for a literate repertoire.

What does this mean for literature-based instruction? The point is that just having literature present in a classroom, or merely "exposing" students to literature, is not enough (although this is not a bad start when contrasted with the starkness of available reading material sometimes witnessed in schools). Mining the richness that literature has to offer takes digging into what an author has presented, and readers spending time and effort in making something of it for themselves. Providing opportunities for meaning-oriented discussions of what students read is a way to take advantage of the rich resource that literature offers.

REFERENCES

Almasi, J. (1995). The nature of fourth graders' sociocognitive conflicts in peer-led and teacher-led discussions of literature. *Reading Research Quarterly, 30*(3), 314–351.

Alvermann, D. E., O'Brien, D. G., & Dillon, D. R. (1990). What teachers do when they say they're having discussions of content area reading assignments: A qualitative analysis. *Reading Research Quarterly, 24*(4), 296–322.

Barr, R., & Dreeben, R. (1991). Grouping students for reading instruction. In R. Barr, M. L. Kamil, P. B. Mosenthal, & P. D. Pearson (Eds.), *Handbook of reading research* (Vol. 2, pp. 885–910). White Plains, NY: Longman.

Beck, I. L., & Carpenter, P. A. (1986). Cognitive approaches to understanding reading: Implications for instructional practice. *American Psychologist, 41*(10), 1098–1105.

Beck, I. L., McKeown, M. G., Sandora, C., Kucan, L., & Worthy, J. (1996). Questioning the author: A year-long classroom implementation to engage students with text. *The Elementary School Journal, 96*(4), 385–414.

Beck, I. L., McKeown, M. G., Sinatra, G. M., & Loxterman, J. A. (1991). Revising social studies text from a text-processing perspective: Evidence of improved comprehensibility. *Reading Research Quarterly, 26*, 251–276.

Bellack, A. A., Kliebard, H. M., Hyman, R. T., & Smith, F. L., Jr. (1966). *The language in the classroom.* New York: Teachers College Press.

Cazden, C. (1986). Classroom discourse. In M. C. Wittrock (Ed.), *Handbook of research on teaching* (3rd ed.) (pp. 433–462). New York: Macmillan.

Chiesi, H. L., Spilich, G. J., & Voss, J. F. (1979). Acquisition of domain-related information in relation to high and low domain knowledge. *Journal of Verbal Learning and Verbal Behavior, 18*, 275–290.

Guszak, F. J. (1967). Teacher questioning and reading. *The Reading Teacher, 21*, 227–234.

Just, M. A., & Carpenter, P. A. (1987). *The psychology of reading and language comprehension.* Boston: Allyn and Bacon.

McKeown, M. G., & Beck, I. L. (1990). What young students understand from their textbooks about the American Revolution. In *Subject specificity in social studies: How does the nature of the subject matter affect curriculum theory and practice?* Symposium at the annual meeting of the American Educational Research Association Annual Meeting, Boston.

McKeown, M. G., Beck, I. L., & Sandora, C. A. (1996). Questioning the author: An approach to developing meaningful classroom discourse. In M. G. Graves, M. M. Taylor, & P. van der Brock (Eds.), *The first R: A right of all children.* (pp. 97–119). New York: Teachers College Press.

Mehan, H. (1979). *Learning lessons: Social organization in the classroom.* Cambridge, MA: Harvard University Press.

O'Flahavan, J. F., Hartman, D. K., & Pearson, P. D. (1988). Teacher questioning and feedback practices: A twenty year retrospective. In *Dialogues in literacy research* (pp. 183–208). Chicago, IL: National Reading Conference.

Rosenblatt, L. M. (1982). The literacy transaction: Evocation and response. *Theory into Practice, 21*, 268–277.

Villaume, S. K., Worden, T., Williams, S., Hopkins, L., & Rosenblatt, C. (1994). Five teachers in search of a discussion. *The Reading Teacher, 47*(6), 480–487.

An Agenda for Teacher Educators

●————————●

Diane Stephens, University of Hawaii

Like all good ideas, the future of literature-based instruction often is discussed independently of the people who advocate for that idea. As advocates, we wonder what will happen to it, and act as if we played no role in its acceptance or decline. However, because teacher educators teach present and future teachers, because we are simultaneously connected to K–12 and university classrooms, and because our work requires us to be part of a national network, our actions can substantially impact the future of literature-based instruction. In order to access this potential, we need to become proactive. We need to move from the sideline of wondering what will happen into the flow of making things happen. We need to become actively engaged in (1) rethinking our classroom-based practice, (2) revising the academic structures within which pre- and inservice teachers learn, (3) critically examining our work that occurs outside our immediate academic contexts, (4) learning to see from the perspectives of those we teach, and (5) taking responsibility for the implementation of the lessons we teach.

RETHINKING PRACTICES

Our proactive agenda needs to begin with an examination of the usefulness of our practices from the perspective of the pre- and inservice teachers who enroll in our programs. In one of my language and literacy classes, for example, I learned the hard way that what I was teaching was not what the students needed to learn. It was a first semester preservice course and I wanted to help the students understand how children learned language and how they as teachers could use literature to support the language learning process. I started by having the students read articles about language acquisition and on cue systems in language. I wanted the students to understand reading as a strategic process and, as part of that, asked them to do a miscue analysis

(Goodman, & Burke, 1982) on a child they worried about as a reader. Meanwhile, the students were spending 5–7 hours a week in a K–6 classroom. We expect them to be highly involved in the classroom, working alongside the teacher. Indeed, by the end of the first eight weeks, we expect them to be able to independently "take over" the first hour of the morning.

One of the students was having a hard time managing even small parts of the teacher's morning structure. In order to help him, we spent time talking with him and the teacher about each of the parts: morning business, read-aloud, and so on. One of our doctoral students, Kerri-Ann Hewett, does an outstanding job when she reads books with children and I asked her to spend some time helping this student plan his read-aloud. During my conversation with her, it occurred to me that the other students should also have access to her expertise and I so asked her if she would conduct a lesson for the entire methods class. She agreed to do so.

I remember so clearly what that day was like. Kerri-Ann started by reading a book to the class and, afterwards, talked with them about what she had done. She talked about how she had chosen the book she wanted to read, about practicing it at home, and about where she had decided to sit and how she had decided to hold the book. She explained to students the other options that were available—for example, she could have walked around the room, showing the pictures. She also talked about the questions she had decided to pose to the group before, during, and after reading as a way of helping them make connections to the book.

What struck me, as I sat on the sidelines watching, was how incredibly attentive the students were to her lesson. They seemed to be with her every step of the way—smiling, nodding, taking notes. I could feel their appreciation for what she was offering.

Once she had finished making her planning explicit, she asked the students to each choose a book to read to a small group, plan, practice, read and then give each other feedback. "Joyful" might be too strong a word to describe their response to this task but it certainly captured my sense of their reaction. I was simultaneously (and painfully) aware that this was not the reaction I got when I asked students to do a miscue analysis or when I discussed the results of their miscue analysis with them.

Later, in their journals, the students talked extensively about how valuable this learning experience had been for them. Many of them noted that, before this lesson, they had not given much, if any, thought to choosing what book to read. Many also said that they had no idea that they should pick the book in advance and practice it before reading to the children. They had also not thought about what questions and responses they might make as part of the read-aloud.

Watching the students that day and reading what they wrote in their journals, I became acutely aware that my teaching had been off the mark. In my need to "cover" what I thought they needed to know, I had failed to take their needs into account. I was trying to teach miscue analysis, which they were not ready to learn; I had not been planning to teach them how to read a book to a child, something they recognized that they needed to know.

REVISING ACADEMIC STRUCTURES

At too many of our universities, pre- and inservice teachers are required to take a collection of courses, each of which has a professor-driven, pre-determined curriculum. In too many universities, students do not have the opportunity to make connections between their field experiences (if they have them) and these classes. All too often, when there are field experiences, the person teaching the course is not in the field with the student.

In too many universities, classroom teachers do the university a "favor" by taking a preservice teacher into their classroom and they are not part of a university–public school partnership that determines what preservice teachers need to learn and how the partners can work together to help the students learn those things. Even when teacher educators teach preservice students on K–12 sites, we do not have structures in place that allow us to learn with and from the K–12 teachers at those sites.

At nearly every university I know, then, at both the undergraduate and at the graduate level, "method" and "theory" is kept separate from practice. How can we possibly think anyone can learn to teach or improve their teaching under those conditions? How can we expect pre- or inservice teachers generatively to "try out" literature-based approaches and critically reflect on them? How can such a structure support them as they do so? How can we sensibly expect our classes to impact the current or future practices of K–12 teachers?

The structures within the public schools often do not do a much better job of helping teachers improve their practices. Often the topics of inservice sessions are based on the current "hot topic" (critical thinking, cognitive coaching, literature-based instruction) and are not grounded in the questions that teachers currently have about their practices. Even when the topic is of genuine interest, the inservice sessions are frequently so brief that teachers can only develop a cursory understanding of the topic being presented. Sources that should be a long-term part of the school culture are brought in, short-term, from outside the culture. There often are neither follow-up sessions nor even books or videos in a professional library that would help teachers subsequently broaden or deepen their knowledge base. This makes it difficult for teachers to make connections between "in-service" sessions and classroom practices.

If we are going to be genuinely helpful to K–12 teachers, teacher educators need to work collaboratively, within the university and within the K–12 school settings, to create structures that support teachers' learning what they need to know and having new information connected to what they already know. This is new action for many of us, and it is also political action. But I am convinced that "great ideas" will not become the norm unless we empower ourselves to change the structures within which we work.

These new structures do not have to be complex. For example, teachers at one school here in Hawaii recently talked about the possibility of "trying out" a literature-based approach to reading but felt that it was too complicated to choose and organize books. The school, however, was part of a university–public school partnership, and classroom and university faculty had been working together on preservice teacher education. Because those connections were in place, it was easy for the teachers to talk to university faculty about their dilemma. Based on those conversations, a university person volunteered to help. The teachers asked that the help be given in the form of a week-long workshop in which the teachers got credit for learning about how to set up a literature-based curriculum for K–6. For a class "project," the teachers picked and organized the books they wanted to use—and even filled out purchase orders for the books. Because of the school–university partnership, university faculty continued to be a part of the literature-based conversations long after the workshop ended. Books and videos about literature-based instruction were available in the university classroom on the elementary school campus. "Inservice" teacher education became a "win-win" situation.

CRITICALLY EXAMINING WORK
OUTSIDE IMMEDIATE CONTEXTS

Too often, via our publications and in the presentations we give away from our home campuses, teacher educators start very far from the "average" classroom. We start with where we are, with what we think the field needs to know, or where we think the field needs to go.

Consider, for example, the good intentions of the authors and editors of this volume. In the introduction, they mention many of the questions they imagine teachers have raised and, in turn, address many of those questions. There are, however, a number of questions that teachers often ask that are not addressed in this volume. Teachers wonder, for example, what the relationship should be between basals and literature. Should literature replace basals? What exactly does that mean? Would teachers then be expected to teach reading using literature? What would that look like? And, perhaps more fundamentally, how do children learn to read and how can literature help them do that?

There are also questions about what it means to "teach" literature. Is using literature to teach reading the same thing as "teaching the literature"? If not, what does it mean to "teach the literature"? If we use literature to teach reading and literature to teach skills is that enough? Just what is a student supposed to "get" from reading literature? Can one story/book serve multiple functions? Should it?

I worry that when we start with questions within literature-based instruction, as these editors and authors have done, we leave out the teachers who have questions about the very idea of using literature in the classroom. It can be argued, of course, that this book is not for them. What worries me is that I do not know who is writing for the teachers who are trying to figure out whether to even introduce literature into their curriculum. Individually and collectively, we need to find ways to invite all teachers into this conversation. Otherwise, fear that literature-based instruction, like other great ideas that have come before and will come after, will have a short half-life and during its lifetime may serve more to fuel debates than to improve practice.

LEARNING TO SEE FROM OTHER PERSPECTIVES

With the best of intentions, teacher educators too often privilege their own agenda and have a hard time seeing from the perspective of others. This practice broadens, not narrows, the gaps between our visions and our practices. I have seen this shortcoming in myself many times. One semester, for example, I had agreed to work with teachers once a week for 13 weeks, in their schools, during the day, helping them to better assess the children they worried about as readers. We met three times as a group to negotiate the experience. During one of those sessions, I mentioned the powerfulness of miscue analysis (Goodman and Burke, 1982). Later, one of the teachers pointed out to me that she was not sure she wanted to participate in this experience. She said she was a "whole language" and "literature-based" teacher and it sounded to her as if this "miscue analysis" stuff came out of an older, more traditional paradigm.

I don't know if this story surprises you, but it most definitely surprised me. From my perspective, "we" (the field) had learned about how children learned oral language (from people such as Brown, 1970 and Halliday, 1975) and how people learned written language (from people such as Ferreiro & Teberosky, 1982; Harste, 1984; Read, 1975; Smith, 1982; and Wells, 1986) and, based on those understandings, began to learn about the specifics of reading (from people such as Goodman, 1972). All of that knowledge led to a commitment on the part of some of us to keep language "whole" so that children could learn language authentically from whole to part in a "literature-based," language-rich environment. I therefore was very surprised to hear a teacher define herself as a "whole language/literature-based" teacher independent of that knowledge base. This experience led me to wonder about how many times we think we are communicating but, instead, are miscommunicating. How often do our words not mean what each one of us thinks they mean?

As teacher educators, we need to learn to see from other perspectives. We need to understand our students as learners. We need to have serious and long conversations within our community so that we understand each other's inquiries and what each other considers newsworthy. This year, I have been having these kinds of conversations informally and from them I have learned that some teachers consider the following things newsworthy:

Children who are read to are more successful, generally, than those who are not.

Children who read in school make more progress as readers and do better on standardized tests than those who do not.

Children who read at home also make more progress as readers.

Children who choose to read are confident readers who have fallen in love with books.

Confident readers:

believe that they can read

believe that text makes sense (is meaningful)

have a variety of strategies for making meaning from print (re-read, skip for now, substitute a word that fits the meaning of the sentence, sound-out, use structural clues, ask someone)

use those strategies flexibly and appropriately to make meaning

use those strategies independently (not just when cued to do so by the teacher)

Children learn from what they see others doing.

Teachers need to surround children with books worth reading.

I learned all these things from teachers after the fact (in their end-of-semester reflections) or along the way (through conversations and via journals). In the future, I need to start my classes by trying to understand the information and beliefs that teachers carry in their heads when they begin their learning journey with me. For years, we have understood from cognitive psychology about schemes and the need to access and make connections to prior knowledge. In our college classrooms, however, we too often have treated pre- and inservice teachers as if their minds were empty slates or made untested assumptions about their background knowledge. We often teach about Vgotsky's Zone of Proximal Development (Vgotsky, 1962) but do not consistently gather the information we need to teach within it.

RESPONSIBILITY FOR THE "LESSONS" WE TEACH

As a part of our work with pre- and inservice teachers, we sometimes talk with them about the contexts in which they teach and learn to teach. Rarely, however, do we take action to help teachers work within those contexts. This realization is the most recent of all for me and I am currently trying to map out just what I think my responsibilities are. I have come to understand— quite powerfully—that it is not ethical for me to teach "great ideas" unless I can concurrently help teachers understand how to execute those "great ideas," without reprisals, within the contexts in which they teach. For too long, I considered "application" as someone else's problem, not mine. This is perhaps the most political agenda of all and the one that will involve the most conversations and the most thoughtful change agenda.

LOOKING AHEAD

Editors Au and Raphael asked the authors of articles in this section to talk about the future of literature-based instruction. Such thinking is often focused on practices within the K–12 classroom. As I hope I have made clear, in order to ensure the life-line of literature-based instruction, or of any great idea, the practices and the thinking of teacher educators need to change first, or, at the least, simultaneously with those of K–12 teachers. Until we do, we will continue to live with the current cycles: great ideas existing as practices in only a few K–12 and college classrooms; the traditional practices of one generation mapping onto another; university and K–12 teachers working out their lives in mutually exclusive contexts; a citizenry no more educated tomorrow than exists today.

University educators are well known for advocating changes in the K–12 classroom. It is time we focused our advice on our own classrooms and our own practices. By doing so, we stand a better chance of helping universally accepted "great ideas" become universally accepted great practices. By so doing, when we open tomorrow's classroom doors we may find "great ideas" in common practice.

REFERENCES

Brown, R. (1970). *Psycholinguistics*. New York: Macmillan.

Ferreiro, E., & Teberosky, A. (1982). *Literacy before schooling*. Exeter, NH: Heinemann.

Goodman, Y. M., & Burke, C. L. (1972). *Reading miscue inventory*. New York: Macmillan.

Halliday, M. A. K. (1975). *Learning how to mean: Explorations in the development of language*. London: Edward Arnold.

Harste, J. C., Woodward, V. A., & Burke, C. L. (1984). *Language stories and literacy lessons*. Portsmouth, NH: Heinemann.

Read, C. (1975). Lessons to be learned from the pre-school orthographer. In E. H. Lennenberg & E. Lenneberg (Eds.), *Foundations of language development: A multi-disciplinary approach (Volume 2)*. New York: Academic Press.

Smith, F. (1982). *Understanding reading*. New York: Holt, Rinehart & Winston.

Vygotsky, L. S. (1962). *Thought and language*. Cambridge, MA: M.I.T. Press.

Wells, G. (1986). *The meaning makers: Children learning language and Using language to learn*. Portsmouth, NH: Heinemann.

Essay 8

Literature Will Survive

●───────●

Bernice E. Cullinan, New York University

When I began teaching I was very young and very scared. I was 17 years old and had completed a cadet teacher certificate scrunched into a summer-winter-summer course. I had written enough lesson plans to last for the first two days of school but after that, I was in big trouble. There were two times every day, however, that I knew I was in charge. One was on the playground. When I saw Elmer chase Nedra across the jungle gym, I snapped my fingers and ordered them down. They listened to me because I spoke with authority and knew I was in charge. The other time during each day when they listened was during story time. I would pick up a book and walk slowly toward the reading area. The 27 six-year-olds followed me like I was the Pied Piper. I sat on a small first-grade chair, lowered my voice an octave or two, and read stories and poems with expression. I read aloud at least once every day, sometimes twice—because it was my Sarah Bernhardt moment. I read the dialogue with the voice of each character; I added tension and suspense by changing the drama in my voice. The children hung onto every word I read and showed their appreciation by yelling "Read it again." And, of course, I did.

I kept track of that class, the first group of children I ever taught to read—and a few years ago I returned to a school reunion. I would not have known the big, six-foot-four man who came up to me if it had not been for the warm brown eyes, the same ones that had stared at me so trustingly from a six-year-old's face. We sat under a tree and drank lukewarm lemonade while we caught up on the news in each other's lives. He has four children, all in school except one. I asked him what I ask every parent, "Do you read to them?" He answered, "Yes, I do. And I still hear the sound of your voice in my ear." That legacy—a young man who reads to his children because I once read to him—is really quite satisfying for me as a teacher. It helps me to address a question about the future of literature-based programs with confidence. Literature is memorable—it is sturdy—it will survive.

Years later, I completed my doctorate at The Ohio State University and worked on a federally funded research project, The Critical Reading Project (Wolf, Huck, & King, 1967). Our research team learned that immersing students in literature was a necessary but not a sufficient step in creating literate students; they needed lots of books, but they also needed to learn to read them critically—to evaluate what they read. We learned that it was necessary to evaluate fiction and nonfiction with different criteria. In fiction students made intertextual links; they compared characters, themes, and plots across books. For example, they observed that Huck Finn, Ramona Quimby, and Anastasia Krupnik, though somewhat similar, were very different characters. They discovered that the theme of inner beauty being valued over outward appearance is found in *Beauty and the Beast* (De Beaumont, 1990) as well as in other stories. Students found that the struggle between good and evil is represented as forces of light and darkness in *The Dark Is Rising* (Cooper, 1981), and as a shadow of oneself in *The Wizard of Earthsea* (LeGuin, 1968, 1991). In nonfiction, students learned to detect persuasive techniques used in writing. They did not accept all information they found in print but learned to evaluate what they read. Students interpreted texts differently depending upon their background knowledge. The illusion of a single right reading was no longer possible. It became clear that the price of freedom from censorship was educated citizens who critically evaluate everything they read. This holds implications for literature-based programs.

SIGNS FOR THE FUTURE

The future of literature-based programs hinges on several factors—knowledge from research about how children learn language, book publishing trends, and development of technology.

Research on Language Learning

Recent research on brain development shows the importance of engaging infants and toddlers in meaningful communication; children need parents who talk to them. We had no idea how much talk children understand but even very young infants respond to their mother's voice by sucking faster or by following a light moving about on the mother's face. Around 18 months of age children learn language so rapidly that it is called a language explosion; they learn a new word every two hours. Children of talkative mothers have more than twice as many words in their vocabulary as children of quiet mothers. The size of a child's vocabulary compounds exponentially as the child grows. Many families understand the importance of communication; they read to their children from the very beginning. Parents hear repeatedly that the single most important thing they can do to make their children successful readers is to read aloud to them. They buy books, have them in the home, and read to their children.

The trend toward the widespread use of literature will be affected by further research on language learning and optimal learning situations for developmental stages. We already know that the complexity of language children learn is directly related to the complexity of the language they hear. We also know that book language is more complex than spoken language. Children who are read to have larger vocabularies and comprehend their world in a way that children without books cannot know (Wells, 1986).

What will happen to literature-based programs in the next ten years? Some things that will happen have already started happening. For example, researchers showed that students get good at what they practice; if they read voluntarily they become good readers. The research showed that students do not read outside of school very much, but the ones who do read even 20 minutes a day score at the top of reading achievement tests (Anderson, Wilson, & Fielding, 1988). Students are more likely to read outside of school if someone reads aloud to them and if they read on their own in school. Teachers, therefore, use classroom sets of paperbacks with groups formed by interest in a book or topic instead of by ability levels. Teachers read aloud sections of the books, students follow along in their copy, read on their own in school, and take the books home for voluntary reading. I believe that these practices will spread.

Book Publishing Trends

The number of children's books published increases almost every year: it's now around 5,000 a year. Publishers enjoy growth in sales. Families buy books for children to read at home. Librarians buy books for school and public libraries. Teachers spend school funds and add their own money for books for their classrooms because they need them desperately. They know they cannot build a love of reading without having good books available. Books today reflect our nation's cultural diversity and most children can now see themselves in books. Members of varied ethnic groups are writing and publishers are publishing them. Books appeal to students when they can identify with the characters in them.

There has been an explosion in publishing excellent nonfiction informational books. Beautiful photo-essays depict nearly any topic in the school curriculum. Teachers need not teach from a single textbook; they can have an array of books at different readability levels so that every student finds a book at an appropriate reading level on a topic of interest. Topics are clearly presented so that students of varying ability levels can understand. There are different points of view from various writers. This creates the need for students to read critically, to compare differing points of view, to critically analyze information, to evaluate the authenticity of the information, and to detect the biases of the writer. These skills are needed for survival in our media-drenched world. The need will grow and the trend will continue.

Distribution and marketing of children's and young adult books open new avenues of access. Books are for sale in family and home stores, such as K-Mart, Bed Bath & Beyond, Price Club Warehouse Stores. Children's book sections in Borders, Barnes & Noble, and other superstores are well stocked; they offer discounts, and they are crowded. Bookstores are pleasant places to visit. You can have a cup of tea, visit with friends, and discover new books. Bookstores have story hours for children with readers on standby to read to small clusters of children who gather at regularly scheduled intervals. New marketing strategies bring books to the center of our attention. It is not only that bookstores are more fun, books are more fun, too. Jon Scieszka (1989) showed us what happens when you tell the *True Story of the Three Little Pigs* from the wolf's viewpoint. Versions of fractured fairy tales give kids a great laugh and encourage them to create spoofs on other tales. People recognize the value of the books they had as a child, such as *Millions of Cats* (Gag, 1928), *Madeline* (Bemelmans, 1962), *Caps for Sale* (Slobodkina, 1947), *Make Way for Ducklings* (McCloskey, 1941, 1963), *Brown Bear, Brown Bear, What Do You See?* (Martin, 1992). It means that we have more great books to entice young readers. Books are available for every age group beginning with board books, ABC books, counting books, books for infants, toddlers, day care centers. Kids are exposed to books earlier. Publishers are attracted to the wider market; they don't put out a book without a stuffed animal, doll, tape, film, sequins, audio tape, activity book, lift the flap. That's not all bad. Kids spend more time with interactive books. Creative people will always find new ways to create exciting books. This trend will continue.

Development of Technology

Technology affects the use of literature but not as drastically as you might think. Students who work on computers read a lot while they are using technology but they turn to books and magazines for pleasure reading. Access to computers is almost mandatory in today's world. One educator said, "If you're in the second grade and not able to surf the Internet, you're in big trouble."

We Americans never seem to be able to do anything in moderation. When we get a new idea, we go overboard to the extreme. When we discover that we have gone overboard in one direction, we change course and go to the opposite extreme. We often throw out the baby with the bathwater.

Ten years from now children will still learn how to read—regardless of the methods used to teach them and regardless of their use of technology.

They will still need exciting books, parents who read to them, enthusiastic teachers, and significant others such as grandparents, to share books with them. Books will not disappear because of technology. You cannot curl up in bed with a computer. It is not easy to carry a computer out under a tree. To paraphrase Isaac Asimov: What we need is something small, portable. It doesn't need to be plugged in. We can carry it around. We already have that; it's called a book.

CONCLUDING COMMENTS

Literature will survive because it enriches our lives, it is part of our cultural heritage, and it is engaging. Literature allows us to live more than the one life we have to live. We can go beyond our one lived experience and, through imagination, know other possiblities. We can understand and respond sympathetically to people whose experience differs from ours. We can try on different life styles and, in the process, come to know who we are. Literature helps us define ourselves.

Literature contains our cultural heritage and helps us to know parallel cultures through other literature. Literature conveys the values, beliefs, and concerns of previous generations that we will never know until we read about them. We can walk beside our ancestors or beside ancient Greeks who established the civilizations we inherit. We do not know our present until we know our past. Literature helps us to know both.

Finally, literature is an art form. It contains beautiful language and images that shape our knowledge of ourselves and our world. Authors deliberately craft works of fiction, nonfiction, and poetry to express humankind's longing for self-knowledge. Literature pushes back the clouds of confusion to show us a way of knowing. The language we use frames the world we know. Literature expands our world.

There has never been an age in which people did not learn how to read, regardless of the methods used to teach reading. Whether they were taught with hornbooks, New England primers, Dick and Jane readers, phonics workbooks, SRA kits, Distar, the language experience approach, basal readers, or literature-based reading programs, students learned how to read. One major attempt to identify the best method, the U.S. Office of Education Cooperative Research Program in First-Grade Reading Instruction, produced mixed results (Bond & Dykstra, 1967). Approaches that included some form of systematic phonic instruction consistently produced better word recognition, but approaches that included both systematic phonics and considerable emphasis on connected reading and meaning surpassed the basal-alone approaches on virtually all outcome measures. Method was not the strong determining factor in finding differences among approaches to teaching reading as had been suspected; there was as much variation within a method as between methods (Bond & Dykstra, 1967). The distinguishing factor was the teacher—if the teacher was excited and enthusiastic about reading, students learned to read whatever approach was used.

In a democracy where each citizen shares responsibility for decisions in government, for nurturing children, for creating communities, and for preserving the environment, it is imperative that members of society have the ability to understand printed matter and to evaluate ideas presented there. Freedom from censorship requires citizens to be discriminating readers. If students are to be adequately prepared to serve as fully functioning members of society, they need to practice reading critically in literature throughout their schooling. Literature will survive.

REFERENCES

Anderson, R. C., Wilson, P. T., & Fielding, L. (1988). Growth in reading and how children spend their time outside of school. *Reading Research Quarterly, 23,* 285–303.

Bond, G. L., and Dykstra, R. (1967). The cooperative research program in first-grade reading instruction. *Reading Research Quarterly,* 2, 5–142.

Wells, G. (1986). *The meaning makers: Children learning language and using language to learn.* Portsmouth, NH: Heinemann.

Wolf, W., Huck, C. S., & King, M. L. (1967). Critical reading ability of elementary school children. U.S. Office of Education, Department of Health, Education, and Welfare. Project No. 5-1040, Contract No. OE-4-10-187.

CHILDREN'S BOOKS CITED

Bemelmans, L. (1962). *Madeline.* New York: Viking.

Cooper, S. (1981). *The dark is rising.* New York: Atheneum.

De Beaumont, M. (1990). *Beauty and the beast.* Illus. Hilary Knight. New York: Simon & Schuster.

Gag, W. (1928). *Millions of cats.* New York: Coward McCann/Putnam.

LeGuin, U. (1968, 1991). *The wizard of earthsea.* New York: Atheneum.

Martin, B. Jr. (1992) *Brown bear, brown bear, What do you see?* Illus. Eric Carle. New York: Holt.

McCloskey, R. (1941, 1963). *Make way for ducklings.* New York: Viking.

Scieszka, J. (1989). *True story of the three little pigs.* Illus. Lane Smith. New York: Viking.

Slobodkina, E. (1947). *Caps for sale.* New York: HarperCollins.

Editors and Contributors

Kathryn H. Au, Professor in the College of Education at the University of Hawaii at Manoa, has previously worked as a researcher, curriculum developer, teacher educator, and classroom teacher at the Kamehameha Elementary Education Program (KEEP) in Honolulu. Her research interest is the school literacy development of students of diverse cultural and linguistic backgrounds. She has published over 60 articles on this topic, as well as a textbook, *Literacy Instruction in Multicultural Settings*. Currently, she is president of the National Reading Conference and of the Aloha

State Council of the International Reading Association and has served as a vice president of the American Educational Research Association (AERA). Kathy received the first National Scholar Award presented by the National Association for Asian and Pacific American Education. She was recognized as a Distinguished Scholar by the AERA Standing Committee on the Role and Status of Minorities in Educational Research and was named a fellow of the National Conference on Research in Language and Literacy.

Taffy E. Raphael is a Professor in the Department of Reading and Language Arts, Oakland University, where she teaches courses in literature-based reading instruction. She has conducted research on strategy instruction in reading and writing, children's and teachers' classroom talk about text, and teacher inquiry. Her research has been published in journals such as *The Reading Teacher*, *Language Arts*, and *Reading Research Quarterly*. She has coauthored *Creating an Integrated Approach to Literacy Instruction* and *Early Literacy Instruction* with Elfrieda H. Hiebert, published

by Harcourt Brace. She has co-edited *The Book Club Connection: Literacy Learning and Classroom Talk* (Teachers College Press), and coauthored *Book Club: A Literature-Based Curriculum* published by Small Planet Communications (www.smplanet.com). She was selected as Outstanding Teacher Educator in Reading in 1996 by the International Reading Association.

Tanja L. Bisesi is a doctoral candidate in Educational Psychology at Michigan State University. Her primary research interest is literacy assessment, particularly alternative performance-based assessment. She also teaches preservice and inservice courses in educational psychology, and classroom literacy assessment. Tanja formerly taught as a public school, speech-language pathologist.

Devon Brenner is a Ph.D. candidate at Michigan State University, focusing on literacy and social studies teacher education. Her ongoing research includes exploring the stories of schooling in children's literature and examining the role of portfolio assessment in teacher development.

Cynthia H. Brock is an Assistant Professor in the Department of Reading and Bilingual Education at Texas Woman's University. She was a public school teacher for 9 years prior to receiving her Ph.D. from Michigan State University. Her research interests include literature-based reading instruction and literacy learning and instruction for second language learners at the elementary school level.

Bernice Cullinan is a Professor of Reading and Children's Literature at New York University. A noted scholar in the area of children's literature, she is the co-author of *Literature and the Child* (Harcourt Brace) with Lee Galda, and co-author of *Language, Literacy and the Child* (Harcourt Brace) with Lee Galda and Dorothy Strickland. Cullinan edited *A Jar of Tiny Stars*, published by National Council of Teachers of English and Boyds Mills Press.

Jenny Denyer, Assistant Professor of Teacher Education at Michigan State University, received the Excellence-in-Teaching Award in recognition of her contributions to teacher preparation. Her research interests focus on teacher and student talk in the context of classroom literacy events, such as writing conferences and book discussions. She has published in journals such as *Teaching and Teacher Education*. She teaches courses in methods of reading and writing instruction at both the undergraduate and graduate levels, as well as doctoral seminars in classroom discourse.

Barbara Diamond received her Ph.D. from Michigan State University. She is currently a Professor of Education at Eastern Michigan University where she teaches courses in multicultural literacy and reading and writing methods in urban settings. She is co-author of *Multicultural Literacy: Mirroring the Reality of the Classroom* (Longman), which chronicles her research and collaborative work with public schools.

Susan Florio-Ruane is Professor of Teacher Education and Coordinator of the Literacy Masters Program at Michigan State University. Her teaching and research interests include sociolinguistics, autobiography, and improving teacher learning about the cultural foundations of literacy and its development. She has coordinated the Learning Community Teacher Preparation Program at Michigan State University and taught courses about writing at the undergraduate, masters, and doctoral levels. She is codirector of the Autobiography Book Club Project, focused on highlighting issues of culture as they relate to literacy learning and instruction. Florio-Ruane recently completed her term as president of the Anthropology and Education Society of the American Anthropology Association.

Lee Galda is a Professor in the Department of Language Education at the University of Georgia where she teaches courses in children's literature and language arts methods. A former Children's Books column editor for *The Reading Teacher*, she is the author of many articles and chapters on children's literature and the classroom, published in a variety of professional journals. She is coauthor of both *Language, Literacy, and the Child* and *Literature and the Child*, both published by Harcourt Brace.

James R. Gavelek is an Associate Professor in the Department of Reading and Language Arts at Oakland University, teaching courses on the relationships between language, literacy, and thought. His scholarly interests focus on the socio-cultural bases of emotion, motivation, and literary response. He has published chapters and articles articulating a sociocultural approach to literacy instruction, most recently appearing in *Language Arts*.

Violet J. Harris received her Ph.D. from the University of Georgia. She is currently an Associate Professor at the University of Illinois at Urbana–Champaign. Her research interests include children's literature, and literacy methods created for African-American children prior to 1950. She is the author of *Teaching Multicultural Literature in Grades K–8* and *Using Multiethnic Literature in the K–8 Classroom*, published by Chrisopher-Gordon.

Elfrieda H. Hiebert is professor and chair of the Literacy, Language, and Learning Disabilities program at the University of Michigan's School of Education. She received her Ph.D. in Educational Psychology from the University of Wisconsin–Madison. Hiebert began her career as a teacher of primary-level students in central California and has also taught at the Universities of Kentucky and Colorado–Boulder. Her research on how instructional and assessment practices influence literacy acquisition, especially among low-income children, has been published in numerous journals and volumes, including *Early Literacy Instruction* (1997, co-authored with Taffy Raphael).

Kathy Highfield, a fifth-grade teacher in the Holly Public Schools, received her M.A. In Literacy Instruction from Michigan State University. She has over ten years of teaching experience, serving as a tutor from grades Kindergarten to 12 in a range of subjects, including French. She has engaged in teacher research examining students' written and oral response within her Book Club instructional program and has been a member of the Teacher Inquiry Group for five years. As a member of that group, she coauthored an article describing its goals and benefits that appeared in the *Teacher Research Journal*. In addition, she is coauthor of *Book Club: A Literature-Based Curriculum* (Small Planet Communications, Inc.)

Marjorie Y. Lipson is Professor of Education at the University of Vermont where she teaches both graduate and undergraduate courses in literacy. Lipson is currently serving as Director of the university reading clinic. She regularly teaches a special topics course entitled New Perspectives on Teaching with Themes. Lipson has been especially intersted in the ways in which interdisciplinary instruction, organized around powerful themes, can enhance reading and writing instruction. She has published widely in a number of edited volumes and in a variety of journals such as *The Reading Teacher, Language Arts, Reading Research Quarterly*. She is a co-author, with Karen Wixson of the book, *Reading and Writing Disability: An Interactionist Perspective*. Most recently, her research has been supported by the Spencer Foundation and has focused on how state policy influences teachers' writing instruction and assessment.

Margaret McKeown is a Research Scientist at the Learning Research and Development Center of the Univeristy of Pittsburgh. Her work involves applying theory and cognitive research to practical, current problems that classroom teachers and their students face. McKeown received her Ph.D. in education from the University of Pittsburgh in 1983. Her dissertation received the Outstanding Dissertation Award for 1985 from the International Reading Association. McKeown was awarded a Spencer Fellowship from the National Academy of Education in 1988 for a research project on developing dictionary definitions for young learners. McKeown was Program Chair of Division C for the 1996 AERA meeting, and will assume the vice presidency of Division C of the American Educational Research Association in 1998.

Susan I. McMahon is an Assistant Professor in the Department of Curriculum and Instruction at the University of Wisconsin–Madison. She spent over 25 years teaching in public and private schools, as well as at the university levels. She cofounded the Book Club Project while at Michigan State University and is coeditor of *The Book Club Connection: Literacy Learning and Classroom Talk* (Teachers College Press). Her current research focuses on classroom instructional support for the development of literacy and learning of literature and social studies, a study funded by the United States Office of Educational Research as part of the Center fo English Learning and Achievement. Her articles have appeared in journals such as *Teaching and Teacher Education, Language Arts*, and *The Reading Teacher*. An article she coauthored in *The Journal of Educational Research* was awarded the Harold E. Mitzel Award for Meritorious Contributions to Educational Practice Through Research.

Mary McVee is a Ph.D. candidate at Michigan State University. Her past research has explored how ESL students and their parents and teachers think about language growth and assessment and how writing groups can assist adult ESL students in learning the writing process. Her current research focuses on the use of oral and written narrative in educating teachers.

Laura S. Pardo spent fourteen years as a classroom teacher before taking her current position as an educational consultant. Her teaching has been highlighted in videotapes including the Center for the Study of Reading's *Reading Instruction in the Content Areas* and Silver Burdett & Ginn's *Literature-Based Instruction*. Ms. Pardo received her M. A. in Reading Instruction from Michigan State University and was involved with the Book Club Project as teacher and teacher researcher from 1990–1996. She is coauthor of *Book Club: A Literature-Based Curriculum* (Small Planet Communications, Inc.).

P. David Pearson, Hannah Professor of Education at Michigan State University, is known for his ground-breaking research in comprehension instruction, standards in the English language arts, and assessment practices. He edited the *Handbook of Reading Research*, volumes I and II, as well as numerous other volumes in the area of literacy instruction and research. He has published widely in journals such as *Reading Research Quarterly*, *American Educational Research Journal*, *Language Arts*, and *The Reading Teacher*. He is past president of National Reading Conference and has served on the board of the International Reading Association. During his tenure at the University of Illinois, he codirected the Center for the Study of Reading and was Dean of the College of Education.

Charles W. Peters is an English Language Arts consultant for Oakland Intermediate School District in Waterford, Michigan. One of his primary responsibilities is to assist the 28 local school districts he serves with curriculum development and performance assessment. He was written a number of articles and book chapters in these areas. Two of his most recent publications are "Developing State Standards in English Language Arts: A Case Study" in the *Handbook for Literacy Educators: Research on Teaching and Communication and Visual Arts* (Macmillan) and "The Case for Integrated Standards in English Language Arts" in *Language Arts*. He has worked with several national and state committees on assessment, including the National Assessment of Educational Progress (NAEP) and the Michigan Educational Assessment Program (MEAP).

Melodye Rosales, illustrator of children's books and publications is known for her research and attention to detail. Ms. Rosales is widely known for her three books in the award-winning Addy series: *Meet Addy* (1993 Cuffy award: Best New Series and *Publishers Weekly* "All-Time Best Selling Book category"). Born in Los Angeles, California, she began her Fine Arts studies at the University of Illinois, Urbana–Champaign and continued her education in Barcelona, Spain at the Unversidad de Barcelona, The School of the Art Institute of Chicago and Columbia College. Ms. Rosales lives in Champaign, Illinois with her her husband and three children.

Robert Rueda, Professor and Chairperson of the Division of Educational Psychology at the University of Southern California (USC), is also a member of faculty in the Language, Literacy, and Learning Doctoral Program. His research has focused on interactive relationships between social processes, cognitive development, and academic achievement in language minority and learning handicapped students, with a special focus on literacy. Recent professional contributions include serving on the Technical Advisory Panel for the Los Angeles Annenberg Metropolitan Project; serving as a Co-director of the Professional Development Research Program Strand for the National Center for Research on Education, Diversity, and Excellence at the University of California, Santa Cruz; and serving on the National Advisory Board of the National Center for Research on Evaluation, Standards, and Student Testing at UCLA.

Loukia K. Sarroub is a doctoral student in teacher education at Michigan State University. A recipient of one of the Spencer Foundation research training grants at MSU, Ms. Sarroub's research interests include work in literacy education and education policy and social analysis.

Kathy G. Short has focused her work on children's literature, curriculum as inquiry, and collaborative learning environments for teachers and children. She teaches graduate courses in children's literature and currriculum at the University of Arizona in the Department of Language, Reading and Culture. Her publications include *Literature as a Way of Knowing* (Stenhouse), *Creating Classrooms for Authors and Inquirers* with Jerome Harste (Heinemann) and *Talking about Books* with Kathryn Mitchell Pierce (Heinemann). She co-edits *The New Advocate*, a journal for all those concerned with young people and their literature.

Lawrence R. Sipe is an Assistant Professor in the Graduate School of Education at the University of Pennsylvania. As a member of the Reading/Writing/Literacy faculty, he teaches courses in literature for children and adolescents. His 19 years of school-based experience include teaching in a one-room school (grades one through eight) in a small fishing village in Newfoundland, Canada; a multi-grade (K–2) class in a private school in Princeton, NJ, and being the coordinator for language arts, early childhood education, and special services for a school district in Newfoundland. Dr. Sipe is particularly interested in the various ways in which children respond to literature; how literature can both reinscribe and challenge cultural and social practices; and the complex relationships between literature and literacy.

Diane Stephens is a Professor at the Univeristy of Hawaii–Manoa where she teaches language and literacy courses. She is actively involved in field-based teacher education programs and collaborative research with teachers. She and the teachers with whom she works wrote a book called *What Matters*, an article for *Language Arts* and wrote and edited an issue of *Primary Voices*, a National Council of Teachers of English (NCTE) journal by and for teachers. She recently was honored by the local chapter of IRA for her contributions to literacy education. At the national level, she has served as Director of NCTE's Commission on Reading and endeavors to stay connected to the national conversations through her writing, committee work, task forces and conference presentations.

Barbara M. Taylor is the Guy Bond Professor of Reading and Literacy at the University of Minnesota where she teachers courses in reading methods and children's literature. Her research focuses on classroom reading intervention in grades 1–4. She regularly spends several mornings a week in the schools helping teachers increase their success in working with their struggling readers. Her co-authored textbook, *Reading Difficulties: Instruction and Assessment*, is in its second edition. She has co-edited *Getting Reading Right from the Start: Effective Early Interventions* with Elfrieda Hiebert and has published researach articles in journals such as *Reading Research Quarterly, American Educational Research Journal, Journal of Reading Behavior,* and *The Reading Teacher*.

Sheila Valencia is Associate Professor of Curriculum and Instruction at the University of Washington where she teaches graduate courses in literacy theory, instruction, and asssessment. She studies classroom-based assessment, professional development, and the active engagements of teachers and students in their own learning. For the past 6 years, she has participated in a collaborative portfolio project with local teachers investigating how portfolios influence instruction and assessment. In addition, she is now in Year 2 of a 4 year study of teachers' transitions into teaching, which focuses on how literarcy teachers appropriate pedagogical and conceptual understandings from their preservice training into their first two years of teaching.

Sean Walmsley is a Professor in the Reading Department at the State University of New York at Albany. He received his Ed.D. in Reading at Harvard University. He has taught in the United Kingdom and in the U.S. in both elementary and secondary schools. In addition to writing several books, Dr. Walmsley has published for the research community in jounals such as *Reading Research Quarterly* and *Curriculum Inquiry,* and for teachers in *Language Arts, Journal of Reading, Elementary School Journal,* and *Instructor Magazine.* For the past seven years, he has been researching the teaching and learning of literature in elementary and middle schools.

Karen K. Wixson is a Professor of Education and Associate Dean for Graduate Studies in the School of Education at the University of Michigan. Prior to receiving her doctorate in reading education at Syracuse University, she worked both as a remedial reading and a learning disabilities teacher. She has published widely including articles in *Language Arts, Reading Research Quarterly,* and the *Review of Educational Research* in the areas of literacy curriculum, instruction, and assessment and is co-author of a text on the assessment and instruction of reading and writing problems. Her awards include the IRA Celebrate Literacy and the AERA Professional Service Award for her work in translating reading research into goals and assessments for the state of Michigan. Most recently, she was co-director of the federally funded Michigan English Language Arts Framework (MELAF) standards project.

Jo Ann Wong-Kam currently teaches at the Punahou School. Prior to that, she was an elementary teacher for 21 years at the Kamehameha Elementary School in Honolulu, Hawaii. Her work with assessment started four years ago when she and several of her colleagues at Kamehameha began using progress folios. Since that time they have learned more about goal setting and linking evaluation to instruction. In the classrooms the students and their parents responded positively to the active roles they play in assessment and evaluation. The feeling developed that all are working for the success of the learner.

Index